ISBN 978-1-332-07082-4
PIBN 10280186

1 MONTH OF
FREE
READING

at
www.ForgottenBooks.com

By purchasing this book you are eligible for one month membership to ForgottenBooks.com, giving you unlimited access to our entire collection of over 700,000 titles via our web site and mobile apps.

To claim your free month visit:

www.forgottenbooks.com/free280186

English
Français
Deutsche
Italiano
Español
Português

www.forgottenbooks.com

Mythology Photography **Fiction**
Fishing Christianity **Art** Cooking
Essays Buddhism Freemasonry
Medicine **Biology** Music **Ancient
Egypt** Evolution Carpentry Physics
Dance Geology **Mathematics** Fitness
Shakespeare **Folklore** Yoga Marketing
Confidence Immortality Biographies
Poetry **Psychology** Witchcraft
Electronics Chemistry History **Law**
Accounting **Philosophy** Anthropology
Alchemy Drama Quantum Mechanics
Atheism Sexual Health **Ancient History**
Entrepreneurship Languages Sport
Paleontology Needlework Islam
Metaphysics Investment Archaeology
Parenting Statistics Criminology
Motivational

THE

THEORY AND PRACTICE

OF

BY THE LATE

HORACE FORD

CHAMPION ARCHER OF ENGLAND FOR THE YEARS 1850 TO 1859 AND 1867

NEW EDITION

THOROUGHLY REVISED AND RE-WRITTEN

BY

FOR MANY YEARS HON. SECRETARY OF THE ROYAL TOXOPHILITE SOCIETY

LONDON

1887

No EXCUSE need be offered to archers for presenting to them a new edition of the late Mr. Horace A. Ford's work on the Theory and Practice of Archery. It first appeared as a series of articles in the columns of the 'Field,' which were republished in book form in 1856; a second edition was published in 1859, which has been long out of print, and no book on the subject has since appeared. Except, therefore, for a few copies of this book, which from time to time may be obtained from the secondhand booksellers, no guide is obtainable by which the young archer can learn the principles of his art. On hearing that it was in contemplation to reprint the second edition of Mr. Ford's book, it seemed to me a pity that this should be done without revision, and without bringing it up to the level of the knowledge of the present day. I therefore purchased the copyright of the work from Mr. Ford's representatives, and succeeded in inducing Mr. Butt, who was for many years the secretary of the Royal Toxophilite Society, to undertake the revision.

A difficulty occurred at the outset as to the form in which this revision should be carried out. If it had been possible, there would have been advantages in printing Mr. Ford's text untouched, and in giving Mr. Butt's comments in the form of notes. This course would, however, have involved printing much matter that has become entirely obsolete, and, moreover, not only would the bulk of the book have been increased to a greater extent even than has actually been found necessary, but also Mr. Butt's portion of the work, which contains the information of the latest date, and is therefore of highest practical value to young archers, would have been relegated to a secondary and somewhat inconvenient position. Mr. Butt has therefore rewritten the book, and it would hardly perhaps be giving him too much credit to describe the present work as a Treatise on the Theory and Practice of Archery by him, based on the work of the late Horace A. Ford.

In writing his book, Mr. Ford committed to paper the principles by means of which he secured his unrivalled position as an archer. After displaying a clever trick, it is the practice of some conjurers to pretend to take the spectators into their confidence, and to show them ' how it is done.' In such cases the audience, as a rule, is not much the wiser ; but a more satisfactory result has followed from Mr. Ford's instructions.

Mr. Ford was the founder of modern scientific archery. First by example, and then by precept, he changed what before was ' playing at bows and arrows ' into a scientific pastime. He held the Champion's medal for eleven years in succession —from 1849 to 1859. He also won it again in 1867. After this time, although he was seen occasionally in the archery field, his powers began to wane. He died in the year 1880. His best scores, whether at public matches or in private prac tice, have never been surpassed. But, although no one has risen who can claim that on him has fallen the mantle of

Mr. Ford, his work was not in vain. Thanks to the more scientific and rational principles laid down by this great archer
any active lad nowadays can, with a few months' practice,
make scores which would have been thought fabulous when
George III. was king.

The Annual Grand National Archery Meetings were started
in the year 1844 at York, and at the second meeting, in 1845,
held also at York, when the Double York Round was shot
for the first time, Mr. Muir obtained the championship, with
135 hits, and a score of 537. Several years elapsed before
the championship was won with a score of over 700. Nowadays, a man who cannot make 700 is seldom in the first
ten, and, moreover, the general level both among ladies and
gentlemen continues to rise. We have not yet, however,
found any individual archer capable of beating in public the
marvellous record of 245 hits and 1,251 score, made by Mr.
Ford at Cheltenham in 1857.

One chief cause of the improvement Mr. Ford effected was
due to his recognising the fallacy in the time-honoured saying
that the archer should draw to the ear. When drawn to the
ear, part of the arrow must necessarily lie outside the direct
line of sight from the eye to the gold. Consequently, if the
arrow points apparently to the gold, it must fly to the left
of the target when loosed, and in order to hit the target, the
archer who draws to the ear must aim at some point to the
right. Mr. Ford laid down the principle that the arrow must
be drawn directly beneath the aiming eye, and lie in its whole
length in the same vertical plane as the line between the eye
and the object aimed at.

It is true that in many representations of ancient archers
the arrow is depicted as being drawn beyond the eye, and

consequently outside the line of sight.   No doubt for war
purposes it was a matter of importance to shoot a long heavy
arrow, and if an arrow of a standard yard long or anything like
it was used, it would be necessary for a man to draw it beyond
his eye, unless he had very long arms indeed.   But in war,
the force of the blow was of more importance than accuracy
of aim, and Mr. Ford saw that in a pastime where accuracy
of aim was the main object, this old rule no longer held good.
This was only one of many improvements effected by Mr. Ford ;
but it is a fact that this discovery, which seems obvious enough
now that it is stated, was the main cause of the marvellous
improvement which has taken place in shooting.

   The second chapter in Mr. Ford's book, entitled ' A Glance
at the Career of the English Long-Bow,' has been omitted.   It
contained no original matter, being compiled chiefly from the
well-known works of Roberts, Moseley, and Hansard.   The
scope of the present work is practical, not historical ; and to
deal with the history of the English long-bow in a satisfactory
manner would require a bulky volume.   An adequate history
of the bow in all ages and in all countries has yet to be
written.

   In the chapters on the bow, the arrow, and the rest of the
paraphernalia of archery, much that Mr. Ford wrote, partly
as the result of the practice and experiments of himself and
others, and partly as drawn from the works of previous writers
on the subject, still holds good ; but improvements have been
effected since his time, and Mr. Butt has been able to add a
great deal of useful information gathered from the long experience of himself and his contemporaries.

   The chapters which deal with Ascham's well-known five
points of archery—standing, nocking, drawing, holding, and

loosing—contain the most valuable part of Mr. Ford's teaching, and Mr. Butt has endeavoured to develope further the principles laid down by Mr. Ford. The chapters on ancient and modern archery practice have been brought up to date, and Mr. Butt has given in full the best scores made by ladies or gentlemen at every public meeting which has been held since the establishment of the Grand National Archery Society down to 1886.

The chapter on Robin Hood has been omitted for the same reasons which determined the omission of the chapter on the career of the English long-bow, and the rules for the formation of archery societies, which are cumbrous and old-fashioned, have also been left out.

The portrait of Major C. H. Fisher, champion archer for the years 1871-2-3-4, is reproduced from a photograph taken by Mr. C. E. Nesham, the present holder of the champion's medal.

In conclusion, it is hoped that the publication of this book may help to increase the popularity of archery in this country. It is a pastime which can never die out. The love of the bow and arrow seems almost universally planted in the human heart. But its popularity fluctuates, and though it is now more popular than at some periods, it is by no means so universally practised as archers would desire. One of its greatest charms is that it is an exercise which is not confined to men. Ladies have attained a great and increasing amount of skill with the bow, and there is no doubt that it is more suited to the fairer sex than some of the more violent forms of athletics now popular. Archery has perhaps suffered to some extent from comparison with the rifle. The rifleman may claim for his weapon that its range is greater and that it shoots more accurately than the bow. The first position may be granted freely, the second only with reserve. Given, a well-made weapon of Spanish or Italian yew, and arrows of the best modern make, and the accuracy of the bow is measured only by the skill of the shooter. If he can loose his arrow truly, it will hit the mark ; more than that can be said of no weapon. That a rifleman will shoot more accurately at ranges well within the power of the bow than an archer of similar skill is certain ; but the reason is that the bow is the more difficult, and perhaps to some minds on that account the more fascinating, weapon. The reason why it is more difficult is obvious, and in stating it we see one of the many charms of archery. The rifleman has but to aim straight and to hold steady, and he will hit the bull's-eye. But the archer has also to supply the motive force which propels his arrow. As he watches the graceful flight of a well-shot shaft, he can feel a pride in its swiftness and strength which a rifleman cannot share. And few pastimes can furnish a more beautiful sight than an arrow speeding swiftly and steadily from the bow, till with a rapturous thud it strikes the gold at a hundred yards.

C. J. LONGMAN.

CONTENTS.

PLATES.

ARCHERY

CHAPTER I.

OF THE ENGLISH LONG-BOW

Of the various implements of archery, the bow demands the
first consideration.   It has at one period or another formed
one of the chief weapons of war and the chase in almost every
nation, and is, indeed, at the present day in use for both these
purposes in various parts of the world.   It has differed as much
in form as in material, having been made curved, angular, and
straight; of wood, metal, horn, cane, whalebone, of wood and
horn, or of wood and the entrails and sinews of animals and
fish combined : sometimes of the rudest workmanship, sometimes finished with the highest perfection of art.

No work exists which aims at giving an exhaustive description of the various forms of bows which have been used by
different nations in ancient and modern times, and such an
undertaking would be far beyond the scope of the present
work.   The only form of the bow with which we are now
concerned is the *English long-bow,* and especially with the
English long-bow as now used for target-shooting as opposed
to the more powerful weapon used by our forefathers for the
purposes of war.   The cross-bow never took a very strong
hold on the English nation as compared with the long-bow,

and, as it has never been much employed for recreation, it need not be here described.

It is a matter of surprise and regret that so few genuine specimens of the *old* English long-bow should remain in existence at the present day. One in the possession of the late Mr. Peter Muir of Edinburgh is said to have been used in the battle of Flodden in 1513 : it is of self-yew, a single stave, apparently of English growth, and very roughly made. Its strength has been supposed to be between 80 and 90 lbs. ; but as it could not be tested without great risk of breaking it, its actual strength remains a matter of conjecture only. This bow was presented to Mr. P. Muir by Colonel J. Ferguson, who obtained it from a border house contiguous to Flodden Field, where it had remained for many generations, with the reputation of having been used at that battle.

There are likewise in the Tower two bows that were taken out of the ' Mary Rose,' a vessel sunk in the reign of Henry VIII. They are unfinished weapons, made out of single staves of magnificent yew, probably of foreign growth, quite round from end to end, tapered from the middle to each end, and without horns. It is difficult to estimate their strength, but it probably does not exceed from 65 to 70 lbs. Another weapon now in the Museum of the United Service Institution came from the same vessel. Probably the oldest specimen extant of the English long-bow is in the possession of Mr. C. J. Longman. It was dug out of the peat near Cambridge, and is unfortunately in very bad condition. It can never have been a very powerful weapon. Geologists say that it cannot be more recent than the twelfth or thirteenth century, and may be much more ancient. Indeed, from its appearance it is more probable that it is a relic of the weaker archery of the Saxons than that it is a weapon made after the Normans had introduced their more robust shooting into this country.

Before the discussion of the practical points connected with the bow is commenced, it must be borne in mind that these pages profess to give the result of actual experience, and nothing that is advanced is mere theory or opinion unsupported by proof, but the result only of long, patient, and practical investigation and of constant and untiring experiment. Whenever, therefore, one kind of wood, or one shape of bow, or one mode or principle of shooting, &c., is spoken of as being better than another, or the best of all, it is asserted to be so simply because, after a full and fair trial of every other, the result of such investigation bore out that assertion. No doubt some of the points contended for were in Mr. Ford's time in opposition to the then prevailing opinions and practice, and were considered innovations. The value of theory, however, is just in proportion as it can be borne out by practical results; 'and in appealing to the success of his own prac tice as a proof of the correctness of the opinions and principles upon which it was based, he professed to be moved by no feeling of conceit or vanity, but wholly and solely by a desire to give as much force as possible to the recommendations put forth, and to obtain a fair and impartial trial of them.

The English bows now in use may be divided primarily into two classes—the *self-bow* and the *backed bow*; and, to save space and confusion, the attention must first be confined to the self-bow, reserving what has to be said respecting the backed bow. Much, however, that is said of the one applies equally to the other.

The self-bow of a single stave is the real old English weapon—the one with which the mighty deeds that rendered this country renowned in bygone times were performed; for until the decline and disappearance of archery in war, as a consequence of the superiority of firearms, and the consequent cessation of the importation of bow-staves, backed bows were unknown. Ascham, who wrote in the sixteenth century, when archery had already degenerated into little else than an amusement, mentions none other than self-bows; and it may therefore be concluded that such only existed in his day. Of the woods for self-bows, yew beyond all question carries off the palm.   Other woods have been, and still are, in use, such as lance, cocus, Washaba, rose, snake, laburnum, and others ; but they may be summarily dismissed (with the exception of lance, of which more hereafter) with the remark that self-bows made of these woods are all so radically bad, heavy in hand, apt to jar, dull in cast, liable to chrysal, and otherwise prone to break, that no archer should use them so long as a self-yew or a good backed bow is within reach.

The only wood, then, for self-bows is yew, and the best yew is of foreign growth (Spanish or Italian), though occasionally staves of English wood are met with which almost rival those of foreign growth.   This, however, is the exception ; as a rule, the foreign wood is the best : it is straighter, and finer in grain, freer from pins, stiffer and denser in quality, and requires less bulk in proportion to the strength of the bow.

The great bane of yew is its liability to knots and *pins,* and rare indeed it is to find a six-feet stave without one or more of these undesirable companions.   Where, however, a pin occurs, it may easily be rendered comparatively harmless by the simple plan of raising it—i.e. by leaving a little more wood than elsewhere round the pin in the belly and back of the bow.   This strengthens the particular point, and diminishes the danger of a chrysal or splinter.   A pin resembles a small piece of wire, is very hard and troublesome to the bow-maker's tools, runs right through the bow-stave from belly to back, and is very frequently the point at which a chrysal starts.   This chrysal (also called by old writers a ' pinch ') is a sort of disease which attacks the belly of a bow.   At first it nearly resembles a scratch or crack in the varnish.   Its direction is always diagonal to the line of the bow, and it gradually eats deeply into the bow and makes it appear as if it had been attacked with a chopper.   If many small chrysals appear, much danger need not be feared, though their progress should be watched ; but if one chrysal becomes deeply rooted, the bow should be sent to the bowmaker for a new belly. A chrysal usually occurs in new bows, and mostly arises from the wood being imperfectly seasoned; but it occasionally will occur in a well-seasoned bow that has been lent to a friend who uses a longer draw and dwells longer on the point of aim, thus using the weapon beyond its wont. Another danger to the life of a bow arises from splinters in the back. These mostly occur in wet weather, when the damp, through failure of the varnish, has been able to get into the wood. Directly the rising of a splinter is observed, that part of the bow should be effectually glued and wrapped before it is again used. After this treatment the bow will be none the worse, except in appearance. Yew and hickory only should be used for the backs of bows. Canadian elm, which is occasionally used for backs, is particularly liable to splinter. It is obvious whenever a bow is broken the commencement of the fracture has been in a splinter or a chrysal, according as the first failure was in the back or the belly; therefore in the diagnosis of these disorders archers have to be thankful for small mercies. The grain of the wood should be as even and fine as possible, with the feathers running quite straight, and as nearly as possible consecutively from the handle to the horn in each limb, and without curls; also, care should be taken, in the manufacture of a bow, that the sap or back be of even depth, and not in some places reduced to the level of the belly. The feathering of a yew bow means the gradual disappearance of some of the grain as the substance of the bow is reduced between the handle and horn. A curl is caused by a sudden turn in the grain of the wood, so that this feathering is abruptly interrupted and reversed before it reappears. This is a great source of weakness in a bow, both in belly and back. There should be nothing of the nature of feathering in the back of a bow, and it is believed that the best back is that in which nothing but the bark has been removed from the stave. Any interruption of the grain of the back is a source of weakness and a hotbed of splinters. A bow that follows the string should never be straightened, for the same reason that

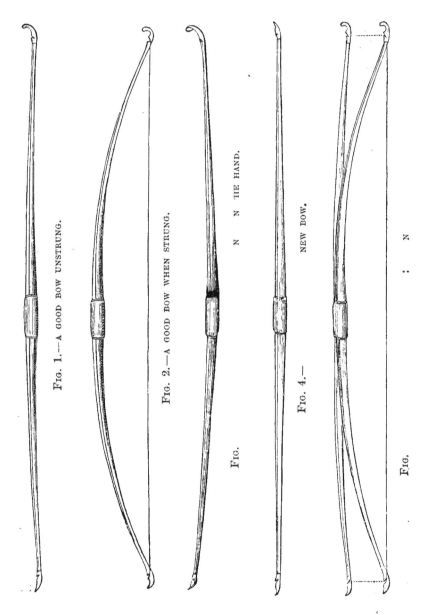

Fig. 1.—A GOOD BOW UNSTRUNG.

Fig. 2.—A GOOD BOW WHEN STRUNG.

Fig.   N   N   THE HAND.

Fig. 4.—   NEW BOW.

Fig.   N

anything of the nature of a carriage-spring should on no account be reversed in application. The wood should be thoroughly well seasoned and of a good sound hard quality. The finest and closest dark grain is undoubtedly the most beautiful and uncommon ; but the open or less close-grained wood, and

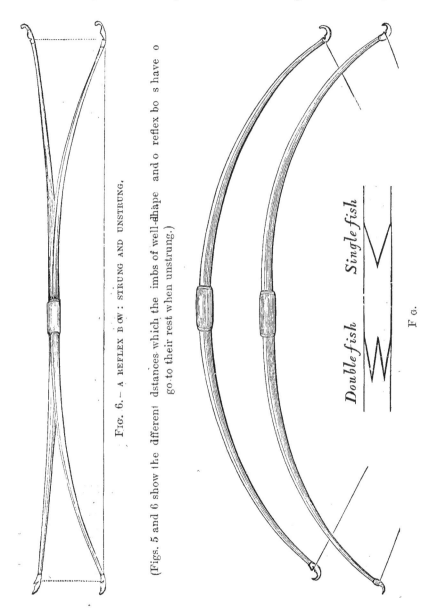

FIG. 6.— A REFLEX BOW : STRUNG AND UNSTRUNG.

(Figs. 5 and 6 show the different distances which the limbs of well-shape and o reflex bo s have o go to their rest when unstrung.)

Double-fish   *Single-fish*

F G.

wood of paler complexion, are nearly, if not quite, as good for use.

The self-yew bow may be a single-stave—that is to say,

made of a single piece of wood, or may be made of two pieces
dovetailed or united in the handle by what is called a fish. In
a single-stave bow the quality of the wood will not be quite the
same in the two limbs, the wood of the lower growth being
denser than that of the upper ; whilst in the grafted bow, made
of the same piece of wood, cut or split apart, and re-united in
the handle, the two limbs will be exactly of the same nature.
The joint, or *fishing* (fig. 7), should be double, not single. The
difference, however, between these two sorts of self-yew bows is so
slight as to be immaterial. In any unusually damp or variable
climate single staves should be prepared ; and in the grafted
bows care should be taken in ascertaining that they be firmly
put together in the middle. A single-stave bow has usually a
somewhat shorter handle, as it becomes unnecessary to cover
so much of the centre of the bow when the covering is not
used as a cover to the joint, but for the purpose of holding the
bow only.

In shape all bows should be full and inflexible in the centre,
tapering gradually to each horn. They should never bend
in the handle, as bows of this shape (i.e. a continuous curve
from horn to horn) always jar most disagreeably in the hand.
A perfectly graduated bend, from a stiff unbending centre of
at least nine inches, towards each horn is the best. Some
self-yew bows are naturally reflexed, others are straight, and
some follow the string more or less. The slightly reflexed bows
are perhaps more pleasing to the eye, as one cannot quite
shake off the belief that the shape of Cupid's bow is agreeable.
Bows which follow the string somewhat are perhaps the most
pleasant to use.

The handle of the bow, which in size should be regulated
to the grasp of each archer, should be in such a position that
the upper part of it may be from an inch to an inch and a
quarter above the *true centre* of the bow, or the point in the
handle whereon the bow will balance. If this centre be lower
down in the handle, as is usual in bows of Scotch manufacture,

the cast of the bow may be somewhat improved, but at the cost of a tendency to that unpleasant feeling of kicking and jarring in the hand. Again, if the true centre be higher, or, as is the case in the old unaltered Flemish bows, at the point where the arrow lies on the hand, the cast will be found to suffer disadvantageously. If the handle be properly grasped (inattention to which will endanger the bow's being pulled out of shape), the fulcrum, in drawing, will be about the true balancing centre, and the root of the thumb will be placed thereon. Considering a bow to consist of three members—a handle and two limbs—the upper limb, being somewhat longer, must of necessity bend a trifle more, and this it should do. The most usual covering for the handle is plush ; but woollen binding-cloth, leather, and india-rubber are also in constant use.

The piece of mother-of-pearl, ivory, or other hard sub stance usually inserted in the handle of the bow, at the point where the arrow lies, is intended to prevent the wearing away of the bow by the friction of the arrow ; but this precaution overreaches itself, as in the course of an unusually long life the most hard-working bow will scarcely lose as much by this friction as must, to start with, be cut away for this insertion.

The length of the bow, which is calculated from nock to nock—and this length will vary a little from the actual length, according as it may be said to hold itself upright or stoob, i.e. follow the string—should be regulated by its strength and the length of the arrow to be used with it. It may be taken as a safe rule that the stronger the bow the greater its length should be ; and so also the longer the arrow the longer should be the bow. For those who use arrows of the usual length of from 27 to 28 inches, with bows of the strength of from 45 lbs. to 55 lbs., a useful and safe length will be not less than 5 ft. 10 in. If this length of arrow or weight of bow be increased or diminished, the length of bow may be proportionally increased or diminished, taking as the two extremes 5 ft. 8 in. and 6 feet. No bow need be much outside either of these measurements. It may be admitted that a short bow will cast somewhat farther than a longer one of the same weight, but this extra cast can only be gained by a greater risk of breakage. As bows are usually weighed and marked by the bowmakers for a 28-inch arrow fully drawn up, a greater or less pull will take more or less out of them, and the archer's calculations must be made accordingly.

To increase or diminish the power of a bow, it is usual to shorten it in the former case, and to reduce the bulk in the latter; but to shorten a bow will probably shorten its life too, and mayhap spoil it, unless it be certain that it is superfluously long or sufficiently strong in the handle. On the other hand, to reduce a bow judiciously, if it need to be weaker, can do it no harm; but the reduction should not be carried quite up to the handle. It is a good plan to choose a bow by quality, regardless of strength, and have the best bow that can be procured reduced to the strength suitable. In all cases the horns should be well and truly set on, and the nocks should be of sufficient bulk to enclose safely the extremities of the limbs of the bow running up into them, and the edges of the nocks should be made most carefully smooth. If the edge of the nock be sharp and rough, the string must be frayed, and in consequence break sooner or later, and endanger the safety of the bow. The lower nock is not unfrequently put on or manufactured a trifle sideways as to its groove on the belly side. This is done with a view to compensate the irregularity of the loop: but this is a mistake, as it is quite unnecessary in the case of a loop, and must be liable to put the string out of position when there is a second eye to the string—and this second eye every archer who pays due regard to the preservation of his bows and strings should be most anxious to adopt as soon as possible.

From all that can be learned respecting the backed bow, it would appear that its use was not adopted in this country until archery was in its last stage of decline as a weapon of war, when, the bow degenerating into an instrument of amusement, the laws relating to the importation of yew staves from foreign countries were evaded, and the supply consequently ceased. It was then that the bowyers hit upon the plan of uniting a tough to an elastic wood, and so managed to make a very efficient weapon out of very inferior materials. This cannot fairly be claimed as an invention of the English bowyers, but is an adaptation of the plan which had long been in use amongst the Turks, Persians, Tartars, Chinese, and many other nations, including Laplanders, whose bows were made of two pieces of wood united with isinglass. As far as regards the English backed bow (this child of necessity), the end of the sixteenth century is given as the period of its introduction, and the Kensals of Manchester are named as the first makers—bows of whose make may be still in existence and use—and these were generally made of yew backed with hickory or wych-elm. At the time of the revival of archery— at the close of the last century, and again fifty years ago—all backed bows were held in great contempt by any that could afford self-yews, and were always slightingly spoken of as 'tea-caddy' bows; meaning that they were made of materials fit for nothing but ornamental joinery, Tunbridge ware, &c.

The backed bows of the present day are made of two or more strips of the same or different woods securely glued, and compressed together as firmly as possible, in frames fitted with powerful screws, which frames are capable of being set to any shape. Various woods are used, most of which, though of different quality, make serviceable bows. For the backs we have the sap of yew, hickory, American, Canadian, or wych-elm, hornbeam, &c.; and for the bellies, yew, lance, fustic, snake, Washaba, and letter-wood, which is the straight grained part of snake, and some others. Of all these combinations Mr. Ford gave the strongest preference to bows of yew backed with yew. These he considered the only possible rivals of the self-yew.

Next in rank he classed bows of yew backed with hickory. Bows made of lance backed with hickory, when the woods used are well seasoned and of choice quality, are very steady and trustworthy, but not silky and pleasant in drawing like bows made of yew. One advantage of this combination of bow is that both these woods can be had of sufficient length to avoid the trouble in making and insecurity in use of the joint in the handle. Of bows into which more than two woods are introduced, the combination of yew for the belly, fustic or other good hard wood for the centre, and hickory for the back cannot well be improved upon, and such bows have been credited with excellent scores. There is also a three-wooded modification of the lance and hickory bow. In this a tapering strip of hard wood is introduced between the back and belly; this strip passes through the handle and disappears at about a foot from the horn in each limb. The lancewood bows are the cheapest, and next to these follow the lance-and-hickory bows, and then those of the description last mentioned. On this account beginners who do not wish to go to much expense whilst they are, as it were, testing their capacity for the successful prosecution of this sport, would do well to make a start with a bow of one or other of these descriptions. It will often be useful to lend to another beginner, or to a friend, to whom it might not be wise to lend a more valuable bow; or it may even be of use to the owner at a pinch. Bows have often been made of many more than three pieces; but nothing is gained by further complications, unless it be necessary in the way of repair.

Next in importance to the consideration of the material of which backed bows should be made comes the treatment of their shape. Judging from such specimens of backed bows, made by Waring and others, before the publication of Mr. H. A. Ford's articles on archery in the 'Field,' as have survived to the present day, and whose survival may be chiefly attributed to the fact that they were so utterly harsh and disagreeable in use that it was but little use they ever got, the author was probably right in saying that they all bent in the handle more or less when drawn, and were too much reflexed. There is but little doubt that—as the joint in the handle, necessitating extra bulk and strength, could be dispensed with in these bows— the makers considered it an excellent opportunity to give their goods what (however erroneously) was then considered the best shape (when drawn), namely, the perfect arc ; and this harmonious shape they obtained most successfully by making the bows comparatively weak in the handle and unnecessarily strong towards the horns ; with the result that these 'tea-caddy bows' met the contemptuous fate they well deserved. Modern archers have to be thankful to Mr. Ford for the vast improvement in backed bows (even more than in the case of self-bows), which are now perfectly steady in hand, and taper gradually, and as much as is compatible with the safety of the limbs, and this in spite of their being still made somewhat more reflex when new than appears necessary in the manufacture of self-yew bows. Yet Mr. Ford was perfectly right to condemn all reflexity that does not result in a bow becoming either straight or somewhat to follow the string after it has been in use sufficiently long for its necessary training to its owner's style. The first quality of a bow is steadiness. Now this quality is put in peril either by a want of exact balance between the two limbs—when the recoil of one limb is quicker than that of the other—or by undue reflexity. These causes of unsteadiness occur in self-bows as well as in backed bows, and are felt in the shape of a jar or kick in the hand when loosed. This unsteadiness from want of balance in the limbs may be cured by a visit of the bow to the maker for such fresh tillering (as it is called) as will correct the fault of one or other limb. If the unsteadiness arise from excessive reflexity, which cannot be reduced by use, a further tapering of the limbs must be adopted. No bow of any sort that cannot be completely cured of kicking should be kept, as no steady shooting can be expected from such a bow. A bow that is much reflexed will be more liable to chrysals and splinters, as the belly has to be more compressed and the back more strained than in a bow of proper shape ; also, such a bow is much more destructive to strings, as a greater strain is put upon the strings by the recoil of the limbs than is the case with a bow that follows the string or bends inwards naturally. It is the uneven or excessive strain upon the string after the discharge of the arrow that causes the kicking of the bow.

When the question arises, ' Which is the best sort of bow ? ' it is found that the solution has only been rendered more complicated since 1859 by the great improvement in the manufacture of various sorts of backed bows : as the following remarks, then applied to the comparison between the self-yew and the yew-backed yew only, must now be extended to all the best specimens of backed bows of different sorts. The advocates of the self-yew affirm that good specimens of their pet weapon are the sweetest in use, the steadiest in hand, the most certain in cast, and the most beautiful to the eye ; and in all these points, with the exception of certainty of cast, they are borne out by the fact. This being the state of the case, how is it, then, that a doubt can still remain as to which it is most profitable for an archer to use ? Here are three out of four points (two of which are most important) in which it is admitted that the self-yew is superior ; and yet, after much practical and experimental testing of all sorts, it must be left to the taste and judgment of each man to decide for himself. The fact undoubtedly is, that the self-yew is the most perfect weapon. But it is equally an undoubted fact that it requires more delicate handling ; since, its cast lying very much in the last three or four inches of its pull, any variation in this respect, or difference in quickness or otherwise of loose, varies the elevation of the arrow to a much greater extent than the same variation of pull or loose in the others, whose cast is more uniform throughout. Now, were a man perfect in his physical powers, or always in first-rate shooting condition, there would be no doubt as to which bow he should use, as he would in this case be able to attain to the difficult nicety required in the management of the self-yew; but as this constant perfection never can be maintained, the superior merits of this bow are partially counteracted by the extreme difficulty of doing justice to them; and the degree of harsh ness of pull and unsteadiness in hand of the others being but trifling, the greater certainty with which they accomplish the elevation counterbalances, upon average results, their inferiority in other respects.   Another advantage the self-yew possesses is, that it is not so liable to injury from damp as are the backed bows; but then the latter are much less costly, and, with common care, need cause no fear of harm from damp, as an inch of lapping at either end covering the junction with the horns will preserve them from this danger.   As regards chrysals, and breakage from other causes than damp, bows of all sorts of wood are about equally liable to failure.   The main results of the comparison, then, resolve themselves into these two prominent features : namely, that the self-yew bow, from its steadiness, sweetness, and absence of vibration, ensures the straightness of the shot better than backed bows; whilst the latter, owing to the regularity of their cast not being confined quite to a hair's breadth of pull, carry off the palm for greater certainty in the elevation of the shot.

It is almost unnecessary to say that there are bad bows of all sorts, many being made of materials that are fit for nothing but firewood; and yet the bowmakers seem to be almost justified in making up such materials by the fact that occasionally the most ungainly bow will prove itself almost invaluable in use, while a perfect beauty in appearance may turn out a useless slug.

Though it may be no easy matter to decide which particular sort of bow an individual archer should adopt, yet, when that individual has once ascertained the description of bow that appears to suit him best, he will be wise to confine his attention to that same sort in his future acquisition of bows. An archer who shoots much will find his bowmaker's account a serious annual matter if he keep none but the best self-yew bows; and therefore any who find it necessary to count the cost of this sport should do their best to adapt themselves to the cheaper though not much inferior backed bows. This also may be further said of the difference between self-yews and backed bows—namely, that there appears to be a sort of individuality attached to each self-yew bow, apart from the peculiarities of its class, which makes it difficult (not regarding the cost) to remedy the loss of a favourite self-yew bow. It is very much easier to replace any specimen of the other sorts of bows, as there is much less variation of character in each class.

The ' carriage bow ' is made to divide into two pieces by means of a metal socket in the handle, after the fashion of the joint of a fishing-rod. The object of this make of bow is to render it more convenient as a travelling-companion ; but, as the result is a bow heavy in hand and unpleasant in use, the remedy appears to be worse than the disease.

It is often asserted that the best bows should be made of steel, as superior in elasticity to wood ; but this is not borne out by the results of experiment. The late Hon. R. Hely-Hutchinson, a member of the R. Tox. Soc., took a great deal of pains to have long-bows manufactured of steel both in England and in Belgium. The best of these, weighing about 50 lbs. for the 28-inch draw, with the aim and elevation which with a good wooden bow would carry an arrow 100 yards, scarcely carried its shaft as far as 60 yards, so deadly slow appeared the recoil ; and besides this, the actual weight in the hand of the implement was so considerable that it would be a most serious addition to the toil of the day, on account of its being so frequently held out at arm's length, to say nothing of its having to be carried about all day.

CHAPTER II.

HOW TO CHOOSE A BOW, AND HOW TO USE AND PRESERVE IT WHEN CHOSEN.

THE next point to be considered is the strength of the bow to be chosen; and respecting this, in the first place, the bow must be completely under the shooter's command—within it, but not much below it. One of the greatest mistakes young archers (and many old ones too) commit is that they *will* use bows that are too strong for them. In fact, there are but few to whom, at one or other period of their archery career, this remark has not applied. The desire to be considered strong appears to be the moving agent to this curious hallucination; as if a man did not rather expose his weakness by straining at a bow evidently beyond his strength, thereby calling attention to that weakness, than by using a lighter one with grace and ease, which always give the idea of force, vigour, and power. Another incentive to the use of strong bows is the passion for sending down the arrows sharp and low, and the consequent employment of powerful bows to accomplish this; the which is perhaps a greater mistake than the other, for it is not so much the strength of the bow as the perfect command of it that enables the archer to obtain this desideratum. The question is not so much what a man can pull as what he can loose; and he will without doubt obtain a lower flight of arrow by a lighter power of bow under his command, than he will by a stronger one beyond his proper management. This mania for strong bows has destroyed many a promising archer, in an archery sense of the term. Not only did one of

C

the best shots of his day, a winner of the second and first prizes at successive Grand National Meetings, dwindle beneath mediocrity in accuracy through this infatuation, but another brought himself to death's door by a dangerous illness of about a year's duration, by injury to his physical powers, brought on by the same failing, only carried to a much greater excess. And, after all, the thing so desired is not always thus attained.

Let the reader attend any Grand National Archery Meeting, and let him observe some fifty or so picked shots of the country arranged at the targets, and contending with all their might for the prizes of honour and skill. Whose arrows fly down the sharpest, steadiest, and keenest ? Are they those of the archers who use the strongest bows ? Not at all. Behold that archer from an Eastern county just stepping so unpretendingly forward to deliver his shafts. See ! with what grace and ease the whole thing is done !—no straining, no contortions there ! Mark the flight of his arrows—how keen, and low, and to the mark they fly ! None fly sharper, few so sharp. And what is the strength of that beautiful self-yew bow which he holds in his hand ? Scarce 50 lbs. ! And yet the pace of his shaft is unsurpassed by any ; and it is close upon five shillings in weight too. There is another. Mark his strength and muscular power ! Possibly a bow of 80 lbs. would be within his pull ; yet he knows better than to use any such, when the prizes are awarded to skill, not brute force. The bow he employs is but 48 lbs. ; yet how steady and true is the flight of his arrow ! And so on all through the meeting : it will be found that it is not the strongest bows, but those that are under the perfect command of their owners, that do their work the best.

Inasmuch, then, as the proper flight of an arrow from any bow depends almost entirely upon the way in which it is loosed, the strength of the bow must not be regulated by the mere muscular powers of the individual archer ; for he may be able to draw even a 29-inch arrow to the head in a very powerful bow without being able during a match to loose steadily a bow of more than 50 lbs. Not the power of drawing, but of loosing steadily, must therefore be the guide here. The bow must be within this loosing power, but also well up to it; for it is almost as bad to be *under-* as *over*-bowed. The evils attendant upon being over-bowed are various : the left (bow) arm, wrist, and elbow, the fingers of the right (loosing) hand and its wrist, are strained and rendered unsteady ; the pull becomes uncertain and wavering, and is never twice alike ; the whole system is overworked and wearied ; and, besides this, the mind is depressed by ill-success ; the entire result is disappointment and failure. On the other hand, care must be taken not to fall into the opposite extreme of being underbowed, as in this case the loose becomes difficult, and generally unsteady and unequal. The weight of the bows now in general use varies from 45 lbs. to 54 lbs., stronger ones forming the exception ; and the lowest of these weights is ample for the distances now usually shot. Each archer must therefore find out how much he can draw with ease and loose with steadiness throughout a day's shooting, and choose accordingly. If a beginner, 50 lbs. is probably the outside weight with which he should commence ; a few pounds less, in most cases, would even be better for the starting-point. As lately as twenty years ago bows were very carelessly marked in the indication of their strength, many bows being marked as much as 10 lbs. above their actual measure ; but in the present day all the bowmakers incline towards the custom of marking a new bow to weigh rather less, perhaps by 3 lbs., than its actual weight. The reason of this is that in the opinion of the marker the bow will arrive at the strength marked in the course of use. It is indeed a very rare case when a new bow does not with use get somewhat weaker.

Besides keeping the bows for his own use mostly of the same description, every archer should also keep them of just about the same weight; and if he shoot much he should possess at the fewest three, as much alike as possible, and use them alternately. This will prove an economy in the end, as each will have time to recover its elasticity, and will thus last a much longer time. It is an agreeable feature in bows that they have considerable facility in recovery from the effects of hard work. This fact may be easily tested by weighing a bow on a steelyard before and after shooting a single York round with it, when a difference of one pound or more will be found in the strength of it, more particularly if the day be hot ; but with a few days' rest this lost power will be regained by the bow.

In the choice of a bow a beginner should secure the assistance of an experienced friend, or content himself with an unambitious investment in a cheap specimen of backed-bow or a self-lance, on which he may safely expend his inexperience. When an archer is sufficiently advanced to know the sort and weight of bow that best suits him, let him go to the maker he prefers, and name the price he can afford to give—the prices of trustworthy self-yews vary from twenty to five guineas, of yew-backed yews from five to three guineas, and of other backed bows from three guineas to thirty shillings ; whilst self-lance bows may be procured for as little as twelve shillings—and he will soon find what choice there is for him. If there appears one likely to suit, let him first examine the bow to see that there be no *knots, curls, pins, splinters, chrysals,* or other objectionable flaws ; then let him string it, and, placing the lower end on the ground in such a position that the whole of the string shall be under his eye and uppermost, let him notice whether the bow be perfectly straight. If it be so, the bow, so balanced between the ground at the lower and a finger at the upper end, will appear symmetrically divided by the string into two parts. Should there appear to be more on one side of the string than on the other in either limb, the bow is not straight, and should be rejected. A bow is said to have a *cast* when it is tilted in its back out of the perpendicular to the plane passing through the string and the longitudinal centre of the bow. Any bow that has this fault should also be rejected. This fault, if it should happen to exist, will be easily detected by reversing the position of the bow just previously described, i.e. by holding the bow as before, but with the back upwards. The next step is to watch the bow as it is drawn up, so as to be able to judge whether it bend evenly in both its limbs and show no sign of weakness in any particular point. The upper limb, as before stated, being the longest, should appear to bend a trifle the most, so that the whole may be symmetrical, when considered as bending from the real centre. It may next be tested, to ascertain whether it be a kicker; thus the string must be drawn up six inches or so and then loosed (of course without an arrow). If the bow have the fault of kicking ever so little, experience will easily detect it by the jolt in the hand. But on no account in this experiment should the string (without an arrow) be fully drawn and loosed. Care should be taken that the bow be sufficiently long for its strength. What has hitherto been said applies to all bows; but in self-bows attention must be paid to the straightness of the feathering of the wood. As a general rule, the lightest wood in a yew-bow will have the quickest cast, and the heaviest will make the most lasting implement. Between two bows of the same strength and length, the one being slight and the other bulky, there will be about the same difference as between a thoroughbred and a cart-horse. Therefore the preference should be given to bows that are light and slight for their strength. Light-coloured and dark yew make equally good bows, though most prefer the dark colour for choice. Fine and more open grain in yew are also equally good, but the finer is more scarce. If there be no bow suitable—i.e. none of the right weight—let the choice fall upon the best bow of greater power, and let it be reduced. Failing this, the purchaser may select an unfinished stave and have it made to his own pattern ; but it is not easy to foretell how a stave will make up.

There remains one point about a bow, hitherto unnoticed, and this is its section, as to shape. This may vary, being broad and flat across its back, or the contrary—deep and pointed in the belly. Here again extremes should be avoided—the bow should in shape be neither too flat nor too deep. If it be an inch or so across the back just above the handle, it should also have about the same measurement through from back to belly. This much being granted, it is further declared that the back should be almost as flat and angular as possible, showing that it has been reduced as little as may be after the removal of the bark ; but the belly should be rounded ; and as the back should not be reduced in its depth towards the horns, and should not get too narrow across, it will follow that the chief reduction, to arrive at the proper curvature when the bow is drawn, must be in the belly, and therefore towards the horn. A well-shaped bow will in measurement become somewhat shallower from back to belly than it is across the back as it advances towards the horns.

Bows are broken from several causes : by means of ne-glected chrysals in the belly, or splinters in the back ; by a jerking, uneven, or crooked style of drawing ; by dwelling over-long on the point of aim after the arrow is fully drawn ; by the breaking of the string ; by damp, and oftentimes by careless-ness ; and even by thoughtlessness. Bows, moreover, may be broken on the steelyard in the weighing of them. A few years ago, when the Americans first took up archery very keenly, one of their novices wrote to a prominent English archer saying that he had broken nearly seventy bows in a couple of years, and asking the reason. He was told that he must either keep his bows in a damp place or the bows must be very bad ones, or else (to which view the writer inclined) he must be in the habit of stringing them the reverse way with the belly outwards. This would certainly have a fatal effect, but it is true that the Americans bought a number of very bad bows about that time from inferior makers in England. Whenever chrysals appear they must be carefully watched, and, as has already been said, if they become serious, a new belly must be added. This will not be a serious disfigurement, even to a self-yew bow. A splinter should be glued and lapped at once, but no one nowadays seems to care to have the covering patch painted as formerly, to represent as nearly as possible the colours of the different parts of the bow. Care should be taken not to stab the belly of the bow with the point of the arrow when nocking it ; and the dents in the back of the bow made with the arrow as it is carelessly pulled out of the target should be avoided. A glove-button will often injure the back of the bow whilst it is being strung. As other ornaments—buttons, buckles, &c.—may also inflict disfigurements, it is better to avoid their presence as far as possible. Breakages from a bad style of drawing, or from dwelling too long on the aim, can only be avoided by adopting a better and more rational method. In order to avoid fracture through the breaking of strings, any string that shows signs of failure from too much wear or otherwise should be discarded ; and strings that are too stiff, too hard, and too thin should be avoided. If a string break when the arrow is fully or almost drawn, there is but little hope for the bow ; but if it break in the recoil after the arrow is shot, which fortunately is more frequently the case, the bow will seldom suffer. Yet if after the bow is strung the archer should observe that the string is no longer trustworthy, and decide to discard it, he should on no account cut it whilst the bow is braced, as the result of so doing will be an almost certain fracture. If the string be looped at both ends and the loop at either end be made too large, so that it slip off the nock in stringing, the bow may break, so that an archer who makes his own loops at the lower end of the string must be careful not to make them too loose. Breakage from damp is little to be feared in self-bows, except in localities where it

is exceptionally moist, or, after long neglect, when damp has
taken possession of the joint in the handle. In these cases
single staves only are safe. Amongst backed bows there is
much mortality from this cause. Commonly, it will be the
lower limb that will fail, as that is most exposed to damp,
arising either from the ground whilst shooting, or from the
floor when put away. If the bow has been used in damp
weather it should be carefully dried and rubbed with waxed
flannel or cloth. A waterproof case, an 'Ascham' raised an
inch or so above the floor in a dry room, and the bow hung up,
not resting on its lower horn, are the best-known precautions.
Half an inch of lapping, glued and varnished, above and below
the joint of the horn is also a safe precaution against damp ;
also an occasional narrow lap in the course of the limb will
assist to 'fast bind, fast find.' As regards the danger of carelessness, bows have been broken through attempts to string
them the wrong way, or by using them upside down ; and
thoughtlessness will lead the inexperienced to attempt to bring
a bow that follows the string upright, to its infinite peril. In
such cases the verdict of ' Serve him right' should be brought
against the offender if he be the owner. In weighing a bow
on the steelyard care must be taken to see that the peg indicating the length to be drawn be at the right point ; otherwise a
lady's bow, for instance, may be destroyed in the mistaken
attempt to pull it up twenty-eight inches, or three inches too
much.

It has already been stated that a belly much injured by
chrysals may be replaced by a new belly ; any incurable failure
of the back may also be cured by its renewal. A weak bow or
limb may also be strengthened by these means. Also, if either
limb be broken or irretrievably damaged, and the remaining
one be sound, and worth the expense, another limb may be
successfully grafted on to the old one. If possible, let this be
an old limb also, as the combination of new and old wood
is not always satisfactory ; the former (though well seasoned,

being unseasoned by use), being more yielding, is apt after a little use to lose its relative strength, and so spoil the proper balance of the bow. This grafting of one broken limb upon another may be carried to the length of grafting together two limbs of different sorts. Mr. P. Muir, who was as good a bowyer as he was an accurate shot, had a favourite bow, that did him good service in 1865 at Clifton, when he took the third place at the Grand National Archery Meeting. This bow in one limb was yew-backed yew, and in the other lance backed with hickory. A bow that is weak in the centre, and not sufficiently strong to allow of the ends being further reduced, may be brought to the required shape, and strengthened by the addition of a short belly.

With regard to unstringing the bow during the shooting, say, of a York Round of 144 arrows, at the three distances, a good bow will not need it, if the shooting be moderately quick, excepting at the end of each of the distances. If there happen to be many shooters, or very slow ones, it may be unstrung after every three or four double ends; and of course it should be unstrung whenever an interruption of the shooting may occur from rain, or any other cause; but it certainly appears unnecessary to unstring the bow after each three shots, as this is an equally uncalled-for strain upon the muscles of the archer and relief to the grain of the wood. In a discussion on this subject, however, between Mr. James Spedding and Mr. P. Muir, the latter maintained that to be unstrung at each end was as agreeable to the bow as to rest on a camp-stool was to the archer. Some archers contend that it is better to have the bow strung some few minutes before the commencement of the shooting.

All that has been said respecting men's bows, with the exception of strength and length, applies equally to those used by ladies. The usual strength of these latter varies from 24 lbs. to 30 lbs. In length they should not be less than five feet. The usual length of a lady's arrow being twenty-five inches, whilst that of a gentleman is twenty-eight inches, it appears that, when fully drawn, a lady's bow must be bent more in proportion to its length than that of a gentleman. The proportion between the bows being as 5 to 6, whilst that of the arrows is as $6\frac{1}{4}$ to 7; yet ladies' bows appear to be quite capable of bearing this extra strain safely.

As bows of three pieces are seldom to be met with manufactured for the use of ladies, their choice of weapons is limited to self-yews, yew-backed yews, yew backed with hickory, and lance backed with hickory; also self-lance bows for beginners, &c. Ladies' bows of snake and other hard woods are still to be met with; but they are so vastly inferior to those above-mentioned that it is scarcely necessary to refer to them.

It is too common a practice amongst archers to throw the consequences of their own faults upon the bowmakers, accusing the weapon of being the cause of their failures, instead of blaming their own carelessness or want of skill. But, before this can be justly done, let each be quite certain that he has chosen his bow with care, and kept it with care; if otherwise, any accidents occurring are, ten to one, more likely to be the result of his own fault than that of the bowmaker.

CHAPTER III.

OF THE ARROW

THE arrow is perhaps the most important of all the implements of the archer, and requires the greatest nicety of make
and excellence of materials; for, though he may get on without absolute failure with an inferior bow or other tackle, unless
the arrow be of the best Robin Hood himself would have aimed
in vain. Two things are essential to a good arrow, namely,
perfect straightness, and a stiffness or rigidity sufficient to
stand in the bow, i.e. to receive the force of the bow as
delivered by the string without flirting or gadding; for a weak
or supple is even worse than a crooked arrow—and it need
hardly be said how little conducive to shooting straight is the
latter. The straightness of the arrow is easily tested by the
following simple process. Place the extremities of the nails
of the thumb and middle finger of the left hand so as just to
touch each other, and with the thumb and same finger of the
right hand spin the arrow upon the nails at about the arrow's
balancing-point; if it revolve truly and steadily, keeping in
close and smooth contact with the nails, it is straight; but if it
jump in the very least the contrary is the case. In order to
test its strength or stiffness the arrow must be held by the
nock, with its pile placed on some solid substance. The hand
at liberty should now be pressed downwards on the middle of
the arrow. A very little experience as to whether the arrow
offer efficient resistance to this pressure will suffice to satisfy the
archer about its stiffness. An arrow that is weaker on one side
than on the other should also be rejected.

Arrows are either *selfs* or *footed*; the former being made
of a single piece of wood (these are now seldom in use, except
for children), and the latter have a piece of different and
harder wood joined on to them at the pile end. ' A shaft,'
says old Roger Ascham, ' hath three principal parts—the *stele*,
the *feather*, and the *head*.' The stele, or wooden body of the
arrow, used to be, and still is occasionally, made of different
sorts of wood ; but for target use, and indeed for any other
description of modern shooting, all may be now discarded save
one—red deal, which when clean, straight of grain, and well
seasoned, whether for selfs or footed shafts, is incomparably
superior to all others. For the footing any hard wood will
do ; and if this be solid for one inch below the pile it will be
amply sufficient. Lance and Washaba are perhaps the best
woods for this purpose; the latter is the toughest, but the
former Mr. Ford preferred, as he thought the darkness of the
Washaba had a tendency to attract the eye. The darker
woods, however, are now mostly in use. This footing has
three recommendations : the first, that it enables the arrow to
fly more steadily and get through the wind better; the second,
that, being of a substance harder than deal, it is not so easily
worn by the friction it unavoidably meets with on entering the
target or the ground ; and the third, that this same hardness
saves the point from being broken off should it happen to strike
against any hard substance—such, for instance, as a stone in
the ground or the iron leg of a target-stand. Before the shooting is commenced, and after it is finished, the arrows should
be rubbed with a piece of oiled flannel. This will prevent
the paint of the target from adhering to them. If in spite
of this precaution any paint should adhere to them, sand-
paper should on no account be used to clean them : this is
most objectionable, as it will wear away the wood of the
footing. Turpentine should be applied, or the blunt back of
a knife.

Before entering upon the subject of the best shape for the

'stele' of the arrow for practical use, it is necessary to say a few words upon a point where the theory and practice of archery apparently clash.

If the arrow be placed on the bowstring as if for shooting, the bow drawn, and an aim taken at an object, and if the bow be then slowly relaxed, the arrow being held until it returns to the position of rest—i.e. if the passage of the arrow over the bow be slow and gradual—it will be found, if the bow be held quite firmly during this action, that the arrow does not finally point to the object aimed at, but in a direction deviating considerably to the left of it—in fact, that its direction has been constantly deviating more and more from the point of aim at each point during its return to the position of rest. This is, of course, due to the half-breadth of the bow, the nock of the arrow being carried on the string, in a plane passing through the string and the axis of the bow's length; and this deviation will be greater if the arrow be chested (i.e. slighter at the pile than at the nock), and less if it be bobtailed (i.e. slighter at the nock than at the pile) than if the arrow be cylindrical throughout. If the same arrow, when drawn to the head, be loosed at the object aimed at—i.e. if the passage of the arrow over the bow be impulsive and instan taneous—it will go straight to the object aimed at, the shoot ing being in all respects perfect.

How, then, is the difference of the final direction of the arrow in the two cases to be explained?

It must be observed that the nock of the arrow being con- strained to move, as it does move in the last case, causes a pressure of the arrow upon the bow (owing to its slanting position on the bow, and its simultaneous rapidity of passage), and therefore a reacting pressure of the bow upon the arrow. This makes the bow have quite a different effect upon the deviation from what it had in the first case, when the arrow moved slowly and gradually upon the bow (being held by the nock), the obstacle presented by the half-breadth of the bow then causing a deviation *wholly* to the left. The pressure now considered, however, has a tendency to cause deviation to the left only during the first part of the arrow's passage upon the bow, whilst during the second part it causes a deviation to the right; or, more correctly speaking, the pressure of the bow upon the arrow has a tendency to cause a deviation to the left *so long as the centre of gravity of the arrow is within the bow, and vice versâ.* So that, if this were the only force acting upon the arrow, its centre of gravity (this is, of course, the point upon which the arrow, balanced horizontally, will poise) should lie midway in that part of the arrow which is in contact with the bow during the bow's recoil. There is another force which contributes towards this acting and reacting pressure between the arrow and the bow at the loose if the nocking-place of the string be properly fitted to the arrow, but not otherwise. As the fingers are disengaged from the string they communicate a tendency to spin to the string, and this spin immediately applies the arrow to the bow if it should happen to be off the bow through side-wind or that troublesome failing of beginners and others of a crooked pinch between the' fingers upon the nock of the arrow. It will be observed that if the nocking-place be too small to fill the nock of the arrow this tendency to spin in the string will not affect the replacement of the arrow; but if the nocking-place be a good fit to the nock, the former must be a trifle flattened, and so communicate the spin of the string to the arrow in the shape of a blow upon the bow. It is not pretended that no arrow will fly straight unless the nocking-place fit the arrow. If the string be home in the nock the shot will still be correctly delivered, because the very close and violent pressure of the string on the nock will arrest the spin and so apply the arrow; but if the string be not home in the nock at the delivery of the loose, there is great danger that the nock will be broken, either from the nocking-place being too small, or from the other fault of its being too big. It is this spin given to the string as the arrow is loosed that necessitates the delivery of the arrow from the other side of the bow when the thumb-loose of the Oriental archer is employed, because this loose communicates the same spin, but reversed, to the string.

The struggle of these forces is clearly indicated by the appearance of the arrow where it comes in contact with the bow when it leaves the string. It is here that the arrow always shows most wear. It is also shown by the deep groove that gets worn by the arrow in a bow that has seen much service.

The nature of the dynamical action may be thus briefly explained. The first impulse given to the arrow, being instantaneous and very great (sufficient, as has been seen, to break the arrow if the string be not home in the nock) in proportion to any other forces which act upon it, impresses a very high initial velocity in the direction of the aim, and this direction the arrow recovers notwithstanding the slight deviations caused by the mutual action between the arrow and bow before explained—these in fact, as has been shown, counteracting each other.

The recoil of the bow, besides the motion in the direction of aim, impresses a rotary motion upon the arrow about its centre of gravity. This tendency to rotate, however, about an axis through its centre of gravity is counteracted by the feathers. For, suppose the arrow to be shot off with a slight rotary motion about a vertical axis, in a short time its point will deviate to the left of the plane of projection, and the centre of gravity will be the only point which continues in that plane. The feathers of the arrow will now be turned to the right of the same plane, and, through the velocity of the arrow, will cause a considerable resistance of the air against them. This resistance will twist the arrow until its point comes to the right of the plane of projection, when it will begin to turn the arrow the contrary way. Thus, through the agency of the feathers, the deviation of the point of the arrow from the plane of projection is confined within very narrow limits. Any rotation of the arrow about a horizontal axis will be

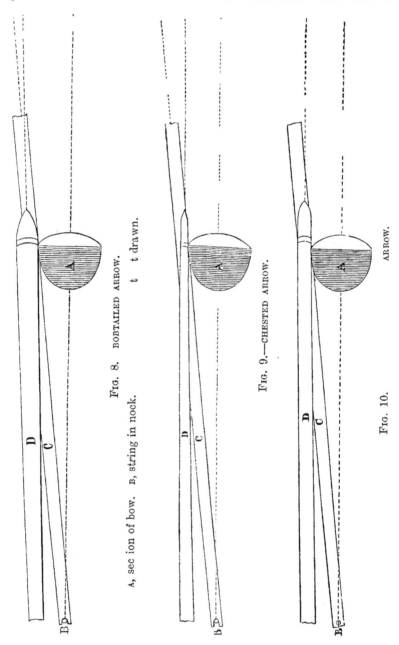

FIG. 8. BOBTAILED ARROW.

FIG. 9.—CHESTED ARROW.

FIG. 10.

A, section of bow. B, string in nock. C, arrow at rest. D, arrow at moment string is drawn.

counteracted in the same way by the action of the feathers. Both these tendencies may be distinctly observed in the actual initial motion of the arrow. In the discussion of these rotations of the arrow about vertical and horizontal axes the bow is supposed to be held in a vertical position.

If the foregoing reasoning be carefully considered, it will be seen how prejudicial to the correct flight of the arrow in the direction of the aim any variation in the shape of that part of it which is in contact with the bow must necessarily be; for by this means an additional force is introduced into the elements of its flight. Take for example the chested arrow, which is smallest at the point and largest at the feathers : here there is during its whole passage over the bow a constant and increasing deviation to the left of the direction of aim, caused by the arrow's shape, independent of, and in addition to, a deviation in the like direction caused by the retention of the nock upon the string. Thus this description of arrow has greater difficulty in recovering its initial direction, the forces opposed to its doing so being so much increased. Accordingly, in practice, the chested arrow has always a tendency to fly to the left. These chested arrows are mostly *flight-arrows*, made very light, for long-distance shooting, and they are made of this shape to prevent their being too weak-waisted to bear steadily the recoil of very strong bows.

As regards the *bobtailed arrow*, which is largest at the point and smallest at the feathers, the converse is true to the extent that this description of arrow will deviate towards the left less than either the straight or chested arrow; moreover, any considerable bobtailedness would render an arrow so weakwaisted that it would be useless.

There is another arrow, known as the *barrelled arrow*, which is largest in the middle, and tapers thence towards each end. The quickest flight may be obtained with this sort of arrow, as to it may be applied a lighter pile without bringing on either the fault of a chested arrow or the weak-waistedness of a bobtailed arrow.

D

If the tapering be of equal amount at each end of the arrow, the pressure will act and react in precisely the same manner as in the case of the cylindrical arrow, with the result that this arrow will fly straight in the direction in which it is aimed.   The cylindrical and the barrelled shapes are therefore recommended as the best for target-shooting.   And as the barrelled is necessarily stronger in the waist and less likely to

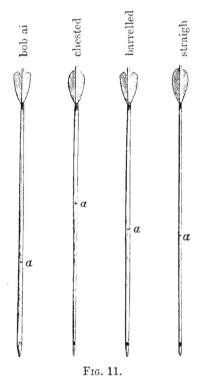

Fig. 11.

a, different balancing points of thin arrows.

flirt even if a light arrow be used with a strong bow this shape is perhaps better than the cylindrical.

The *feathering* of the arrow is about the most delicate part of the fletcher's craft, and it requires the utmost care and experience to effect it thoroughly well.   It seems difficult now to realise why the feathering of the arrow came to have grown to the size in use during Mr. Ford's time, when the feather occupied the whole distance between the archer's fingers and the place on the bow where the arrow lies when it is nocked previous to shooting—i.e. the length of the feather was up. wards of five inches. Mr. H. Elliott was the first archer who, about fifteen years ago, reduced the dimensions of the feathers of his arrows by cutting off the three inches of each feather furthest from the nock. He found this reduction enabled the arrow to fly further. Others soon followed his example, and in the course of about twelve months all the arrow-makers had supplied their customers with arrows of the new pattern, which, however, cannot be called a new pattern, as Oriental arrows, and many flight-arrows, were much less heavily feathered. The long feathering is now scarcely ever seen, except occasionally when it is erroneously used to diminish the difficulty of shoot_ ing at sixty yards. Mr. Ford recommended rather full-sized feathers ' as giving a steadiness to the flight.' With the re- duced feathers arrows fly as steadily, and certainly more keenly towards the mark. A fair amount of rib should be left on the feather, for if the rib be pared too fine the lasting quality of the feather will be diminished. The three feathers of an arrow should be from the same wing, right or left ; and as none but a raw beginner will find any difficulty in nocking his arrow the right way—i.e. with what is known as the cock feather upwards, or at right angles to the line of the nock—with- out having this cock feather of a different colour, it is advisable to have the three feathers all alike. Perhaps the brown feathers of the peacock's wing are the best of all, but the black turkey- feathers are also highly satisfactory. The white turkey feathers are also equally good, but had better be avoided, as they too readily get soiled, and are not to be easily distin guished from white goose-feathers. These last, as well as those of the grey goose, though highly thought of by our fore- fathers, are now in no repute, and it is probable that our ancestors, if they had had the same plentiful supply of pea- fowls and turkeys as ourselves, would have had less respect for the wings of geese. The reason why the three feathers

must be from the same wing is that every feather is outwardly
convex and inwardly concave. When the feathers are correctly applied, all three alike, this their peculiarity of form
rifles the arrow or causes it to rotate on its own axis. This
may be tested by shooting an arrow through a pane of glass,
when it will be found that the scraping against the arrow of
the sharp edges of the fracture passes along the arrow spirally.
Some years ago a very unnecessary patent was taken out for
rifling an arrow by putting on the feathers spirally, over-

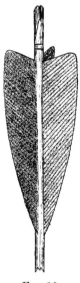

FIG. 12.   FIG. 13.

doing what was already sufficient. As regards the position of
the feather, it should be brought as near as possible to the nock.
Some consider an inch in length of feather quite sufficient.
It is certain that any length between two inches and one
inch will do; so each individual may please himself and suit
the length of the feathering to the length and weight of his
arrows. The two shapes in use are the triangular and the
parabolic or balloon-shaped. Of these both are good—the
former having the advantage of carrying the steerage further
back, whilst the latter is a trifle stiffer.

The feathers are preserved from damp by a coat of oil paint laid on between them and for one-eighth of an inch above and below them. This should afterwards be varnished, and the rib of the feather should be carefully covered, but care must be taken to avoid injuring the suppleness of the feather with the varnish. Feathers laid down or ruffled by wet may be restored by spinning the arrow before a warm fire carefully.

The *pile,* or point, is an important part of the arrow. Of the different shapes that have been used, the best for target-shooting—now almost the only survivor—is the square-shouldered parallel pile. Its greatest advantage is, that if the arrow be overdrawn so that the pile be brought on to the

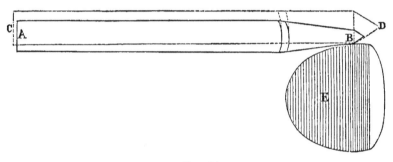

FIG. 14.

bow, the aim will not be injured, as must be the case with all conical piles so drawn. (Very light flight-arrows, for which the piles provided for ladies are considered too heavy, must still be furnished with the conical piles used for children's arrows.) This parallel pile is mostly made in two pieces—a pointed cone for its point, which is soldered on to the cylindrical part, which itself is made of a flat piece of metal soldered into this form. This same-shaped pile has occasionally been made turned out of solid metal; but this pile is liable to be so heavy as to be unsuitable for any but the heaviest arrows, and the fletchers aver that it is difficult to fix it on firmly owing to the grease used in its manufacture. Great care should be taken, in the manufacture of arrows, that the footing exactly fits the pile, so as to fill entirely the inside of it ; unless the footing of the arrow reach the bottom of the pile, the pile will either crumple up or be driven down the stele when the pile comes in contact with a hard substance. It is, of course, fixed on with glue ; and to prevent its coming off from damp, a blow, or the adhesiveness of stiff clay, it is well to indent it on each side with a sharp hard-pointed punch fitted for the purpose with a groove, in which the arrow is placed whilst the necessary pressure is applied.. This instrument may be procured of Hill & Son, cutlers, 4 Haymarket.

The *nock* should be strong, and very carefully finished, so that no injury may be done by the string or to the string. Of course the nock must be of the same size in section as the stele of the arrow ; and this furnishes an additional argument against the bobtailed arrow, which is smallest at this end. The notch or groove in which the string acts should be about one-eighth of an inch wide and about three-sixteenths of an inch deep. The bottom of this notch will be much improved by the application of a round file of the right gauge, i.e. quite a trifle more than the eighth of an inch in diameter ; but great care must be taken to apply this uniformly, and the nock must not be unduly weakened. This application will enable the archer to put thicker, and therefore safer, lapping to the nocking-place of the string, and the danger of the string being loose in the nock will be lessened. It is possible that this additional grooving of the nock may to a very trifling extent impede the escape of the arrow from the string. Mr. Ford recommended the application of a copper rivet through the nock near to the bottom of the notch to provide against the danger of splitting the nock. But it is so doubtful whether any rivet fine enough for safe application would be strong enough to guard against this danger, that the better plan will be to avoid the different sorts of carelessness that lead towards this accident.

As regards the *length* of the arrow no arbitrary rule can

be laid down. The arrow most generally in use is twenty-eight inches in length from the point of the pile to the bottom of the groove of the nock. This arrow may be easily drawn up by any man of average height—the twenty-seven inches, or the clothyard length of the old English archer, leaving the inch of pile undrawn. A taller man may venture to draw the pile. An arrow of twenty-nine inches may be adopted by those who have very long arms or are unusually tall. Those who are short of stature or short in limb may adopt the shorter arrow of twenty-seven inches. Shorter arrows than this will be found to fly unsteadily, and the longer arrows, if thoroughly drawn up, are very trying to the bows. The shorter arrows of twenty-seven inches in length have been in much more frequent use since about 1862, when the late T. L. Coulson adopted them, and advocated that it was better to draw up a shorter arrow than to leave a longer one undrawn. The fault of drawing not far enough is so much more frequent than that of overdrawing, that archers are strongly recommended to avoid shortening their arrow unadvisedly, and rather to draw the longer ones as far as they reasonably can. The fault of overdrawing is so dangerous to the archer, his tackle, and others, that, though an unfrequent fault, a caution against it must not be omitted. Whatever be the length of the arrow, it should always be drawn up to exactly the same point.

The *weight* of the arrow must to a certain extent be regulated by its length and by the strength of the bow with which it is to be used; for if an arrow be a long one it must have bulk sufficient to ensure its stiffness, and stiffness also in proportion to the strength of the bow. 4s. for the lowest, and 5s. 6d. for the highest weight, are the two extremes within which every length of arrow and strength of bow may be properly fitted, so far as gentlemen are concerned. For ladies, 2s. 6d. and 3s. 6d. should be about the limits. It should be borne in mind that light arrows, unless dictated by physical weakness, are a mistake in target-shooting. For flight-shooting very light-chested arrows may be procured stiff enough for any strength of bow; but in this style of shooting distance to be covered is of more importance than accuracy of aim. It would be much better if the arrow-makers, instead of selling their arrows in sets, progressing by three silver pennyweights, would sell them also weighed to the intermediate penny-weights. As the matter stands now, supposing the archer's favourite weight to be 4s. 9d., he may have at one time a set weighing rather less than 4s. 8d., and at another time rather more than 4s. 10d. As all the intermediate weights of arrows are manufactured, there can be no sufficient reason why the lighter set should not be marked and sold as 4s. 8d., and the heavier as 4s. 10d. A careful archer should attend also to the balance of his arrows. By this is meant that the same centre of gravity should pervade the whole set. Longer or shorter, lighter or heavier footing will vary this balancing-point, as also any variation in the weight of the piles.

As the variation of elevation, or distance to be shot, should not be managed by a change of weight in arrows, it is decidedly advisable to keep arrows all of the same weight, &c. Indeed it is a great mistake to change any part of the tackle, bow or arrow, during the shooting, except in unavoidable cases. The scoring will seldom be bettered by such means.

Formerly only two arrows were shot at each end, and three were carried, and called an 'archer's pair,' including the spare one. Now it is the almost universal custom to shoot three arrows at each end. Some spare ones should, of course, be at hand in case of accidents. It must be remembered that if the slightest variation in shape or weight occurs amongst those in use, the line or elevation is sure to be affected, to the serious detriment of accurate hitting; therefore too much care cannot be taken in their choice.

Whether it be for store or for daily use, the arrow should be kept in a quiver or case made on such a plan that each shall have its separate cell, and they should be kept upright when possible, and so be insured from warping, or from having their feathers crushed. It is too much the custom to squeeze a quantity of arrows into a small quiver. Let not any archer who values his tackle be guilty of this folly. An arrow that has had one of its feathers crumpled from this cause will, maybe, wobble and stagger all the rest of its life, though in all other respects it be in perfect repair. Arrows will be found to wear out quite speedily enough without being subjected to ill-usage or neglect to hurry them through their short lives

It appears to be well authenticated that if a light-chested flight-arrow be feathered at each end, with the feathers trimmed lower at the nock than at the pile end, when shot against the wind it will return back again like a boomerang. And if the same-shaped arrow be feathered in the middle only, it will in its flight make a right angle, and no power of bow can send it any considerable distance.

Mr. R. Hely-Hutchinson, already mentioned as having made experiments in modern times with steel bows, had another peculiarity. On the back of his bow he had a flat piece of hard wood or metal fixed at right angles to the length of his bow. An upright piece of the same material was fitted into a groove in this, whose outside distance was about an inch from the place where the arrow usually touches the bow above the handle. He used always to shoot with his arrow resting, not on the bow, or on his hand, but in the outside angle between this projection and the upright piece of it. He aimed as other archers do, and has been seen to make excellent hitting at the distance of one hundred yards, even when far advanced in years. In this case the axis of the arrow, or the line of aim, was distant from the plane through the string and the axis of the bow an inch in addition to the usual half-width of the arrow and half-width of the bow. Yet the arrow appeared to fly quite steadily and truly. It is not known why he adopted this peculiarity, and it is unnecessary to inquire ; but it will serve as a useful peg whereon to hang a further consideration of the difficulties an arrow has to contend with in getting straight to the point of aim, and its determined resolution to overcome these difficulties. In addition to the forces already discussed as acting upon the arrow, there is also the force of gravity, the resistance of the air, and the interference of the wind ; but these forces affect in the same way all arrows, however shot. The same may be said of all the other forces implicated, until there is an artificially increased impediment interposed in addition to the natural one of the half-bow and half-arrow. Now, supposing the distance of the nock from the centre of the bow be such when the arrow is drawn that a perpendicular let fall from the centre of the bow to the line of aim will mark off twenty-seven inches of draw, the resolution of the force acting in the line from the nock to the centre of the bow will be correctly represented by twenty-seven in the direction of the point of aim and three-eighths at right angles to that direction ; or the relation between the straight part of the whole force and its remainder will be as 216 to 5.

But when Mr. Hutchinson's peculiar method of shooting is compared with this natural way, it will appear that the relation between these same resolved forces will be as 216 to 13 ; showing that the obstruction in this latter case has been considerably more than doubled—the keenness of flight will be diminished, and increased *friction* will be shown between the arrow and its resting-place at the instant of the loose.

Besides the spin given to the string at the loose, there is also a push, at right angles to the direction delivered, by the more or less unavoidable obstruction of the fingers as they liberate the string ; but this push, occurring before the liberation of the string, is the final difficulty of the aim and loose.

Immediately the string is loosed the arrow has, as it were, the nocking-place between its teeth in the nock, and contributes to the direction of its course to the point of rest ; and it is highly probable that the path of the nocking-place from the loose to rest is not confined to the plane of the string and axis of the bow.

Greater or diminished friction between the bow and arrow would be another way of representing greater or less obstruction to the aim of the arrow. As the arrow deepens the groove made by its passage over the bow the obstruction will be diminished, but the surface exposed to this friction will be increased.

If a bow could be so constructed that an arrow could be shot through it just above the handle, the opening must be large enough to admit free passage for the feathering as well, and the opening must be contrived so that the 'stele,' true to the point of aim throughout its passage through the bow, shall never swerve from the right side of the opening.

CHAPTER IV.

OF THE STRING, BRACER, AND SHOOTING-GLOVE

THE best bowstrings are all of Belgian make, and cannot be considered of such good quality as they used to be twenty-five years ago. Then the best bowstrings were obtained from a maker at Liège, by name Meeles, the last of his race, who, with his wife, kept most jealously the secret of the manufacture, which had been transmitted through many generations in the one family, and they died childless without communicating it to anyone. Their residence was kept with the windows on the street side constantly barred up, so as to make sure that they could not be overlooked, and they depended entirely for the air and light necessary for their labour on the private garden at the back of the house.

In the choice of a string see that it has three, not two, strands; and care must be taken to avoid those that are too hard and stiff, as they are liable to be brittle and to break very soon. The next thing to be attended to is that the string is smooth and round throughout, and sufficiently increased in bulk at the ends where are the eye and loop. It cannot be doubted that a quicker cast may be obtained from a *thin string* than from a *very thick one*; but it will be better to choose strings strong enough in proportion to the strength of the bows to ensure their (i.e. the bows') safety rather than to pay too much regard to this quickness of cast. When the string is chosen its eye must be fitted into the groove of the lower horn of the bow. In order to make *the loop* at the other end the string must now be applied to the back of the unbent bow,

and the first rounded turn of the loop must be made at about
three inches from the groove of the upper horn, or two and a
half inches in the case of a lady's bow. At about the distance
of one inch and a quarter beyond—and one inch in the case of
a lady's string—the crown of this rounded turn the string must
be sharply bent back, and this sharp bend applied round the
string on the other side of the rounded turn. Slip the sharp
turn a little further down the string towards the eye, and
twist the remaining reversed end of the string three times
round the looped part of the string, beginning inwards. The
sharp turn must then be pushed back into the first bent position. The eye must now be passed over the upper horn, and
passed far enough down the bow to allow the loop to be passed
over the lower horn and into its groove, and the loop should
be so applied into this groove that the waste end of string shall
lie between the sharp turn and the horn (see fig. 16). If the
waste end of the string be then knotted firmly, and the remainder
cut off, the loop will be finished, and, if successfully managed,
will never shift or stretch when it has once reached its bear-
ings. The virtue in this loop is that it is quite fast and tight
when in use, and yet it can be very readily slipped off and
opened for readjustment on the same bow, or for application to
another bow of different length. By far the neatest finish to
a bowstring is the addition of a *second eye* instead of the *loop*,
and this is now very readily done by the bowmakers for their
customers at a small additional charge; but every handy
archer should learn how to make this second eye for himself.
The following method is recommended. When the loop has
been correctly adjusted, so that the string, when the bow is
braced, is at a suitable distance from the bow (i.e. six inches
or so for a man's bow, or five and a half inches for a lady's bow)
mark with ink the crown of the rounded turn before mentioned
(i.e. the point of the string, not of the waste twisted round the
string in the loop nearest to the upper horn). Now unbrace
the bow and take off the string. Undo the loop and straighten

out the string (see fig. 15).   At the distance of one inch and a
quarter (one inch is sufficient for a lady's string) from the
ink-mark, and on each side of it, tie tight round the string a

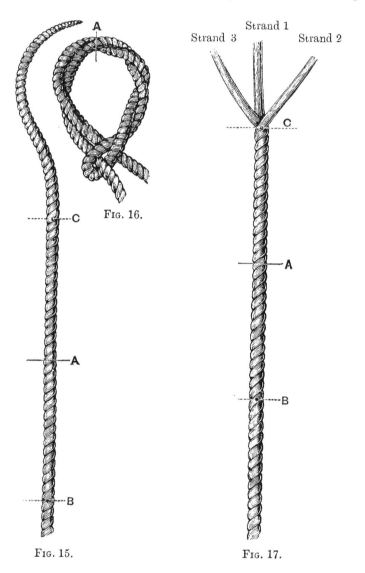

FIG. 16.

FIG. 15.   FIG. 17.

small piece of fine waxed thread; cut off the waste end of the
string at the knot made in finishing the loop.   Keep the part
of the string between the two ties well wound up during the
whole of the succeeding stages of the manufacture of this

part into an eye so as to correct the necessary unwindings. Unwind up to c, fig. 17, completely separate, and straighten out the three strands (1), (2), (3), fig. 17, of the remaining portion of the waste end of the string up to its tie at c. Pass a small marlinespike or stiletto between each of the three strands of the string, just beyond the other tie at b, and as close to it as possible. Flatten out the three unwound strands of the waste end fingerwise (fig. 17). Bend (keeping it wound up) the part of the string between the two ties b and c, so as

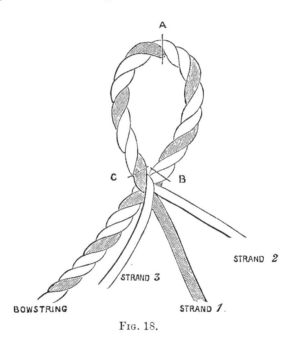

FIG. 18.

to bring these two ties exactly together, with the separated strands (1), (2), (3) lying across the string at right angles to its worm (see fig. 18). Now insert the middle strand (1), fig. 19 (taking care to cross the worm of the string), with the help of the marlinespike under that strand of the string across which it lay in fig. 18.

Give the commenced eye a quarter turn to the left (see fig. 20), so that it is seen edgewise, tie c being now out of sight.

Strand (2) now lies across the strand of the string under

which strand (1) has just been passed, and the next strand of
the string. Insert it (2) under this latter strand, and give the
eye another quarter turn, showing strand (2) inserted (see
fig. 21).

Strand (3) as shown in fig. 21 must now be bent to the left
across the central upright strand of the string, and passed
under that strand and brought out and back towards the right
again (see fig. 22).

The loop will now be an *eye,* as soon as the two ties B

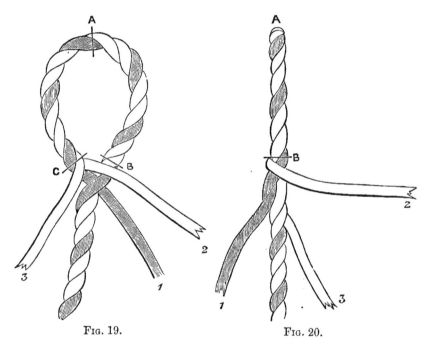

Fig. 19.   Fig. 20.

and c have been brought close together again, and the three
strands, loosened by constant manipulation, have been carefully waxed and wound up again.

From this point there are two methods of proceeding : the
one, which will complete the eye so as to resemble the manu
factured eye, by winding each waste strand round and round
its own corresponding strand ; and for this method the waste
strands should now be *tapered* before they are wound in.
By the other method each waste strand in turn should be

passed over the next strand and under the next but one.
The waste strands will again occupy alternate positions
between the other strands. Wind up and wax the waste
strands again carefully. Enough has now been done to secure
the safety of the *eye-splice*; but it will be best to splice in
once again each of the waste strands; then bind tightly over
the waste for about half an inch down the string, and cut off
the remaining waste strands.

In order to taper the waste strands, divide each into two

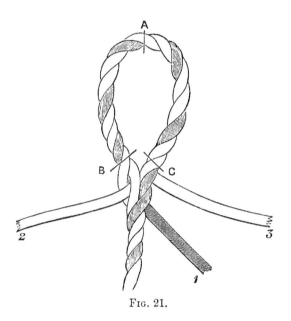

Fig. 21.

equal parts, lengthwise, after the position shown in fig. 22
has been completed, and with a blunt knife fine down each
of the two parts gradually till each tapers to nothing at the
length of about two and a half inches from the string; now
work in as much wax as possible, flattening each of the divided
portions in so doing; readjust the divided portions, and
wind them carefully together again. The waste ends may
then be wound round and round the appropriate strands until
they disappear; or the first method of splicing may be continued till they fade off and disappear, so that the finishing

E

process of binding and cutting off the waste ends may be
dispensed with.   Don't bind the eye with string, leather, or
any other material.   If the string was originally sufficiently
thicker at this part, its final failure is very unlikely to occur
at either of the eyes, and there is a general belief that any
unnecessary clothing of the eye interferes with the cast of the
string.   If the waste strands, *untapered,* be spliced in and
in very frequently, the string will be somewhat shortened.
A string that is too short—i.e. too far from the bow when

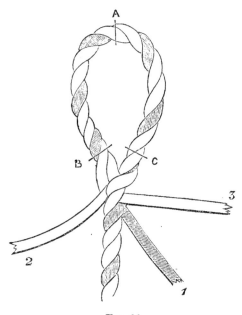

Fig. 22.

braced—cannot be lengthened without altering the loop or
remaking the eye, but a string that is slightly too long—i.e.
not giving sufficient distance between the string and bow when
braced—can be shortened by spinning it up tighter ; but care
must be taken not to attempt this operation with a hard-
cemented, new string, as it will almost certainly prove fatal
to the string, which will snap in two at the loose ; and no
string should be much spun up.

The next thing to be considered is the *necessary clothing* of the string, called its *lapping*. Without doubt the best *lapping* of all is a thin strip of *whalebone,* of the width of about one-eighth of an inch. This may be fastened on to the string at about two inches and a half from its (the string's) centre (this is calculated for the case of a bow whose centre or fulcrum is one inch below the top of the handle: if the centre be at the top of the handle, as in old Flemish bows, the lapping need not be so long, and if the centre be lower down than one inch, as in the Scotch make of bows, the lapping must be still longer) with very fine string, waxed thread, or silk, so that the whalebone lapping may be wrapped closely round the string in the reversed direction to the grain or worm of the string.

Let an arrow be now applied, resting on the top of the bow hand as if the hand holds the handle of the bow in shooting, and exactly at right angles to the braced string. This exact right angle must be carefully attended to, because, if the upper angle be an acute angle between the arrow and string, cast or force will be lost in the force of the cast being resolved, as shown previously in the case of an increased impediment, acting as an obstruction to the right line of force : the arrow will beat itself wastefully on the top of the hand in overcoming the unnecessary impediment ; and, if this upper angle be an obtuse angle, the difference between the lower and upper portions of the string will be increased, to the manifest injury of the pre-arranged balance of the limbs of the bow. Mark carefully on the lapping the exact position of the centre of the nock of the arrow, and overlap with two or three strands of waxed filoselle very tightly for about one-third of an inch, with the mark under its centre. This is the nocking-place. The whalebone lapping must be carried down to the length of five inches in order to save the string from being frayed against the sleeve, armguard, &c. ; and it will be found that this length of lapping will be sufficient for another nocking-place if the string, already provided with two eyes, be turned over. The occasional use of the second nocking-place will be found to lengthen the life of the string by changing the position of the wear and tear. A narrow strip of vellum used

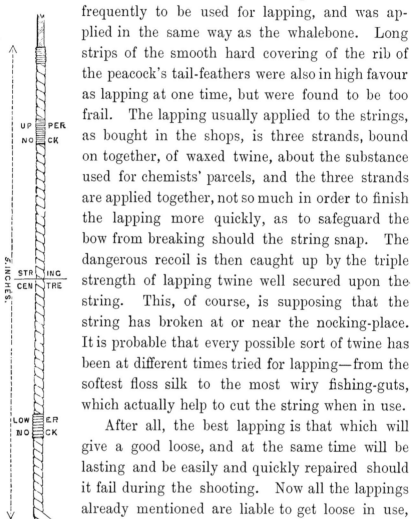

frequently to be used for lapping, and was applied in the same way as the whalebone. Long strips of the smooth hard covering of the rib of the peacock's tail-feathers were also in high favour as lapping at one time, but were found to be too frail. The lapping usually applied to the strings, as bought in the shops, is three strands, bound on together, of waxed twine, about the substance used for chemists' parcels, and the three strands are applied together, not so much in order to finish the lapping more quickly, as to safeguard the bow from breaking should the string snap. The dangerous recoil is then caught up by the triple strength of lapping twine well secured upon the string. This, of course, is supposing that the string has broken at or near the nocking-place. It is probable that every possible sort of twine has been at different times tried for lapping—from the softest floss silk to the most wiry fishing-guts, which actually help to cut the string when in use.

After all, the best lapping is that which will give a good loose, and at the same time will be lasting and be easily and quickly repaired should it fail during the shooting. Now all the lappings already mentioned are liable to get loose in use, and it takes time to refasten them. The following somewhat tedious process, the result of more than twenty years of experience, is recommended.

Fig. 23.

Take a naked string with two eyes, and make a pencil-mark on it for the exact central position of each of the two nocking-places. Wax the string well. Wrap two strands nine inches long of waxed (yellow) filoselle tightly upon the string at each nocking-place for the third of an inch, with the pencil-mark under the centre of this third. Fasten off so that the waste ends shall come out close to these centres. Do not cut off the waste ends. Now take three strands of waxed filoselle of another colour (red), and in length from one yard to four feet. Wrap this tightly round the string, commencing from one and a quarter inch above the one nocking-place, and ending at the same distance below the other. Apply this wrapping the contrary way to the worm of the string, and let the waste ends of the previous wrapping (it does not signify which way this is applied) pass out between the wraps as they occur. Now take other three strands of (green) waxed filoselle, of the same length, and wrap them tightly on over all the last wrapping of red; but this time wrap the same way as the worm of the string. Again let the first ends of the yellow wrapping pass out. The principal wrapping is now complete, and the waste ends of (yellow) filoselle are ready in place to complete the necessary thickening for the nocking-places. This lapping is very firm and lasting. It cannot get loose in use, and it is in every part capable of almost instantaneous repair, and the archer has no need to carry about him any other materials than a few pieces of filoselle, some wax, and a knife.

The most convenient position for lapping a string is assumed by passing the left leg through between the braced bow and its string and sitting down with the string upper-most and the bow stave under the thigh. This description of the operation of lapping will be incomplete without instructions for fastening off, for the benefit of beginners.

In the commencement of lapping the end is passed under, and the wrapping is tightly bound over it five or six times, till it is considered sufficiently secure. To finish off, the same operation is reversed, thus : arrest the lapping by passing the filoselle, or whatever the material in use may be, over the thumb of the left hand, interposed between the lapping-material and the string.   Wrap the lapping material upon the string the reverse way to that in which it has been previously wrapped about five or six times (see fig. 22).   Keep the material *a b* tight-drawn with the left thumb whilst this is being done.   Now draw the end *c* (fig. 24) close to the string, and along its length, so that it may lie close between part *a* and the string.   Now take the piece *a b* from off the left thumb, and draw the part *a* up to the lapping already applied. Bind part *a* on to the string.   This binding will unwind the part *b*.   Continue this till all *b* is unwound from the string and wound on again.   Now hold tight the remainder unwound

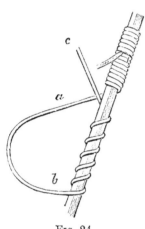

of *a b* with the left hand.   Draw it through under the lapping with the right hand ; but the surplus portion of *a b* to be drawn through must be kept tight to the last by the insertion of the left little finger to prevent kinking and cockling, which would spoil the finish.   With the same object in view, keep the waste part *a b* as short as possible.   Filoselle, being a loosely wound material, easily passes through this finish, but the kinking of some of the other tight-wound materials renders this finish trouble some if it have to be drawn under many wraps.

Fig. 24.

The Bracer or Armguard.

The object of the *armguard* or *bracer* is to protect the left arm and wrist from the blow of the string *in the event of* this striking upon it when loosed.   The expression 'in the event of ' is especially meant to imply that in most cases no need exists for the string's striking the arm at all ; but if the bow be low-strung—or follow the string, as it is called—it is impossible to avoid an occasional smart blow in the neighbourhood of the left wrist, and this must be guarded against. For this purpose a short armguard, covering the wrist and that half of the forearm, will be all-sufficient. As regards the blow of the string upon this limited sort of armguard, it may be observed that it cannot injuriously affect the flight of the arrow, as it occurs most probably after the arrow has left the string. This protection for the wrist should extend up the arm, but very little beyond the point where the bowstring would touch the arm when the properly-braced bow is extended at arm's length. For this armguard a piece of thin leather, laced closely at the back of the forearm, answers very well. Should this be too thin to save the arm from the blow of the string, let a piece of stiff card be slipped between the sleeve and the wrist. The sleeve about the wrist should be made to fit as closely as possible, and all other materials—cuffs, shirt-sleeves, &c.—discarded, or rolled up above the elbow. Care must also be taken to avoid all wrinkles and folds in the sleeve between the guard and the elbow. This can be best managed by having the sleeve no atom too long, and drawing it as far down the hand as possible whilst the guard is being fixed. It is unfortunate that the seam along the inside of almost every sleeve occurs just where it helps to manufacture folds and pro-jections ready to act as impediments to the passage of the string. Some archers use stout elastic webbing, and others wrap round the wrist strong braid, &c. The main object of all these guards is to avoid the blow of the string until the string shall have advanced so far in its course to rest as to be unable to interfere with the direction of a properly aimed arrow. Some archers, shooting with the bow in the left hand, aim with the left (not with the right) eye, and this peculiarity makes it rather more difficult to avoid hitting the forearm at some point between the elbow and the short guard. With others, when the left arm, holding the bow, is extended straight out, and stiffened at the elbow, it will be found to bend inwards—knock-kneed, as it were. In such cases it would probably be better to widen the handle of the bow, so as to remove the inner outline of the arm farther from the plane in which the string acts, than to increase the certainty of an aim-disturbing blow by adding the thickness of an armguard to the already existing impediment ; or—but this is only mentioned as an alternative, not recommended for general adoption—the arm may be slightly bent outwards at the elbow. Some try to avoid this unnecessary hitting of the arm by keeping their bows very high-strung ; but this should be avoided, as it is very trying to both the bow and the string, and it is generally believed that by keeping a bow high-strung some of its cast is lost.

The old-fashioned bracer, of which there are still many modern representatives—although Mr. Ford, in his book, successfully demolished the ' armguard-hitting theory,' which was upheld by most previous writers on the subject—was, and is, certainly admirably calculated to be hit as much as possible, being often made of very thick leather, and lined and padded as well. If something of this sort, failing other expedients to avoid hurting the arm, must be used, let it be as thin and close-fitting as possible, and in particular close-fitting for the four inches or so next to the wrist, where the reckless old armguards used to project as much as half an inch, ready to welcome the blow of the string several inches sooner than need be. And, to avoid the worst blow of all—that delivered upon the top of the armguard where it is shaped to the bend of the elbow—let the upper strap be carried round above the elbow so that it draws the front of the guard tight as the arm is straightened. In spite of all that has been said above, it cannot be denied that, such is the persistent determination of arrows well aimed and well loosed to reach the target, they will certainly very often succeed, notwithstanding frequent interruptions from an armguard in addition to the natural difficulties. Too much care cannot be taken to see that when fastened no edge or corner of the armguard protrudes that can by possibility obstruct the free passage of the string. In spite of good old Ascham's statement that 'the string, gliding quickly and sharply off it' [the bracer], 'may make a sharper shoot' (he also advised that the bow be high-strung, so that this hitting may be avoided), the guard should be made of moderately soft and yielding but perfectly smooth leather, and not of any hard material. The silver armguard, which may be fitting enough as a trophy for the Field Captain of the Royal Toxophilite Society, would be about as much out of place during the shooting of the York Round as the ancient Scorton arrow would be amongst the shafts in use during one of the annual Yorkshire meetings.

The Shooting-Glove, and other Protections for the Fingers.

The old-fashioned archer's glove—still in use in Scotland, and perhaps occasionally elsewhere—resembles a boxing-glove, being made of thick buckskin, and calculated to protect the hand from some of the accidents of war. It was provided with a pocket for extra strings, wax, and other necessaries on its back; and no doubt owned a companion glove for the bow hand, also calculated to protect *it* from injury. This glove has pieces of hard leather sewn on to the ends of the fingers as a further protection against the string; and leather straps, passing round the roots of the fingers and along the back of the hand, are tied tightly round the wrist to prevent the finger-guards from being dragged forward out of place at the loose.

The protection for the fingers, which is probably best known to beginners and old-fashioned archers, consists of three conical tips or thimbles of leather, each sewn up at the back of the finger, and attached—also at the back—to long strips of leather, connected at the back of the hand so as to form one piece, which is fixed upon a strap which passes round the wrist and is fastened securely by a buckle (fig. 25). There is nothing to be said against this description of shooting-glove if a thimble can be got to fit each of the fingers accurately; but, as it can seldom happen that in a ready-made article a perfect fit can be found, this form of finger-guard has become unfashionable, and has gone out of favour. It was probably never made with the thimbles of the right sort of leather (horse-butt), as the softer and more pliable sorts of

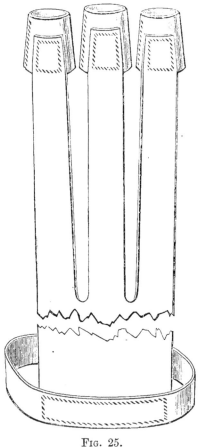

leather would be more suitable to fit all comers. It effectually obviates one of the difficulties which occurs to most beginners —that of recovering their tips when they have been scattered all over the shooting-lawn.

The 'tab' (see fig. 26) is probably one of the most ancient of finger-guards, and it has so many merits that it can never be altogether discarded. Any archer may quickly manufacture it out of almost any sort of leather, and it is very readily altered or replaced, and it is no impediment to the free use of the fingers for other purposes than loosing an arrow. The whole of the first finger of the right hand is passed right through the opening A from the side not seen, and the tip

Fig. 25.

of the finger is placed on *a*. The third finger is similarly passed through B, and its tip lies on β. The middle finger is now placed on *b*. It will be found that the 'tab' is now securely fastened for use, the string being applied to the side not seen. The tab can be readily turned down into the palm of the hand whilst the arrow is applied to the string. The tab is then replaced on the tips of the fingers and applied to the string, with the arrow at the bottom of the opening between the parts *a* and *b*. The one drawback to this description of finger-guard is that the arrow comes into actual contact with the sides of the first and second fingers, and beginners are specially perplexed with the difficulty of keeping the arrow applied to the proper place on the side of the bow during the operation of pulling up, owing to too tight a pinch between the fingers, given by the bent string. This same difficulty occurs also with other guards, but the results are not so painful, as the corner of the nail is protected by leather

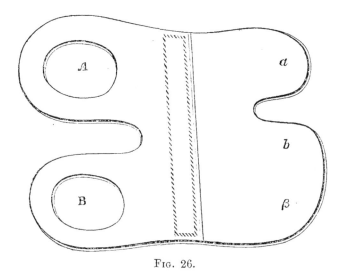

Fig. 26.

from the nock of the arrow. The tab is not, therefore to be recommended for the use of beginners. Should any archers be tempted to use it when the first difficulties are overcome, it will be found that the insertion of a piece of cork or leather between the first and second fingers will overcome the trouble caused by this pinch. The tab, as before mentioned, may be made of one piece of leather ; but it is better to have it made of two pieces sewn together, as shown in the sketch (see fig. 26), the part applied to the string being made of 'horse-butt,' which is a brittle sort of leather, the part through which the fingers are passed being made of some more supple leather.

Before the more elaborate and scientific finger-stall or guards come to be considered the remaining simple and old-fashioned ones must be completed.

Next in order comes an ordinary glove, which has lately come prominently to the front, because the constant use of a good thick dogskin glove has enabled the Champion of 1884 to keep his place in 1885 and 1886. To this may be applied the dogmatic words of Mr. Ford (slightly altered) with reference to the tab: ' This does not, however; alter my opinion as to its being decidedly an inferior method, as who shall say how much more [he] might have excelled had [he] adopted a different and [less] rational one ? '

FIG. 27.

A well-fitting glove may be improved by sewing small pieces of pigskin or other smooth sound leather over the tips of the fingers (see fig. 27).

Constant practice on the harp has been known to enable a lady to dispense with any artificial protection, and to make three golds at one end at one of the Leamington meetings.

Another method of preparing the fingers for naked application to the bowstring is to use them industriously as pipe-stoppers ; but as some archers do not smoke, and it might not be easy for a non-smoker to get employment as a pipe-stopper to others who do, a more convenient way of hardening the fingers would be by dropping on hot sealing-wax, and then dipping the finger into salt.

It is undeniable that permanently successful shooting depends mostly upon an even, certain, and unvarying loose, and such a loose can only be attained by the help of the most suitable glove, tips, tab, or other protection for the fingers. The archer must have the perfect command of the string, and of the exact ' how ' and ' when ' it shall be allowed to quit the fingers. If the glove &c. be too loose or too tight, this neces-

sary command is lost. In the first case, the feeling of inse
curity gives a hesitating uncertainty to the loose ; and in the
second, the power of the fingers is so cramped that a sensation of distortion cripples their best efforts. Further, too thick
a glove &c. interferes with the proper ' feel ' of the string ;
whilst one that is too thin, by hurting the fingers, causes
them to flinch from the proper degree of crisp sharpness
requisite for a perfect loose. Still further, with too hard a
substance—metal, for instance : finger-tips have been occasionally made of silver—the string cannot be with certainty
retained till the proper instant of loosing, whilst with leather
that is too soft and sodden, the string cannot be quitted without a jerk that staggers the bow-arm.

It will be seen, therefore, that positive rules cannot be laid
down as to either the size, make, shape, or material of the
finger-guards ; as each individual must be suited according
to the peculiar nature of his own fingers, be they callous or
tender, strong or weak, clumsy or dexterous.

In 1859 it may have been good advice to archers to manufacture their own finger-guards, though Mr. Ford candidly
confessed ' that the endeavours of ten years have hardly succeeded in producing finger-stalls perfectly to my satisfaction.'
It may be safely asserted, however, that it is better to use
the thinner leather (provided it be thick enough to protect
the fingers from pain), and the stalls must be constructed so
as to confine the hand and cramp the knuckles as little as
possible.

The ' Mason ' finger-stall, described by Mr. Ford, consisted
of a piece of leather partly surrounding the tip of the finger,
and connected over the nail with vulcanised india-rubber,
and kept in place by a ring, also of india-rubber, or preferably of silver, passing over both joints of the finger, and
connected inside the hand with the stall by means of a thin
tongue of india-rubber about an inch or an inch and a
half long; a guard or stop is placed upon each stall, about

half an inch from the top, by which (stop) the line of the
fingers and position of the string is regulated, &c. A very
similar finger-guard, produced by Mr. Buchanan of 215
Piccadilly, was made, closed at the finger-end, so as to protect
the top of the finger from possible injury.

In these finger-guards the stop or catch of leather on the
inside of the finger first makes its public appearance, but the
contrivance in its entirety has completely gone out of favour
—probably owing to the untrustworthiness of india-rubber,
even though it be vulcanised. The connecting ring removed
the objection to these separate tips that, unless they were
glued on or too tight (both undesirable), they were sadly liable
to slip off at the loose. Also the connecting tongue of india-
rubber might enable the lower part of the finger to contribute
some trifle of support to the tip of the finger at its fullest
strain, and certainly it would assist to catch the finger-tip
back from the sprawled position (much objected to by some
instructors in this craft) sometimes assumed after a dead
loose.

Mr. James Spedding and Mr. H. C. Mules, about the same
time that Mr. H. A. Ford and others were making experiments in the construction of their own finger-tips, contrived
a little brass nutted screw-bolt for securing the finger-tips
safely upon the fingers without the uncertain action of india-
rubber, or in any way cramping the action of the finger-joints.

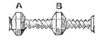

FIG. 28.

This little contrivance is three-quarters of an inch long. The
nut A is fixed, but the nut B can be moved to any position on
the screw-bolt.

This contrivance is passed through the holes at *a* and *b*
(see fig. 29) of a finger-tip shaped thus. Of course the end
of the screw-bolt over which the nut B is passed after the

screw bolt-has been passed through *a* and *b* must be clinched afterwards to prevent nut B coming off again. The lacing together of the six corresponding holes on each side of the

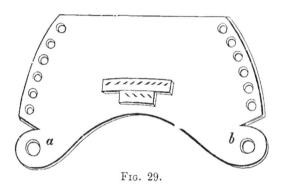

Fig. 29.

guard at the back of the finger over the nail can be tight or loose, according to taste ; but it should be laced with fine strong cord, not elastic, as generally supplied by the makers. The brass bolt passes over the top-joint of the finger when the guard is put on the finger, and may then be tightened so as to keep the guard in its place and to prevent it escaping at the loose. Leather catches may easily be added of any shape or in any position that is preferred.

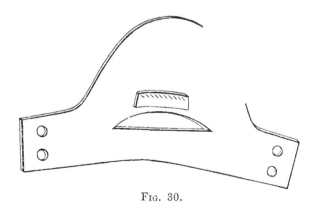

Fig. 30.

The elementary tip, that anybody may cut out of a piece of pigskin (fig. 30), further sophisticated, became the tip registered by Messrs. Aldred in 1868 (fig. 31) as the 'Paragon,' with the Mules-Spedding contrivance added, and also a catch, and a strap over the nail, for keeping it in position.

The *parrot-beak* (fig. 32) is a further development of the Mules-Spedding tip, with the brass bolt omitted.   This is not

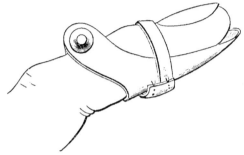

Fig. 31.

an improvement, as the sewing, if it suddenly failed, could not be readily replaced.

Mr. J. Spedding had a further contrivance which brought the little finger in to the assistance of the third finger.   This was managed by securing a loop to the guard for the third finger.   This loop was passed over the little finger, which was tightly curled up towards the palm of the hand, thus support-

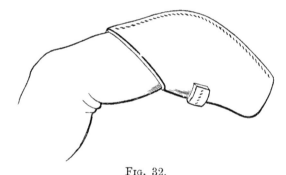

Fig. 32.

ing the third during the strain of the aim.   The little finger was, of course, uncurled at the instant of loose.

Soon after 1859 Mr. H. A. Ford began to lose the almost perfect command which he had, during about ten years, possessed over the bow.   Whether this failure arose from the use of bows

that were too strong, causing actual physical injury to some
of the muscles engaged in the action of pulling up or loosing;
or whether it arose from shooting too much; or whether it
arose from loss of nerve and confidence, through over-anxiety
to excel, and keep in front of all the opponents who, profiting
by his instruction, began to tread close upon his heels, will
never be known; but certain it is that before he reappeared
as Champion at Brighton in 1867, with his fourth best Grand
National score of 1,037 (his better scores being, 1,251 at
Cheltenham in 1857, 1,076 at Exeter in 1858, and 1,074 at
Shrewsbury in 1854), he had taken to weak bows and light
arrows, and had tried several different combinations of fingers
for loosing.   Thus he contrived a finger-tip for the little finger,
to the back of which he attached the third finger, so that these
two might combine to do the work of one finger.   This did not
prove successful; but he was satisfied with his final experiment, which consisted of a tip for the first finger, on to the
back of which his second finger was also applied; and he has
been heard to declare his belief that if he could have tried
this loose in his best days he might have improved upon his
best scores.

Occasionally the second and third fingers are furnished
with a double-cell tip for the parallel action of these two
fingers; but as contrivances of this sort are but the play-
things of broken-down archers—of whom, alas, there are too
many—they are not mentioned with any view of recommend-
ing them until, after patient trial, the other simpler finger-
guards have failed.

A piece of strong quill is sometimes sewn upon the inside
of the tip with the leather catch so as to prevent the string
from getting embedded in the leather, and to quicken the loose;
but its interference with the ' feel ' of the string argues against
its employment.

It is even doubtful whether anything but the most cautious
use of the leather catch to the finger-tip may not be most

dangerous. Many of the best shots do not use it ; and though no doubt the certainty of the one best position for the string on the fingers, when the archer is at his best, will produce most excellent results, yet, the possibility that a permanent break-down may be the result of the use of the same catch when the archer is out of condition or practice, or perhaps tired, should make every archer careful to avoid the loss of liberty of hold that may be found advisable under varying circumstances.

CHAPTER V.

OF THE GREASE-BOX, TASSEL, BELT, ETC

THE GREASE BOX.

The grease-box was, no doubt, an important part of an archer's equipment when prepared for battle, as he had to be out in all weathers, and the grease it contained could alone help him to avoid the ill consequences of moisture about his shooting-glove. The modern archer is seldom called upon to shoot more than, possibly, one end in a sudden shower ; and many now never carry a grease-box at all. Yet there is no objection to its use. It should contain vaseline, which may be occasionally applied to the finger-guards, and to the lapping where in contact with the fingers ; also, the arrows about the footing may be greased to prevent the paint from the target-faces adhering to them.

THE TASSEL.

He must be a good archer indeed who can dispense with this necessary addition to his equipment. The tassel is usually made of green worsted, and its primary use is to remove any dirt that may adhere to the arrow when it is drawn from the ground, but the head of it may be used for carrying a few pins, and concealed within the outer fringe may be kept a small piece of oiled flannel, to be applied to the arrow occasionally, so as to prevent the paint from sticking on to the shaft. The tassel should be of moderate dimensions—in fact, the smaller the better, provided it be big enough for use. It is usually hung on to a button of a gentleman's coat, but ladies usually wear it attached to their girdles.

The Belt, Quiver, etc.

In former days a leather belt was considered absolutely necessary, and some have been known to consider themselves more fully dressed for an archery contest with the green baize bag for the bow surrounding the waist. It was certainly useful, and kept together the various things then in use, namely, the glove, the quiver, the tassel, the grease-box, the tablets for scoring, the pricker for the same purpose, the armguard, &c. A well-appointed archer of the present day devotes a coat specially for the purposes of archery, and this is fitted with a long leather-lined pocket let into the back of the coat, to the left of the left back-button. This pocket holds his arrows, and becomes his quiver. The tassel is attached to a front button. Any suitable note-book with a pencil goes into a pocket, taking the place of the tablet and pricker. As a belt is not the most convenient receptacle for the rest of his equipment, no belt is carried. As ladies are not yet so well provided with pockets as gentlemen, they still find it almost absolutely necessary to carry a belt for their various requisites, and some will even voluntarily (or perhaps involuntarily, in the case of the Championess of the West) handicap themselves by carrying the whole apparatus in solid silver.

The Scoring Apparatus.

Any ordinary note-book fitted with a pencil is by far the best thing for keeping the correct record of an archer's score. Very convenient scoring-books are to be bought at the archery shops, and these contain usually the forms for York Rounds for gentlemen, and National Rounds for ladies, to be filled up with plain figures entered in the right places as the scores are made. The objection to these books is that the rounds shot are not invariably York and National rounds. That the ingenious may be saved the trouble of re-inventing the best

scoring-apparatus of past times it is here described. A card
3½ inches by 2½ inches was slipped into a silver frame, which
was much like the contrivance used for direction cards for
luggage in travelling. Between the card and the back of the

1	2	3	4	5	6	7	8	9	10	11	12	H	S	1	2	3	4	5	6	7	8	H	S	1	2	3	4	H	S
												8	8																
												4	42										3	15				2	6
												15	75									15	75				5	25
												21	147									12	84				10	70
												8	72									14	126				7	63

100Yds 1st Round					66	34	80Yds			47	301	60Yds 24 164		Score
a strength uncertain wind!!													33	177
										11			35	237
Total 137 · 809 ...													36	246
													104	654

| 2nd Round | | | | | | | | | | | | | | |
| Double Round | | | | | | | | | | | | | | |

Mr. Ford shot another dozen arrows at 60 yards, scoring 80, and shows his score
in the St. George's Round to be 654 from 104 hits.

Fig. 33.

silver frame was a leather pad of the same size as the card.
A pricker was used to record the score on the card, and the
leather pad protected the point of the pricker from the silver
back. The card had engraved upon it the form of the round
usually shot. The form for a York Round is here
given. The figures on the left-hand side indicate
the twelve double ends of six arrows each—72
arrows shot at 100 yards; the middle figures
indicate the eight double ends of six arrows each
—48 arrows at 80 yards; and the figures on the
right-hand side indicate the four double ends at
60 yards—24 arrows. This form is now filled up
with the best York Round that Mr. H. A. Ford
ever made, as recorded by himself, and here given
in facsimile. It is believed that the wonderful
score here recorded of 809, from 137 hits, in the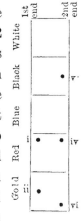
York Round, was made at Cheltenham about September 4
1855; but, through an unaccountable want of courtesy on
the part of the Ford family, the accurate date of this score
cannot be given as a fact. It is not entered in the way

invented by the Rev. J. Bramhall, which indicates not only the hits made, but also the order in which the arrows were shot. Thus (see p. 69) say the first arrow, shot at 100 yards, hit the red ; the second was a gold, and the third a miss ; the fourth arrow was a red; the fifth was a black, and the sixth a gold. Each set of vertical spaces for whites, blacks, blues, reds, and golds is allotted to a double end of six arrows. The result of the first arrow is marked on the left-hand side at the top, the second on the left-hand side in the middle, and the third on the left-hand side at the bottom. The same is done with the next three arrows on the right-hand side. Of course, when an arrow misses the target, no mark is made, and the order of the misses is shown by the hits.

A translation into the modern method of Mı Ford's best score is here given.

100 Yards				Hits	Score			
97	973	971	731	= 11	63			
753	755	711	973	= 12	60			
753	75	973	53	= 10	54			
75	751	953	97	= 10	58			
731	73	977	775	= 11	63			
551	553	733	531	= 12	46			
						Hits	Score	
80 Yards						66	344	Totals
977	97	955	973	= 11	77			
953	993	975	975	= 12	80			
975	973	755	755	= 12	74			
951	775	953	955	= 12	70			
60 Yards						47	301	Totals
995	997	995	775	= 12	90			
977	753	775	773	= 12	74			
						24	164	Totals
				Grand totals		137	809	

The incurable fault of this method of scoring by prick-marks is that it is impossible to correct a mistake or to verify the accuracy of scores as recorded. (Is there not the Hibernian story of the archer who, in perfect good faith, believed that he made seventy-three hits with seventy-two arrows at sixty yards ?)

So much that was unpleasant transpired after the Crystal Palace Meeting in 1871, that in 1872 the system of scoring at the public meetings by means of these prick-marks in the different colours was finally abandoned, and the scoring by the figures 1, 3, 5, 7, 9 introduced instead. This scoring by figures had then already been for some years in vogue amongst the West Kent archers, introduced by the hon. secretary, Mr. R. B. Martin, and the members of the Royal Toxophilite Society had mostly, for many years previously, kept their private scores in plain figures.

In this method no attempt is ever made to record the order in which the hits at any end fall; neither is it considered advisable to do so, though it would be equally easy to enter the figures in the same order, when known, as the hits are made; but this is a matter of no importance.

THE REGISTER.

Every archer is most strongly recommended to keep a careful and accurate record of all the shooting he does, not only by entering in a scoring-book every arrow shot during the day (which will act as a check to irregular and careless practice), but also by keeping a register, or book of record, in which the results of each day's shooting should be entered. Those who have not been in the habit of booking all their successes and shortcomings have no idea of the great interest with which this record invests the most solitary practice, and how conducive it is to its steady and persevering continuance. It begets a great desire to improve: for no man likes to have evidence before his eyes of his pains and exertions being of no avail, and of himself at a standstill in any pursuit he takes an interest in; it ensures a due carefulness in the shooting of every arrow, since without it the score will be bad and therefore disagreeable to chronicle; it excites emulation, by enabling the average of one man's shooting to be compared with that of another, and restrains by its sternly demonstrating figures those flights of imagination occasionally indulged in by the owners of inaccurate memories as to feats performed and scores achieved. By taking note also in this register of the causes of failure at different times, a lessened chance will exist of their occurring again, as it will keep the same always in view, and the necessity of their avoidance prominently before the attention. In short, the archer will find the little trouble the keeping of it occasions him so abundantly repaid in a variety of ways, that when it is once commenced he will never afterwards be induced to abandon its use.

Whilst the subject of register is under consideration the beginner's attention should be called to the 'Archer's Register,' edited by Mr. J. Sharpe, which is issued annually, and gives a full account of all the public archery meetings of the previous year, and of the doings of all the principal societies in the kingdom.

THE 'ASCHAM.'

This term is applied to an upright narrow cupboard, contrived for the purpose of holding all the implements of archery. It is constructed so that the bows may stand or hang upright in the back part, and in the front each individual arrow may stand, also upright, and sufficiently apart from its neighbour to avoid the possibility of any injury to the feathers. In height this *Ascham* should be upwards of six feet, so that there may be sufficient room for the longest bows, and the bows should all, if standing, be on a bottom raised some few inches above the floor of the apartment, as an additional security against damp, which is a most fatal enemy to the bow. In damp situations, and particularly at the seaside, great care must be taken to keep out all moisture. Also, as far as possible, a tolerably even temperature should be maintained. The long box in which an archer keeps his stock of bows, arrows, &c., when travelling, is also called an *Ascham*.

THE TARGETS.

The backing of the *target* is made of thrashed or unthrashed straw (rye-straw is the best) firmly bound together whilst wet with strong tarred string, and in construction is somewhat similar to the make of beehive, only it is made flat. It is circular, and the front of this straw *boss* (as it is called), intended for the canvas facing, is worked up with a flat surface, so that the facing may lie upon it more evenly than it could upon the other side. The canvas facing must also be circular, and exactly four feet in diameter; of course the straw *boss* should also be as nearly as possible of the same size, but on no account less. The canvas facing is divided into a central circle of gold, surrounded by concentric rings of red, blue, black, and white, arranged in this order of colour from the centre outwards. The radius of the golden centre and the breadth of each of the surrounding rings should be the same, namely, one-fifth of four feet, i.e. four inches and four-fifths of an inch. Each hit in these colours is valued as follows nine in the gold, seven in the red (formerly called scarlet), five in the blue (still occasionally known as inner white), three in the black, and one in the white. These figures, however, do not correctly represent the value of the rings according to their respective areas. The area of a circle is proportional to the square of its radius. Therefore the area of the circle containing the gold and red together is four times as large as the area of the gold circle alone; and it follows that if the gold circle be removed from this larger circle the remaining red ring will be three times the size of the gold circle. In the same manner, the circle containing the gold, red, and blue will in area be nine times as large as the gold circle alone; and if the combined gold and red circle be removed the remaining area of the blue ring will be five times as large as the gold. Again, the area of the circle containing the gold, red, blue, and black will be sixteen times larger than the gold;

and if the gold, red, and blue be removed, an area seven times as large as the gold will be left for the black ring. Finally, the entire face of the target contains an area twenty-five times at large as the gold, and the white ring is nine times as large as the gold. Thus we get the target divided into twenty-five parts, of which one part is gold, three parts are red, five are blue, seven are black, and nine are white. But it does not correctly follow that, nine being taken to represent the value of a hit in the gold, and one as the value of a hit in the white (because the white ring is nine times larger than the gold circle), a hit in the red ring should count as seven, a hit in the blue as five, and a hit in the black as three. The proportion of the areas between the white and black rings is as nine to seven, giving the value of $1\frac{2}{7}$ for each hit in the black, or 1·28571 in decimals. Similarly, the proportion of area between the white and blue rings is as nine to five, giving the value of $1\frac{4}{5}$, or 1·8, as the value of each hit in the blue circle. The proportion of the area between the white and the red rings is as nine to three, giving the value of three for each hit in the red ring.

It may be taken that these values of 9, 7, 5, 3, 1, representing the hits in gold, red, blue, black, and white, are the best that can be adopted, and in their sum represent the twenty-five parts, the size of the gold, into which the target may be supposed to be divided.

There appears to be no exaggeration of the value of the gold as compared with the white, and the exaggerated value of the other colours very properly rewards superior skill, as shown by central hitting of the target.[1]

In the days when handicapping was done by taking off rings instead of percentages it might have been better to reduce the values of these reds, blues, and blacks when made by the more skilful.

---

[1] See Sir John F. W. Herschel's *Familiar Lectures on Scientific Subjects,* ' Estimation of Skill in Target-shooting,' p. 495.

The old exploded custom of adding hits to score was only a roundabout method of reducing the values of the hits from 9, 7, 5, 3, 1 to 5, 4, 3, 2, 1.

Targets are now all made of the same size, as already mentioned; but for many years after the revival of archery in 1781 four-feet targets were only used at the long distances of 120, 100, and 90 yards, whilst targets of three feet and two feet in diameter were used at the shorter distances and by ladies. In still older times our modern target-practice was represented by what was called the *Paper Game*, from paper being employed instead of the oil-painted canvas now in use.

It was an old fashion to score in money, thus: a gold was 2*s*. 6*d*., a scarlet 2*s*., an inner white 1*s*. 6*d*., a black 1*s*., and a white 6*d*.; and this is still the custom with the Woodmen of Arden, whose members still receive in cash at the end of a prize meeting the total value of their scores. The same custom also prevails at the Annual Scorton Arrow Meeting, except that each archer pays 6*d*. into the pool for every hit he makes in the white.

Formerly, unless an arrow was entirely in one colour, it was counted as a hit in the inferior of the two colours between which its position was divided; but now, except with the Woodmen of Arden, the contrary custom prevails, and the arrow will count as a hit in the superior colour, unless it be quite surrounded by the inferior colour. It is right that the archer should have the benefit of any doubt in this matter.

The purchasers of targets should ascertain that they have well-painted and well-seasoned facings. The American-cloth facings sometimes to be met with are most unsatisfactory, and occasionally there is too much of a sticky compound laid on the facings previous to the paint, which adheres to the arrow, and helps to denude the target of colour.

It is not generally acknowledged that the colours of the target at present in use are well adapted for most accurate shooting. They are too bright and glaring, confusing to the eye, and drawing the attention away from the centre, so that it is most difficult to avoid aiming at the target generally, rather than the gold. Now that the scoring is kept in figures, and no longer in colours, there would be no difficulty in substituting other colours that would assist to concentrate the aim, if only a general agreement about the nature of the change could be arrived at.

The usual custom of fixing targets is, that the centre of the gold shall be four feet from the ground, and as the target is always sloped with its lower part advanced towards the shooter, it follows that the correct distance of the bottom of the target from the ground is a trifle more than two feet and one inch.

The Target-Stands.

The most usual *target-stands* are of iron in three pieces, each of about six feet in length, hinged together at the top, and painted green, forming a tripod for the support of the target, which is caught on to it by a hooked spike at the top of the stand, and kept from shifting its position thereon by a spike about half way up each of the front legs. These stands are so destructive to any arrows that hit them, even through the targets, that, for home use, they should be padded in front with a strip of thick felt, secured with strong twine, and then carefully wrapped with strong binding and painted.

The late Mr. James Spedding first invented this method of covering the stands which he had made for the Royal Toxophilite Society, of three long ash poles, united together at the top with iron nutted screw-bolts. When the stand is so treated it is almost impossible that an arrow can be injured by contact with the stand, and the extra expense (which is, however, considerable) is soon saved by the saving in arrows at 2s. 6d. apiece.

The Meyler stand, a very expensive machine, was a strong iron arm, fitted into a metal socket fixed in the ground, and at the upper end provided with three prongs, upon which the target was fixed; but it possessed the same incurable fault as the old earthen butts, in that it was immovable (except to the places where the necessary sockets were).

THE QUIVER.

The tin *quiver*, made in different sizes to contain six, a dozen, or more arrows, with sometimes a receptacle at the top for spare strings, wax, thread, silk, file, &c., is too handy an article to be ever altogether discarded, though the arrows in it do occasionally suffer by being indiscriminately jumbled together. The arrow-boxes of wood now made to hold different quantities of arrows are, of course, to be preferred. But the best receptacle for arrows on a journey is a properly fitted compartment in the bow-box, and the method invented by the Rev. J. M. Croker is the best of all. This is fitted with a hinge, so that any arrow in it can be removed without shifting any of the others.

CHAPTER VI.

OF BRACING, OR STRINGING, AND NOCKING

In the previous chapters such plain directions have been given concerning the various implements of archery as will enable each archer to provide himself with the best of the kind that his inclinations or means may lead him to adopt, and to enable him to avoid such as are in themselves radically bad, or likely to add to the difficulties he is sure to meet with before arriving at any great or satisfactory proficiency in the art. Having been thus enabled to form a choice as to his weapons, he must now be guided in their use; and, in the first place, there are a few minor matters that cannot be altogether passed over in silence. The first of these is the *bracing* or *stringing* of a bow, which may be considered as the first preliminary operation to actual shooting. This is the act of *bending* the bow, when unstrung, sufficiently to enable the archer to slip the upper *eye* of the string into the *nock* of the upper horn. To effect this, the usual method is to set the lower horn of the bow (its back being turned towards the archer) on the ground, against the inside of the right foot, this being turned a little inward so as to prevent the horn from slipping out of place. Then, the handle being firmly grasped with the right hand, and the lower or wrist-part of the left hand being rested upon the upper limb of the bow a few inches below the upper eye of the string, a strong steady pull must be applied with the right hand at the handle (the left hand and right foot forming the *points d'appui*) so that the bow may be bent, whilst the thumb and second joint of the first finger, or preferably the tips of the first and second fingers of the left hand, carry the eye of the string into the nock. Novices must be particularly careful that they do not get either of the fingers entangled between the string and the bow.

In stringing the bow, it is quite unimportant whether it be held in the right or left hand; but if the finger-tips be worn on the right hand, it is better to use this hand for the purpose of grasping the bow, rather than for helping the eye of the string into its place.

To unstring the bow, the action is the same as in the final position of stringing it, except that the eye·of the string is slipped out of the horn.

To string and unstring a bow gracefully and without apparent effort is an affair rather of knack than of much strength or force, and is therefore only to ·be learnt with a certain amount of practice. The archer must keep, as far as possible, an upright position, as to crouch over the operation is ungainly, and interferes with the satisfactory application of the necessary amount of effort.

The bow being now strung, two things must be carefully noted : first, that the bend of the bow be neither too much nor too little ; and secondly, that the string starts from both horns exactly at the centre of each—i.e. no atom either to the right or left, but dividing the bow precisely in half from end to end. If this latter caution be not observed the grain of the bow runs considerable risk of being unnaturally strained, and the bow itself of being pulled away and out of its proper shape, and sooner or later breaking in consequence. It is even possible that the correct cast itself may be more or less disadvantageously affected by any carelessness on this point. This is one of the many minutiæ of archery, which is of more importance than may at first sight appear, and should always be attended to before the bow is allowed to discharge a single arrow. During the shooting, too, attention should be occasionally directed to the string, to observe whether the loop may not have slipped a little away, as it may sometimes unavoidably do. If a second eye has been added to the string in the place of the loop, the string will be much more easily adjusted, and then there will be no fear of its getting away during the shooting. As regards the first point—namely, the amount of bend in a bow when strung—it has been already stated that in a man's bow the distance of the inside of the handle from the string should scarcely ever be less than six inches. The advantages of having the bow low-strung are that the bow casts quicker and farther (owing to the greater length the arrow is acted upon by the string), and that the bow, and also the string, are less strained, and consequently in less danger of breaking ; but to be balanced against these advantages is the fact that the danger of striking the arm-guard before the extreme point of the string's recoil (already shown to be fatal to accurate shooting) is greater, and the cast may be somewhat less steady.

It has been immemorially customary to ascertain the amount of the bend of the bow when strung, by placing the fist upright upon the inside of the handle (at the centre of the bow), at the same time raising up the thumb towards the string ; if the string then just touches the extremity of the thumb the bracing is supposed to be tolerably correct. This is not, however, an infallible test, as the size of hands of different individuals varies considerably ; but each archer can ascertain how far his own hand, placed in the above way, varies from the old-fashioned measure of six inches, known as a *fistmele*, and, bearing this constantly in mind, may ascertain the bracing of his bow as accurately as if his own fistmele were the exact six inches.

The *nocking* of the arrow must now be considered. This is the application of the nock of the arrow to its proper place on the string. Simple as this operation may at first sight appear, yet there is a right way and a wrong way of doing it ;

and as the wrong way leads to the injury and disfigurement of the bow, let the beginner acquire the right method at first, as follows :—

The bow being held somewhat downwards by the handle with the left hand, with the string upwards, let the arrow be placed with the right hand *over* the string (not on any account *under* the string, as this latter method of nocking is sure to lead sooner or later to the disfigurement of the belly of the bow, by numerous stabs inflicted upon it by the sharp point of the arrow) upon that part of the bow (close to the forefinger of the left hand) upon which it is to lie ; the thumb of the left hand (not the forefinger) being then gently placed over it will serve to hold it perfectly under command, whilst the forefinger and thumb of the right hand take hold of the nock end of the arrow, and manipulate with perfect ease the application of the *nock* to the proper *nocking-place* on the string. Five minutes' practice will suffice to render this method of nocking easy and familiar. But if the archer be afraid of unsteadying his hold upon the handle of the bow by shifting his left thumb on to the arrow, as above described, let him hold the arrow with his right hand just above the feathers, and so apply the nock to the string without assistance from the left thumb. This method is, however, somewhat more awkward-looking.

The centre of the nocking-place should be exactly upon that point of the string which is opposite to the spot on the bow over which the arrow will pass when shot—i.e. the arrow when nocked must be precisely perpendicular to the string. If the arrow be nocked at a lower point, it will beat itself against the forefinger of the left hand, and thereby waste some of the energy that should be applied to its flight. On the other hand, if the arrow be nocked at a higher point, the drawing will be commenced from a point not contemplated in the manufacture of the bow when the compensated strength of the upper and lower limbs is arranged for a fulcrum not exactly central. Care must be taken that the nocking-part of the string exactly fits or fills the nock of the arrow. The hold of the nock upon the string must be neither too tight nor too loose ; if the first, the nock may, and probably will, be split ; and if the second, the shaft is apt to slip whilst in the act of being drawn, and the nock will be broken, or the correct elevation and proper flight of the arrow will be lost.

A word of warning must be added for the young archer against attempting to alter the range of his arrow by varying the nocking-place. For the reasons above given, a worse system could not be adopted.

CHAPTER VII.

OF ASCHAM'S FIVE POINTS, POSITION STANDING, ETC.

THE various implements of archery having been now described, the proper use of these by the archer claims attention.

Roger Ascham stated in 1545 that ' fayre shootynge came of these thynges: of standynge, nockynge, drawynge, howld-yuge, and lowsynge '; and these his well-known *five points of archery* have been followed by most other writers on the subject in this same order. He has set out so well ' all the discommodities whiche ill custome hath grafted in archers ' that ' can neyther be quycklye poulled out, nor yet sone reckened of me, they be so manye,' that it will be excusable to quote them for the benefit of beginners, for their avoidance before they have been acquired.

' Some shooteth his head forwarde, as though he woulde byte the marke ; an other stareth wyth hys eyes, as though they shoulde flye out ; another winketh with one eye, and looketh with the other. Some make a face with writhing theyr mouthe and countenance so ; another blereth out his tonge ; another byteth his lyppes ; another holdeth his neck a wrye. In drawynge some set suche a compasse, as thoughe they woulde tourne about and blysse all the feelde ; other heaue theyr hand nowe vp, nowe downe, that a man cannot decerne wherat they wolde shote ; another waggeth the vpper ende of his bow one way, the neyther ende an other waye. An other wil stand poyntinge his shafte at the marke a good whyle, and by-and-by he wyl gyue a whip, and awaye, or a man wite. An other maketh suche a wrestling with his

gere, as thoughe he were able to shoote no more as longe as
he lyued.   Another draweth softly to ye middes, and by-and-by
it is gon, you cannot knowe howe.

'Another draweth his shafte lowe at the breaste, as thoughe
he woulde shoote at a rouynge marke, and by-and-by he lifteth
his arme vp pricke heyghte.   Another maketh a wrynching
with hys back as though a manne pynched hym behynde.

'Another coureth downe, as though he shoulde shoote at
crowes.

'Another setteth forwarde hys lefte legge, and draweth backe
with head and showlders, as though he pouled at a rope, or
els were afrayed of the marke.   Another draweth his shafte
well vntyll wythin ii fyngers of the head, and then stayeth to
looke at hys marke, and that done pouleth it vp to the head,
and lowseth; whiche waye, although summe excellent shoters
do use, yet surely it is a faulte, and good mennes faultes are
not to be followed.[1]

'Summe men drawe to farre, summe to shorte, summe to
slowlye, summe to quickely, summe holde over longe, summe
let go over sone.

'Summe sette theyr shafte on the grounde, and fetcheth
him vpwarde.   Another poynteth vp towarde the skye, and so
bryngeth hym downewardes.

'Ones I sawe a manne whyche used a brasar on his cheke,
or elles he had scratched all the skynne of the one syde of his
face with his drawynge hand.

'An other I sawe, whiche at everye shoote, after the loose,
lyfteth vp his ryght legge so far that he was ever in ieopardye
of faulyng.

---

[1] It should seem possible that Roger Ascham's condemnation of this style
may be insincere, as he speaks of it as 'the waye of summe excellent shoters,'
and further as good 'mennes faultes.'   May it not be hoped that he refers to
this as his own style when he says (see further on) ' of these faultes I have
verye manye myself,' modestly classing his own excellence as possibly faulty.
See Mulcaster, who says he (R. A.) 'hath showed himself a cunning Archer,' but
this refers to his capacity for 'trayning the Archer to his bowe.'

'Summe stampe forwarde, and summe leape backwarde. All these faultes be eyther in the drawynge or at the loose; with many other mo, whiche you may easelye perseyue, and so go about to auoyde them.

'Now afterwardes, when the shafte is gone, men haue manye faultes, which euell custome hath broughte them to, and specially in crynge after the shafte and speakynge woordes scarce honest for suche an honest pastyme.

'And besyde those whiche must nedes have theyr tongue thus walkynge, other men vse other fautes: as some will take theyr bowe and writhe and wrinche it, to poule in his shafte when it flyeth wyde, as yf he draue a carte. Some wyll gyue two or iii strydes forwarde, daunsing and hoppynge after his shafte, as long as it flyeth, as though he were a madman. Some which feare to be to farre gone, runne backewarde as it were to poule his shafte backe. Another runneth forwarde when he feareth to be short, heauynge after his armes, as though he woulde helpe his shafte to flye. An other writhes or runneth a syde to poule in his shafte strayght. One lifteth up his heele, and so holdeth his foote still, as longe as his shafte flyeth. Another casteth his arme backewarde after the lowse. An other swynges his bowe aboute hym, as if it were a man with a staffe to make roume in a game place. And manye other faultes there be, whiche nowe come not to my remembraunce. Thus, as you have hearde, manye archers wyth marrynge theyr face and countenaunce wyth other partes of theyr bodye, as it were menne that shoulde daunce antiques, be farre from the comelye porte in shootynge whiche he that woulde be excellent muste looke for.'

He then frankly confesses that, though teaching others ' of these faultes, I have verie manye my selfe ;' but I talk not of my shootynge, but of the generall nature of shootyng. Now ymagin an archer that is clean, wythout all these faultes, and I am sure euerye man woulde be delyghted to se hym shoote.'

Another will suddenly crouch down on his hams, as

though he were marking a bird's flight to pluck it down, or it were out of sight.

'Another will call himself uncomely names, whilst another casteth away his bow as though he would break it for faultes that are his own ; and yet another will treat himself at faulte with such harsh usage that he shall scarce shoot again without black eyes for manye a daie.'

As the term *standing* seems insufficient to include all that has to be said respecting the attitude and general bearing of the archer whilst in the act of shooting, the expression *position* is adopted instead, as more applicable and comprehensive, and under *position* will be included, not only the footing or standing, but also the manner in which the hand should grasp the bow, and therefore, as well, the exact position of the bow itself.

In an endeavour to lay down such plain directions as may prevent the assumption of attitudes inimical to good shooting, and as may also assist in the avoidance of such other attitudes as do violence to gracefulness and are repulsive to the looker-on, it would be venturing too far to assert that but *one* position is good, or even that any particular *one* is the best; yet some general rules can with sufficient confidence be laid down for the purpose of controlling mannerisms and of confining them within harmless limits.

As regards the footing or standing and the attitudes of archers, it may be safely asserted that there are as many varieties as there are archers to call them into existence; that no two are exactly alike in all particulars; and that no one archer has yet been seen to combine all the excellences that might be centred in a perfect archer.

That an archer's general position may be a good one it must possess three qualities—firmness, elasticity, and grace: *firmness*, to resist the strain and the recoil of the bow—for if there be any wavering or unsteadiness the shot will probably prove a failure; *elasticity*, to give free play to the muscles, and the needful command over them—which cannot be the case should the position be too rigid and stiff; and *grace*, to render the archer and his performance agreeable, and not ludicrous, to the spectator. It so far, fortunately, happens that the third requirement—that of grace—is almost a necessary consequence of the possession of the other two: as the best position for practical results is, in fact, the most graceful one. Experience proves that an awkward ungainly style of shooting is very seldom successful. All these three requisites must be kept constantly in mind in every endeavour to arrive at the best position for combining them.

To the first part of position—that of *footing*, or *standing*—but little can be added to what has already been recommended in other books on the subject.

The heels should be, not close together, but about six or eight inches apart—thus avoiding the position that gives too little steadfastness in a wind in the one extreme, and an ungainly straddle in the other. The feet must be firmly planted on the ground, symmetrically, so as to form an angle of from 45° to 60° by the joining of the lines passing through the feet behind the heels. As regards the position of the heels with reference to the target to be shot at, undoubtedly the best position is that in which a line through the centres of the heels points to the centre of the target (fig. 34); but as many good shots have modified this position in the one or other direction, it may be allowed that any position of the feet—varying from that in which a line through the left or forward foot is at right angles to the line from the shooter's eye to the centre of the target (fig. 35) to that in which the line through the right foot is at right angles to the same line towards the target (fig. 36) (an extreme variation of 60°)—may be adopted without extreme violence to either freedom of action or grace. The fault of tipping forward towards the target shot at, caused by throwing the balance unduly upon the forward foot, may be cured by raising the heel of that foot. This is by no means an uncommon fault, and should be carefully guarded against as very fatal to shooting, and liable to result in most ridiculous developments. As the opposite fault has almost overtaken some of the best shots, it may be classed amongst exaggerated virtues, and is little likely to embarrass beginners. The legs should be perfectly straightened at the knees, and not on any

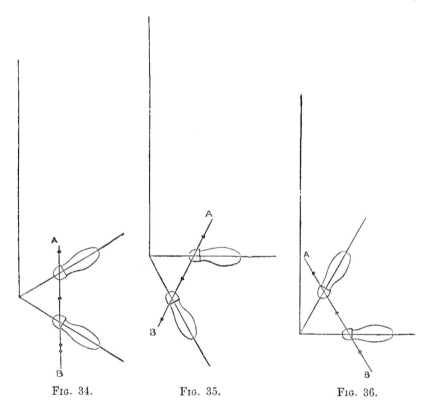

Fig. 34.   Fig. 35.   Fig. 36.

account bent forward and yet the knees should not be so rigidly locked back as to interfere with the elasticity of the position.

It will be observed that in fig. 34 only, the left and right shoulders, at points A and B respectively, come naturally into the best position for shooting at the target; but by adopting the position shown in fig. 36, a full-bodied archer may be enabled to draw a trifle further before the bowstring comes in contact with the chest; whilst in the position shown in fig. 35

an archer of supple figure can easily get the shoulders into the best position in the course of drawing up.

The body should be naturally upright, but not stiff; the whole person well balanced; and the face turned round so as to be nearly fronting the target.

During the brief period of time between the nocking of the arrow (already described in pp. 80-2) and the loosing of it, some slight alteration of the body's attitude, as arranged when the archer assumes his footing, will take place, as in the combined act of drawing and aiming, the right shoulder will be brought a little forward, and the left shoulder will be taken a little backward, before the shoulders resume their former relative positions previous to the loose, which in that position only can be most advantageously executed. The slightest possible inclination forward should be given to the head and chest, that the arrow may be brought directly under the right or aiming eye, without bringing the line of aim so close to the line through the left shoulder and bow as to make it impossible that the string can clear the forearm at the loose.

Many archers bend the body considerably forward from the waist, and quote the following passage from Bishop Latimer's sixth sermon—My father 'taught me how to drawe, how to lay my bodye in my bowe, and not to drawe with strength of armes, as other nacions do, but with strength of bodye '—in justification of this practice. Here, laying the body in the bow means taking up the best position for shooting. An archer in olden times was said to shoot *in* a bow, not *with* a bow.

' Not stooping, nor yet standing straight upright,' as Nicholl's ' London Artillery ' hath it, expresses the right position correctly.

The second part of *position* which is most important also, is the manner in which the hand should grasp the bow, and the attitude of the bow itself—i.e. whether this should be vertical, or more or less oblique.

It may be stated at once that the most natural and easy method of grasping the bow is also the best; in fact this remark is applicable to almost every point connected with archery, and cannot be too much or too often insisted upon. If the wrist and hand be in any way unnaturally employed bad results immediately follow. For instance, if the grasp be such as to throw the fulcrum much below the centre of the bow, its lower limb runs great risk of being pulled away and out of shape, which sooner or later will cause it to chrysal or break. Again, the Waring method, which used to be in high favour, ' of turning the wrist in as much possible,' causes the left arm to be held in such a straightened position, that it will not only present a constantly recurring obstacle and diverting influence to the free passage of the string, but will also be the cause of an increased strain and additional effort to the shooter, besides taking the spring and elasticity out of that all-important member the bow-arm. If the reverse of this method be adopted, and the wrist be turned intentionally and unnaturally outwards, it will be found that in avoiding Scylla Charybdis is at hand, and, though the string is well clear of the armguard, the wrist cannot sustain either the strain of the bow at full stretch or its recoil at the loose. Thus, as in every other instance, the extremes are bad, and the correct position will be found at the balancing-point between them.

When the *footing* has been taken, with the arrow nocked, let the bow lie easily and lightly in the left hand, the wrist being turned neither inwards nor outwards, but allowed to remain in the position most easy and natural for it; as the drawing of the bow commences, the grasp will intuitively tighten, and by the time the arrow is drawn to the head the position of the hand and wrist will be such as to be easiest for the shooter and best for the success of his shot.

It will be observed in the three figures giving the correct and wrong positions of the hand on the bow-handle, that the upper part of the bow hand, including the whole of the thumb and first finger, is above the upper line of the wrist (line AB), whilst the fulcrum, or working centre of the bow, is also above that line, or even in such bows as have their centres in the middle of the handle but little below that line. It is pretty clear

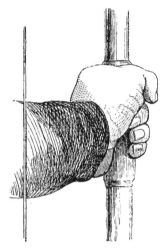

Fig. 37.—WRONG POSITION.

Fig. 39.—WRONG POSITION.

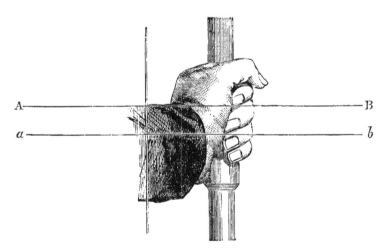

Fig. 38.—RIGHT POSITION.

that if the hand had been originally constructed solely with a view to its application to the bow, or even as a weapon in the noble art of self-defence, it might have been constructed so as to be a more evenly-balanced hammer at the end of its handle, the arm, than it is at present. Possibly its narrow escape from being another foot has interfered with its proper development from an archer's point of view. However this may be, it would be better, as a mechanical contrivance, for drawing a bow, if the strain applied by the loosing hand could pass directly along the line through the centre of the arm, with centre or fulcrum of the bow in the same line—i.e. in line $a\ b$ (fig. 38).

The nearest approach to this condition of a perfect archer's hand was possessed by Mr. G. Edwards, the first archer to displace Mr. H. A. Ford from the position of Champion, in 1860, who, though he may never have made the extraordinary scores credited to Mr. Ford, was an excellent shot, and, when at his best, had the steadiest bow-arm and the firmest grip ever seen on a bow. Through a gun accident, he lost entirely his left thumb, and held his bow with his four fingers, pressing it against a leather pad inserted between the bow and his wrist, much in the position the thumb would occupy if it could be placed downwards across the palm of the hand. This altered formation shifted the position of his arm so that the line through the fulcrum of the bow was well below the upper line of his wrist.

Some archers acquire the habit of extending the thumb upwards along the belly of the bow. This method of grasping the bow tends to weaken and unsteady the drawing power, but as a point of drill for the acquisition of such a grasp of the bow with the fingers, before the thumb is placed in position to assist, as will enable the archer to clear his armguard, its trial is strongly recommended. A steadier hold of the bow is in the end obtained by keeping the upper part of the thumb off the bow, so that the hold is between the root of the thumb and the fingers. As the first finger is often used to assist in adjusting the position of the arrow on the bow, care must be taken to replace it at the commencement of the draw. Unless the bow be held firmly between the four fingers and the thumb and heel of the hand, at the loose and recoil an unpleasant jar will be felt, with the further ill-consequence of blisters, &c. The position of the bow should be straight across the palm of the hand, so that the fingers when closed in position to hold it lie as nearly as possible at right angles to the axis of the bow.

A lateral projection on the left side of the handle of the bow is sometimes added, if the archer's hand be hollow, and this contrivance assists the bowstring to avoid the arm guard.

Before the consideration of the final position of the bow at the loose, as to whether it should be vertical or oblique, a glance must be taken at the horizontal position which should be adopted by all those who disbelieve in the possibility of aiming with bow and arrow whilst the arrow is discharged from the side of the bow, because in that position the arrow cannot be thrown to the left of the mark aimed at. This position is so cramped and awkward as to be practically useless for shooting at a horizontal aim, when a full-length arrow cannot be drawn up, as the string comes too soon in contact with the left side. Yet archers have been known to make successful scores in this style, using weak bows and light arrows.

The vertical position of the bow (but not as sometimes adopted, when the bow is thus set up at the end of a horizontal arm to be hauled at until the beginner's arrow is discharged) is an assistance in clearing the bowstring from the chest when a full-length arrow is fully drawn ; and a tendency towards this position at the instant of loose will correct the curious habit many archers acquire of throwing the upper limb of the bow down and the lower limb up after the loose, as if part of the loosing or drawing action had been a mutually antagonistic screw between the holding and loosing hands.

The chief advantage of the oblique position is that the arrow is not so likely to be blown away from its contact with the bow by a high wind from the bow side.

CHAPTER VIII.

DRAWING

Ascham seems to be right in declaring that ' Drawyne *well* is the best parte of shootyng '; and, as it is in the course of this part of the act of shooting that all the ridiculous antics already quoted may be exhibited, and without drawing well it is almost impossible to *take aim* or *loose* with any chance of success, every archer must pay the utmost attention to the acquisition of the best and easiest method of drawing. Yet it is not pretended that there is but one best method of drawing.

Here two things have to be previously considered, namely, the strength of the bow to be used, and the length of the arrow, or rather how much of its length must be drawn up. First as regards the strength of bow to be used, it should be observed that when, in modern times, the practice of shooting isolated arrows was discontinued in favour of three arrows shot by each archer consecutively at each end throughout a York Round, the possibility of making the delivery of each arrow a supreme effort became impossible, and the more frequent repetition of an effort, which, though considerable (as it should always be), is not quite a *tour de force*, is now accepted as more likely to exhibit grace in the execution and accuracy in the result, with the natural consequence that the average strength of bows now in use is scarcely so great as it used to be; though it must not be lost sight of that bows now are more accurately weighed, than they were before the invention of the York and National Rounds; and also that now a large proportion of archers pull their arrows well up, hold, and aim with them, whereas none did so in the old times when no archer had so much as dreamed that it was possible to take an aim with bows and arrows. Yet still at any public archery meeting it is easy to observe, in one or other of the many varieties of style of drawing represented, the germs of all possible contortions ; but in nearly all these cases of contortion it will be found that the ' very head and front of the offending ' is in the archer's vain attempt to employ a bow that is beyond his control ; whilst, if the weapon be well within his control, it is as needless to distort even a muscle of the face as it is for a short-sighted person to make a grimace when fixing the glass in his eye. Still it will also be a mistake to be under-bowed with a plaything, as wasting part of the power of covering distance and overcoming wind, &c. Whilst bows varying in measure from 40 lbs. to 56 lbs. and arrows varying in weight from 4s. to 5s. can be easily procured, every archer's weakness or strength can be appropriately suited. For ladies there is the range in strength of bows from 20 lbs. to 35 lbs., and in weight of arrows from 2s. 6d. to 3s. 6d.

. Next as regards the length of arrow to be drawn at each discharge. The variation in the arrows themselves may be only from 26 to 29 inches in those of men, and from 24 to 26 inches in those of ladies ; but there is a much wider variation in the part of the arrow drawn up by different archers. There appears to be a widespread belief that in olden times the archer soldiers used arrows a yard long ; but only a few archers participate in this belief, and join in treating this as a proof of the degeneracy of modern archers. Ascham, in his treatment of the subject of arrows, mentions them of many different lengths and thicknesses, without any precision, and no doubt they were much more various in his time than now. The ' clothyard ' or the ' clothier's yard,' not the standard yard, is almost always mentioned by old writers when treating of the length of draw employed by English archers ; and many con siderations (supposing positive proof to be altogether wanting) point to the conclusion that this 'clothyard' was the length of 27 inches. In the absence of any representative surviving war-arrow the evidence of an ancient model may be taken, and such a model exists in the possession of the Royal Toxophilite Society, described thus in 'A History of the Royal Toxophilite Society 1870.' 'The most ancient piece of plate possessed by the Society is an arrow, $28\frac{1}{4}$ inches long, the "stele" being of iron very thickly plated with silver, and the barbed pile ($1\frac{1}{4}$ inch long), of solid silver. The three feathers are also of solid silver. On the "stele" are these inscriptions ·

> SIR REGINALD FOSTER, Kt. and Bart.
> WARWICK LEDGINGHAM, Esq.
> *Stewards in Finsbury.*
> Anno Dom. 1663.

This arrow was presented to the Society by Mr. Philip Constable.' This Mr. Philip Constable is mentioned as one of the oldest Finsbury archers in Daines Barrington's essay on Archery in the seventh volume of 'Archæologia.' The ancient Scorton arrow (1672) is of no greater length, but has been broken and repaired and has no date on it. There is an act of Parliament (Irish ?) 5 Edward IV. ch. 4, which provides that every Englishman, and Irishman dwelling with Englishmen, and speaking English, being between sixteen and sixty years of age, shall have an English bow of his own length, and a fistmele at least between the nocks, and *twelve shafts of the length of three-quarters of the standard.* This points to the length of 27 inches as the regulation length for the stele of an arrow. The danger of breaking a bow increases the further it is drawn up, and there is no scarcity of bows that are broken at even a shorter draw than 27 or 28 inches. How many more broken bows would there have been then if the usual length of arrows drawn were 36 inches ; and this in the course of a battle, when a broken bow meant an archer temporarily disabled, as an archer ? The material used in the manufacture of bows, the wood, must have been the same as now, and, from the specimens extant, their length does not appear to have been much beyond those now in use. In fact, the length of a bow must always be limited so as to be within the reach of the archer who strings it, and the average stature of the human race does not appear to have diminished.

It is not pretended that no arrows were longer than 27 inches. Doubtless long and light arrows were employed to annoy an enemy whilst still at a distance ; but for a war-arrow, with a heavy barbed pile, to be an effective missile, it must have been provided with a strong and stiff stele, and this cannot also have been unusually long.

As dictionaries seem to avoid the compound words *cloth-yard* and *clothier's yard*, no better evidence can be found than the statement that the 27 inches constitute a Flemish yard, and that Flemish bows, arrows, and strings were always in high.repute. So the dispute must still be left for further consideration.

Hansard, in ' The Book of Archery,' 1840, treats the matter as fully as possible perhaps, and apparently leans towards the belief that the tallest and most stalwart archers may have drawn up huge bows a full yard of the standard ; yet, as he contends, at p. 191, that ' great numbers of Welsh served at Crecy and Poictiers, and it is somewhere said that a consider able portion consisted of archers,' it seems unlikely that at the same time the average archer at those battles was of gigantic stature. Ascham might have settled the matter, but he ventures no further than the statement (p. 87 of Arber's reprint) that ' at the battel of Agincourt with vii thousand fyght-yugé men, and yet many of them sycke, beynge suche archers, *as the Cronycle* sayeth, that mooste parte of them drewe a yarde,' &c.

Apart from the historical consideration of what used to be the average draw of the old English archers, it must be

H

admitted that modern archers err on the side of not pulling up
enough rather than on the side of over-drawing.   Therefore it
is strongly recommended to every archer to employ as long an
arrow as he can conveniently use, and to bear in mind that
the portion of it to be drawn up at each loose should bear some
reasonable proportion to the length of arm, &c., in each individual case.   It may be safely stated that no archer will find
that he can conveniently draw fully up and loose evenly an
arrow of greater length than the space between the left centre
joint of the collarbone and the knuckle of the left-hand index-
finger when the bow-arm is fully extended.

But few experienced archers now extend the bow-arm fully
and take their aim before they commence drawing at all.
Neither can this method be commended, as it has an awkward
appearance, from the necessity that exists of stretching the
other arm so far across the body in order to reach the string,
and it materially increases the exertion necessary to pull the
bow.   Yet this method is not without its use as a preliminary
drill for a beginner, that he may learn the necessity and the
difficulty of drawing his arrow up, whilst keeping it constantly
and exactly on the line which the arrow is afterwards to follow
towards the object to be hit when it is loosed; at the same
time not yet attending to the second and equally great difficulty of a beginner, namely, that of shooting the exact length
as well; also that he may learn how to cover different lengths
by higher and lower positions of the bow-hand.

Much diversity of opinion exists as to the best method of
getting the bow-hand into position for the aim and loose, as to
whether, in the course of drawing up, the arrow shall be brought
into the line of aim from below or from above, or from the right
to the left; and here it would seem that to make the motion of
drawing from the right to the left and upwards at the same
time is the simplest and most direct plan, since, after the
nocking of the arrow, the drawing commences most naturally
from beneath and to the right of the object to be hit.

There seem to be three successful methods of drawing—namely, first, to draw the arrow home ı at once, loosing when it has been aimed, without any further draw; secondly, to draw the arrow within an inch or a little more of home,[1] aiming then, and loosing after the completion of the draw; and thirdly, the method of combining the operations of drawing and aiming so continuously that the loose is the uninterrupted completion of the draw. It is unnecessary to consider the distinct method of drawing up and letting out again before the loose, or the uncertain method of fraying up and down, or playing as it were at fast-and-loose a bit before the loose, as no archer would adopt any such uncertain style as a matter of choice; though such stuttering and hiccoughing performances may occasionally bring back an erring arrow to its duty, or may arise from the loss of nerve and the departure of the crisp finish from what was once steady and unhesitating. Any movement of the bow-hand in drawing up from the left towards the right should be avoided, as that movement tends to contract instead of expanding the chest; therefore great care should be taken, when lateral movement is used in drawing up, to avoid passing the line of aim in moving the bow-hand towards the left.

Though the theory and practice of aiming will be fully treated in another chapter, some reference must here be made to *aiming*, although it may lead to apparently unnecessary repetition. Reference has already, somewhat prematurely, been made to the *line of aim*, and also to the *length* to be shot. Now it is clear that the success of a scientific shot must be the result of the exact combinations of the *right line of aim*, and the correct *level* of the bow- and loosing-hands by which to attain the *length*. In drawing, the process by which the *line of aim* and the *level* are arrived at must be associated in *practice*, but may be *considered* separately. Advice has already

---

[1] By 'drawing the arrow home' the full length of the arrow is not necessarily intended, but so much of its length as each archer *should* draw.

been given to avoid—as soon as possible after the beginner has
got through the first elements—the setting-up of the bow-hand
with the arrow already on the line of aim to be then hauled
at, and this for reasons already given.   But now comes in the
apparently contradictory advice, to get it planted there to be
hauled at in good time before the conclusion of the operation
of drawing, so that *that conclusion* may be certainly in the
right line of aim.   And the further advice at this stage of
drawing is that the loosing-hand be kept well back, and never
allowed to advance between the archer's face and the object
aimed at.   In previous editions of this book it was laid down
that ' the arrow shall be at least three-fourths drawn when
brought upon the [line of] aim.' But this is far from sufficient
at this point of the process.   About nine-tenths of drawing
should be by that time accomplished, or the archer will be
in a still worse position for applying his strength to the loose
with advantage should there be any pause at this stage of
drawing to combine the *level* with the *line of aim*.   Next come
the considerations whether the arrow should be held quiescent
for a short time, whilst the perfect aim is found, or whether
the entire drawing should be one continuous act from the
first moment of pulling and raising the bow to the loose.
Neither of these methods appears to have much advantage
over the other, if well executed.   The former will be a little
more trying to the bow, and, if the finish be imperfect, may
lead to letting the arrow out, which is known as a *creeping-loose*.
The latter may lead to an arrow being occasionally imperfectly
drawn ; but the bow will have no cause of complaint, and full
advantage will always be taken of all the work that is done.

The method of drawing the arrow home at once, which has
still to be considered, has this point apparently in its favour
—that it ensures the arrow's being always drawn to the same
point.   But it is very trying to the bow, the arms, and the
fingers, and, ending in what is called a *dead-loose*, at the
best scarcely produces results commensurate with the labour

undoubtedly taken, and whenever it is imperfectly finished a creeping-loose results.

Ascham, quoting Procopius, says that 'Leo, the Emperoure, would have hys souldyers drawe quycklye in warre, for that maketh a shaft flie a pace. In shootynge at pryckes, hasty and quicke drawing is neyther sure nor cumlye. Therefore, to draw easely and uniformely . . . is best both for profit and semelinesse.' The modern style of shooting the York Round, &c., is the same as used in his days to be called shooting at pricks, and his advice as to the manner of drawing cannot be much improved.

A few lines before the passage above quoted he says, ' And one thynge commeth into my remembrance nowe, when I speake of drawynge, that I never red of other kynde of shootynge, than drawing wyth a mans hand either to the breste or eare.' This he says when referring to the invention of cross-bows. But it is curious that to no writer on the subject of archery it occurred that ' under the eye ' might possibly be a better direction for ' drawing ' than either to the *breste* or to the *eare*. Yet so it is that until the first appearance of Mr. H. A. Ford's ' Theory and Practice of Archery ' in 1855 there existed no intermediate styles between the one, that was too low, and the other, which, though in the opposite extreme, was then so highly regarded as the grand old English style, that the author, though annually Champion since 1849, must have been a bold man to give the first indication of the new, and now almost universally admitted, best style for target-practice of drawing ' *to such a distance that the wrist of the right hand come to about the level of the chin,*' and the level of the arrow shall be a shade lower than that of the chin ; its nock being in the vertical line dropped from the right eye.

One of the main features of good *drawing* is that the distance pulled be precisely the same every time ; that is to say, the same length of the arrow must be drawn identically, whether this length be to the pile, or any shorter distance.

Unless this be unerringly accomplished with every shot the *length* must be more or less uncertain, since the power taken out of the bow will be greater or less according to the longer or shorter draw.

A great many devices have been tried and practised to make this exact similarity in the distance drawn a matter of certainty, such as by notching the end of the arrow, so that the left hand may feel it when the right length of draw has been reached ; or by touching some point of the face, neck, or chin, collar, button, or other fixed point with some part of the drawing hand.   But it will be found infinitely better to arrive at an exact repetition of the same action by careful practice rather than by dodges, which may, however, be useful as experiments.   These mechanical devices are unlikely to have a beneficial result when constantly in use, as, when the eye and mind are fixed and concentrated (as they should be) on the aim, if anything occurs to distract either, the loose is almost sure to become unequal.

The pile of the arrow should not be drawn on to the bow. It is far better that no arrow be drawn further than exactly to the pile ; and every arrow should be longer, by at least as much as the pile, than the archer's actual draw.   The danger of overdrawing, in that the arrow at the loose gets set inside the bow, to its own certain destruction and to the bow's and the archer's infinite risk, is very considerable.   Nothing can be gained by the violation of this rule.   In cases where a beginner may be likely to overdraw, a string of the correct length to be drawn may be tied between the bow string and the handle of the bow, which will effectually prevent such an occurrence.

It is believed that all archers, good, bad, and indifferent, are (more or less) constantly subject to one failing, namely, that in completing the draw, after the aim is taken, a slightly different line to that occupied by the arrow (if correctly aimed) is taken, instead of making the line of finish (as they should do) an exact continuation of the arrow's axis, dropping the right hand, or letting it incline to the right, or both ; the effect being to cast the arrow out of the direction it had indicated, and by means of which the aim had been calculated. Here nothing but the most minute attention and constant practice will save the archer ; but he must be prepared for participation in this common failing, and it is one of which he will be often quite unconscious, though the cause of his frequently missing the target. The very best archer needs to bear constantly in mind the necessary avoidance of this fault ; for, however skilful he may be, however experienced and practised a shot, he may be quite sure that it is one into which he will be constantly in danger of falling. Failure in wind is frequently caused more by this failing than by the effect of the wind itself ; for instance, the aim, perhaps, is designedly taken so as to make some allowance for a side-wind, and then the loose is delivered as if no allowance had been made. The difficulty all experience in shooting correctly on a ground where the distant level is not horizontal is more or less connected with this dangerous failing. Here, though the archer be perfectly aware that the distance slopes, however slightly, one way or the other to the correct horizon, yet at the instant of the loose he will unconsciously overlook this, and expect to have his unfortunate arrow travel in a plane vertical to the mock horizon instead of in a really vertical plane such as it must travel in, unless diverted from it by wind. Another way of accounting for this universal failing is that there is an unconscious detection of error at the last moment, and a convulsive attempt to correct this error before the completion of the loose by altering the line of the loose. Every archer is strongly advised, when he detects an error in the aim at the last moment that cannot be corrected before the discharge except in the action of the loose, to take down his arrow and begin the shooting of it afresh. The capacity to do this, when needful, is an excellent test of nerve.

As far as possible the right hand must always be drawn identically to the same point for all kinds of target-practice, whatever the distance to be shot may be. To the left arm alone should be left the delicate task of the elevation or depression necessary when a longer or a shorter distance from the target is adopted. It will be obvious that when the left hand is, according to this rule, higher or lower for the purpose of shooting a longer or shorter distance the relative positions of the two hands must vary from a greater to a less divergence from an horizontal level between them, and this leads to a most important consideration in the action of drawing, namely, the position of the right elbow. This, being necessarily out of the archer's sight whilst aiming, is too frequently forgotten, and a faulty weak position of the elbow is much more easily contracted than cured. Treated as a mechanical contrivance for drawing up an arrow, the only correct position of the right elbow with reference to the arrow is that the arrow's axis should pass through the point of the bent elbow, and in this position only can the archer apply his full strength. Yet, probably from the fact that the elbow must pass through positions of less advantage in the course of drawing before the full draw is reached, it will be observed that many archers at the loose have the elbow below the level of the arrow's axis ; and not a few have the elbow projecting forwards from the same axis. These faults are believed to be the causes of the constant and otherwise unaccountable, but most frequent, downfall of successful archers, generally attributed to the failure of nerve. Yet the nerves cannot certainly be altogether at fault, for the same archer, whose arrow takes its flight into its own hands, when applied to target practice, can steadily draw and hold the same arrow when it is not to be shot. It can doubtless be observed that in such cases the arrow in the one case is drawn up with a faulty wavering of the elbow, whilst in the other the elbow is brought steadily into correct position. When a position of the elbow higher than the axis of the arrow comes to be considered, it appears to partake of the nature of an exaggerated virtue rather than a fault; is an assistance in the earlier processes of drawing; and, when in excess though not graceful, will probably cure itself. Much the same may be said of the much less frequent fault of drawing the right elbow into a position further back than the axis of the arrow. This can only be brought about by overdrawing, and is seldom observable except in beginners who are anxious ' to do all they know ' with too long an arrow.

The treatment of the elbow of the bow-arm remains to be considered. Here trouble is more likely to arise with beginners than in an archer's after-career. If a beginner, in obedience to the instructions of Waring and the older masters of the craft, hold out the bow-arm ' as straight as possible ' i.e. locked tight at the elbow, a sprain difficult to cure may not unlikely be the result, and, at any rate, a vast deal of unnecessary arm or armguard thrashing. On the other hand, a bent bow-arm, such as may appear to be recommended in the earlier editions of this work, will lead to but poor results if a bow equal to the archer's power be used. Here again the best advice that can be given is to hit off the happy mean between the too rigid arm and that which is too slack. Let the bow-arm be straightened naturally as the strain of the loosing hand is applied to it, and by careful drill each archer will arrive at a method of rendering the recoil of the bow string harmless to the course of the arrow as well as to a naked wrist, which, it is now almost universally admitted, need not be brought into contact with the armguard.

A marked variation of the method of drawing has occasionally been adopted, with considerable success, with weapons of light calibre. The nocked arrow is placed horizontally a little below the shoulder-level. The draw then commences with the extension of the bow-arm, whilst the right hand and elbow take the position for loosing, the arrow being kept all the time on the line of aim.

One not altogether uncommon distortion must be mentioned for careful avoidance. This consists of a stiffening of the right wrist, with the hand bent backwards, at the time the fingers are applied to the bowstring. This antic of course cripples considerably the draw. The action of the wrist should be quite free and unconstrained until the commencement of the draw, and during the draw the back of the hand should be kept as nearly as possible in the same line as the forearm.

The left shoulder requires most careful attention. It must not be allowed to rise too high when the bow is drawn, nor to shrink inwards, as it will sometimes do with beginners when using bows that are too strong. Moreover, this shoulder must be kept so close to the line between the bow and the right shoulder that it shall project neither before nor behind that line.

CHAPTER IX.

AIMING

THE *aim* is undoubtedly the most abstruse and scientific point connected with the practice of archery. It is at the same time the most difficult to teach and the most difficult to learn · and yet, of all points, it is the most necessary to be taught. Upon the acquisition of a correct method of aiming depends all permanently successful practice; yet respecting this important point the most sublime ignorance prevails amongst the uninitiated.

Unless the archer acquires a perfect understanding of the science of aiming, an almost impassable barrier is presented to his progressing a single step beyond the commonest mediocrity, whilst his interest in his practice is increased tenfold as soon as he has discovered that hitting or missing the object he aims at may be removed from the mysterious condition of an unaccountable sympathy between the hand and eye to the safer ground of positive knowledge.

It is perhaps quite natural that most beginners should assume that at any rate as regards the application of their eyes to the shooting of arrows they can have nothing to learn. Have they not had the full and constant use of their eyes from their earliest infancy? and have not these been with sufficient frequency applied in such a manner as must secure the necessary qualifications for such a simple task as aiming with bows and arrows? There cannot, surely, be any science wanted in the use of weapons that any child can not only use but even make? Was it ever necessary to take lessons in

order to secure accuracy in throwing stones? or can any
amount of abstract study of optics contribute the smallest
improvement or finish to a bowler? So it is in this matter
of aiming that beginners, and still more those who are more
advanced in practice, seem most to resent interference and
advice; partly because they object to being told that they are
making a wrong or incomplete use of their own eyes—looking
upon it as a direct accusation of folly—when they feel that
they must surely know better than their adviser all about those
useful members, which, though almost constantly in employ,
have never given any trouble, and have never even seemed to
require any training or education; and partly with the more
advanced, who have met with considerable success in hitting
with their purblind (as it may be called) method of aiming,
because they fear to weaken their not wholly complete *Ÿaith* [1]
in their own system by admitting even the possibility of a
better. Thus in this matter of aiming it will be better that the
inexperienced archer should be referred to written instruction;
and whilst on the subject of instruction it should be thoroughly
well enforced that nothing is more unpleasant than the un-
solicited interference and advice of the officious busybody, and
—particularly at an archery meeting—no unasked advice or
instruction should ever be offered.

It need now be no matter of surprise that before the first
appearance of this work, in 1855, no writer on archery had
been able to grapple intelligently with the subject of aiming.
When firearms first took the place of bows and arrows as
weapons of war and the chase, the firearms themselves were so

[1] It must have been from the absence of this complete faith that the cele-
brated archer mentioned by Montaigne in his seventeenth chapter was con-
strained to decline the offer made to him when condemned to die, that 'to save
his life he should exhibit some notable proof of his art; but he refused to try,
fearing lest the too great contention of his will should make him shoot wide,
and that, instead of saving his life, he should also lose the reputation he had
got of being a good marksman.' And again in the case of Tell the same
scarcity of faith became apparent from his securing in his quiver that second
quasi-historical arrow.

inaccurate that chance went almost, if not quite, as far as science in the use of them. Their improvement was but slow and gradual; and for the firing of them the invention of percussion instead of flint and steel, which in its turn had displaced the original fuse, belongs to quite modern times. The neglected bows and arrows naturally gained no improvement; yet, until the invention of rifling firearms, bows and arrows, except for the greater inherent difficulty in the use of them, might have had a better chance to hold their own against Brown Bess and the bullet (it was commonly believed that it cost the expenditure of about a ton of lead to kill a single enemy in battle) had aiming with them been well understood. It cannot be doubted that many an archer (besides those who converted their knuckles into pincushions, and resorted to other dodges) must have hit upon an intelligent method of aiming for himself in early times; but such early experts must have resorted to the expedient of getting the arrow under the eye by pulling low, and would have to bear the withering scorn of all their brethren, who blindly upheld that the grand old English style of aiming from the ear was alone worthy of a man; and such despised experts would be most likely to keep their better knowledge to themselves for the same selfish but valid reason that Kentfield the inventor of the side-stroke in billiards, kept his own counsel as long as he could; and also because any crusade having as its object the deposition of the pull to the ear in favour of the pull to the breast must always have proved quixotic. So it came about that Mr. H. A. Ford was the first who, after five or six years of successful practice and many diligent and careful experiments conducted in combination with Mr. J Bramhall, braved the danger of being anathematised as a heretic for daring to impugn the dear old legend of the 'pull to the ear,' and preached in favour of a style of shooting that brought the arrow as directly under the archer's eye as is the barrel of a rifle in the hands of a marksman, without resorting to the justly condemned style of pulling as low as the breast.

Much about the same time great improvements were effected in firearms, which brought the accuracy of rifles much closer to perfection. The Volunteer movement, followed by the establishment of the annual Wimbledon rifle meeting, at which a Ross (then an illustrious name) was the first Queen's Prizeman in 1860, brought the scientific practice of aiming to a pitch of perfection that had never previously been dreamed of. Thus it will be seen that archery was not behind firearms in scientific advancement.

It is stated in 'Scloppetaria'—a scarce book on the rifle, published by Colonel Beaufoy in 1812—that ' as the deflection from the original line of flight was an inconvenience from which arrows were not found so liable as bodies projected from firearms, it naturally led to an inquiry how that could arise. The prominent feature of an arrow's flight is to spin with considerable velocity all the time of its flight, and therefore attention was directed towards attaining the same advantage for firearms'; and it is not without interest to notice that the modern rifle is thus directly derived from the clothyard shaft.

The improvement of the conical bullet is a later offspring of the same ancient missile.

An archer holds an intermediate position between a sportsman, who, in his attacks upon moving game, must waste no time in taking aim, and a rifleman, who, even in a standing position, can use the utmost deliberation. If he be as quick as the sportsman he will increase the difficulty of reproducing with each discharge exactly the same accuracy of pull and position. He must not be too hesitatingly slow, or he will spoil his bows and involve himself in unnecessary toil. Further, the rifleman has plenty of leisure to close the eye with which he does not aim ; and such closing assists, and in no way hinders, his taking his aim, by bringing the bead at the end of his weapon and the mechanical sight by which the ' length ' (distance from the target) is compassed to bear upon the centre of the target, or such other point at some trifling distance from it as the conditions of wind or weather may command; whilst the sportsman, whose weapon cannot be sighted for all the different distances at which the game he fires at may be from himself, must keep both eyes open, so that he may be better able to calculate distances and attend to such other surrounding circumstances as with the then more perfect indirect vision he will be able to do, taking in a much wider field than can be obtained when one eye only is open.

In the cases of the comparatively few archers who have but one eye, or where, from the natural but not unfrequent difference in the two eyes, one only is habitually used in aiming, the following considerations of binocular vision can have but an abstract interest. The binocular difficulties, moreover, will not occur to those archers who have acquired the habit of closing one eye whilst aiming. But the habitual closing of the non-aiming eye is not recommended, for the reason that any archer in full use of both eyes can much more readily and clearly watch the flight of his arrow towards the mark with both eyes open. There is as much enjoyment to be obtained by following the course of a well-shot arrow as there is necessity for watching the errors of those that fly amiss that the causes of such errors may if possible be avoided.

But before the demonstration of the true and only scientific mode of aiming can be proceeded with, a few words must be said on the subject of *direct* and *indirect vision*.

When both eyes are directed upon the observation of any single object—say the centre of the gold of the target at 100 yards—the axes of the eyes meet at that point, and all parts of the eyes having perfect correspondence as regards that point, the sensation of perfect vision is given, i.e. the best and most accurate image that can be obtained on the retinæ of the point to which the entire attention of both eyes is directed. But at the same time there are images formed on the retinæ, of other objects nearer (those more distant need not be con

sidered) than this point, and to the right and left of it, as well
as above and below it ; and all such objects are included within
the attention of indirect vision. The exact correspondence of
the images formed on the two retinæ applies only to the point
of direct vision, and the images of all other objects—i.e. the
objects of indirect vision—are differently portrayed on each
retina. Any object embraced in this indirect vision will be
seen less or more distinctly according to its remoteness or
otherwise from one or other of the axes in any part of its
length ; and it will be, or at any rate naturally should be,
clearest to the indirect vision of that eye to the axis of which
it most approximates.

Now, in aiming with an arrow, to arrive at anything like
certainty, it is necessary to have in view three things, namely,
the mark to be hit (the gold of the target) ; the arrow, as
far as possible in its whole line and length (otherwise its
real future course cannot be appreciated) ; and the point of
aim.

It may be well to explain here that by the *point of aim* is
meant the spot which the point of the arrow appears to cover.
This spot, with the bow, is seldom identical with the centre of
the gold, or if it be so with any individual archer at one particular distance, it will not be so at other distances, because
the arrow has no adjusting sights such as are provided to
assist the aim with a rifle. As an example, let it be supposed
that an archer is shooting in a side-wind, say at 80 yards,
and that this distance is to him that particular one where, in
calm weather, the point of his arrow and the gold are identical
for the purposes of aiming. It is clear that, if he *now* treat
them so, the effect of the wind will carry his arrow to the
right or left of the mark according to the side from which
it blows. He is therefore obliged to aim on one side of his
mark, and the point of his arrow consequently covers a spot
other than the target's centre. And this other spot in this
instance is to him his *point of aim*. Under the parallel cir-

cumstances of a long range and a side-wind the rifle will be found subject to the same rule.

. Now it will be understood that it is necessary for the archer to embrace within his vision the gold, the point of aim, and the true line in which the arrow is directed.

Direct vision can only be applied to one object at a time, and as direct vision should be applied as little as possible to the arrow during the aim, it has to be shown in what way the arrow must be held in order that the archer may, by means of his *indirect vision*, clearly appreciate the *true line* in which it points at the time of aiming. The discussion as to whether the gold or the point of aim shall be the object of direct vision may be postponed for the present.

Now it may be positively asserted as an incontrovertible axiom in archery that this true line cannot be correctly appreciated by the shooter unless the arrow lie, in its whole length, directly beneath the axis of the aiming eye. This is most confidently maintained, in spite of the fact that the strongest, the most deliberate, and the most successful archer of the present day systematically keeps his arrow a trifle out-side his right eye. It must be remembered that Ascham ordains that ' *good mennes faultes are not to be followed.*'

The indirect vision of both eyes can never be used here, for if it were, according to the law of optics, two arrows would be seen ; but this is never the case with the habitual shooter —though both his eyes be open, habit, and the wonderful adapting power of the eye, preventing such an untoward effect equally well as (nay, better than) if the second eye be closed. To state this more correctly : an expert archer with both eyes open is in the same condition with two similar eyes as a person who, with imperfect sight, habitually wears a spy-glass to improve the sight of the one eye, with which improved eye alone he sees, to the complete neglect of all that is taken in by the other eye, though constantly open. Those who have shot both right- and left-handed—and there are not a few such- -can answer for it that, though a different indirect vision of the arrow is observed with each eye, either can at will be used without any inconvenience arising from the un-necessary presence of the other. Another unusual exception may here be mentioned of a style of aiming which, though eminently successful through a good many years in the case of a Championess, cannot be recommended for imitation.

She kept her direct vision only on the point of her arrow, thus seeing the nock end of the arrow gradually diverging from its point towards each eye by indirect vision, and also by indirect vision seeing two targets, or two sets of targets, from which she had to select the correct one to secure the right direction for the loose. Many archers close the non-aiming eye, and it will be well for all beginners to do so to avoid a very possible trouble, in the case of an archer whose non-aiming eye is the best and most used of the two, of this better eye officiously interfering to do wrong what its neighbour only can do right.

But to return to the statement that the arrow in its whole length must lie directly beneath the axis of the aiming eye, which is now assumed to be the right eye, as it is so in ninety-nine cases out of a hundred. From fig. 40 it will appear that it must be so, because otherwise the shooter will be deceived as to the true line it has to take; for so long as the point of the arrow touches the axis of the aiming eye, the arrow may appear to that eye to be pointing in a straight line to the object looked at, though really directed far away to the right or left of it, as shown in fig. 41; where the arrow cB, though really pointing in the directions bcE, may, through touching the axis of the eye from B to D at c, falsely appear to the archer to be aimed at the object D.

(In figs. 40 to 43 the distances between A and B are sup-posed to represent the possible two inches or so between the two eyes, and the distances between A and D and B and D to be not less than fifty yards.)

For instance: suppose the archer to be shooting at such a

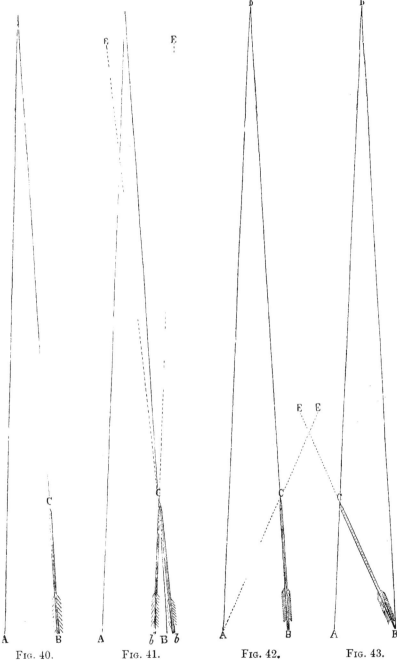

FIG. 40. FIG. 41. FIG. 42. FIG. 43.

A B, the two eyes.
B, the aiming eye.
C, the arrow.
D, the object *directly* looked at.
A D and E D, the axes of the eyes.
E. false point of aim.

A B, the two eyes.
A, the aiming eye.
C, the arrow.
D, the object directly looked at.
A D and B D, the axes of the eyes.
E, false point of aim.

I 2

distance that his point of aim is included in the gold ; he of
course will bring the point of his arrow to bear upon it, just as
a rifleman would his sights ; that is, the point will touch the
axis of the aiming eye.   But if the arrow itself be inclined, say
to the right of the axis (as in the pull to the ear it would be),
it will fly away some distance to the left of the object looked at.
And the converse of this will be true also ; for if it incline to the
left of the axis it will then fly off to the right; the archer in
these cases being in the position of a marksman who instead
of keeping his foresight in a line with his backsight has de-
liberately adjusted the aperture of his backsight to the right or
left of the bead at the muzzle of his weapon with reference to
the object aimed at.

An example that came within Mr. Ford's personal knowledge will afford a perfect illustration, and will be useful for
the possible solution of similar cases.   An archer had shot
for many years, but invariably found that if ever his arrow
pointed (as it seemed to him) in a straight line with the centre
of the target it persistently flew off to the left of it five or
six yards, even at the short distances (see fig. 43, where the
arrow BC, though pointing in the direction BE, appeared
to the shooter to be aimed at D).   He was therefore obliged
to make an allowance and to point his arrow that much to
the right (see fig. 42, where the arrow BC, though pointed
straight to D, appeared to the archer to be pointing in the
direction AE).   In vain he sought a solution of this anomaly.
All could tell him that there was something faulty ; but, as
everything in his style and mode of action appeared correct,
that something remained a mystery, until it was ultimately
discovered that, though the arrow was held directly beneath
the axis of the *right* eye (this being also open), this archer
actually used his *left* eye to aim with.   It will be readily
seen why the discrepancy existed between his aim and the
flight of his arrow, the fact being that the arrow did not
appear to the shooter to be pointing towards the object at D

until it touched the axis of his left eye, and consequently not until its direction pointed far away to the left of the mark (see fig. 43). On closing the left eye the direction of the arrow's flight and the aim coincided, because the eye beeath whose axis the arrow lay became the eye with which the aim was taken.

As to whether the *direct* vision should be applied to the mark to be hit or to the *point of aim*, the argument is all in favour of the latter. For the point of aim must of necessity be in relation to the mark—either in the same vertical line with it or outside that line. If outside, then the direct vision must certainly be upon the point of aim ; otherwise the arrow cannot lie directly beneath the axis of the aiming eye, which has already been shown to be necessary. Therefore the only question remaining to be decided is, When the *mark* falls in the same vertical line with the *point of aim*, which of the two should be *directly* looked at ? Here again an argument can be adduced to determine the choice in favour of the latter ; for when the point of aim is above the mark the latter will be hidden from the right or aiming eye by the necessary raising of the left or bow hand, as may be easily proved by the closing of the left eye ; therefore the direct vision cannot be applied to the mark, though it may be applied to the point of aim. There now remains but one case, namely, when the point of aim falls below the mark, but in the same vertical line with it ; and here (though either of them may in this case be regarded with the direct vision) as no reasoning or argument can be adduced for violating or departing from the rule shown to be necessary in the other cases ; and as it is easier to view the point of aim directly and the mark indirectly than the contrary, because the point of aim will necessarily lie between the mark and the arrow's axis ; and as uniformity of practice is highly desirable, the application of direct vision to the point of aim in every case is most strongly recommended. This teaching was quite contrary to that taught by all the old-fashioned writers, who maintained that the eye, or eyes, should be kept always intently fixed upon the mark to be hit. It is probable that even those archers who imagine that they regard directly the mark only, do so only in the case when the mark and the point of aim coincide (which with each archer may be called his *point-blank* [1] range); and this is analogous to all rifle practice, where from any cause allowance must be made.

It must be borne in mind that all these remarks apply only to target lengths. As regards aiming at very long distances, when the mark and the point of aim are too far apart to be sufficiently seen in conjunction, no scientific principle can be laid down for the guidance of an archer. Practice alone will give him a knowledge of the power of his bow, and the angle of elevation required to throw up the arrow as far as the mark. If the distance to be shot be a known and a fixed one—for instance, two hundred yards—the necessary calculations are more or less attainable; but the great distance renders the result so uncertain as to prevent anything approaching to the accuracy of aim attainable at the customary target distances. If the mark be a varying and uncertain one, as in Roving, the archer is entirely dependent upon his judgment of distances. This sort of shooting, though very interesting, must be attended with a great amount of uncertainty; but, as in every other case, the more judicious practice be applied the greater will be the success.

No hard-and-fast rules can be laid down for deciding where the point of aim ought to be at any particular distance, as this is dependent upon a great variety of circumstances—as strength of bows, and the sharpness and dulness of their cast, heavy or light arrows, a quick or sluggish loose, and the varying force of different winds. One archer will find his point-blank range at 120 yards, whilst another can get a point-blank aim on the target, at 60 yards even, by raising

---

[1] 'Point-blank' can have no other meaning in Archery.

his loosing hand so high that the angle between the axis of his aiming eye and the axis of the arrow is very small. It is now many years ago since two toxophilites, using bows of about fifty pounds in weight, with five-shilling arrows of the old-fashioned manner of feathering, and employing the same position (about three inches below the chin) of the right hand for the loose at each of the three usual distances of 100, 80, and 60 yards, found that the point of aim at 100 yards was about the target's diameter (4 feet) above the target, whilst the point of aim at 80 yards was about the same measure below the target, and the point of aim at 60 yards was at a spot about fifteen paces from the shooter.

It would have been highly interesting if Mr. H. A. Ford, who was always most faithful to his own dogma that the loosing hand must be brought to the same position at the loose, had published some account of his own points of aim, which must have had a very wide range of variation from those of his best period, when he was using 56 lb. bows, and arrows 29 inches in length, up to the time of his last appearance as Champion, in 1867 at Brighton, when, with weak bows and light arrows, his score was 1,037, with 215 hits.

The late ingenious Mr. James Spedding, who always touched some button on his coat-collar with his loosing hand, contrived a 'sight' upon his bow, which obviated the necessity of a point of aim. This was a bright metal bead such as is at the muzzle of a gun. This at the upper end of a slight metal rod (in fact, a bright-headed pin), and fitted into a groove added to the back of the bow (in which it could at will be lowered or raised), gave him a point of aim on the centre of the target at distances where his natural (may it be called ?) point of aim would have been beneath the target. With this contrivance, the slightest variation in the slope of the bow distorted the aim.

The American contrivance of the *peep-sight* is a very minute instrument, with a still smaller aperture. This is shifted up and down the bowstring, and, when correctly adjusted, the aiming eye should just catch sight of the centre of the target through the aperture. This instrument is confessedly useless except for very weak bows, and the smallest trembling even would put it off the aim, and blind, as it were, the aiming eye.

An Irish shot, the late Captain Whitla, succeeded in getting his aim on the target at all the three distances by varying the strength and cast of his bows, using his best and strongest at 100 yards, then one that was slower and weaker at 80 yards, and trusting himself to a slug like a broomstick at 60 yards.

Another archer (with the same bow at all distances) got his aim upon the target when shooting at 100 yards by touching with the thumb of his right hand about the position of the right collar-bone. When shooting at 80 yards he got his aim again on the target by raising his hand so high that his thumb, now coiled up and close to the root of the first finger, with its top joint touched beneath the chin. And at 60 yards he still obtained an aim on the target by raising the loosing hand higher, so that the same point of the thumb touched the right corner of his mouth. It is believed that in this case the gradual contraction of the angle between the axis of the eye and of the arrow led to a shorter draw at the nearer distances.

One class of archers, though implied in previous discussions, should also be treated separately, as they may be more in number than is generally supposed, namely, those who, because the left eye is the best of the two, or, from constant and incurable habit, aim with the left eye, though shooting, as it is called, right-handed, i.e. holding the bow in the left hand. Such archers should, if the peculiarity be detected in time, be recommended to shoot with the bow in the right hand. Possibly more than one most promising archer has been kept on the top rung but one of the ladder of fame by trying to force his weaker right eye to do the work that might have been much better done by the left one. It has also been already explained that, where physical peculiarities admit it, this right-handed shooting with the left eye gives the archer a slight mechanical advantage, as the divergence from the line of force may be thus contracted.

To conclude the subject of aiming, it is not pretended that shutting one eye and aiming with the other is wrong, but that it is better, though occasionally closing one eye for experiments, to use the other eye for aiming with, the one being diligently trained to keep in the background, attending solely to its own subordinate functions.

CHAPTER X.

OF HOLDING AND LOOSING

HOLDING.

By *holding* is meant keeping the arrow fully drawn before it is loosed. Ascham has made this his fourth point of archery; and but little can be added to what he has said on the subject. 'Holding,' he says, 'must not be longe, for it bothe putteth a bowe in ieopardy, and also marreth a man's shoote; it must be so lytle yat it may be perceyued better in a man's myndè when it is done, than scene with a man's eyes when it is in doyng.' This represents so exactly what holding, at its best, should be, that it needs only be added that this almost imperceptible pause before the act of loosing serves to steady the arm and perfect the aim, and is a great assistance to the obtaining of a certain and even loose. It is therefore, in company with the other points of archery, most necessary to be cultivated if successful hitting is to be the result. But let no archer think to arrive at this perfection of holding by grasping his bow as tight as he possibly can from first to last. The grasp should be gradually tightened as the strain of the draw is increased; otherwise too much toil is given to the bow-hand, and it will fail in the loose. One very successful shot had so many faults that his success was always a surprise; yet he had this invariable virtue, that, though it was obvious that he held his bow quite loosely during the draw, at the final pause his grasp was visibly tightened most firmly.

Mention should not be omitted of the sadly false concep-

MAJOR C. H. FISHER, CHAMPION ARCHER
FOR THE YEARS 1871-2-3-4.

tion many archers have of holding when fully drawn. This they exhibit by constantly letting the arrow creep out whilst they appear to be taking aim, as though they were quite incapable of checking its impatience to be off. This is a most dangerous fault, and must be most carefully guarded against.

Loosing.

After the bow has been drawn up to its proper extent, and the aim correctly taken, there still remains one more point which the archer must achieve successfully before he can ensure the correct and desired flight of his arrow to its mark ; and this is the point of *loosing*, which term is applied to the act of quitting or freeing the string from the fingers of the right hand which retain it. It is the last of Ascham's famous ' Quintette,' wherein, though he does not say much, yet what he does say is so much to the point that it may well be quoted. ' It must be so quycke and hard yet it be wyth oute all guides, so softe and gentle that the shafte flye not as it were sente out of a bow case. The meane betwixt bothe, whyche is the perfyte lowsynge, is not so hard to be folowed in shootynge as it is to be descrybed in the teachyng. For cleane lowsynge you must take hede of hyttynge anythynge aboute you. And for the same purpose Leo the Emperour would haue al archers in war to haue both theyr heades pouled and there berdes shauen, lest the heare of theyr heades should stop the syght of the eye, the heere of theyr berdes hinder the course of the strynge.'

This loosing is the archer's crowning difficulty ; for no matter how correct and perfect may be all the rest of his performance, the result will infallibly prove a failure, and end in disappointment, unless the loose also be successfully mastered. Upon this the flight of the arrow mainly depends, and to how great an extent this may be affected by it may be gathered from the fact that the same bow with a like weight of arrow

and length of pull will cast many yards further in the hands
of one man than it will in those of another, owing solely and
entirely to the different manner in which the string shall have
been quitted.

No arguments are necessary to prove how delicate an
operation it is in archery to loose well, and to accomplish,
with the evenness, smoothness, and unvarying similarity necessary for accurate hitting, the consummating effort, including
as it does on the one side of an instant the greatest exertion
of muscles that on the other side of that instant are in per
fect repose.   But considerable misapprehension exists amongst
archers as to what is a good loose, it being often thought
that if an extreme sharpness of flight be communicated to
the arrow, it is conclusive evidence as to the goodness of the
loose, without reference to the consideration that this extreme
sharpness of loose seldom produces steadily successful hitting
at any distance, and still less frequently is effective at all the
distances.   A thoroughly good loose cannot exist unless accuracy of hitting as well as keenness of flight be the combined
result ; and if the two cannot be obtained together, a slower
flight with accuracy rises immeasurably superior to the rapid
flight with uncertainty.

The flight of an arrow keenly loosed is as fair to view as
that of any bird, whilst the flight of an arrow that is badly
loosed is as uninteresting as the staggerings of a drunken
man.   This is quite apart from the consideration of hitting
the object aimed at ; but when the question resolves itself into
this practical form—'Is it possible for the same mode of loosing
to give the utmost rapidity of flight and at the same time
certainty of line and elevation ?' —the consensus of experience
should be in the negative.   There is no denying that a few successive arrows may be shot accurately in this way, but during
any prolonged period the inaccuracy of flight is sure to be
such as to render the average shooting inferior.   The difficulty,
amounting almost to an impossibility, of obtaining a loose

which shall combine great sharpness and accuracy of flight at
the same time arises from the fact that such a loose requires,
to obtain that sharpness, that the fingers of the right hand
be snatched away from the string with such suddenness and
rapidity as to compromise the second quality of accuracy—
such a sudden jerk of the string endangering the steadiness
of the left arm at the final moment, and, by its unavoidable
irregularity, not only having a tendency to drag the string
and consequently the arrow out of the proper line of flight,
but also simultaneously to vary the elevation. Excepting for
long-distance shooting, then, a very sharp loose cannot be
recommended; nevertheless, in case he may be at any time
engaged therein, the archer perfect at all points should have
it under his command.

The different looses may now be divided into the *slashing*
loose, which may degenerate into the snatch or may be improved into the steady *continuous* loose. The chief contrast
to this is the *dead* loose, which in strong hands is very useful. This consists of the simple opening of the fingers for the
escape of the string, and is liable to degenerate into the
creeping loose, which need not be further referred to except
for the purpose of again urging its avoidance. Another loose,
which may be called an *active* loose, is an appreciable improvement upon the dead loose in that the fingers at the
loosing instant are withdrawn from the string, though without
any further draw, and will be found, after the escape of the
string, to have resumed their previous position—i.e. curled
up instead of being sprawled out straight as is the case in
the dead loose. The only remaining loose may be called the
lively loose, and consists of a short and quick additional draw,
after the aim has been taken, of say from half an inch to
three inches, and finished with an *active* loose, and care
must be taken to prevent the degeneration of this into a
snatch.

Before the final treatment of the loose be entered upon, it

will be useful to consider how the different sorts of shooting-gloves and finger-tips affect this intricate operation. Doubtless in the times when the English archer was in such high repute in battle, the only loose suitable to the old glove was the *slash*, as the only method of quitting the string, which, with the strongest bow each individual could use, must, for the longest pull on such bow, have been gripped as close as possible to the inside of the knuckles of the last joints of the two or three fingers used. No other loose could be employed with any chance of obtaining full results from the work done, and it is evident from the Acts of Parliament on the subject that in the archer's drill none but long-distance shooting was countenanced. The comparatively modern finger-tips or thimbles connected by straps at the back of the hand and buckled on round the wrist must have been used with the same slashing sort of loose. But, with the old tab made of horse-butt leather, and all the different neatly-fitting tips with catches that have been invented long since the commencement of the public meetings at which York Rounds are shot, a much steadier and quieter loose may be obtained without wasting any of the work done; but, it must be admitted, with the general result that there is some slight decrease in the average strength of the bows that are used now. Moreover, it has been found that in the closely-contested matches of the present times the slashing sort of loose stands at a positive disadvantage at the shorter ranges.

With the glove and tab and tips without catches the best loose may be obtained with the fingers extended as far as is compatible with the retention of the string; and, by applying the fingers almost diagonally to the string, a very firm grip is secured combined with much facility of liberation (fig. 46, p. 128). With the help of catches on the tips the string can be taught to rest at any intermediate point on the last joint or third phalanx of either of the fingers—it will be found more convenient here to use the word *phalanx* for each part of the finger, each finger having three phalanges, first, second, and third—and the most entirely different hold on the string to the one previously described is that where the fingers are almost completely curled up (fig. 45) ; with an *active* or *lively* loose the string may be very sharply quitted with this hold, but it is more liable to strain the fingers, unless the bow be weak, and the high-set catch, though more .popular twenty years ago, is now very little used. With a strong common glove and all four fingers on the string, this extreme position has been known to contribute to first-rate scores at all the dis-

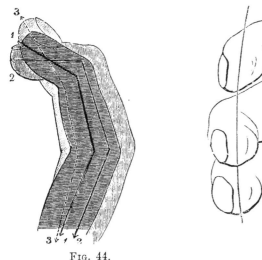

FIG. 44.   FIG. 45.

tances, and it is probably the necessary position when four fingers are used.

The intermediate position between these two extremes will probably be found the best, and this may be thus described.

The third phalanx of the middle finger should be as nearly as possible at right angles with the line of the drawn-up arrow.

The second phalanx will make an obtuse angle with the third, and the first about the same obtuse angle with the second ; and these obtuse angles will vary in individual instances according to the stiffness or suppleness of the finger-joints.

The back of the hand will incline slightly away from the line through the forearm, so that the line from the elbow through the wrist may be quite straight with the same line continued through the wrist to the position of the string on the fingers at A.   The positions of the phalanges of the first and third fingers will vary from those of the second finger, as shown in fig. 44.

This position of the string across the fingers should be neither too near to nor too far from the tips, as too great a grip necessitates a drag or a jerk to free the fingers, besides

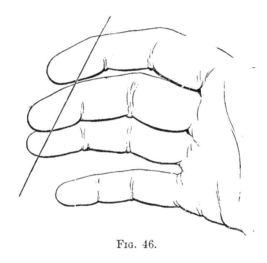

Fig. 46.

exposing more surface to the friction of the string in passing over it ; whilst an insufficient hold of the string weakens the shooter's command over it, and renders the giving way of the finger a constant occurrence.   It is therefore recommended that the string be placed as nearly as possible midway between the tips and first joints of the fingers.

Now a good loose may be described as possessing the characteristic that the fingers do not go forward one hair's breadth with the string, but their action is, as it were, a continuance of the draw rather than an independent movement, yet accompanied with just enough additional muscular action in a direction away from the bow and simultaneous expansion of the last joints of the fingers at the final instant of quitting the string as to admit of its instantaneous freedom from all and each of them at the same identical moment of time; for should one finger linger on the string but the minutest moment longer than its fellows, or should all or any of them follow forward with the string in the slightest degree, the loose will be faulty and the shot a probable failure. So slight, however, is this muscular movement that, though a distinct and appreciable fact to the mind of the shooter, it is hardly if at all perceptible to the lookers-on, as in a good loose the fingers should instantly recover their holding position, but will be at a slight though appreciable distance further from the bow consequent upon the combined effect of the removal of the pulling weight of the bow and the loosing effort. A passage out of Mr. Townsend's article, 'How should the String be Loosed,' in the 'Archer's Register for 1866-7,' may here be quoted. 'The string of the bow having been pulled to the fullest extent intended, and the pause having been felt or made, next comes the loose; and, as this *must be effected by an opening of the fingers*, the tendency of the string would be to run forward, if ever so little, during the opening; and, as the whole spring [cast] of the bow is not given to the string [and arrow] until it is altogether freed from the fingers, so, to prevent [the] loss of power, the pulling hand and arm are drawn so much further back, as the opening of the fingers would allow the string to run forward before it is altogether released. Thus the string in reality remains stationary or nearly so [quite so] during the loose; and the fingers are freed without going one hair's breadth forward with the string.

As an assistance towards this instantaneous recovery of the loosing fingers, some archers wore silver rings round the first phalanges of their three fingers, and these rings were connected by india-rubber straps with the finger-tips, thus compelling the first and third phalanges to approximate, as described in the *Mason* tips.

K

Mr. Townsend's 'india-rubber practising apparatus' has not been seen for many years, though of great assistance in experiments and in correcting faults and general improvement of drawing and loosing.

Some archers use only the first and second fingers, and the loose thus obtained possesses the advantage that the string when quitting the fingers has less surface in contact with it.

Mr. Ford's own latest loose was from the first and third fingers, with the second finger packed upon the back of the first finger for its support; and he has been heard to declare that this arrangement of the fingers gives the best loose possible, as already described.

One of the commonest faults at the present day is the habit of making the third finger do more than its fair share of work. Evidence of this failing may be found in the fact that blisters are far more common on the third finger than on either of the others, and a frequent result is that the muscles of the third finger get strained and even partially torn from their attachments. This is one of the most frequent causes of the breakdown of archers who practise much. This may be avoided and the loose much improved by turning the backs of the fingers while drawing slightly upwards, and inwards, and thus exerting more pressure with the forefinger. An example of what is meant may be seen in the picture (opp. p. 122) of Major Fisher, whose loose is remarkably good. Here it will be seen that the line of the knuckles is not perpendicular, but slopes outwards and downwards from the knuckle of the forefinger to that of the fourth.

The utility of catches on the finger-tips has already been explained in a previous chapter, but may be further mentioned in connection with the loose as contributing by an invariable hold on the string to a constant repetition of exactly the same loose.

Especial care must be taken that, whilst loosing, the left arm must maintain its position firmly and unwaveringly, and must not give way at the final moment in the slightest degree in the direction towards the right hand, as arrows constantly dropping short are the certain consequence of any such shrinking of the bow-arm—the same injurious effect being produced on their flight as when the fingers of the right hand are allowed to go forward with the string. This yielding of the left arm is of more constant occurrence than archers will generally admit, and is the cause of many an arrow, otherwise correctly treated, missing its mark. This failing is not unfrequently the result of too much practice. All must be firm to the last, and the attention of the shooter should never be relaxed for a single instant until the arrow has actually left the bow. But, though this firmness be necessary for the shooting of an arrow it is not necessary, however satisfactory the result or good the attitude, to remain for some seconds in rivalry with the Apollo Belvedere ; the bow-arm should, if possible, be instantly and quietly moved to the left whilst the next arrow is procured from the quiver or whilst the shooting station is given up to the next in order ; and this leftward motion of the left arm will correct the very general tendency there is to throw the upper horn of the bow to the right and downwards convulsively, which is a very frequent and unsightly antic. Many of the other objectionable antics already referred to are brought to perfection at this instant, and should also be most carefully avoided.

CHAPTER XI.

OF DISTANCE SHOOTING, AND DIFFERENT ROUNDS.

The attention may now be turned to the results obtained by the use of the bow and arrow.

The best notion of the old practice of archery may be gained from a review of the ancient butts or shooting-fields of our ancestors. These shooting-grounds were evidently attached to every town (if not also village) in the kingdom, as may be gathered from the universal survival of the local name of Butts. There is extant ' A plan of all the marks belonging to the Honourable Artillery Company in the fields near Finsbury, with the true distance as they stood, Anno 1737, for the use of long-bows, cross-bows, hand guns, and artillery.' These marks all have different appellations, and there is but one single instance of a repetition of the same distance between one of these marks and the other.

The ground on which these marks were situated appears to extend from a mark called *Castle*[1] to *Islington Common*, and there were two sets of actual butts at the Islington end. The distance between the one pair of these butts is given as six score and ten yards—i.e. 130 yards. The distance between the other pair is not given in the plan, but it appears to be less than half of the other, and is probably about sixty yards. The whole length of these shooting-fields appears to be about one mile on the plan; and this is about the actual distance between the Artillery Ground and the ' Angel,' Islington.

[1] Possibly now the ' Castle ' publichouse, 9 Finsbury Pavement.

The longest distance between any of the two marks is thirteen score and five yards—i.e. 265 yards—between Turk's Whale and Absoly. Here follow the names of the marks; and these may possibly be still traced in the neighbourhood in some instances. The distances are also given.

The start is made from 'Castle.'

	Score yards	Yards
From Castle to Gard stone	9·5	185
„ Gard stone to Arnold . .	10·0	200
„ Arnold to Turk's Whale	8·4	164
„ Turk's Whale to Lambeth	3·13	73
„ Lambeth to Westminster Hall . . .	11·7	227
„ Westminster Hall to White Hall . . .	11·2	222
„ White Hall to Pitfield . .	7·17	157
„ Pitfield[1] to Nevil's House or 'Rosemary Branch'	9·17	197
Total yards	. .	1425

At 'Nevil's House' there appears to be a break in the marks, but they are taken up again at the 'Levant.'

	Score yards	Yards
From the Levant to Welch Hall	8·18	178
„ Welch Hall to Butt (1)	11·11	231
„ Butt (1) to Butt (2) on Islington Common .	6·18	138
And, on going back to Welch Hall, from Welch Hall to Egg-Pye	10·10	210
Total yards	. .	757

Here there is another break.

To continue the round of the marks on the return journey without going over the same distance twice, return to Pitfield.

---

[1] The 'Rosemary Branch' publichouse, 2 Shepperton Road, Islington, N., is perhaps too far off the line to be identical. The same may be said of Pitfield Street, Hoxton.

	Score yards	Yards
From Pitfield to Bob Peek		
„ Bob Peek to Old Absoly		
„ Old Absoly to Pitfield		
„ Pitfield to Edw. Gold		
„ Edw. Gold to Jehu		
„ Jehu to Old Absoly		
„ Old Absoly to Scarlet		
Scarlet to Edw. Gold		
„ Edw. Gold to White Hall		
„ White Hall to Scarlet		
„ Scarlet to Jehu		
„ Jehu to Blackwell Hall		
„ Blackwell Hall to Scarlet		
„ Scarlet to Star or Dial		
„ Star or Dial to White Hall		
Total yards		2725

Returning to Star or Dial :—

	Score yards	Yards
From Star or Dial to Westminster Hall . . .	8·8	168
„ Westminster Hall to Dial or Monument .	8·4	164
„ Dial or Monument to Star or Dial .	9·9	189
„ Star or Dial to Blackwell Hall . . .	9·5	185
„ Blackwell Hall to Old Speering . . .	6·9	129
„ Old Speering to Star or Dial	9·16	196
Total yards		1031

Returning to Blackwell Hall :—

	Score yards	Yards
From Blackwell Hall to Dial or Monument . .	10·16	216
„ Dial or Monument to Lambeth . . .	6·10	130
„ Lambeth to Old Speering	10·8	208
Total yards		554

Returning to Lambeth :—

	Score yards	Yards
From Lambeth to Day's Deed	8·14	174
„ Day's Deed to Turk's Whale . .	9·12	192
„ Turk's Whale to Absoly (longest) . . .	13·5	265
„ Absoly to Arnold	9·1	181
„ Arnold to Blood House Bridge . .	7·14	154
Total yards		966

Returning to Day's Deed :—

	Score yards	Yards
From Day's Deed to Absoly	9·11	191
„ Absoly to Gard stone	9·15	195
Total yards		386

The sum of all these distances amounts to about 4½ miles, being actually 4 miles and 804 yards. There is a pathway extending the whole distance from Blood House Bridge to Islington Common. There are boggy places set down as lying between Turk's Whale and Absoly, and Turk's Whale and Day's Deed. There is also a bog located between the two nearest butts, which must have been inconvenient; also a pond on one side, and another bog on the other side of them.

Two other measurements are given—namely, fifteen score and eight yards, or 308 yards, for the length of a garden wall lying some yards to the right of the White Hall and Pitfield marks; and sixteen score and two yards, or 322 yards, in the same neighbourhood, close by the pathway, and indicating about the distance between Star or Dial and Edw. Gold.

The widest part of these shooting-fields seems to be at about this same part—viz. from White Hall to Scarlet 242 yards, and on to Jehu 82 yards, a total width of 324 yards ; and the narrowest part extends from Nevil's House to Islington Common, in which narrow part are both the sets of butts.

There appear to be some eight or ten fields included in the plan, with hedges indicated, but there is no appearance of either a road or a pathway crossing them.

These marks, giving a great variety of distances, from the shortest of 73 yards between Turk's Whale and Lambeth to the longest of 265 already particularised, seem admirably calculated for the training of the old English archer and the teaching him readily to calculate the various distances at any time between himself and his enemy ; and it is worthy of observation that all these distances are well within the belief of modern archers as such distances as—bearing in mind that there is no evidence of general deterioration—our ancestors could easily compass, seeing that there are well-authenticated instances of lengths somewhat beyond 300 yards having been attained in modern times without any lengthened special training.

In these fields no doubt was seen the *clout shooting*, which is still kept up by the Woodmen of Arden, at Meriden in War wickshire, and by the archers of the Scottish Bodyguard at Edinburgh.

This style of shooting is so called from the aim having been taken at any white mark (cloth, etc.), placed at a fixed distance ; but the clout in use now is a white target with a black centre, set slantwise on the ground. The distances vary from 180 to 240 yards, and this latter distance may be taken as about the extreme range of this style of shooting in olden times ; as Shakespeare mentions (2 Henry IV. iii. 2) that ' old Double,' who ' drew a good bow,' and ' shot a fine shoot,' ' would have clapped i' the clout at twelve score, and carried you a forehand shaft a fourteen and fourteen and a half, that it would have done a man's heart good to see.' As the clout is but rarely hit, the arrow nearest to it at each end, if within three bows' lengths (about eighteen feet) of it, counts as in bowls and quoits.

When the Grand National Archery Meeting was held at Edinburgh in 1850, some of this shooting was introduced, with the result that, out of 2,268 shots at 180 yards, there were 10 hits, and out of 888 shots at 200 yards there were 5 hits.

At the meetings at Meriden stands a marker right in front of this clout, whose duty it is to signal back to each archer, when he has shot, whether his arrow fall short, or go too far, or wide, and—to avoid being hit himself.

The ordinary target arrows may be used in this practice up to the distance of 200 yards, but beyond this distance much stronger bows or flight arrows must be employed.

In these fields, too, would be kept up the practice of *roving*, or taking, as the object to be aimed at, not these or any known mark, but some stray or accidental mark. This practice must have been valuable in olden times in testing the knowledge of distances acquired at the different fixed marks, and it would still be interesting as an amusement, but it is not now so easy to find grounds sufficiently open for the purpose. Where there is sufficient space for golf links, roving might still be practised, and already the golfer's ball and the archer's arrow have been matched together between hole and hole.

Of *flight-shooting*, or shooting with *flight* or light arrows, it may be said that such practice was probably in vogue in old times for the purpose of annoying the enemy whilst at a distance, or in such a ruse as is described by Hall in his account of the battle of Towton in 1461, when 'The Lord Fawconbridge, which led the forward of King Edwardes battail, beinge a man of great Polyce, and of much experience in Marciall feates, caused every archer under his standard to shoot one flight (which before he caused them to provyde), and then made them to stand still. The Northern men, felyng the shoot, but by reason of the snow not wel vewyng the distaunce betwene them and their enemies, like hardy men shot their schefe arrowes as fast as they might, but al their shot was lost and their labor vayn, for thei came not nere the Southern men by xl. tailors' yerdes.'

Flight-shooting has also been used in experiments to determine the extreme casts of different weights and kinds of bows, and the greatest range attainable by the power and skill of individual archers. As a result of such experiments, it may be stated that very few archers can cover more, or even as much as, 300 yards. To attain this range, a bow of at least sixty-two or sixty-three pounds must not only be used but thoroughly mastered, not merely as regards the drawing, but in respect of quickness and sharpness of loose also.

The only remaining style of shooting in vogue in old times —that at the butts or mounds of earth—was known as *prick-shooting*, a small mark being fixed upon the butt and shot at from various distances. This style of shooting was probably popular even then, as many of the Acts of Parliament are levelled against it, on account of its interfering with the more robust practice of the long distances necessary for the purpose of war. This prick-shooting next became known as the *paper game*, when cardboard, and paper stretched on canvas, were placed on the butts. It is not very clear when such targets as are now in use came into fashion, with their gaudy heraldic faces. The distances employed for this butt-shooting appear to have been differently calculated from the lengths in the longer-distance shooting, an obsolete measure of 7½ yards, known as an *archer's rood*, having been employed; and the butt-shooting in vogue at the revival of archery in 1781 was at the distances of 4, 8, 12, and 16 roods, or 30, 60, 90, and 120 yards; and the modern distances of 60 yards, 80 yards, and 100 yards do not seem to have come into use until they were mentioned towards the end of the last century as *Princes' lengths* at the annual contests held in the grounds of the Royal Toxophilite Society, for the possession of the silver bugles presented by their patron, George IV., then Prince of Wales.

About the date of the Introduction of the *York Round* in 1844, two other rounds were in use amongst archers and in archery clubs. These were the *St. Leonard's Round*, which first consisted of 75 arrows at 60 yards only, but afterwards of 36 arrows at 80 yards, and 39 arrows at 60 yards; and the *St. George's Round*, consisting of 36 arrows at each of the distances of 100 yards, 80 yards, and 60 yards, the round of the St. George's Archers, who occupied grounds in St. John's Wood, near London.

The *York Round*, having been now firmly established for more than forty years as the round appointed to be shot at all the public archery meetings, has become the acknowledged test of excellence in bow practice, and all other rounds have dropped out of use with the exception of the round known as the *National Round*, which is practised by ladies at the public meetings, and consists of 48 arrows at 60 yards and 24 arrows at 50 yards; and of 48 arrows at 80 yards and 24 arrows at 60 yards, as practised by gentlemen at meetings where the 100 yards shooting is omitted.

CHAPTER XII.

ARCHERY SOCIETIES, 'RECORDS,' ETC.

PRINCE ARTHUR, the elder brother of King Henry VIII., enjoys the reputation of having been an expert archer, and it is believed that in his honour a good shot was named after him ; but as he was born in 1486 and died in 1502, his skill in the craft cannot have had time to arrive at maturity, though even in modern times a stripling has occasionally snatched the palm of success from the more mature experts.

That King Henry VIII. took a deep interest in archery as necessary for the safety and glory of his kingdom is quite certain, and the various Acts of Parliament passed in the course of his reign (3 Henry VIII. ch. 3, 4, 13 ; 6 Henry VIII. ch. 2, 11, 13 ; 14 & 15 Henry VIII. ch. 7 ; 25 Henry VIII. ch. 17 ; and 33 Henry VIII. 6 & 9) sufficiently prove his determination to stimulate the more frequent use of the long bow. But, apart from his public encouragement of archery, he took personal interest in it himself, and, being a famous athlete, he was no doubt as successful with his bow as his natural impatience would allow. The following extracts from the accounts of his privy purse for the year 1531, when he was forty-one years of age, may be taken as the nearest approach to his actual scores that can be reached. The late Lord Dudley's score at 60 yards, when shooting with one of the best shots at that distance, at one guinea per arrow, must have shown an equally unfavourable balance :—

' 20 March.—Paied to George Coton for vij shottes loste by

the Kinges Grace unto him at Totehill at vj*s*. viij*d*. the shotte xlvj*s*. viij*d*.

' 29 March.—Paied to George Gifford for so moche money he wanne of the Kinges Grace unto him at Totehill at shoting xij*s*. vj*d*.

' 13 May.— Paied to George Coton for that he wanne of the Kinges Grace at the Roundes the laste day of April iij*l*.

' 3 June.— Paied to George Coton for so moche money by him wonne of the Kinges Grace at bettes in shoting vij*l*. ii*s*.'

And again on the last day of June there were ' paied to the iii Cotons for three settes which the King had lost to them in Greenwich Park xx*l*. and vj*s*. viij*d*. more to one of them for one up shotte.'

This George Coton (Cotton) is probably the same person who was governor to the Duke of Richmond, the King's natural son.

On January 31, 1531, 'paied to Byrde Yoeman of the Kinges bowes for making the Roundes at Totehill by the Kinges commandment xij*s*. viij*d*.'

The musters, or what we should now call reviews, were at this time held in the Tothill Fields.

Sir W. Cavendish, the historian of Cardinal Wolsey, thus speaks of his interview with the King in 1530, when he was the bearer of the news of the death [1] of Wolsey to the King, then staying at Hampton Court. (See Cavendish's ' Wolsey,' 1827, p. 396.)

' Upon the morrow (of St. Nicholas Eve, 1530) I was sent for by the King to come to his grace ; and being in Master Kingston's chamber in the Court (Hampton Court), had knowledge thereof, and repairing to the King, found him shooting at the rounds in the park, on the backside of the garden.

' And perceiving him occupied in shooting, thought it not my duty to trouble him : but leaned to a tree, intending to

---

[1] Wolsey died November 30, 1530

stand there, and to attend his gracious pleasure. Being in a
great study, at last the King came suddenly behind me, where
I stood, and clapped his hand upon my shoulder ; and, when
I perceived him, I fell upon my knee. To whom he said,
calling me by name, " I will," quoth he, " make an end of my
game, and then will I talk with you," and so he departed to
his mark, whereat the game was ended.

'Then the King delivered his bow unto the yeoman of
his bows, and went his way inward to the palace, whom I
followed.'

Sir Thos. Elyot, the first edition of whose book, the
'Governour,' was printed in 1531, devoted chapter xxvii. to
the praise of the long bow, and was the earliest writer on the
subject of archery, unless the unknown author of the 'Book
of King Modus,' which is said by Hansard ('Book of
Archery,' 1840, p. 210) to be 'preserved in the royal library at.
Paris,' wrote about two centuries and a half before the 'Toxo-
philus,' by Roger Ascham, was printed in 1545.

Neither Elyot nor Ascham makes any mention of the
societies of archers known as the Fraternities of St. George
and of Prince Arthur, but something of the kind is plainly
indicated by Richard Mulcaster in his book, the 'Positions,'
published in 1581, where he quaintly says, 'This exercise'
(archery) ' I do like best generally of any rounde stirring without the dores, upon the causes before alleaged : which, if I
did not that worthy man our late learned countriman Maister
Askam, would be halfe angrie with me though he were of
milde disposition, who both for the trayning of the Archer to
his bowe and the scholler to his booke, hath showed himselfe
a cunning archer and a skilful maister.

'In the middest of so many earnest matters I may be
allowed to intermingle one which hath a relice of mirthe : for
in praysing of Archerie as a principall exercise to the pre-
seruing of health how can I but prayse them who profess
it thoroughly and maintain it nobly, the friendly and franke

fellowship of Prince Arthur's knights in and about the Citie of London which of late yeares have so reuiued the exercise, so countenaunced the artificers, so inflamed emulation, as in themselues for friendly meting, in workmen for good gayning, in companies for earnest comparing, it is almost growne to an orderly discipline, to cherishe louing society, to enriche labouring pouerty, to maintaine honest actiuitie, which their so encouraging the under trauellours, and so increasing the healthfull traine, if I had sacred to silence would not my good friend in the Citie, Maister Heugh Offley, and the same my noble fellow in that order, Syr Launcelot, at our next meeting haue giuen me a sowre nodde, being the chief furtherer of the fact, which I commend, and the famousest knight of the fellowship, which I am of? Nay, would not even Prince Arthur himself, Maister Thomas Smith, and the whole table of those wel known knights, and most actiue Archers haue layd in their challeng against their fellow knight, if, speaking of their pastime, I should haue spared their names? Where-unto I am easily led bycause the exercise deseruing suche prayse, they that loue so prayseworthy a thing, neither can themselues, neither ought at my hande to be hudled up in silence.'

In 'the Auncient order Societie and unitie laudable of Prince Arthure and his Knightly Armory of the Round Table London, 1583,' Richard Robinson says, 'King Henry VIII. not onely . . . proceeded with what his Father had begun,' by keeping up a body guard of archers, 'but also added greater dignity . . . by his gracious charter confirmed unto the worshipful citizens (of London) . . . this your now famous Order of Knights of Prince Arthure's Round Table or Society.'

But when the practice of archery was enforced by Act of Parliament, and there were shooting butts and fields at hand almost everywhere for the use of those who took a genuine interest in the exercise, there could be but little reason for the introduction of archery societies and clubs.   The meetings for the exhibition of skill would be the regular musters.

How different the position of archery would have been if, instead of clamouring for and getting passed irksome Acts of Parliament, compelling all to shoot, archers, bowmakers, fletchers and others had started a National Long-Bow Association with State sanction and encouragement for the promotion of this exercise and the reward of the most successful shots !

As in early times there were great musters or reviews of companies of archers, of whom the sole actual survivor is the Royal Body-Guard of Scotland (the Archers Company of the Honourable Artillery Company, itself originally a body of archers, was revived late in the last century, and is now represented by the Royal Toxophilite Society) for military display; and local festivities, and wardmotes, as still maintained by the Woodmen of Arden (revived in 1785) and the Scorton Arrow Meetings (dating back to 1673), for the glorification of the best local shots; and the daily use of the long-bow for exercise and sport, i.e. killing of game ; so now there are the meetings of the Grand National Archery Society, established for the peaceable purpose of annually rewarding the champion and championess and other illustrious archers, as hereafter set out in the full account of these meetings, and also the local public meetings of similar character also given ; and in addition to these there are the meetings of the numerous archery societies and clubs in different localities, and the constant private practice either at home or on club grounds. .

Nothing is now to be gained by insisting upon the marked inferiority of the 'incomparable archers' who flourished towards the close of the eighteenth and in the first half of the present centuries, as compared with the many strong and accurate shots who have displayed their skill since the establishment of the Grand National Archery Meetings.   Mr. H. A. Ford seems to have been unable to find any records of shooting at 100 yards where more than one-half of the shots were hits, though he says (p. 112), ' I have seen a letter as late as 1845, from good old Mr. Roberts' (the author of the 'English Bowman,' 1801), ' who was well acquainted with the powers of all the best archers of the preceding half-century, in which he states " he never knew but one man that could accomplish it." ' This one man was probably Mr. Augustus L. Marsh, Royal Toxophilite Society, who owned, and was able to use, the magnificent self-yew bow of 85 lbs. now in the possession of Mr. Buchanan, of 215 Piccadilly, as may be seen from the following records of his best scores in 1837 :—

1837
June 1 at 4 ft. targets, 100 shots at 100 yards
  ,, 27   ,,   ,,   ,,
  ,, 29
July 6   .
  ,, 11
  ,, 20   .
  ,, 21

These would be considered even respectable performances now when hits in the *petticoat* count, and all hits between the colours count in that of higher value, also when three arrows are shot consecutively, instead of two separately, at each end. Competitive examinations had not then been brought to their more recent perfection, and standards of excellence in athletics were as yet unrecorded. Professor John Wilson's (' Christopher North ') wonderful long jump remained as unsurpassable as the ' Douglas cast,' unless it were, perhaps, beaten or preceded by the deeds of the wondrous athlete who could clear a full-sized billiard-table lengthwise, though in his first attempt to do so he failed through knocking the back of his head against the far side of the table.

Mr. Frederick Townsend, in 1865, made the best ' record ' of shooting at 100 yards, at a wardmote of the Woodmen of Arden, when all the old customs just referred to were still, as now, in vogue, his score being 322 from 80 hits out of 150 shots.

There is now left for consideration the subject of ' record,' or standard of highest excellence at the public meetings, and it appears that Mr. A. P. Moore's performance at Derby in 1849 of 747, when, however, Mr. H. A. Ford became champion by the points, was the earliest notable score.   Mr. H. A. Ford improved upon this in the next year at Edinburgh by scoring 899, and in 1854, at Shrewsbury, he made an advance to 1,074. In 1857, at Cheltenham, he took the record on to 1,251 score with 245 hits, and there it now remains.

The first eminent score by a championess was 634, made by Miss H. Chetwynd at Cheltenham, also in 1857.   Mrs. Horniblow took the record on to 660 at Worcester in 1862, Miss Betham next advanced it, at the Alexandra Park Meeting in 1864, to 693.   At Bath, in 1870, Mrs. Horniblow took it further to 700, and also still further to 764, with 142 hits, in 1873 at Leamington, and at that point it now remains, though very closely approached by Miss Legh's score of 763 at Sutton Coldfield in 1881.

Miss Legh's still better score of 840, with all the 144 hits, was made at the Grand Western Meeting at Bath in 1881 ; and Mrs. Piers F. Legh outstripped this ' record ' by scoring 864 with 142 hits at the Leamington and Midland meeting in 1885 ; 33 of the hits on this occasion were golds.

The best ' record ' of target practice at 120 yards is to be found amongst the doings of the Royal Toxophilites.   Mr. H. O'H. Moore, in 1872, on the Norton prize-day, shooting 144 arrows, scored 213 with 43 hits, and Mr. G. E. S. Fryer, on the similar occasion in 1873, scored 273 with 67 hits.

In the shooting at 100 yards of the same society, on the Crunden day in 1854, shooting 144 arrows, Mr. H. A. Ford scored 362 with 88 hits.   This score remained unbeaten, though surpassed in hits by Mr. G. E. S. Fryer in 1873 (361 score, 91 hits), until it was fairly outstripped by Mr. C. E. Nesham, who scored 478 with 104 hits in 1883.   He also made 435 score with 95 hits in 1886.

In 1866 Mr. T. Dawson, Royal Toxophilite Society, presented a challenge medal for the reward of excellence in shooting at 80 yards, 144 arrows being shot, and in the first year this medal was taken by Mr. T. Boulton with 501 score from 113 hits. This record he took on further in 1875, with 591 score from 125 hits. This has been nearly approached only by Mr. C. E. Nesham in 1886, with 576 score from 124 hits.

The record for the 60 yards (144 arrows being shot) medal, presented by the same gentleman in 1866, was also started in that same year by Mr. T. Boulton, with 824 score from 142 hits. This record was surpassed by Mr. W. Rimington in 1872, his score being 840 from the same number of hits.

A good record for best shooting at 100 yards at the annual West Berks meeting, when 216 arrows are shot at that distance, was first reached by Major C. H. Fisher in 1871, when he made 140 hits with 556 score. In 1877 he carried the record on to 572 score with 136 hits. Mr. C. H. Everett made a still further advance with 155 hits and 633 score in 1880 ; and in 1881 Mr. H. H. Palairet made 153 with 623 score.

To Mrs. Butt (then Miss S. Dawson) still belongs the best ' record ' for the ' Ladies' Day ' of the Royal Toxophilite Society, the largest annual gathering of ladies, when the single National Round of 48 arrows at 60 and 24 arrows at 50 yards is shot. She made 70 hits with 406 score in 1867 ; in 1875 she scored 401 with 69 hits ; and in 1885 Mrs. P. F. Legh made 70 hits with 400 score.

CHAPTER XIII.

THE PUBLIC ARCHERY MEETINGS AND THE DOUBLE
YORK AND OTHER ROUNDS,

In 1791, ten years after the revival of archery by the esta
blishment of the Royal Toxophilite Society, a public meeting
of all the Archery Societies, which had already become very
numerous in the United Kingdom, was held on Blackheath.
and this meeting was followed by other similar meetings in
1792 and 1793. Here ended this series of National Archery
Meetings, and in the early part of the present century the use
of the bow appears to have languished.

The records of the Scorton Arrow Meetings go back, in
an almost uninterrupted succession of annual meetings, to the
year 1673. These meetings, though originally confined to a
limited locality—'six miles from Eriholme-upon-Tees,' near
Richmond, in Yorkshire—were open to all comers. In 1842
and 1843 these meetings were held at Thirsk, in Yorkshire,
and to those present thereat the establishment of an annual
Grand National Archery Meeting is certainly owing.

The first Grand National Archery Meeting was held at
York on August 1 and 2, 1844, the Scorton Arrow Meeting
having been again held at Thirsk on July 30 in the same
year. It was originally intended that the meeting should
occupy one day only, but the weather proved so unfavourable
on the first day that the Round had to be finished on the
second day. To the enterprising archers of Yorkshire is also
due the invention of the York Round, which has since become

the almost universally acknowledged test of the comparative excellence of all archers. This Round—which is now always shot on each of the two days of a public archery meeting—consisting of six dozen arrows at 100 yards, four dozen arrows at 80 yards, and two dozen arrows at 60 yards, was so arranged in the belief that about the same scores would then be made at each distance; and this has been proved tolerably correct as regards the average of archers, though not so as regards Mr. H. A. Ford, Major C. H. Fisher, Mr. H. H. Palairet, Mr. C. E. Nesham, and some others, when shooting in their best form, as it would be clearly impossible for them to score, in four dozen arrows at 60 yards, the 495 which Mr. H. A. Ford made in twelve dozen arrows at 100 yards at Cheltenham in 1857, or the 466 which he made on the same occasion in eight dozen arrows at 80 yards. Efforts have occasionally been made to reduce the quantity of shooting at 100 yards, for the benefit of those who look upon 80 yards as a long distance; and it has also been suggested that a few arrows might be taken from 80 yards and added to 60 yards; but it is generally acknowledged that the York Round cannot well be mended.

The Ladies' National Round of four dozen arrows at 60 yards, and two dozen arrows at 50 yards, shot on each of two days, did not become the established Round until 1851, and then the only reason of its adoption was that it corresponded in quantities with the shooting of the gentlemen at 80 yards and 60 yards.

In the year after the Third Leamington Grand National Archery Meeting—i.e. in 1854—the Leamington Meeting was started, and has ever since been an annual institution, except in those years when the Grand National Meeting has been again held at Leamington.

The first Crystal Palace Archery Meeting was held in 1859, and has since been repeated annually.

The Grand Western Archery Meeting was started at

Taunton in 1861, and has been repeated annually at different places, except in 1865, when the Grand National Meeting was held at Clifton, and in 1867, when no Grand Western Archery Meeting was held. In 1886 this meeting was combined with the Grand National Archery Meeting when held at Bath.

Occasionally an extra public meeting has occurred—as at Aston Park, Birmingham, in 1858 and in 1868; at the Alexandra Park, Muswell Hill, in 1863, and again in 1873 and 1882; also at Hastings, in 1867.

The first of a series of Grand Northern Meetings was established in 1879. This meeting has since been repeated annually.

In 1881 the Royal Toxophilite Society, in celebration of their centenary, gave a Double York Round meeting, which, though not strictly speaking a public meeting, was so well attended that it cannot be omitted from the records of the York Round. This meeting has also been repeated annually ever since 1881.

Almost the largest attendance of gentlemen at a public Archery Meeting consisted of one hundred and ten at York in 1845, when there were only eleven ladies shooting. At Cheltenham, in 1856, there were seventy-two ladies and one hundred and twelve gentlemen shooting. The best attended meeting was in 1860, at Bath, when there were one hundred and nine gentlemen and ninety-nine ladies. This was just before the beginning of the Grand Western Meetings, and there was a full meeting of ninety gentlemen and ninety-three ladies in 1865, in which year no Grand Western Meeting was held.

With the exception of the Seventh Grand National Archery Meeting, which was held in Edinburgh in 1850, all the Grand National Archery Meetings have occurred in England.

Two Double York Round Scottish National Meetings were

held in Scotland in the years 1865 and 1866 ; but they were not largely attended.

In Ireland, in the course of the years 1862 to 1866, Irish National and other public meetings were held, mostly in the grounds of the Dublin Exhibition ; but though the Double York Round was shot, and some good shooting was done by the Irish and also by English visitors, the meetings were mostly small, and there seems but little probability of their revival.

A few words should be said about the scoring at public meetings. The original plan was for the Captain at each target to mark, with a pricker made on purpose, the hits made by each shooter in a space representing each of the colours of the target—gold, red, blue, black, and white. In 1872 an improved plan was adopted of keeping a proper space for the hits made at each end, in which is entered each hit in the figure representing its value, as 9, 7, 5, 3, or 1. When no hit is made at any end, this fact should also be recorded ; and thus the progress of the shooting is always kept accurately noted, and the possibility of mistakes in the scores is very much diminished.

Mr. H. A. Ford often mentions the St. George and St. Leonard's Rounds—the former being three dozen arrows at each of the distances of 100, 80, and 60 yards, and the latter (originally 75 arrows at 60 yards only) being three dozen arrows at 80 yards, and three dozen and three at 60 yards. The practice of these Rounds has now entirely disappeared from amongst archers.

During the whole of the period from 1844 to 1886 inclusive the appointed Round has been completed (except at the Leamington Meeting in 1862, when the weather rendered it quite impossible); and this says a great deal for the steadfastness of archers, as they have frequently had to submit to the ill-treatment· of pitiless downpourings of rain and arrow-breaking storms of wind in order to get the Round finished.

No approach has been made to Mr. H. A. Ford's best public score of 1,251, made at Cheltenham in 1857, or to his second best record of 1,162 at Leamington in 1856 ; but his other scores of over 1,000 are easily counted—namely, 1,076 at Exeter in 1858, 1,014 at Leamington in 1861, 1,037 at Brighton in 1867, 1,087 at Leamington in 1868, and 1,032 at Leamington in 1869.   Major C. H. Fisher made 1,060 at Sherborne in 1872.   Mr. Palairet made 1,025 at the Crystal Palace in 1882, and 1,062 in the Regent's Park in 1881.   Mr. C. E. Nesham made 1,010 in the Regent's Park in 1883, and 1022 at Bath in 1886.   No other archers have reached 1,000 at a public match.

Miss Legh's score at Bath in 1881 of 840, when she made all the 144 hits, stood foremost amongst ladies' achievements until it was beaten by Mrs. Legh's score of 864 with 142 hits at Leamington in 1885.   Miss Legh in 1882, at the Crystal Palace, scored 792, and in 1885 809 with 143 hits.   Mrs. Butt's score of 785 at Leamington in 1870 ranks next. Then come Mrs. Horniblow's scores of 768 at Leamington in 1871, and of 764—also at Leamington—in 1872.   Mrs. Piers F. Legh scored 763 at Sutton Coldfield in 1881. Mrs. V. Forbes scored 752 at the Crystal Palace in 1870. Mrs. Marshall scored 744 at the Crystal Palace in 1884. Miss Betham's best score was 743 at Leamington in 1867. Mrs. P. Pinckney scored 729 at the Crystal Palace in 1873 ; and Mrs. Pond scored 700 in 1874, also at the Crystal Palace.   No other ladies appear to have made as much as 700.

Other scores of 700 and upwards have been—

MRS. HORNIBLOW		MISS BETHAM			MRS. P. F. LEGH	
1871	746	1864 . . 735			1882 . . 750	
1873	733	1867	733		1879	. 743
1873 .	. 719	1866 . . 701			1881 . . 723	
1872	. 712				1883	712
1863	706				1884	. 701
1870	. 700					

The summary of Public Meetings is—

43 Grand National Archery Meetings.
31 Leamington Archery Meetings.
28 Crystal Palace Archery Meetings.
24 Grand Western Archery Meetings.
7 Grand Northern Archery Meetings.
2 Alexandra Park Archery Meetings.
1 Hastings Archery Meeting.
2 Aston Park Archery Meetings.
6 Royal Toxophilite Society's Archery Meetings.

144 Meetings.

When attention is turned towards the meetings at which most gentlemen have made more than 600, and most ladies have made over 500, it is found that in 1860, at Bath, seventeen gentlemen reached or passed the score of 600, but at the same time only two ladies passed 500. This still remains the largest meeting which has yet been held, two hundred and eight shooters having been present. At the Alexandra Park Meeting in 1864, sixteen gentlemen and six ladies attained the same amount of excellence. At Brighton, in 1867, seventeen gentlemen and seven ladies passed the same levels. But, in 1882, at the Crystal Palace, the corresponding numbers were ten gentlemen and nineteen ladies, and at Leamington in the same year, fourteen gentlemen and sixteen ladies; whilst in 1883, at Cheltenham, nineteen gentlemen passed 600 and fourteen ladies passed 500, though the shooters competing at this meeting were only one hundred and thirty-one. At Windsor in 1884, thirteen ladies scored more than 500, and twelve gentlemen more than 600. This shows clearly that, although the number of attendances has diminished since the extraordinary start given to archery by Mr H. A. Ford's book (and this is possibly due to the multiplication of public matches), yet the average of excellence, particularly amongst the ladies, has made considerable progress. This is a most encouraging symptom for the future of archery.

The First Grand National Archery Meeting was held on August 1 and 2, 1844, at Knavesmire, near York.

GENTLEMEN	100 Yards		80 Yards		60 Yards		TOTALS	
	Hits	Score	Hits	Score	Hits	Score	Hits	Score
Rev. J. Higginson . .	18	66	21	93	14	62	53	221
Rev. E. Meyrick . .	15	65	24	76	19	77	58	218

Sixty-five gentlemen shot, and no ladies appeared at the targets.

The single *York Round* (72 arrows at 100 yards, 48 arrows at 80 yards, and 24 arrows at 60 yards) was shot first on this occasion.

The Second Grand National Archery Meeting was held on June 25 and 26, 1845, at the same place.

LADIES	60 Yards	
	Hits	Score
Miss Thelwall . . .	48	186
Miss Townshend . . .	45	163
Miss Emma Wylde . .	33	161
Miss Jane Forster . .	40	152

Eleven ladies shot 96 arrows, all at 60 yards.

GENTLEMEN	100 Yards		80 Yards		60 Yards		TOTALS	
	Hits	Score	Hits	Score	Hits	Score	Hits	Score
Mr. Peter Muir . .	53	185	46	182	36	170	135	537
Mr. J. Jones . . .	28	110	63	243	38	146	129	499
Rev. E. Meyrick . .	42	150	42	146	32	150	116	446
Mr. Blackley . . .	27	113	44	176	30	128	101	417

One hundred and ten gentlemen shot at this meeting, and the York Round, as before described, was shot on each day and at all the following meetings.

The Third Grand National Archery Meeting was held on July 29 and 30, 1846, at the same place.

GENTLEMEN	100 Yards		80 Yards		60 Yards		TOTALS	
	Hits	Score	Hits	Score	Hits	Score	Hits	Score
Mr. R. G. Hubbock . .								
Rev. E. Meyrick . .								
Rev. T. Meyler . .								
Mr. Glasgow . . .								
Mr. C. Garnett . .								
Mr. J. P. Marsh . .								
Rev. J. Higginson . .								
Mr. A. Radcliff . .								

Eighty-three gentlemen shot at this meeting, but no ladies appeared.

The Fourth Grand National Archery Meeting was held on July 28 and 29, 1847, at Derby.

—	60 Yards	
	Hits	Score
Miss Wylde	65	245

The ladies, who numbered only six, again shot—at 60 yards only—the same number of arrows as in 1845, namely, 96.

GENTLEMEN	100 Yards		80 Yards		60 Yards		TOTALS	
	Hits	Score	Hits	Score	Hits	Score	Hits	Score
Mr. Peter Muir . .				2				
Mr. Hutchons . . .				6				
Mr. E. Maitland . .				9				
Mr. E. Marr . . .				4				
Rev. J. Bramhall . .				9				
Mr. C. Garnett . .				5				
Rev. T. Meyler . .								
Mr. G. Attwood . .								
Rev. E. Meyrick . .								

Fifty-eight gentlemen shot at this meeting, and on the following day—July 30—half a York Round was shot for a bow (Buchanan's) and two other prizes.

—	100 Yards		80 Yards		60 Yards		Totals	
	Hits	Score	Hits	Score	Hits	Score	Hits	Score
Rev. J. Bramhall won the bow	18	58	16	74	9	41	43	173

The Fifth Grand National Archery Meeting was held on July 19 and 20, 1848, at the same place.

Ladies	60 Yards		50 Yards		Totals	
	Hits	Score	Hits	Score	Hits	Score
Miss J. Barrow . . .	14	54	33	113	47	167 .
Miss Temple . . .	18	80	26	80	44	160

Only five ladies shot, and they shot 72 arrows at 60 yards, and 72 at 50 yards.

Gentlemen	100 Yards		80 Yards		60 Yards		Totals	
	Hits	Score	Hits	Score	Hits	Score	Hits	Score
Mr. E. Maitland . .	55	245	44	206	36	130	135	581
Rev. J. Bramhall . .	45	145	52	218	35	151	132	514
Mr. C. Wilkinson . .	45	161	40	150	28	134	113	445
Mr. E. Marr . . .	42	170	47	167	29	99	118	436
Mr. Willis . . .	35	117	38	156	34	146	107	419
Mr. J. Wilson . . .	42	152	41	141	29	109	108	402

Seventy-four gentlemen shot at this meeting. Horace A. Ford here made his first public appearance, scoring—

100 Yards		80 Yards		60 Yards		Totals	
Hits	Score	Hits	Score	Hits	Score	Hits	Score
31	81	38	142	32	118	101	341

He stood fifteenth in the list.

The Sixth Grand National Archery Meeting was held on July 18 and 19, 1849—again at Derby.

LADIES	60 Yards		50 Yards		TOTALS	
	Hits	Score	Hits	Score	Hits	Score
Miss Temple . . .	36	122	19	67	55	189
Miss Mackay . . .	24	98	19	65	43	163
Miss Billing	25	89	14	62	39	151

Eight ladies attended this meeting, and the *National Round* (96 arrows at 60 yards, and 48 arrows at 50 yards), equally divided between the two days, was shot now for the first time, and has been ever since shot by the ladies, except at the next meeting at Edinburgh.

GENTLEMEN	100 Yards		80 Yards		60 Yards		TOTALS	
	Hits	Score	Hits	Score	Hits	Score	Hits	Score
Mr. A. P. Moore . .	62	238	68	318	43	191	173	747
Mr. H. A. Ford . .	69	231	63	264	44	208	176	703
Mr. G. Attwood . .	65	255	49	235	35	125	149	615
Mr. E. Meyrick . .	52	196	41	183	29	161	122	540
Mr. G. Ollier . . .	38	130	49	187	41	199	128	516
Mr. J. Wilson . . .	30	108	58	218	37	177	125	503

Forty-six gentlemen shot at this meeting, and the Champion's medal was first awarded on this occasion, and won by Mr. H. A. Ford, who won most points [1] (5), Mr. Moore having won 4—namely, hits and score at 80 yards, and gross score—and Mr. Attwood won the points for score at 100 yards.

[1] The points for the Champion's medal are

2 points each for gross score and gross hits.
1 point each for score and hits at 100 yards.
1 point   ,,   ,,   80 yards.
1 point   ,,   ,,   60 yards.
         Total, 10 points.

The Seventh Grand National Archery Meeting was held on July 24, 25, and 26, 1850, at Edinburgh, in Warrender Park.

LADIES	60 Yards		50 Yards		TOTALS	
	Hits	Score	Hits	Score	Hits	Score
Mrs. Calvert. . . .	27	89	20	72	47	161
Miss E. Forster . . .	29	113	13	43	42	156

Eight ladies shot at this meeting, and the round, which, owing to the condition of the weather, was all shot on the third day, consisted of 72 arrows at 60 yards, and 36 arrows at 50 yards.

GENTLEMEN	100 Yards		80 Yards		60 Yards		TOTALS	
	Hits	Score	Hits	Score	Hits	Score	Hits	Score
Mr. H. A. Ford . .	79	343	70	314	44	242	193	899
Mr. C. Garnett . .	65	249	61	221	40	168	166	638
Rev. G. Mallory . .	59	197	55	235	30	150	144	582
Mr. G. W. Willis . .	45	175	46	184	39	181	130	540
Mr. J. Wilson . . .	50	192	49	203	36	140	135	535
Mr. O. K. Prescot . .	58	224	41	165	35	125	134	514
Mr. J. Turner . . .	50	208	44	196	31	101	125	505

Eighty-three gentlemen shot, and the Champion's medal was won by Mr. H. A. Ford, who made all the points.

At this meeting there was also some shooting at 200 yards, 180 yards, and at 100 feet, in addition to the usual double York Round.

The Eighth Grand National Archery Meeting was held on July 25 and 26, 1851, on Wisden's Cricket-ground at Leamington. At this meeting thirty-three ladies shot the National Round.

Mr. H. A. Ford won all the points for the Champion medal except that for score at 80 yards, which was won by Mr. K. T. Heath.

	60 Yards		50 Yards		Totals	
—	Hits	Score	Hits	Score	Hits	Score
Miss Villers, afterwards } Mrs. Davison	73	323	35	181	108	504

Miss Villers's score showed a rapid stride in advance amongst the ladies, as she was more than 100 points ahead of the second lady, Miss Eaton—73 hits, 297 score—and the third, Mrs. Thursfield—75 hits, 293 score.

GENTLEMEN	100 Yards		80 Yards		60 Yards		Totals	
	Hits	Score	Hits	Score	Hits	Score	Hits	Score
Mr. H. A. Ford . .	76	308	72	324	45	229	193	861
Mr. K. T. Heath . .	61	235	67	327	40	214	168	776
Rev. J. Bramhall . .	65	283	71	273	42	204	178	760
Mr. P. Muir . . .	67	243	51	197	41	228	160	668
Mr. H. Garnett . .	61	257	52	186	35	163	148	606

Ninety gentlemen shot at this meeting.

On the 27th a handicap sweepstake match was shot.

The Ninth Grand National Archery Meeting was held on July 7 and 8, 1852, at the same place, in Leamington.

LADIES	60 Yards		50 Yards		Totals	
	Hits	Score	Hits	Score	Hits	Score
Miss Brindley . . .	45	155	39	181	84	336
Miss M. Peel . . .	51	217	33	113	84	330
Miss Villers	49	197	30	132	79	329

At this meeting thirty-six ladies and seventy-eight gentlemen shot.

Mr. H. A. Ford won the Champion's medal with 6 points,

Mr. Bramhall having won 2 points for hits and score at 100 yards, and Mr. J. Wilson 2 points for hits and score at 60 yards.

GENTLEMEN	100 Yards		80 Yards		60 Yards		TOTALS	
	Hits	Score	Hits	Score	Hits	Score	Hits	Score
Mr. H. A. Ford . .	72	306	74	282	42	200	188	788
Rev. J. Bramhall . .	84	352	61	249	39	177	184	778
Mr. J. Wilson . . .	68	238	55	207	44	204	167	649
Mr. H. Garnett . .	68	230	59	229	34	152	161	611

This match had a most exciting finale. When the last three arrows alone remained to be shot, Mr. Bramhall was 2 points ahead in score. It was then a simple question of nerve, and Mr. Ford's proved the best, as he scored 14 to his opponent's 2. The two gentlemen were placed at adjoining targets, and Mr. Bramhall's nerve was further disturbed by his hearing some one noisily offer to bet heavily in favour of Mr. Ford. Mr. Ford shot first at his target, and Mr. Bramhall second at his.

Mr. Ford's score on July 9, in the handicap match, amounted to 485.

The Tenth Grand National Archery Meeting was held on July 6 and 7, 1853—again at Leamington.

LADIES	60 Yards		50 Yards		TOTALS	
	Hits	Score	Hits	Score	Hits	Score
Mrs. Horniblow . . .	54	230	35	135	89	365
Miss M. Peel . . .	44	180	40	184	84	364
Miss Clay . . .	46	192	35	145	79	337
Mrs. Tennant (née Temple) .	48	190	31	129	79	319

The silver bracer for the Lady Championess, presented by the Norfolk Bowmen, was first competed for at this meeting, and won by Mrs. Horniblow, who won 6 of the 8 points, Miss M. Peel having secured the 2 points for hits and score at 50 yards.

GENTLEMEN	100 Yards		80 Yards		60 Yards		TOTALS	
	Hits	Score	Hits	Score	Hits	Score	Hits	Score
Mr. H. A. Ford . .	78	322	77	367	47	245	202	934
Rev. J. Bramhall . .	56	212	66	300	45	221	167	733
Mr. C. Garnett . .	55	197	57	251	39	157	151	605

Mr. Ford won all the Champion's points, and now first began to show his marked superiority.

Fifty ladies and eighty-two gentlemen shot.

The Eleventh Grand National Archery Meeting was held on July 5 and 6, 1854, on the racecourse at Shrewsbury.

LADIES	100 Yards		80 Yards		TOTALS	
	Hits	Score	Hits	Score	Hits	Score
Mrs. Davison (*née* Villers) .	68	318	41	171	109	489
Mrs. Horniblow . . .	56	212	40	186	96	398
Miss Baker	61	245	34	152	95	397

Mrs. Davison won the silver bracer with 7 points, Mrs. Horniblow, who made a score of 325 on the handicap day, having secured the eighth point with the highest score at fifty yards.

GENTLEMEN	100 Yards		80 Yards		60 Yards		TOTALS	
	Hits	Score	Hits	Score	Hits	Score	Hits	Score
Mr. H. A. Ford . .	101	411	87	415	46	248	234	1,074
Rev. J. Bramhall . .	62	270	77	329	37	149	176	748
Mr. H. Hilton . . .	62	230	66	260	39	175	175	667
Mr. H. Garnett . .	54	214	61	249	41	205	156	668
Mr. P. Muir . . .	67	229	52	206	41	197	160	632

Mr. Ford won all the points of the Champion's medal, and made a further stride in front of all other competitors, making over **1,000.**

Sixty-six ladies and ninety-four gentlemen shot.

The First Grand Leamington and Midland Archery Meeting was held in the Jephson Gardens, on July 19 and 20, 1854.

LADIES	60 Yards		50 Yards		TOTALS	
	Hits	Score	Hits	Score	Hits	Score
Mrs. Horniblow . . .	73	361	36	146	109	507
Miss Baker	71	277	42	198	113	475

GENTLEMEN	100 Yards		80 Yards		60 Yards		TOTALS	
	Hits	Score	Hits	Score	Hits	Score	Hits	Score
Colonel Clowes . .	57	197	57	237	36	156	150	590
Mr. R. Garnett . .	42	162	44	212	32	134	118	508

The Second Grand Leamington and Midland Archery Meeting was held on June 20 and 21, 1855.

LADIES	60 Yards		50 Yards		TOTALS	
	Hits	Score	Hits	Score	Hits	Score
Mrs. Horniblow . . .	67	265	39	161	106	426
Miss H. Chetwynd . .	54	210	38	162	92	362

GENTLEMEN	100 Yards		80 Yards		60 Yards		TOTALS	
	Hits	Score	Hits	Score	Hits	Score	Hits	Score
Mr. H. A. Ford . .	82	270	79	323	46	268	207	861
Mr. T. G. Golightly .	63	231	55	205	35	151	153	587

The Twelfth Grand National Archery Meeting was held on August 1 and 2, 1855—again at Shrewsbury.

LADIES	60 Yards		50 Yards		TOTALS	
	Hits	Score	Hits	Score	Hits	Score
Mrs. Davison . . .	70	278	45	213	115	491
Mrs. Horniblow . . .	67	277	36	160	103	437
Miss Clay	64	282	36	146	100	428

Mrs. Davison won 7 points, and again secured the silver bracer.

Miss Clay won 1 point for score at 60 yards.

Miss H. Chetwynd made 296 on the handicap day.

GENTLEMEN	100 Yards		80 Yards		60 Yards		TOTALS	
	Hits	Score	Hits	Score	Hits	Score	Hits	Score
Mr. H. A. Ford . .	69	281	65	285	45	243	179	809
Rev. J. Bramhall . .	68	242	63	261	44	206	175	709
Mr. P. Muir . . .	59	251	57	217	39	159	155	627
Mr. J. Wilson . . .	50	164	59	253	45	197	154	614
Mr. H. Hilton . . .	53	195	64	258	34	160	151	613

Mr. Ford won the Champion's medal, having won all the points except that there was a tie between him and Mr. Wilson for hits at 60 yards.

The weather was unfavourable at this meeting, which helps to account for the apparent falling off in the scores.

Fifty-five ladies and eighty-three gentlemen shot.

The series of eighteen articles, out of which this book was afterwards formed, began to appear in the ' Field ' on October 6 in this year.

The Third Grand Leamington and Midland Archery Meeting was held on June 18 and 19, 1856

LADIES	60 Yards		50 Yards		TOTALS	
	Hits	Score	Hits	Score	Hits	Score
Mrs. Horniblow . . .	74	338	41	203	115	541
Miss H. Chetwynd . .	67	299	41	209	108	508

GENTLEMEN	100 Yards		80 Yards		60 Yards		TOTALS	
	Hits	Score	Hits	Score	Hits	Score	Hits	Score
Mr. H. A. Ford . .	105	447	91	431	48	284	244	1162
Mr. G. Mallory . .	65	241	58	220	40	176	163	637
Colonel Phillipps . .	47	185	59	247	44	202	150	634
Mr. G. Edwards . .	61	251	53	221	40	148	154	620

The Thirteenth Grand National Archery Meeting was held on July 2 and 3, 1856, on the College Cricket-ground, at Cheltenham.

LADIES	60 Yards		50 Yards		TOTALS	
	Hits	Score	Hits	Score	Hits	Score
Mrs. Horniblow . . .	68	294	41	193	109	487
Mrs. Davison [1] . . .	68	312	35	149	103	461

GENTLEMEN	100 Yards		80 Yards		60 Yards		TOTALS	
	Hits	Score	Hits	Score	Hits	Score	Hits	Score
Mr. H. A. Ford . .	81	299	87	439	45	247	213	985
Rev. J. Bramhall . .	82	346	69	271	40	168	191	785
Mr. P. Muir . . .	65	289	65	253	34	146	164	688
Mr. C. Garnett . .	68	260	51	211	39	189	158	660
Mr. W. Peters. . .	57	189	57	235	32	160	146	584

Mrs. Horniblow won the silver bracer with six points, Mrs. Davison having won the point for score at 60 yards, and

[1] Did not shoot the last six arrows at 50 yards, being prevented by indisposition.

having made the same number of hits as Mrs. Horniblow at that distance. Miss H. Chetwynd made the same number of hits at 50 yards as Mrs. Horniblow.

Mr. Ford again secured the Champion's medal with eight points, his old opponent Mr. Bramhall having won the points for hits and score at 100 yards.

Seventy-two ladies and 112 gentlemen shot at this meeting.

The first edition of ' The Theory and Practice of Archery ' was published in the course of this year.

The Fourth Grand Leamington and Midland Archery Meeting was held on June 10 and 11, 1857.

LADIES	60 Yards		50 Yards		TOTALS	
	Hits	Score	Hits	Score	Hits	Score
Mrs. Horniblow . . .	66	276	41	183	107	459
Mrs. Litchfield . . .	58	230	38	158	96	388

GENTLEMEN	100 Yards		80 Yards		60 Yards		TOTALS	
	Hits	Score	Hits	Score	Hits	Score	Hits	Score
Mr. H. A. Ford . .	97	387	88	398	45	241	230	1026
Mr. C. H. Fisher . .	59	231	62	212	44	172	165	615

The Fourteenth Grand National Archery Meeting was held on July 1 and 2, 1857—again at Cheltenham.

LADIES	60 Yards		50 Yards		TOTALS	
	Hits	Score	Hits	Score	Hits	Score
Miss H. Chetwynd . .	82	390	46	244	128	634
Mrs. Davison . . .	73	339	41	209	114	548
Mrs. Horniblow . . .	80	346	42	194	122	540
Mrs. R. Blaker . . .	69	325	39	171	108	496

Miss H. Chetwynd won the silver bracer with all the points, and exceeded all the previous performances of ladies in match shooting.

GENTLEMEN	100 Yards		80 Yards		60 Yards		TOTALS	
	Hits	Score	Hits	Score	Hits	Score	Hits	Score
Mr. H. A. Ford . .								
Mr. G. Edwards . .								
Mr. W. J. W. Baynes .								
Mr. P. Muir . . .								
Mr. J. Bramhall . .								
Mr. H. C. Mules . .								
Mr. E. Mason . . .								
Mr. H. Garnett . .								
Mr. H. Hilton . . .								
Mr. J. Wilson . . .								
Mr. C. H. Fisher . .								

Mr. Ford again secured all the points for the Champion's medal, and made the finest score ever yet made in public.

The average of the shooting of all showed a marked improvement at this meeting; and it was gratifying to Mr. Ford to be able to state that several of the leading archers attributed their high positions in the prize-list to their careful following out of the principles and directions laid down in his book.

Sixty-one ladies and ninety-seven gentlemen shot.

Mr. H. C. Mules scored 389 on the handicap day.

The Fifth Grand Leamington and Midland Archery Meeting was held on June 23 and 24, 1858.

— LADIES —	60 Yards		50 Yards		TOTALS	
	Hits	Score	Hits	Score	Hits	Score
Miss H. Chetwynd . .	74	344	41	191	115	535
Miss Dixon	62	270	39	179	101	449

GENTLEMEN	100 Yards		80 Yards		60 Yards		TOTALS	
	Hits	Score	Hits	Score	Hits	Score	Hits	Score
Mr. H. A. Ford . .	100	424	87	463	43	241	230	1128
Mr. G. Edwards . .	77	303	64	298	45	263	186	864
Mr. H. Walters . .	58	256	66	276	43	225	167	757
Mr. W. J. W. Baynes .	60	260	63	239	45	213	168	712
Mr. H. C. Mules . .	56	256	55	225	45	209	156	690
Mr. S. Mason . . .	53	197	59	267	38	172	150	636
Colonel Clowes . .	44	202	49	211	42	214	135	627

Twenty-nine ladies and twenty-nine gentlemen shot.

The Fifteenth Grand National Archery Meeting was held on July 21 and 22, 1858, at Exeter.

LADIES	60 Yards		50 Yards		TOTALS	
	Hits	Score	Hits	Score	Hits	Score
Mrs. Horniblow . . .	58	256	43	201	101	457
Mrs. St. George . . .	58	254	36	174	94	428
Miss H. Chetwynd . .	56	204	43	219	99	423
Mrs. R. Blaker . . .	54	228	38	184	92	412
Lady Edwardes . . .	54	262	31	139	85	401
Miss Turner . . .	59	255	34	136	93	391

GENTLEMEN	100 Yards		80 Yards		50 Yards		TOTALS	
	Hits	Score	Hits	Score	Hits	Score	Hits	Score
Mr. H. A. Ford . .			1				1	
Mr. G. Edwards . .			0					
Mr. J. T. George . .			3					
Mr. W. J. W. Baynes .			0					
Mr. J. Spedding . .			1					
Mr. E. Mason . . .			6					
Mr. H. C. Mules . .			9	255	44			
Mr. P. Muir . . .			0	250	39			

Mrs. Horniblow won the silver bracer with $4\frac{1}{2}$ points. Miss Turner won the point for hits at 60 yards, Lady Edwardes the point for score at 60 yards, and Miss H. Chetwynd won the point for score at 50 yards and divided the point for hits at this distance with Mrs. Horniblow.

Mr. Ford, having won all the ten points, became Champion for the tenth time. He accounted for the apparent falling off in the shooting at this meeting as compared with the previous one by the fact that the weather was rough and the ground difficult.

Eighty-four ladies and eighty-six gentlemen shot.

A Grand Archery Meeting was held in the grounds of Aston Park, near Birmingham, on September 8 and 9, 1858.

GENTLEMEN	100 Yards		80 Yards		60 Yards		TOTALS	
	Hits	Score	Hits	Score	Hits	Score	Hits	Score
Mr. H. A. Ford	87	339	73	343	48	294	208	976
Mr. G. Edwards	63	277	65	255	46	250	174	782
Mr. H. Walters	55	231	53	253	37	193	145	677
Mr. H. Elliott	60	242	63	247	39	185	162	674
Mr. G. L. Aston	35	141	57	243	40	164	132	548
Mr. W. J. W. Baynes	49	185	47	175	41	185	137	545

LADIES	60 Yards		50 Yards		TOTALS	
	Hits	Score	Hits	Score	Hits	Score
Mrs. Horniblow	75	317	42	218	117	535
Miss H. Chetwynd	65	287	39	187	104	474
Miss Aston	67	251	41	175	108	426
Lady Edwards	61	267	32	142	93	409

It was intended, and advertised, that this meeting should be repeated in 1859; but, from insufficient support, it was abandoned, and the first of the series of annual archery meetings held in the grounds of the Crystal Palace was substituted for it.

The Sixth Grand Leamington and Midland Archery Meeting was held on June 15 and 16, 1859.

Thirty ladies and thirty-three gentlemen shot.

LADIES	60 Yards		50 Yards		TOTALS	
	Hits	Score	Hits	Score	Hits	Score
Mrs. Horniblow . . .	70	282	48	262	118	544
Miss H. Chetwynd . .	67	313	39	179	106	492

GENTLEMEN	100 Yards		80 Yards		60 Yards		TOTALS	
	Hits	Score	Hits	Score	Hits	Score	Hits	Score
Mr. G. Edwards . .	93	355	76	350	47	257	216	962
Mr. H. A. Ford . .	75	327	82	382	43	213	200	922
Mr. E. Mason . . .	55	217	67	297	42	240	164	754
Mr. G. L. Aston . .	56	254	56	244	41	205	153	703
Mr. H. C. Mules . .	52	214	65	257	37	185	154	656
Mr. H. Walters . .	44	170	63	253	40	200	147	623

The Sixteenth Grand National Archery Meeting was held on July 6 and 7, 1859—again at Exeter.

Miss Turner won the silver bracer with 5 points, Miss H. Chetwynd having won 2 points for gross hits and 1 point for hits at 60 yards.

LADIES	60 Yards		50 Yards		TOTALS	
	Hits	Score	Hits	Score	H	Score
Miss Turner	77	385	45	245	122	630
Miss H. Chetwynd . .	82	370	43	215	125	585
Mrs. G. Atkinson . . .	76	334	42	207	119	541
Mrs. Horniblow . . .	74	356	38	160	112	536

The Champion's medal for the eleventh consecutive time

was won by Mr. Ford with 8 points, Mr. Edwards having won
the points for hits and score at 80 yards.

GENTLEMEN	100 Yards		80 Yards		60 Yards		TOTALS	
	Hits	Score	Hits	Score	Hits	Score	Hits	Score
Mr. H. A. Ford	5	3					205	
Mr. G. Edwards							184	
Rev. W. J. Richardson							178	
Mr. A. Edmondstone								
Mr. H. C. Mules								
Mr. E. Meyrick								
Mr. J. Rimington								
Mr. J. T. George								
Mr. T. Boulton								
Mr. H. Walters								
Mr. H. B. Hare								
Mr. W. Swire								
Mr. C. H. Fisher								

Eighty-six ladies and eighty-four gentlemen shot.

The second edition of Mr. Ford's book was issued in this
year, and the account of this Grand National Archery Meeting
was not included in it.

A Grand Archery Meeting, under the management of Mr.
Merridew, was proposed to be held in the grounds of Aston
Park, Birmingham, on July 27 and 28, 1859, as mentioned
by Mr. H. A. Ford at page 124; but at the Leamington
meeting of the same year it was decided that this proposed
meeting should be transferred to the grounds of the Crystal
Palace at Sydenham, and thus commenced the annual Crystal
Palace Archery Meetings.

The First Grand Annual Crystal Palace Archery Meeting was held on July 27 and 28, 1859, on the Cricket
ground.

LADIES	60 Yards		50 Yards		TOTALS	
	Hits	Score	Hits	Score	Hits	Score
Miss Turner	66	272	41	203	107	475
Mrs. Horniblow . . .	50	226	40	198	90	424

GENTLEMEN	100 Yards		80 Yards		60 Yards		TOTALS	
	Hits	Score	Hits	Score	Hits	Score	Hits	Score
Mr. H. A. Ford . .	78	314	80	380	48	252	206	946
Mr. G. Edwards . .	64	264	66	252	45	259	175	775
Mr. H. C. Mules . .	67	257	57	285	41	179	165	721
Mr. H. Walters . .	54	186	73	311	42	202	169	699
Mr. T. Boulton . .	54	226	47	181	42	216	143	623

Twenty ladies and forty-one gentlemen shot.

The Seventh Grand Leamington and Midland Archery Meeting was held on June 13 and 14, 1860.

LADIES	60 Yards		50 Yards		TOTALS	
	Hits	Score	Hits	Score	Hits	Score
Mrs. E. Lister . . .	72	336	45	197	117	533
Mrs. Litchfield . . .	72	324	39	163	111	487
Mrs. Horniblow . . .	66	238	46	202	112	440

GENTLEMEN	100 Yards		80 Yards		60 Yards		TOTALS	
	Hits	Score	Hits	Score	Hits	Score	Hits	Score
Mr. H. A. Ford . .	82	336	80	406	47	255	209	997
Mr. E. Mason . . .	70	268	64	266	46	226	180	760
Mr. T. G. Golightly. .	54	228	67	277	44	204	165	709
Mr. T. Boulton . .	49	197	66	284	39	197	154	678
Mr. H. Walters . .	57	217	61	249	43	207	161	673

Thirty-two ladies and thirty-six gentlemen shot.

The Seventeenth Grand National Archery Meeting was held on July 4 and 5, 1860, at Bath.

LADIES	60 Yards		50 Yards		TOTALS	
	Hits	Score	Hits	Score	Hits	Score
Mrs. E. Lister . . .	69	337	43	213	112	550
Mrs. G. Atkinson . . .	79	341	42	190	121	531
Mrs. Rogers	66	306	38	188	104	494

GENTLEMEN	100 Yards		80 Yards		60 Yards		TOTALS	
	Hits	Score	Hits	Score	Hits	Score	Hits	Score
Mr. G. Edwards . .								
Mr. P. Muir . . .								
Mr. H. A. Ford . .								
Mr. H. C. Mules . .								
Mr. W. Rimington . .								
Mr. E. Mason . .								
Rev. W. J. Richardson .								
Mr. H. Walters . .								
Mr. H. B. Hare . .								
Mr. G. T. Golightly .								
Mr. J. Spedding . .								
Mr. J. Wilson . . .								
Mr. T. Boulton . .								
Mr. C. H. Fisher . .								
Mr. J. Turner . . .								
Col. Clowes . . .								
Mr. E. Meyrick . .								

Mrs. Lister won the first score prize, but Mrs. Atkinson won the silver bracer with 4 points.

Mrs. Lister won 2 points for gross score.

Mrs. Horniblow won the point for score at 50 yards, and Mrs. Litchfield won the point for hits at 50 yards.

At this meeting Mr. Edwards won the Champion's medal with 6 points, Mr. Ford, who took third rank, having won 4 points—namely, 2 for gross hits and those for hits at 80 yards and hits at 60 yards.

Ninety-nine ladies and 109 gentlemen shot.

The influence of hits as affecting the position of the winners of the best prizes was now entirely abandoned, and the order of the prizes taken from the gross score only, except when two had a tie in score. In this case the difference (if any) in hits was considered.

Want of space prevents the introduction of all the winners of best prizes, who vary in number at the different meetings from six to twelve, according to the numbers present; but it should be mentioned that at the earliest meetings the second prize was allotted to the maker of most gross hits. This rule prevailed up to 1851. In 1852, 1853, and 1854 the order of prize-winners was in accordance with the order of the gross scores. From that date the first prizes were named 'first, second, third, &c. gross score, and hits,' and the rule by which the order of the prize list was obtained was that the number of each shooter's position in hits was taken and added to the number representing his position in score. The lowest total won the first score and hits prize, and the next lowest the second, and so on. In cases where the totals of two were the same, the highest score would win. The application of this rule may be observed in 1859, when Mr. Richardson made the third score (812), but won the fourth prize; whilst Mr. Edmondstone, who made the fourth score, won the third prize. Mr. Edmondstone was second in hits and fourth in score (total, 6); Mr. Richardson was third in score and fourth in hits (total, 7).

The Second Grand Annual Crystal Palace Archery Meeting was held on July 18 and 19, 1860.

LADIES	60 Yards		50 Yards		Totals	
	Hits	Score	Hits	Score	Hits	Score
Mrs. Horniblow . . .	65	271	39	179	104	450
Miss Turner	58	258	34	132	92	390

GENTLEMEN	100 Yards		80 Yards		60 Yards		TOTALS	
	Hits	Score	Hits	Score	Hits	Score	Hits	Score
Mr. G. Edwards . .	67	247	77	359	46	224	190	830
Mr. H. Walters . .	66	258	72	306	46	220	184	784
Mr. H. A. Ford . .	63	289	64	258	46	226	173	773
Mr. Bradford . . .	66	256	64	256	42	218	172	730
Mr. H. C. Mules . .	60	254	63	257	42	200	165	711
Mr. T. Boulton . .	57	247	57	243	31	133	145	623

Twenty-six ladies and forty-three gentlemen shot.

The Eighth Grand Leamington and Midland Archery Meeting was held in the Jephson Gardens on June 12 and 13, 1861.

Twenty-six ladies and thirty-four gentlemen shot.

LADIES	60 Yards		50 Yards		TOTALS	
	Hits	Score	Hits	Score	Hits	Score
Mrs. Horniblow . . .	78	366	46	230	124	596
Mrs. E. Lister . . .	69	315	44	236	113	551
Mrs. Litchfield . . .	79	351	39	159	118	510

GENTLEMEN	100 Yards		80 Yards		60 Yards		TOTALS	
	Hits	Score	Hits	Score	Hits	Score	Hits	Score
Mr. H. A. Ford . .	83		83			274		
Mr. G. Edwards . .	52		76			279		
Mr. T. G. Golightly . .	69		68			223		
Mr. M. Knapp . . .	77		55			164		
Mr. H. C. Mules . .	65		67			179		
Mr. W. Ford . . .	60		59			177		
Mr. G. Mallory . .	57		49			211		
Mr. W. Swire . . .	52		58			177		
Mr. J. Spedding . .	60		54			137		
Mr. T. L. Coulson . .	46		57			196		
Mr. H. B. Hare . .	50		53			209		

The Eighteenth Grand National Archery Meeting was held on the Racecourse at Aintree, near Liverpool, on July 17 and 18, 1861.

LADIES	60 Yards		50 Yards		TOTALS	
	Hits	Score	Hits	Score	Hits	Score
Mrs. G. Atkinson . . .	73	367	40	208	113	575
Miss Turner	65	291	42	214	107	505
Mrs. Horniblow . . .	67	265	42	212	109	477

Mrs. Atkinson won the silver bracer with 6 points. Miss Turner won the point for score at 50 yards, and Mrs. E. Lister the point for hits (44) at 50 yards.

GENTLEMEN	100 Yards		80 Yards		60 Yards		TOTALS	
	Hits	Score	Hits	Score	Hits	Score	Hits	Score
Mr. G. Edwards . .	68	288	63	235	44	222	175	745
Mr. T. G. Golightly. .	60	250	58	270	41	205	159	725
Mr. P. Muir . . .	49	175	62	266	43	221	154	662
Mr. H. A. Ford . .	54	220	56	200	45	241	155	661
Mr. T. Boulton . .	54	178	58	268	40	196	152	638
Mr. J. Wilson . . .	46	220	56	212	36	164	138	596

The Champion's medal was again won by Mr. G. Edwards with 7 points. Mr. Golightly won the point for score at 80 yards, and Mr. H. A. Ford won two points for score and hits at 60 yards.

The wind at this meeting—on an exposed ground—was tremendous.

Sixty-four ladies and eighty-nine gentlemen shot.

Some better scores—Mr. E. Mason (446), Mr. F. Townsend (374), and Mr. H. C. Mules (365)—were made on July 19 in the handicap match.

The Grand National Archery Society was first established at a meeting of archers held at the Adelphi Hotel in Liverpool on July 19, 1861.

The Third Annual Crystal Palace Archery Meeting was held on July 30–31 and August 1, 1861.

LADIES	60 Yards		50 Yards		TOTALS	
	Hits	Score	Hits	Score	Hits	Score
Miss Turner	77	345	45	255	122	600
Mrs. Horniblow . . .	66	336	44	216	110	552
Miss H. Chetwynd . .	72	326	42	200	114	526

GENTLEMEN	100 Yards		80 Yards		60 Yards		TOTALS	
	Hits	Score	Hits	Score	Hits	Score	Hits	Score
Mr. H. A. Ford . .	80	314	75	319	43	211	198	844
Mr. G. Edwards . .	50	206	79	361	47	251	176	818
Mr. H. Hilton . . .	54	236	51	219	36	142	141	597

No other shooter made as much as 600.

Twenty-two ladies and thirty-seven gentlemen shot.

The First Grand Western Archery Meeting was held at Bishop's Hull, near Taunton, on August 7 and 8, 1861, when fifty-three ladies and forty-two gentlemen shot.

LADIES	60 Yards		50 Yards		TOTALS	
	Hits	Score	Hits	Score	Hits	Score
Miss Turner	80	386	45	259	125	645
Miss Mignon . . .	66	276	41	197	107	473
Miss H. Chetwynd . .	56	236	40	228	96	464
Miss James	59	271	37	165	96	436
Mrs. A. Malet . . .	62	256	34	142	96	398

GENTLEMEN	100 Yards		80 Yards		60 Yards		TOTALS	
	Hits	Score	Hits	Score	Hits	Score	Hits	Score
Mr. G. Edwards . .	59	263	85	381	45	253	189	897
Mr. H. A. Ford . .	65	235	73	319	47	275	185	829
Colonel Clowes . .	53	215	62	272	39	189	154	676
Mr. W. Rimington . .	53	207	58	272	39	191	150	670
Mr. H. B. Hare . .	58	226	56	232	41	205	155	663
Mr. W. Swire . . .	57	205	57	251	36	180	150	636
Mr. H. Walters . .	42	140	57	257	41	223	140	620

The Fourth Annual Crystal Palace Archery Meeting was held on May 29 and 30 1862.

LADIES	60 Yards		50 Yards		TOTALS	
	Hits	Score	Hits	Score	Hits	Score
Mrs. Horniblow . . .	76	328	44	220	120	548
Mrs. H. Walters . . .	73	329	41	209	114	538

GENTLEMEN	100 Yards		80 Yards		60 Yards		TOTALS	
	Hits	Score	Hits	Score	Hits	Score	Hits	Score
Mr. F. Townsend . .	75	299	72	344	41	223	188	866
Mr. H. A. Ford . .	77	319	67	291	43	201	187	811
Mr. G. Edwards . .	58	252	70	312	47	241	175	805
Mr. H. B. Hare . .	54	238	61	305	37	145	152	688
Mr. W. Swire . . .	56	238	64	254	39	189	159	681
Mr. T. Boulton . .	62	220	58	238	39	179	159	637
Mr. J. H. Chance . .	38	144	55	233	44	234	137	611

Twenty-six ladies and forty gentlemen shot.

The Ninth Grand Leamington and Midland Archery Meeting was held in the Jephson Gardens on June 11 and 12, 1862.

N

—	60 Yards		50 Yards		TOTALS	
·	Hits	Score	Hits	Score	Hits	Score
Mrs. Horniblow . . .	?	191	23	143	?	334

This was Mrs. Horniblow's score on the first day. The round on the second day was not completed on account of the bad weather.

GENTLEMEN	100 Yards		80 Yards		60 Yards		TOTALS	
	Hits	Score	Hits	Score	Hits	Score	Hits	Score
Mr. H. A. Ford .	?	186	?	184	23	137	?	507
Mr. G. Edwards . .	29	131	41	169	24	144	94	444

This was the best shooting of the first day.   On the second day only 48 arrows at 100 yards were shot.

Thirty-three ladies and twenty-eight gentlemen shot.

The Nineteenth Grand National Archery Society's Meeting was held at Worcester, on July 17 and 18, 1862.

Sixty-five ladies and eighty-eight gentlemen shot.

LADIES	· 60 Yards		50 Yards		TOTALS	
	Hits	Score	Hits	Score	Hits	Score
Mrs. Horniblow . . .	80	384	48	276	128	660
Mrs. G. Atkinson . . .	76	334	40	208	116	542
Miss Jarrett	68	296	43	229	111	525
Miss H. Chetwynd . .	65	313	40	176	105	489

Mrs. Horniblow won the silver bracer with all the 8 points.

Mr. G. Edwards secured the Champion's medal with 7 points.   Mr. H. A. Ford won the point for score at 80 yards, and the points for score and hits at 60 yards.

GENTLEMEN	100 Yards		80 Yards		60 Yards		TOTALS	
	Hits	Score	Hits	Score	Hits	Score	Hits	Score
Mr. G. Edwards	71	297	78	366	45	239	194	902
Mr. H. A. Ford	67	245	76	376	47	275	190	896
Mr. E. Mason .	65	239	71	339	42	210	178	788
Mr. T. Boulton	63	279	56	230	42	156	161	665
Mr. W. Rimington .	52	204	62	230	41	199	155	633
Mr. H. B. Hare	65	249	51	177	40	200	156	626
Mr. H. Walters	48	194	61	235	40	194	149	623

Some good scores—Mr. H. A. Ford (479), Mr. G. Edwards (447), and Mr. H. B. Hare (386)—were made on July 19 in the handicap match.

The Second Grand Western Archery Meeting was held at West Harnham, near Salisbury, on July 9 and 10, 1862, when sixty-four ladies and fifty-one gentlemen shot.

LADIES	60 Yards		50 Yards		TOTALS	
	Hits	Score	Hits	Score	Hits	Score
Miss H. Chetwynd	65	309	36	154	101	463
Mrs. A. Malet	60	264	37	163	97	427

GENTLEMEN	100 Yards		80 Yards		60 Yards		TOTALS	
	Hits	Score	Hits	Score	Hits	Score	Hits	Score
Mr. G. Edwards	51	189	61	255	45	275	157	719
Mr. H. A. Ford	57	235	63	283	42	188	162	706
Mr. H. B. Hare	50	190	64	244	39	171	153	605

Mrs. A. Malet and Mr. H. B. Hare became respectively the Championess and Champion of the West.

The Fifth Grand Annual Crystal Palace Archery Meeting was held on June 11 and 12, 1863.

Thirty-four ladies and forty-six gentlemen shot.

LADIES	60 Yards		50 Yards		TOTALS	
	Hits	Score	Hits	Score	Hits	Score
Mrs. Horniblow . . .	78	364	43	237	121	601
Mrs. Blaker	61	275	36	188	97	463

GENTLEMEN	100 Yards		80 Yards		60 Yards		TOTALS	
	Hits	Score	Hits	Score	Hits	Score	Hits	Score
Mr. H. A. Ford . .	59	221	72	326	44	244	175	791
Mr. F. Townsend .	58	196	68	284	41	195	167	675
Mr. T. L. Coulson .	53	233	65	281	34	142	152	656
Mr. MacNamara .	49	169	64	292	42	192	155	653
Mr. G. Edwards .	49	185	64	264	42	188	155	637
Mr. A. R. Tawney .	59	245	55	209	26	156	140	610
Colonel Clowes . .	45	173	57	245	36	190	138	608

The Tenth Grand Leamington and Midland Archery Meeting was held in the Jephson Gardens on June 25 and 26, 1863. Twenty-eight ladies and thirty-two gentlemen shot.

LADIES	60 Yards		50 Yards		TOTALS	
	Hits	Score	Hits	Score	Hits	Score
Mrs. Horniblow . . .	90	442	44	264	134	706
Miss B. Edwards . . .	73	305	47	229	120	534
Miss Waller	74	322	42	206	116	528

GENTLEMEN	100 Yards		80 Yards		60 Yards		TOTALS	
	Hits	Score	Hits	Score	Hits	Score	Hits	Score
Mr. H. A. Ford . .					41			
Mr. McNamara . .					46			
Captain Betham . .					37			
Mr. T. L. Coulson . .					40			
Mr. H. B. Hare . .					33			
Colonel Clowes . .					36	1		
Mr. H. Walters . .					39	1		
Mr. J. Spedding . .					33	1		

The Twentieth Grand National Archery Society's Meeting was held on the Christ Church Cricket-ground at Oxford on July 1 and 2, 1863.

LADIES	60 Yards		50 Yards		TOTALS	
	Hits	Score	Hits	Score	Hits	Score
Mrs. Horniblow . . .	73	285	43	193	116	478
Miss H. Chetwynd . .	61	281	39	189	100	468
Miss B. Edwards . . .	60	258	38	192	98	450

Mrs. Horniblow won the silver bracer with all the 8 points.

GENTLEMEN	100 Yards		80 Yards		60 Yards		TOTALS	
	Hits	Score	Hits	Score	Hits	Score	Hits	Score
Mr. P. Muir . . .	72	292	65	295	44	258	179	845
Mr. H. A. Ford . .	62	242	70	290	44	248	176	780
Mr. T. L. Coulson . .	59	219	58	240	41	223	158	682
Mr. G. Edwards . .	54	206	59	245	42	218	155	669
Mr. H. Walters . .	38	160	64	290	45	209	147	659
Mr. F. Townsend . .	55	211	50	200	43	207	148	618

The weather was very rough.

Mr. P. Muir won the Champion's medal with 8 points; Mr. H. A. Ford won the point for hits at 80 yards ; and Messrs. H. Walters and R. W. Atkinson divided the point for hits at 60 yards (45).

Fifty-four ladies and ninety-six gentlemen shot.

Mr. T. L. Coulson (452) shot well on July 3 in the handicap match.

The Third Grand Western Archery Meeting was held at Weymouth on July 15 and 16, 1863, when fifty-nine ladies and sixty-four gentlemen shot.

There was a tie between Miss L. Turner and Miss S Dawson in points; and on drawing lots (not a fair way of deciding the tie) Miss S. Dawson won, and became Championess.

LADIES	60 Yards		50 Yards		TOTALS	
	Hits	Score	Hits	Score	Hits	Score
Miss L. Turner . . .	69	331	42	200	111	531
Miss S. Dawson . . .	71	295	42	200	113	495

GENTLEMEN	100 Yards		80 Yards		60 Yards		TOTALS	
	Hits	Score	Hits	Score	Hits	Score	Hits	Score
Mr. H. A. Ford . .	65	243	77	341	44	242	186	826
Mr. T. L. Coulson . .	70	258	57	277	42	236	169	771
Captain Betham . .	50	194	76	322	43	219	169	735
Mr. W. Rimington . .	64	234	67	249	43	207	174	690
Colonel Clowes . .	56	208	59	243	34	176	149	627

Mr. H. B. Hare (148 hits, 594 score) became Champion of the West.

A Grand Inaugural Archery Fête was held in the Alexandra Park, Muswell Hill, on July 23 and 24, 1863.

LADIES	60 Yards		50 Yards		TOTALS	
	Hits	Score	Hits	Score	Hits	Score
Mrs. Horniblow . . .	78	370	47	269	125	639
Miss H. Chetwynd . .	76	354	40	188	116	542
Mrs. Hare	74	328	43	177	117	505

GENTLEMEN	100 Yards		80 Yards		60 Yards		TOTALS	
	Hits	Score	Hits	Score	Hits	Score	Hits	Score
Mr. G. Edwards . .								
Mr. W. Rimington . .								
Mr. T. L. Coulson . .								
Mr. H. Walters . .								
Colonel Clowes . .								
Mr. T. Boulton . .								
Mr. J. Rogers . . .								
Captain Betham . .								

Mr. J. Buchanan acted as manager of this meeting.
Nineteen ladies and forty-one gentlemen shot.

The Eleventh Grand Leamington and Midland Archery Meeting was held in the Jephson Gardens on June 15 and 16, 1864.

LADIES	60 Yards		50 Yards		TOTALS	
	Hits	Score	Hits	Score	Hits	Score
Miss Betham . . .	88	464	47	271	135	735
Mrs. Horniblow . . .	86	396	46	234	132	630
Mrs. E. Lister . . .	67	313	38	184	105	597

GENTLEMEN	100 Yards		80 Yards		60 Yards		TOTALS	
	Hits	Score	Hits	Score	Hits	Score	Hits	Score
Mr. G. Edwards . .	57	239	82	346	46	258	185	843
Mr. H. Walters . .	55	199	54	284	43	239	152	722
Captain Betham . .	54	212	63	231	47	251	164	694
Mr. G. L. Aston . .	56	208	65	269	41	215	162	692
Mr. T. L. Coulson . .	61	207	58	248	42	230	161	685
Mr. Betham . . .	68	232	58	238	40	194	166	664
Mr. McNamara . .	50	176	60	242	41	185	151	603

Thirty-five ladies and thirty-three gentlemen shot.

The Sixth Grand Annual Crystal Palace Archery Meeting was held on June 30 and July 1, 1864.

Thirty-eight ladies and forty-four gentlemen shot.

GENTLEMEN	100 Yards		80 Yards		60 Yards		TOTALS	
	Hits	Score	Hits	Score	Hits	Score	Hits	Score
Mr. G. Edwards . .					47			
Mr. Betham . . .					46			
Mr. H. Walters . .					43			
Captain Betham . .					45			
Mr. W. Rimington . .					42			
Mr. James Spedding .					43			
Mr. H. B. Hare . .					38			
Mr. J. Rogers . . .					39			

LADIES	60 Yards		50 Yards		TOTALS	
	Hits	Score	Hits	Score	Hits	Score
Miss Betham . . .	76	350	41	253	117	603
Mrs. Horniblow . . .	73	343	45	221	118	564
Miss Turner	72	296	41	225	113	521

The Twenty-first Grand National Archery Society's Meeting was held in the Alexandra Park, Muswell Hill, near London, on July 6 and 7, 1864.

LADIES	60 Yards		50 Yards		TOTALS	
	Hits	Score	Hits	Score	Hits	Score
Miss Betham . . .	83	429	46	264	129	693
Mrs. G. Atkinson . . .	74	392	43	243	117	635
Mrs. Horniblow . . .	76	314	45	227	121	541
Miss A. S. Butt . . .	79	339	46	200	125	539
Miss Quin	68	320	44	208	112	528
Miss Turner	66	300	41	211	107	511

Miss Betham won the silver bracer with $7\frac{1}{2}$ points. Miss A. S. Butt divided the point for hits at 50 yards with her.

GENTLEMEN	100 Yards		80 Yards		60 Yards		TOTALS	
	Hits	Score	Hits	Score	Hits	Score	Hits	Score
Mr. G. Edwards . .								
Mr. P. Muir . .								
Mr. H. Walters . .								
Mr. W. R. Atkinson .								
Captain Betham .								
Mr. James Spedding .								
Mr. Betham . . .								
Mr. T. L. Coulson . .								
Mr. St. J. Coventry .								
Mr. A. R. Tawney . .								
Captain C. H. Fisher .								
Mr H. B. Hare . .								
Mr. J. Wilson . .								
Mr. H. Elliott . .								
Mr. McNamara . .								
Mr. H. Garnett . .								

Mr. G. Edwards secured the Champion's medal with 6½ points. Mr. P. Muir won 2 points for hits and score at 100 yards, and Mr. H. Walters divided the point for hits at 60 yards with Mr. G. Edwards

Eighty-two ladies and eighty-six gentlemen shot.

Good scores appear to have been made in the handicap match on July 8—namely, 356 by Miss Betham, 334 by Mrs. G. Atkinson, and 321 by Miss Turner; 463 by Mr. G. Edwards, 420 by Mr. W. R. Atkinson, and 394 by Mr. W. Rimington.

The Fourth Grand Western Archery Meeting was held at Exeter on August 3 and 4, 1864, when one hundred and seventeen ladies and fifty-eight gentlemen shot.

LADIES	60 Yards		50 Yards		TOTALS	
	Hits	Score	Hits	Score	Hits	Score
Miss S. Dawson . . .	86	416	46	252	132	668
Mrs. C. H. Everett . .	68	330	43	223	111	553
Miss Quin	75	347	42	188	117	535

GENTLEMEN	100 Yards		80 Yards		60 Yards		TOTALS	
	Hits	Score	Hits	Score	Hits	Score	Hits	Score
Mr. G. L. Aston . .	72	280	74	336	44	220	190	836
Captain C. H. Fisher .	80	340	64	250	37	195	181	785
Mr. H. B. Hare . .	53	225	65	251	35	169	153	645
Mr. W. Rimington . .	50	174	45	207	40	204	135	585

Miss S. Dawson and Mr. H. B. Hare became Championess and Champion of the West.

The Twelfth Grand Leamington and Midland Archery Meeting was held on June 14 and 15, 1865, in the Jephson Gardens.

LADIES	60 Yards		50 Yards		TOTALS	
	Hits	Score	Hits	Score	Hits	Score
Miss Betham . . .	86	412	47	259	133	671
Miss S. Dawson . . .	84	404	45	241	129	645
Mrs. Horniblow . . .	86	384	46	240	132	624
Mrs. E. Lister . . .	69	311	40	198	109	509
Miss A. S. Butt . . .	74	300	40	206	114	506
Miss Waller	70	310	40	192	110	502

GENTLEMEN	100 Yards		80 Yards		60 Yards		TOTALS	
	Hits	Score	Hits	Score	Hits	Score	Hits	Score
Mr. G. Edwards . .								
Mr. T. L. Coulson . .								
Mr. Betham . . .								
Mr. H. Walters . .								
Captain Betham . .								
Mr. Chance . . .								
Mr. H. Elliott . .								
Mr. A. R. Tawney . .								

Thirty-two ladies and forty gentlemen shot.

The Seventh Grand Annual Crystal Palace Archery Meeting was held on July 6 and 7, 1865.

LADIES	60 Yards		50 Yards		TOTALS	
	Hits	Score	Hits	Score	Hits	Score
Miss Betham . . .	70	352	46	246	116	598
Miss E. K. Fenton . .	67	307	38	178	105	485
Mrs. Horniblow . . .	70	304	38	176	108	480

GENTLEMEN	100 Yards		80 Yards		60 Yards		TOTALS	
	Hits	Score	Hits	Score	Hits	Score	Hits	Score
Mr. E. A. Holmes . .	71	267	67	263	39	181	177	711
Mr. G. Edwards . .	50	162	63	265	44	246	157	673
Mr. H. Elliott . .	45	181	59	255	40	194	144	630
Mr. H. Walters . .	30	100	65	269	43	225	132	594

Miss H. Chetwynd (afterwards Mrs. Christie) had the management of this meeting, and of the previous one in 1864. Forty ladies and forty-nine gentlemen shot.

The Twenty-second Grand National Archery Society's Meeting was held at Clifton, near Bristol, on College Cricket-ground, on July 26 and 27, 1865.

LADIES	60 Yards		50 Yards		TOTALS	
	Hits	Score	Hits	Score	Hits	Score
Miss Betham . . .	79	385	45	221	124	606
Miss S. Dawson . . .	76	376	45	205	121	581
Mrs. E. Lister . . .	74	362	42	218	116	580
Mrs. P. Becher . . .	71	323	40	212	111	535
Mrs. FitzGerald . . .	73	337	37	185	110	522
Mrs. Horniblow . . .	67	281	43	213	110	494

Miss Betham won the silver bracer with 6½ points. Miss L. J. Butt won the point for score at 50 yards (222) ; and Miss S. Dawson divided the point for hits at 50 yards with Miss Betham.

GENTLEMEN	100 Yards		80 Yards		60 Yards		TOTALS	
	Hits	Score	Hits	Score	Hits	Score	Hits	Score
Mr. E. A. Holmes . .								
Mr. T. Boulton . .								
Mr. P. Muir . . .								
Mr. G. Edwards . .								
Mr. R. W. Atkinson .								
Mr. H. Walters . .								
Mr. E. Mason . .								
Mr. W. Rimington . .								
Mr. T. L. Coulson . .								
Mr. G. L. Aston . .								

Mr. E. A. Holmes became the Champion, having won most points (5). Mr. P. Muir won 2 points for hits and score at 100 yards ; Mr. G. Edwards won the point for score at 80 yards ; and Mr. R. W. Atkinson won the point for score at 60 yards.   Messrs. G. Edwards and H. Walters divided the point for hits at 60 yards.

Ninety-three ladies and ninety gentlemen shot.

No Grand Western Archery Meeting was held this year.

The Thirteenth Grand Leamington and Midland Archery Meeting was held in the Jephson Gardens on June 13 and 14, 1866.

LADIES	60 Yards		50 Yards		TOTALS	
	Hits	Score	Hits	Score	Hits	Score
Miss Betham . . .	82	444	45	257	127	701
Mrs. Horniblow . . .	83	423	46	276	129	699
Miss S. Dawson . . .	91	459	43	187	134	646
Mrs. E. Lister . . .	78	374	42	218	120	592

GENTLEMEN	100 Yards		80 Yards		60 Yards		TOTALS	
	Hits	Score	Hits	Score	Hits	Score	Hits	Score
Mr. G. Edwards . .							184	
Mr. T. L. Coulson							186	
Mr. T. Boulton .							181	
Mr. O. K. Prescot .							158	
Mr. H. Elliott .							169	
Mr. Golightly . .							163	
Mr. Betham . . .							173	
Captain Betham . .							161	
Mr. H. Walters . .							141	

Mr. Golightly scored 405 on June 15 in the handicap match. Thirty-one ladies and thirty-six gentlemen shot.

The Eighth Grand Annual Crystal Palace Archery Meeting was held on June 28 and 29, 1866

Twenty-nine ladies and forty-five gentlemen shot.

LADIES	60 Yards		50 Yards		TOTALS	
	Hits	Score	Hits	Score	Hits	Score
Miss Betham . . .	81	389	44	244	125	633
Mrs. Hosken . . .	78	346	46	234	124	580
Mrs. Horniblow . . .	82	348	44	222	126	570
Miss A. S. Butt . . .	68	338	41	201	109	539
Mrs. P. Becher . . .	72	332	42	194	114	526

GENTLEMEN	100 Yards		80 Yards		60 Yards		TOTALS	
	Hits	Score	Hits	Score	Hits	Score	Hits	Score
Mr. H. Elliott . .				3				
Mr. G. Edwards .			5	2				
Mr. T. Boulton .			9					
Mr. E. A. Holmes .			4					
Mr. T. L. Coulson .			4					
Mr. R. W. Atkinson .			8					
Mr. W. Rimington . .			5					
Mr. F. Townsend . .			4					
Captain C. H. Fisher .			7					
Captain Whitla . .			9					

The Fifth Grand Western Archery Meeting was held at Weymouth on July 18 and 19, 1866, when seventy-seven ladies and fifty-nine gentlemen shot.

Miss S. Dawson and Mr. H. Walrond became respectively Championess and Champion of the West.

During these five Grand Western Archery Meetings Mr. T. Dawson acted as Hon. Secretary. No meeting was held in 1865, when the Grand National Archery Meeting was held at Clifton ; and none was held in 1867.

LADIES	60 Yards		50 Yards		TOTALS	
	Hits	Score	Hits	Score	Hits	Score
Miss Betham . . .	76	384	46	262	122	646
Miss S. Dawson . . .	82	414	41	195	123	609
Miss A. S. Butt . . .	66	296	42	221	108	517

GENTLEMEN	100 Yards		80 Yards		60 Yards		TOTALS	
	Hits	Score	Hits	Score	Hits	Score	Hits	Score
Mr. H. Walrond . .	44	180	66	320	40	198	150	698
Mr. Betham . . .	53	191	62	268	43	223	158	682
Mr. T. G. Golightly .	51	205	56	254	38	202	145	661
Mr. W. Rimington . .	47	177	65	255	39	183	151	615
Mr. H. A. Ford . .	45	123	61	275	45	215	151	613

The Twenty-third Grand National Archery Society's Meeting was held in the grounds of Sir R. Harvey, Bart., at Crown Point, near Norwich, on July 25 and 26, 1866.

LADIES	60 Yards		50 Yards		TOTALS	
	Hits	Score	Hits	Score	Hits	Score
Miss Betham . . .	85	405	45	257	130	662
Mrs. Horniblow . . .	86	428	42	212	128	640
Miss L. J. Butt . . .	72	316	43	189	115	505
Miss A. S. Butt . . .	60	262	44	228	104	490

Miss Betham won the silver bracer with 6 points. Mrs. Horniblow won the 2 points for hits and score at 60 yards.

GENTLEMEN	100 Yards		80 Yards		60 Yards		TOTALS	
	Hits	Score	Hits	Score	Hits	Score	Hits	Score
Mr. G. Edwards . .								
Mr. E. A. Holmes . .								
Mr. W. Rimington . .								
Mr. Betham . . .								
Mr. R. W. Atkinson .								
Mr. F. Townsend . .								
Mr. T. L. Coulson . .								
Mr. H. A. Ford . .								
Captain Whitla . .								
Mr. O. K. Prescot . .								
Captain C. H. Fisher .								
Mr. C. C. Ellison . .								
Mr. F. Partridge . .								
Mr. Chance . . .								

Mr. G. Edwards won all the points, and became the Champion.

Seventy-four ladies and seventy-five gentlemen shot.

The Fourteenth Grand Leamington and Midland Archery Meeting was held in the Jephson Gardens on June 12 and 13, 1867.

LADIES	60 Yards		50 Yards		TOTALS	
	Hits	Score	Hits	Score	Hits	Score
Miss Betham . . .	86	466	47	277	133	743
Mrs. Horniblow . . .	85	423	37	217	122	640
Mrs. E. Lister . . .	84	394	45	237	129	631
Mrs. Litchfield . . .	65	337	31	169	96	506

GENTLEMEN	100 Yards		80 Yards		60 Yards		TOTALS	
	Hits	Score	Hits	Score	Hits	Score	Hits	Score
Mr. H. A. Ford . .								
Mr. O. K. Prescot . .								
Mr. R. Caldwell . .								
Mr. H. Elliott . .								
Mr. Betham . . .								
Mr. T. L. Coulson . .								
Mr. W. Butt . . .								
Mr. Spottiswoode . .								

Mr. R. Caldwell scored 423 on June 14 in the handicap match.

Twenty-five ladies and forty-one gentlemen shot.

The Ninth Grand Annual Crystal Palace Archery Meeting was held on July 18 and 19, 1867.

Mr. O. K. Prescot scored 451 on July 20 in the handicap match.

Forty-nine ladies and sixty-six gentlemen shot.

LADIES	60 Yards		50 Yards		TOTALS	
	Hits	Score	Hits	Score	Hits	Score
Miss S. Dawson . . .	84	378	44	248	128	626
Miss Ripley	70	320	43	201	113	521
Miss Betham . . .	69	281	42	218	·111	499

GENTLEMEN	100 Yards		80 Yards		60 Yards		TOTALS	
	Hits	Score	Hits	Score	Hits	Score	Hits	Score
Mr. H. A. Ford . .								
Mr. O. K. Prescot . .								
Mr. Spottiswoode . .								
Mr. W. Rimington . .								
Mr. E. A. Holmes . .								
Mr. H. Elliott . .								
Mr. Betham . . .								
Captain C. H. Fisher .								
Mr. J. M. Croker . .								
Mr. R. W. Atkinson .								
Admiral Lowe . .								
Mr. St. J. Coventry .								

The Twenty-fourth Grand National Archery Society's Meeting was held at Preston, near Brighton, on July 24 and 25, 1867.

LADIES	60 Yards		50 Yards		TOTALS	
	Hits	Score	Hits	Score	Hits	Score
Mrs. E. Lister . . .	86	454	42	236	130	690
Miss Betham . . .	82	366	47	281	129	647
Miss S. Dawson . . .	88	404	44	242	132	646
Mrs Horniblow . . .	88	450	42	196	130	646
Miss Stephenson . . .	70	310	41	233	111	543
Mrs. J. R. Thomson . .	75	361	35	169	110	530
Miss A. S. Butt . . .	69	319	41	191	110	510

Mrs. E. Lister won the silver bracer of the Championess with 3 points. Miss S. Dawson won the 2 points for most hits, and divided the point for hits at 60 yards with Mrs. Horniblow.   Miss Betham won 2 points for hits and score at 50 yards.

GENTLEMEN	100 Yards		80 Yards		60 Yards		TOTALS	
	Hits	Score	Hits	Score	Hits	Score	Hits	Score
Mr. H. A. Ford . .	94	39						
Mr. E. A. Holmes . .	88	41						
Mr. Spottiswoode . .								
Mr. O. K. Prescot . .								
Mr. W. Rimington. .								
Mr. G. Edwards . .								
Mr. Betham . . .								
Mr. P. Muir . . .								
Mr. R. Caldwell . .								
Admiral Lowe . .								
Mr. H. Elliott . .								
Captain C. H. Fisher .								
Mr. R. W. Atkinson .								
Mr. T. Boulton . .								
Mr. C. Ellison . .								
Mr. T. L. Coulson . .								
Mr. G. Holmes . .								

Mr. H. A. Ford became the Champion for the twelfth and last time.   He won 8 points, Mr. E. A. Holmes having won the point for score at 100 yards, and Mr. O. K. Prescot that for score at 80 yards.   Mr. E. A. Holmes was unwell during the shooting at 60 yards on the second day, when he made only 89 at that distance.   The average value of the first ten on this occasion, all over 700, was 820·7 ; and this still remains the highest average ever yet attained.   Mr. H. A. Ford on this occasion was using very weak bows, not much more than forty pounds in weight, and light arrows.

Seventy-two ladies and eighty-six gentlemen shot.

A Grand Archery Meeting was held, in the Public Recreation Ground at Hastings, on July 31 and August 1, 1867.

Thirty-three ladies and twenty-seven gentlemen shot.

LADIES	60 Yards		50 Yards		TOTALS	
	Hits	Score	Hits	Score	Hits	Score
Miss Betham . . .	88	458	47	275	135	733
Miss A. Betham . . .	76	324	48	238	124	562
Mrs. P. Becher . . .	78	336	39	207	117	543
Miss L. J. Butt . . .	70	294	43	227	113	521

GENTLEMEN	100 Yards		80 Yards		60 Yards		TOTALS	
	Hits	Score	Hits	Score	Hits	Score	Hits	Score
Mr. H. A. Ford . . .			298		230			
Mr. O. K. Prescot . .			302		165			
Mr. Betham . . .			235		210			
Mr. W. Butt . . .			191		231			
Admiral Lowe . .			196		206			
Mr. T. Boulton . .			244		179			
Captain C. H. Fisher .			291		165			
Captain Betham .			230		189			

In the handicap match shot in the Archery Ground, St. Leonards-on-Sea, on the next day—August 2—Captain C. H. Fisher scored 472 and Mr. H. A. Ford 471.

The Fifteenth Grand Leamington and Midland Archery Meeting was held in the Jephson Gardens on June 10 and 11, 1868.

LADIES	60 Yards		50 Yards		TOTALS	
	Hits	Score	Hits	Score	Hits	Score
Mrs. Horniblow . . .	90	474	45	245	135	719
Miss Ripley	80	412	48	244	128	656
Miss Betham . . .	79	411	44	220	123	631
Mrs. W. Butt (Miss S. Dawson)	83	401	43	225	126	626
Mrs. A. Knox (Miss E. A. Betham) . . .	77	385	46	226	123	611
Mrs. P. Becher . . .	70	344	42	222	112	566
Miss Stephenson . . .	72	306	44	230	116	536
Mrs. W. S. Miller. . .	71	317	43	209	114	526
Miss H. Hutchinson . .	75	325	44	194	119	519

GENTLEMEN	100 Yards		80 Yards		60 Yards		TOTALS	
	Hits	Score	Hits	Score	Hits	Score	Hits	Score
Mr. H. A. Ford . .	9	4		405				
Mr. O. K. Prescot . .				334				
Mr. Betham . . .				282				
Captain C. H. Fisher .				291				
Mr. R. Caldwell . .				310				
Mr. H. Elliott . .				313				
Mr. W. Butt . . .				266				
Mr. Coker . . .				268				
Mr. Jenner-Fust . .				250				

Thirty ladies and forty-one gentlemen shot.

A Grand Archery Meeting was held in the Lower Ground, Aston Park, Birmingham, on June 16 and 17, 1868.

LADIES	60 Yards		50 Yards		TOTALS	
	Hits	Score	Hits	Score	Hits	Score
Miss Ripley	82	444	45	249	127	693
Mrs. W. Butt . . .	84	422	44	232	128	654
Miss Betham . . .	80	342 ·	47	253	127	595
Mrs. P. Becher . . .	83	373	41	191	124	564
Miss H. Hutchinson . .	83	391	38	172	121	563
Mrs. A. Knox (Miss A. Betham) . . .	84	358	44	180	128	538

GENTLEMEN	100 Yards		80 Yards		60 Yards		TOTALS	
	Hits	Score	Hits	Score	Hits	Score	Hits	Score
Mr. H. A. Ford . .								
Captain C. H. Fisher .								
Mr. W. Butt . . .								
Mr. O. K. Prescot . .								
Mr. Betham . . .								
Mr. H. Elliott . .								
Mr. R. Caldwell . .								
Mr. Coker . . .								

Twenty-two ladies and thirty gentlemen shot.

This meeting was managed by Mr. N. Merridew for Mr. Quilter.

The Tenth Grand Annual Crystal Palace Archery Meeting was held on **July 2 and 3, 1868.**

LADIES	60 Yards		50 Yards		TOTALS	
	Hits	Score	Hits	Score	Hits	Score
Mrs. W. Butt . . .	87					
Mrs. Horniblow . . .	86					
Miss Betham . . .	83					
Miss H. Hutchinson . .	86					
Miss Ripley						
Miss Ellis						
Miss Adams						
Mrs. A. Knox . . .						

GENTLEMEN	100 Yards		80 Yards		60 Yards		TOTALS	
	Hits	Score	Hits	Score	Hits	Score	Hits	Score
Mr. E. A. Holmes `. .	77	339			40	208		
Mr. W. Rimington. .	84	338			42	228		
Mr. H. A. Ford . .	81	315			39	157		
Mr. Spottiswoode .	62	234			43	219		
Mr. E. N. Snow . .	49	195			44	224		
Mr. F. Townsend . .	52	200			36	172		
Mr. J. M. Croker . .	40	162			42	214		
Mr. Betham . . .	44	160			41	195		
Mr. Jenner-Fust . .	53	209			40	196		
Captain C. H. Fisher .	68	272			43	189		
Mr. H. Elliott . .	54	172			39	171		

Thirty-seven ladies and fifty gentlemen shot.

The Twenty-fifth Grand National Archery Society's Meeting was held at Hereford, on the Racecourse, on July 29 and 30, 1868.

LADIES	60 Yards		50 Yards		TOTALS	
	Hits	Score	Hits	Score	Hits	Score
Miss Betham . . .	80	382	48	290	128	672
Mrs. W. Butt . . .	87	359	47	265	134	624
Mrs. P. Becher . . .	79	401	41	193	120	594
Mrs. E. Lister . . .	72	346	43	247	115	593
Mrs. Horniblow . . .	82	364	44	222	126	586
Miss Ripley	70	330	42	214	112	544

Miss Betham won the silver bracer with 4 points. Mrs. W. Butt won 2 points for most hits and another point for hits at 60 yards. Mrs. P. Becher won the point for score at 60 yards.

GENTLEMEN	100 Yards		80 Yards		60 Yards		TOTALS	
	Hits	Score	Hits	Score	Hits	Score	Hits	Score
Mr. W. Rimington . .								
Mr. O. K. Prescot . .								
Captain C. H. Fisher .								
Mr. E. A. Holmes . .								
Mr. H. A. Ford . .								
Colonel M. F. Ward .								
Mr. J. M. Croker . .								
Mr. H. Elliott . .								
Mr. Betham . . .								
Mr. H. Walrond . .								
Mr. Jenner-Fust . .								
Mr. W. Butt . . .								

Mr. W. Rimington became the Champion with 5 points. Captain C. H. Fisher won 2 points for hits and score at 100 yards. Mr. O. K. Prescot won the point for score at 80 yards; and Mr. J. M. Croker won the points for score and hits at 60 yards

Sixty-three ladies and sixty-nine gentlemen shot.

Mr. W. Rimington scored 433 on July 31 in the handicap match.

The Sixth Grand Western Archery Meeting was held at Bitton, near Teignmouth, on September 9 and 10, 1868.

LADIES	60 Yards		50 Yards		TOTALS	
	Hits	Score	Hits	Score	Hits	Score
Mrs. Horniblow . . .	83	453	44	238	127	691
Miss Ripley	85	397	45	219	130	616
Miss Rowlett . . .	62	268	43	201	105	469

GENTLEMEN	100 Yards		80 Yards		60 Yards		TOTALS	
	Hits	Score	Hits	Score	Hits	Score	Hits	Score
Mr. H. A. Ford . .	70	300	76	364	44	260	190	924
Colonel M. F. Ward .	67	299	68	320	39	217	174	836
Mr. H. B. Hare . .	53	199	73	325	30	198	156	722
Mr. E. N. Snow . .	48	192	63	275	43	237	154	704
Admiral A. Lowe . .	69	283	56	242	34	160	159	685
Mr. C. H. Everett . .	63	221	56	212	37	189	156	622
Mr. H. Walrond . .	58	206	47	207	42	188	147	601

Miss Ripley became Championess, and Colonel Ward Champion of the West.

Fifty-six ladies and thirty-eight gentlemen shot.

The Sixteenth Grand Leamington and Midland Archery Meeting was held on June 9 and 10, 1869, in the Jephson Gardens.

LADIES	60 Yards		50 Yards		TOTALS	
	Hits	Score	Hits	Score	Hits	Score
Miss Betham . . .						
Mrs. Kinahan . . .						
Mrs. P. Becher . . .						
Mrs. Horniblow . . .						
Miss Peel						
Miss Stephenson . . .						
Mrs. E. Lister . . .						
Miss H. Hutchinson . .						
Miss F. Flight . . .						

GENTLEMEN	100 Yards		80 Yards		60 Yards		TOTALS	
	Hits	Score	Hits	Score	Hits	Score	Hits	Score
Mr. H. A. Ford . .	95	403	77	369	48	260	220	1032
Captain C. H. Fisher .	60	250	74	312	43	205	177	767
Mr. O. K. Prescot . .	79	281	65	291	37	161	181	733
Mr. H. Elliott . .	74	286	69	247	39	145	182	678
Mr. T. L. Coulson . .	56	236	59	231	40	164	155	631
Mr. Walford . . .	50	198	52	210	44	220	146	628
Mr. W. Ford . . .	49	195	60	238	35	179	144	612

Twenty-one ladies and thirty-nine gentlemen shot.

The Eleventh Grand Annual Crystal Palace Archery Meeting was held on July 8 and 9, 1869.

LADIES	60 Yards		50 Yards		TOTALS	
	Hits	Score	Hits	Score	Hits	Score
Mrs. Horniblow . . .	88	410	48	266	136	676
Miss Ripley	81	369	46	278	127	647
Miss H. Hutchinson . .	68	308	41	243	109	551
Miss Stephenson . . .	74	336	40	200	114	536
Mrs. P. Becher . . .	69	305	43	229	112	534
Mrs. Kinahan . . .	74	344	40	184	114	528

GENTLEMEN	100 Yards		80 Yards		60 Yards		TOTALS	
	Hits	Score	Hits	Score	Hits	Score	Hits	Score
Mr. W. Rimington . .	80							
Mr. H. A. Ford . .	66							9
Captain C. H. Fisher .	77							2
Mr. H. Elliott . .	60							8
Mr. E. A. Holmes . .	68							
Mr. Walford . . .	38							
Mr. Horlock . . .	54							
Mr. W. L. Selfe . .	63							
Mr. J. M. Croker . .	49							
Admiral Lowe . .	57							
Mr. Betham . . .	57							
Mr. Lea	48							

Forty-two ladies and fifty-seven gentlemen shot.

The Twenty-sixth Grand National Archery Society's Meeting was held in the Aston Park Grounds, near Birmingham, on July 28 and 29, 1869.

LADIES	60 Yards		50 Yards		TOTALS	
	Hits	Score	Hits	Score	Hits	Score
Mrs. Horniblow . . .	78	402	45	227	123	629
Mrs. Kinahan . . .	83	409	40	198	123	607
Mrs. E. Lister . . .	65	299	45	219	110	518
Miss Betham . . .	61	247	43	239	104	486
Miss Stephenson . . .	62	276	41	201	103	477
Miss H. Hutchinson . .	73	321	35	155	108	476

Mrs. Horniblow won the silver bracer with the highest score, as there was a tie between her and Mrs. Kinahan in points. This was said to be the case at the time, but it does not appear to have been so from the published scores, as Mrs. Horniblow had the advantage by one-half a point. Mrs. Horniblow appears to have won 2 points for gross score, 1 point for a tie with Mrs. Kinahan for total hits, and one-half a point for a tie with Mrs. E. Lister for hits at 50 yards— total, $3\frac{1}{2}$ points. Mrs. Kinahan won 2 points for hits and score at 60 yards, and 1 point for the tie in total hits—her total being only 3 points. Miss Betham won 1 point for score at 50 yards. The annual report of this meeting was never issued by the Hon. Secretary, the Rev. O. Luard, so the actual state of the case cannot now be made certain. Of course there may have been an error in the unofficial accounts published.

Mr. W. Rimington won the Champion's gold medal with the highest score, as there was a tie in points between him and Captain C. H. Fisher, each having won 4 points. Mr. W. Rimington won 1 point for score at 100 yards, 1 point for score at 60 yards, and 2 points for gross score. Captain C. H. Fisher won 2 points for score and hits at 80 yards, and 2 for most total hits. Mr. E. A. Holmes won 1 point for

hits at 60 yards, and Mr. O. K. Prescot one point for hits at
100 yards.

GENTLEMEN	100 Yards		80 Yards		60 Yards		TOTALS	
	Hits	Score	Hits	Score	Hits	Score	Hits	Score
Mr. W. Rimington .								
Mr. E. A. Holmes .								
Captain C. H. Fisher								
Mr. H. A. Ford								
Mr. G. Edwards								
Mr. O. K. Prescot								
Mr. H. Elliott								
Mr. H. Walrond								
Mr. C. H. Everett .								
Captain Lewin, R.E.								
Mr. H. B. Hare								
Mr. T. L. Coulson .								

On this occasion it was decided by the Committee that in
future the Champion honours at their meetings should be
decided by gross score and not by points. A handsome silver
cup, value 50 guineas, collected by small subscriptions from
numerous archers, was presented on July 29 to Mr. C. M.
Caldecott, of Holbrooke Grange, near Rugby, who had acted
for many years as judge at these meetings.

Only thirty-six ladies and sixty-nine gentlemen shot at
this meeting.

The Seventh Grand Western Archery Meeting was held in
Mr. Parson's grounds at Bitton, near Teignmouth, on August
4 and 5, 1869.

LADIES	60 Yards		50 Yards		TOTALS	
	Hits	Score	Hits	Score	Hits	Score
Miss Ripley .	76	390	46	270	122	660
Mrs. Kinahan	86	412	36	176	122	588

GENTLEMEN	100 Yards		80 Yards		60 Yards		TOTALS	
	Hits	Score	Hits	Score	Hits	Score	Hits	Score
Mr. C. H. Everett . . .	59	227	74	310	39	175	172	712*
Mr. R. Price . . .	51	211	63	279	40	194	154	684
Mr. H. Walrond . .	45	157	64	296	38	186	147	639
Mr. Jenner-Fust . .	53	233	55	193	40	212	148	638
Colonel M. F. Ward .	56	182	60	266	40	180	158	628

Miss Ripley and Mr. R. Price became Championess and Champion of the West.

Sixty-two ladies and thirty-nine gentlemen shot.

The Seventeenth Grand Leamington and Midland Archery Meeting was held in the Jephson Gardens on June 15 and 16, 1870.

LADIES	60 Yards		50 Yards		TOTALS	
	Hits	Score	Hits	Score	Hits	Score
Mrs. W. Butt . . .	93	525	44	260	137	785
Mrs. Villiers Forbes . .	86	454	43	227	129	681
Miss H. Hutchinson˙ . .	83	403	44	232	127	635
Mrs. Horniblow . . .	83	389	44	236	127	625
Mrs. E. Lister . . .	83	365	44	232	127	597
Miss Joan Ley . . .	76	326	41	223	117	539

GENTLEMEN	100 Yards		80 Yards		60 Yards		TOTALS	
	Hits	Score	Hits	Score	Hits	Score	Hits	Score
Mr. H. Elliott . .								890
Mr. Jenner-Fust . .								780
Mr. Betham								750
Mr. O. K. Prescot .								747
Colonel M. F. Ward .								713
Mr. W. F. Heideman .								668
Captain Lewin, R.E. .								629
Mr. W. Butt . . .								606
Mr. T. L. Coulson . .								605

Twenty-five ladies and forty gentlemen shot.

Mr. O. K. Prescot scored 400 on June 17 in the handicap match.

The Twelfth Grand Annual Crystal Palace Archery Meeting was held on July 7 and 8, 1870.

LADIES	60 Yards		50 Yards		TOTALS	
	Hits	Score	Hits	Score	Hits	Score
Mrs. V. Forbes . . .				45		
Mrs. W. Butt . . .		442		46		
Mrs. Horniblow . . .				45		
Mrs. Kinahan . . .				41		
Miss H. Hutchinson . .				46		
Miss Joan Ley . . .				47		
Miss H. Holmes . . .				42		
Mrs. Hosken . . .				45		

GENTLEMEN	100 Yards		80 Yards		60 Yards		TOTALS	
	Hits	Score	Hits	Score	Hits	Score	Hits	Score
Mr. E. A. Holmes . .								897
Mr. H. Elliott . .								794
Captain C. H. Fisher .								784
Mr. Jenner-Fust . .								722
Mr. H. Walrond . .								718
Mr. Walford . . .								661
Mr. W. Butt . . .								639
Colonel A. Robertson .								612
Mr. T. Boulton . .								608

Forty-eight ladies and thirty-nine gentlemen shot.

The Twenty-seventh Grand National Archery Society's Meeting was held on July 21 and 22, 1870, at Weston, near Bath.

LADIES	60 Yards		50 Yards		TOTALS	
	Hits	Score	Hits	Score	Hits	Score
Mrs. Horniblow . . .	86					
Mrs. V. Forbes . . .						
Mrs. W. Butt . . .						
Mrs. E. Lister . . .						
Miss H. Hutchinson .						
Mrs. P. Pinckney . .						
Miss Hulme						
Miss Joan Ley . . .	69					
Miss Ripley [1] . . .	45					
Mrs. J. R. Thomson . .	60					

Mrs. Horniblow became the Championess by highest gross score. The points happened to be equally divided between her and Mrs. W. Butt.

GENTLEMEN	100 Yards		80 Yards		60 Yards		TOTALS	
	Hits	Score	Hits	Score	Hits	Score	Hits	Score
Mr. E. A. Holmes . .			3					
Captain C. H. Fisher .			2					
Mr. C. H. Everett . .			2					8
Mr. Walford . . .								6
Mr. H. Elliott . .					4			
Mr. W. Rimington . .					4			
Mr. W. Butt . . .								
Mr. E. Ley . . .					3			
Mr. O. K. Prescot . .								
Mr. Betham . . .								
Colonel M. F. Ward .								
Mr. W. F. Heideman .								

Mr. E. A. Holmes became the Champion with the highest score under the rule passed in 1869 abolishing points. He would have become champion by one-third of a point.

The average of the shooting at this meeting was unusually good amongst the gentlemen, being 751·5 for the first ten.

Mr. H. A. Ford was present, but did not shoot.

The weather was excessively hot.

[1] Shot only 15 arrows at 60 yards the first day.

Eighty-three ladies and seventy-nine gentlemen shot.

Good scores were made by Mr. E. A. Holmes (490), Captain C. H. Fisher (443), and Mr. Walford (411), on July 23, in the handicap match.

The Eighth Grand Western Archery Meeting was held in the grounds at Bitton, near Teignmouth, on July 27 and 28, 1870.

LADIES	60 Yards		50 Yards		TOTALS	
	Hits	Score	Hits	Score	Hits	Score
Miss M. Lockyer . . .	91	463	45	235	136	698
Mrs. V. Forbes . . .	81	407	47	275	128	682
Mrs. P. Pinckney . . .	85	403	45	249	130	652
Miss J. Ley	85	387	45	263	130	650
Miss Ripley	78	362	47	283	125	645
Miss H. Hutchinson . .	78	320	45	249	123	569
Mrs. J. R. Thomson . .	83	343	39	205	122	548

GENTLEMEN	100 Yards		80 Yards		60 Yards		TOTALS	
	Hits	Score	Hits	Score	Hits	Score	Hits	Score
Captain C. H. Fisher .								
Mr. H. Walrond . .								
Mr. Betham . . .								
Mr. O. K. Prescot . .								
Mr. E. N. Snow . .								
Mr. W. Rimington .								
Mr. Price . . .								
Colonel M. F. Ward .								

Miss M. Lockyer and Mr. Walrond became Championess and Champion of the West.

Sixty-three ladies and forty-three gentlemen shot.

The Eighteenth Grand Leamington and Midland Archery Meeting was held in the Jephson Gardens on June 14 and 15, 1871.

LADIES	60 Yards		50 Yards		TOTALS	
	Hits	Score	Hits	Score	Hits	Score
Mrs. Horniblow . . .	89	503	47	265	136	768
Mrs. V. Forbes . . .	77	431	48	268	125	699
Mrs. W. Butt . . .	83	403	44	240	127	643
Mrs. E. Lister . . .	76	368	45	221	121	589
Miss Joan Ley . . .	76	348	46	218	122	566
Mrs. P. Becher . . .	71	329	42	176	113	505

GENTLEMEN	100 Yards		80 Yards		60 Yards		TOTALS	
	Hits	Score	Hits	Score	Hits	Score	Hits	Score
Captain C. H. Fisher .								
Mr. T. L. Coulson . .								
Mr. Jenner-Fust . .								
Mr. C. H. Everett . .								
Mr. G. L. Aston . .								
Mr. F. Townsend . .								
Mr. W. Butt . . .								
Mr. H. Elliott . .								

Twenty-three ladies and thirty-six gentlemen shot.

During all these eighteen Leamington meetings Mr. N. Merridew acted as Secretary and Manager, and Mr. C. M. Caldecott as Judge.

The Twenty-eighth Grand National Archery Society's Meeting was held on the College Cricket-ground, at Cheltenham, on June 28 and 29, 1871

At this meeting the system of points for the selection of the Champion and Championess was reintroduced, and Mrs. Horniblow became the Championess with all the points, except that Mrs. V. Forbes and Mrs. Eyre W. Hussey tied her in hits at 50 yards, with 47 hits. This score of 746 was the best yet made, Mrs. Horniblow's own score of 700 at Bath in 1870 being the next best.

LADIES	60 Yards		50 Yards		TOTALS	
	Hits	Score	Hits	Score	Hits	Score
Mrs. Horniblow . . .	91					
Mrs. E. Lister . . .						
Mrs. W. Butt . . .						
Mrs. V. Forbes . . .						
Mrs. Eyre W. Hussey . .						
Mrs. J. R. Thomson . .	73					
Miss Betham . . .	75					
Miss Joan Ley . . .	70					
Miss Hulme	68					
Miss F. Flight . . .						

GENTLEMEN	100 Yards		80 Yards		60 Yards		TOTALS	
	Hits	Score	Hits	Score	Hits	Score	Hits	Score
Captain C. H. Fisher .								
Mr. W. Rimington . .								
Mr. H. Walrond . .								
Mr. Jenner-Fust . .								
Mr. T. L. Coulson . .								
Mr. Walford . . .								
Mr. H. Elliott . .								
Mr. P. Muir . . .								

Captain C. H. Fisher won the Championship with all the points, except that for hits at 60 yards, which was won by Mr. W. Rimington (47). This 955 was the best score yet made by anybody except Mr. H. A. Ford, and Mr. Holmes, whose score was 973 at Brighton in 1867.

Fifty-nine ladies and sixty-eight gentlemen shot at this meeting.

On the next day—June 30—Mr. Aston made 389, Miss Hulme 388, and Mrs. W. Butt 380.

The Thirteenth Grand Annual Crystal Palace Archery Meeting was held on July 12 and 13, 1871.

Twenty-three ladies and thirty-seven gentlemen shot.

LADIES	60 Yards		50 Yards		TOTALS	
	Hits	Score	Hits	Score	Hits	Score
Mrs. W. Butt . . .						
Mrs. Horniblow . . .						
Mrs. Eyre W. Hussey . .						
Miss Ripley						
Miss Betham . . .	7					
Mrs. V. Forbes . . .	7					
Mrs. J. R. Thomson . .	6					
Mrs. Kinahan . . .	7					

GENTLEMEN	100 Yards		80 Yards		60 Yards		TOTALS	
	Hits	Score	Hits	Score	Hits	Score	Hits	Score
Captain C. H. Fisher .								
Mr. H. Elliott								
Mr. C. H. Everett .								
Mr. H. Walrond .								
Mr. T. L. Coulson . .								
Captain Lewin, R.E. .								
Mr. Walford . . .								
Mr. B. P. Gregson . .								
Mr. Jenner-Fust . .								

Mr. R. Butt acted as Hon. Secretary to these meetings from 1867 to 1871 inclusive.

The Ninth Grand Western Archery Meeting was held at Bitton, near Teignmouth, on August 2 and 3, 1871, when fifty-four ladies and thirty-five gentlemen shot.

LADIES	60 Yards		50 Yards		TOTALS	
	Hits	Score	Hits	Score	Hits	Score
Miss Ripley	86	434	45	265	131	699
Mrs. V. Forbes . . .	75	337	44	248	119	585
Mrs. Letts	68	342	39	177	107	519
Mrs. P. Pinckney . . .	70	318	37	177	107	495

GENTLEMEN	100 Yards		80 Yards		60 Yards		TOTALS	
	Hits	Score	Hits	Score	Hits	Score	Hits	Score
Mr. H. Walrond . .	66	296	68	328	45	227	179	851
Admiral A. Lowe . .	79	353	59	265	36	180	174	798
Mr. R. Price . . .	73	283	68	288	42	226	183	797
Captain C. H. Fisher .	73	293	66	302	39	171	178	766
Mr. C. H. Everett . .	58	256	57	243	38	236	153	735
Mr. T. L. Coulson . .	70	268	56	208	38	164	164	640

Miss Ripley and Mr. Walrond became Championess and Champion of the West.

The Nineteenth Grand Leamington and Midland Archery Meeting was held in the Jephson Gardens, on June 12 and 13, 1872.

LADIES	60 Yards		50 Yards		TOTALS	
	Hits	Score	Hits	Score	Hits	Score
Mrs. Horniblow . . .	88	470	46	242	134	712
Mrs. Kinahan . . .	90	434	43	237	133	·671
Mrs. V. Forbes . . .	82	390	48	276	130	666
Mrs. E. Lister . . .	81	381	46	226	127	607

GENTLEMEN	100 Yards		80 Yards		60 Yards		TOTALS	
	Hits	Score	Hits	Score	Hits	Score	Hits	Score
Captain C. H. Fisher .								
Mr. H. Sagar . . .								
Mr. G. E. S. Fryer .								
Mr. G. L. Aston . .								
Mr. Betham . . .								
Mr. W. Ford . . .								
Mr. H. Elliott . .								
Mr. T. L. Coulson . .	8							
Mr. B. P. Gregson . .	0							
Captain Lewin, R.E. .								
Mr. O. K. Prescot . .								

Eighteen ladies and thirty-two gentlemen shot.

The Fourteenth Grand Annual Crystal Palace Archery Meeting was held on July 11 and 12, 1872.

LADIES	60 Yards		50 Yards		TOTALS	
	Hits	Score	Hits	Score	Hits	Score
Mrs. J. R. Thomson . .	81	343	47	261	128	604
Mrs. P. Pinckney . . .	72	328	46	208	118	536
Miss Ripley	69	299	40	200	109	499

GENTLEMEN	100 Yards		80 Yards		60 Yards		TOTALS	
	Hits	Score	Hits	Score	Hits	Score	Hits	Score
Mr. H. Sagar . . .	52	214	73	335	41	197	166	746
Captain C. H. Fisher .	74	258	67	211	45	225	186	694
Mr. G. E. S. Fryer. .	59	195	63	289	41	201	163	685
Mr. H. Elliott . .	55	207	56	222	41	193	152	622

Thirty-six ladies and thirty-three gentlemen shot.

The Twenty-ninth Grand National Archery Society's Meeting was held, in the grounds of the College at Cheltenham, on June 26 and 27, 1872.

LADIES	60 Yards		50 Yards		TOTALS	
	Hits	Score	Hits	Score	Hits	Score
Mrs. Horniblow . . .	88	394	48	266	136	660
Mrs. J. R. Thomson . .	80	372	45	233	125	605
Mrs. Kinahan . . .	75	365	46	216	121	581
Mrs. E. Lister . . .	75	327	41	243	116	570
Miss H. Hutchinson . .	72	320	45	239	117	559
Mrs. Acklom . . .	73	317	41	201	114	518

Mrs. Horniblow won the silver bracer, having secured all the points.

Captain C. H. Fisher became Champion with highest gross score, as he was a tie with Mr. Betham for points, each having 4—Captain Fisher having hits and score at 80 yards and gross score, and Mr. Betham hits and score at 100 yards and gross hits. Mr. Sagar won the 2 points for hits and score at 60 yards.

GENTLEMEN	100 Yards		80 Yards		60 Yards		TOTALS	
	Hits	Score	Hits	Score	Hits	Score	Hits	Score
Captain C. H. Fisher .	64	242	75	347	36	182	175	771
Mr. Jenner-Fust . .	68	250	65	291	43	207	176	748
Mr. Betham . . .	71	269	67	267	40	176	178	712
Mr. G. E. S. Fryer .	63	259	50	216	43	209	156	684
Mr. H. Sagar . . .	37	139	58	250	47	227	142	616
Mr. H. Elliott . .	56	188	59	233	42	194	157	615

Fifty-five ladies and fifty-eight gentlemen shot at this meeting.

Mrs. Thomson made a score of 345 on the following day— June 28—in the handicap match.

The Tenth Grand Western Archery Meeting was held at Sherborne, in Mr. Digby's grounds, on August 7 and 8, 1872, when fifty-four ladies and forty-four gentlemen shot.

LADIES	60 Yards		50 Yards		TOTALS	
	Hits	Score	Hits	Score	Hits	Score
Mrs. P. Pinckney . . .	85	401	47	249	132	650
Miss Lockyer . . .	72	334	43	223	115	557

GENTLEMEN	100 Yards		80 Yards		60 Yards		TOTALS	
	Hits	Score	Hits	Score	Hits	Score	Hits	Score
Captain C. H. Fisher .	95	429	76	370	47	261	218	1060
Mr. G. E. S. Fryer .	68	256	65	299	46	262	179	817
Mr. R. Price . . .	58	234	59	261	41	211	158	706
Mr. H. Walrond . .	52	206	58	256	47	221	157	683
Mr. C. H. Everett . .	55	229	53	199	40	188	148	616
Mr. T. Boulton . .	53	211	60	264	33	141	146	616
Mr. Jenner-Fust . .	66	244	55	217	31	149	152	610

Mrs. P. Pinckney and Mr. Price became Championess and Champion of the West.

No Leamington Archery Meeting was held in 1873, as the Grand National Archery Society's Meeting was held in Leamington in the course of the year.

The Fifteenth Grand Annual Crystal Palace Archery Meeting was held on July 9 and 10, 1873.

LADIES	60 Yards		50 Yards		TOTALS	
	Hits	Score	Hits	Score	Hits	Score
Mrs. P. Pinckney . . .	88	468	47	261	135	729
Mrs. Horniblow . . .	89	477	46	242	135	719
Mrs. Piers F. Legh . .	84	398	46	244	130	642
Miss H. Hutchinson . .	73	317	46	234	119	551
Miss Ripley	77	329	39	221	116	550
Mrs. Mayhew . . .	79	345	35	179	114	524
Mrs. M. Barnard . . .	78	334	38	172	116	506

GENTLEMEN	100 Yards		80 Yards		60 Yards		TOTALS	
	Hits	Score	Hits	Score	Hits	Score	Hits	Score
Mr. C. H. Everett . .								
Mr. G. E. S. Fryer								
Mr. H. H. Palairet								
Mr. H. Sagar .								
Mr. T. Boulton								
Mr. Betham .								
Mr. B. P. Gregson								
Mr. T. L. Coulson								
Mr. A. Henty .								
Dr. R. Harris . . .								

Forty-four ladies and twenty-seven gentlemen shot.

Major Lewin acted as Hon. Secretary to these meetings in 1872 and 1873.

A Grand Archery Meeting was held on the Cricket-ground of the Alexandra Park Company, Muswell Hill, near Hornsey, on July 17 and 18, 1873.

LADIES	60 Yards		50 Yards		TOTALS	
	Hits	Score	Hits	Score	Hits	Score
Mrs. Horniblow . . .	90	460	47	273	137	733
Miss H. Hutchinson . .	77	343	45	239	122	582
Mrs. P. Pinckney . . .	73	321	47	253	120	574
Miss Betham . . .	73	365	40	198	113	563
Mrs. Piers F. Legh . .	76	330	44	228	120	558

GENTLEMEN	100 Yards		80 Yards		60 Yards		TOTALS	
	Hits	Score	Hits	Score	Hits	Score	Hits	Score
Mr. H. H. Palairet . .								
Major C. H. Fisher .								
Mr. G. E. S. Fryer .								
Mr. C. H. Everett . .								
Mr. H. Sagar . . .								
Admiral A. Lowe . .								
Mr. T. Boulton . .								
Mr. Betham . . .								
Mr. G. L. Aston . .								
Mr. R. Braithwaite .								

Mr. T. Aldred had the management of this meeting. Thirty-seven ladies and thirty-four gentlemen shot.

The Thirtieth Grand National Archery Society's Meeting was held at Leamington, in Mrs.Wise's grounds, Shrublands, on July 23 and 24, 1873.

Mrs. Horniblow again won the silver bracer with 6 points. Mrs. P. Pinckney won the points for hits and score at 50 yards.

Major Fisher became Champion with 8½ points. Mr. A.

Henty won the point for hits at 60 yards, and Mr. Fust tied Major Fisher for the point for score at 60 yards.

LADIES	60 Yards		50 Yards		TOTALS	
	Hits	Score	Hits	Score	Hits	Score
Mrs. Horniblow . . .						
Miss Ripley						
Mrs. Piers F. Legh . .	82					
Mrs. P. Pinckney . . .	8					
Miss H. Hutchinson . .	8					
Miss Betham . . .	76					
Mrs. Villiers Forbes . .	75					
Mrs. Hornby . . .	77					
Mrs. Letts	87					

GENTLEMEN	100 Yards		80 Yards		60 Yards		TOTALS	
	Hits	Score	Hits	Score	Hits	Score	Hits	Score
Major C. H. Fisher .								
Mr. H. H. Palairet .								
Mr. C. H. Everett . .								
Mr. T. Boulton . .								
Mr Jenner-Fust . .								
Admiral A. Lowe . .								
Mr. O. K. Prescot . .								
Mr. G. E. S. Fryer .								
Mr. E. N. Snow . .								
Mr P. Muir . . .								
Mr. A. Henty . . .								

In the handicap match on the next day—July 25—Miss Hutchinson scored 350, Mrs. Hornby 312, Major Fisher 462, Mr. Everett 439, and Mr. Fryer 360.

Sixty-three ladies and seventy-six gentlemen shot at this meeting.

The Eleventh Grand Western Archery Meeting was held in Mr. Parson's grounds at Bitton, near Teignmouth, on

August 27 and 28, 1873, when fifty-three ladies and thirty-nine gentlemen shot.

LADIES	60 Yards		50 Yards		TOTALS	
	Hits	Score	Hits	Score	Hits	Score
Mrs. P. Pinckney . . .	83	375	45	273	128	648
Miss Ripley	80	362	47	285	127	647
Mrs. Kinahan . . .	70	308	45	233	115	541
Mrs. Letts	64	290	40	206	104	496

GENTLEMEN	100 Yards		80 Yards		60 Yards		TOTALS	
	Hits	Score	Hits	Score	Hits	Score	Hits	Score
Mr. C. H. Everett . .	60	264	73	323	40	182	173	769
Mr. O. K. Prescot . .	58	264	63	269	38	170	159	703
Mr. H. Walrond . .	47	171	68	294	42	216	157	681
Captain C. H. Garnett .	64	266	60	258	35	151	159	675
Mr. T. L. Coulson . .	57	203	65	273	35	167	157	643
Major C. H. Fisher .	40	158	64	256	41	197	145	611

Mrs. Pinckney and Mr. Walrond became Championess and Champion of the West.

The Twentieth Grand Leamington and Midland Archery Meeting was held on June 24 and 25, 1874.

LADIES	60 Yards		50 Yards		TOTALS	
	Hits	Score	Hits	Score	Hits	Score
Mrs. E. Lister . . .						
Mrs. V. Forbes . . .						
Miss H. Hutchinson . .						
Mrs. Pond						
Mrs. Hornby . . .						
Mrs. Piers F. Legh . .						
Mrs. Mayhew . . .						
Miss M. A. Hollins . .						
Mrs. J. F. Stilwell . .						

GENTLEMEN	100 Yards		80 Yards		60 Yards		TOTALS	
	Hits	Score	Hits	Score	Hits	Score	Hits	Score
Mr. *O. K.* Prescot . .	90	350	65	279	43	195	198	824
Mr. Betham . . .	61	261	71	325	45	217	177	803
Mr. G. E. S. Fryer .	74	288	63	225	44	228	181	741
Mr. G. L. Aston . .	57	211	57	223	41	199	155	633
Mr. H. Sagar . . .	56	244	50	196	38	188	144	628
Captain C. H. Garnett .	39	149	68	296	39	177	146	622
Colonel Norbury . .	44	140	65	279	45	201	154	620

Twenty-four ladies and thirty-eight gentlemen shot.

The Sixteenth Grand Annual Crystal Palace Archery Meeting was held on July 8 and 9, 1874.

LADIES	60 Yards		50 Yards		TOTALS	
	Hits	Score	Hits	Score	Hits	Score
Mrs. Pond	83	421	47	279	130	700
Miss Croker	74	382	42	230	116	612
Mrs. Mayhew . . .	77	339	48	266	125	605
Mrs. J. F. Stilwell . .	75	357	44	236	119	593
Miss H. Hutchinson . .	71	323	44	244	115	567
Mrs. Marshall . . .	83	375	37	189	120	564
Mrs. P. Pinckney . . .	69	311	46	240	115	551

GENTLEMEN	100 Yards		80 Yards		60 Yards		TOTALS	
	Hits	Score	Hits	Score	Hits	Score	Hits	Score
Mr. W. Rimington . .	73	329	78	334	46	250	197	913
Major C. H. Fisher .	80	326	74	354	42	206	196	886
Mr. Betham . . .	67	283	70	304	38	176	175	763
Mr. H. Sagar . . .	61	229	68	310	43	197	172	736
Mr. A. Henty . . .	56	222	68	288	42	160	166	670
Major Lewin, R.E. .	53	195	57	277	35	161	145	633
Mr. *G.* E. S. Fryer .	46	214	55	221	39	183	140	618

Thirty-nine ladies and forty-three gentlemen shot.

The Twelfth Grand Western Archery Meeting was held at Weymouth on July 29 and 30, 1874, when fifty-two ladies and thirty-six gentlemen shot.

LADIES	60 Yards		50 Yards		TOTALS	
	Hits	Score	Hits	Score	Hits	Score
Mrs. Pond	75	327	41	187	116	514
Mrs. Horniblow . . .	72	304	44	200	116	504
Mrs. C. Betham . . .	68	304	41	191	109	495
Miss Betham . . .	60	270	44	212	104	482
Mrs. Piers F. Legh . .	73	289	43	191	116	480
Miss Lowe	66	306	37	169	103	475
Mrs. P. Pinckney . . .	64	244	44	230	108	474

GENTLEMEN	100 Yards		80 Yards		60 Yards		TOTALS	
	Hits	Score	Hits	Score	Hits	Score	Hits	Score
Major C. H. Fisher .	72	246	65	267	42	244	179	757
Mr. H. Walrond . .	55	243	56	286	35	133	146	662
Mr. W. Rimington . .	65	233	60	244	38	156	163	633
Mr. T. L. Coulson . .	49	195	63	297	34	122	146	614
Mr. O. K. Prescot . .	63	239	57	217	34	148	154	604

Miss Lowe and Mr. H. Walrond became Championess and Champion of the West.

The Thirty-first Grand National Archery Society's Meeting was held on August 5 and 6, 1874, on the College Cricket-ground, at Winchester.

Mrs. Pond won the silver bracer with 6 points. Mrs. P. F. Legh won the point for score at 50 yards ; and Mrs. P. Pinckney and Mrs. Horniblow divided the point for hits at 50 yards.

Major C. H. Fisher became Champion, having secured all the points.

Eighty-two ladies and sixty-four gentlemen shot at this meeting.

LADIES	60 Yards		50 Yards		TOTALS	
	Hits	Score	Hits	Score	Hits	Score
Mrs. Pond	87	431				
Mrs. Piers F. Legh . .	7	369				
Mrs. P. Pinckney . . .		362				
Mrs. Horniblow . . .		352				
Mrs. E. Lister . . .	76	330				
Miss Milne	76	384				
Miss Betham . . .	73	351				
Miss E. Martin . . .	73	333				
Mrs. Mayhew . . .	64	280				
Mrs. Holland . . .		308				

GENTLEMEN	100 Yards		80 Yards		60 Yards		TOTALS	
	Hits	Score	Hits	Score	Hits	Score	Hits	Score
Major C. H. Fisher .								
Mr. C. H. Everett . .								
Mr. G. E. S. Fryer .								
Mr. Betham . . .								
Mr. H. Walrond . .								
Mr. O. K. Prescot . .								
Mr. B. P. Gregson . .								
Mr. A. Henty . . .								
Mr. W. Rimington . .								

In the handicap match on August 7, Mrs. E. Lister scored 356, Mrs. Piers F. Legh 333, and Mrs. Horniblow 319; Major C. H. Fisher 443, and Mr. Betham 418.

The Twenty-first Grand Leamington and Midland Archery Meeting was held in the Jephson Gardens, on June 23 and 24, 1875.

LADIES	60 Yards		50 Yards		TOTALS	
	Hits	Score	Hits	Score	Hits	Score
Mrs. W. Butt . . .	86	422	43	235	129	657
Mrs. Pond	82	366	44	258	126	624
Miss M. A. Hollins . .	80	360	48	262	128	622
Miss H. Hutchinson . .	82	328	41	181	123	509
Mrs. Hornby . . .	74	326	37	181	111	507

GENTLEMEN	100 Yards		80 Yards		60 Yards		TOTALS	
	Hits	Score	Hits	Score	Hits	Score	Hits	Score
Mr. W. Rimington . .	74	280	73	339	44	238	191	857
Mr. C. H. Everett . .	82	310	71	265	45	215	198	790
Mr. H. H. Palairet .	62	256	66	276	47	227	175	759
Mr. Betham . . .	58	244	63	253	44	196	165	693
Mr. W. Porter . .	47	185	70	300	33	165	150	650
Mr. H. Elliott . .	55	213	60	238	40	166	155	617

Twenty-four ladies and forty gentlemen shot.

The Seventeenth Annual Crystal Palace Archery Meeting was held on July 28 and 29, 1875.

LADIES	60 Yards		50 Yards		TOTALS	
	Hits	Score	Hits	Score	Hits	Score
Mrs. Horniblow . . .	84	394	48	280	132	674
Mrs. Pond	82	374	46	250	128	624
Mrs. Kinahan . . .	76	310	48	258	124	568
Mrs. Piers F. Legh . .	80	350	43	195	123	545
Miss Legh	75	313	40	184	115	497

GENTLEMEN	100 Yards		80 Yards		60 Yards		TOTALS	
	Hits	Score	Hits	Score	Hits	Score	Hits	Score
Major C. H. Fisher .								
Mr. W. Rimington . .								
Mr. Betham . . .								
Mr. Piers F. Legh . .								
Mr. C. H. Everett . .								
Mr. H. Walrond . .								
Mr. H. H. Palairet .								
Mr. G. E. S. Fryer . .								
Mr. W. Ford . .								

Forty ladies and fifty-seven gentlemen shot.

The Thirty-second Grand National Archery Society's Meeting was held on August 4 and 5, 1875, in the Deer-park at Richmond, Surrey.

LADIES	60 Yards		50 Yards		TOTALS	
	Hits	Score	Hits	Score	Hits	Score
Miss M. A. Hollins . .	88					
Mrs. Horniblow . . .						
Mrs. P. Pinckney . . .						
Mrs. E. Lister . . .						
Mrs. Marshall . . .						
Mrs. Pond						
Miss H. Hutchinson . .	70					
Miss Milne	76					
Mrs. C. E. Hornby . .	59					
Miss Benwell . . .	70					

Miss Hollins won the silver bracer with $7\frac{1}{2}$ points, as she divided the point for hits at 50 yards with Mrs. Lister.

GENTLEMEN	100 Yards		80 Yards		60 Yards		TOTALS	
	Hits	Score	Hits	Score	Hits	Score	Hits	Score
Mr. G. E. S. Fryer . .								
Mr. W. Rimington . .								
Major C. H. Fisher .								
Mr. B. P. Gregson . .								
Mr. Betham . . .								
Mr. H. H. Palairet . .								
Mr. Piers F. Legh . .								
Mr. A. T. D. Berrington .								
Mr. C. H. Everett . .								
Mr. H. Walrond . .								
Mr. W. Butt . . .								

Mr. Fryer became Champion with 6 points. Mr. Rimington won the point for hits and score at 100 yards; Mr. Betham the point for hits at 60 yards; and Mr. Butt the point for score at 60 yards.

Eighty-four ladies and seventy-two gentlemen shot at this meeting.

The Thirteenth Grand Western Archery Meeting was held at Bitton, near Teignmouth, on August 11 and 12, 1875, when forty-seven ladies and twenty-seven gentlemen shot.

	60 Yards		50 Yards		Totals	
	Hits	Score	Hits	Score	Hits	Score
Mrs. Hosken. .	69	313	39	193	108	506

Gentlemen	100 Yards		80 Yards		60 Yards		Totals	
	Hits	Score	Hits	Score	Hits	Score	Hits	Score
Mr. W. Rimington . .	74	286	81	381	47	259	202	926
Major C. H. Fisher .	77	289	77	341	40	206	194	836
Mr. G. E. S. Fryer .	72	290	63	297	38	190	173	777
Mr. H. Walrond . .	64	274	65	275	40	198	169	747
Mr. H. H. Palairet .	60	236	68	316	34	150	162	702
Mr. H. Sagar . . .	65	253	56	242	37	169	158	664
Mr. Grant Dalton . .	45	171	59	257	43	203	147	631

Mrs. Hosken and Mr. Walrond became Championess and Champion of the West.

Major Fisher scored 442, and Mr. Palairet 424, in the handicap match on the following day—August 13.

The Twenty-second Grand Leamington and Midland Archery Meeting was held on June 21 and 22, 1876.

Twenty-nine ladies and thirty-four gentlemen shot.

Ladies	60 Yards		50 Yards		Totals	
	Hits	Score	Hits	Score	Hits	Score
Mrs. W. Butt . . .						
Mrs. Horniblow . . .						
Mrs. Pond						
Mrs. Piers F. Legh . .						
Miss H. Hutchinson . .						
Mrs. E. Lister . . .						
Miss M. A. Hollins . .						
Mrs. Hornby . . .						
Mrs. Kinahan . . .						

GENTLEMEN	100 Yards		80 Yards		60 Yards		TOTALS	
	Hits	Score	Hits	Score	Hits	Score	Hits	Score
Mr. C. H. Everett . .	94	364	70	348	39	185	203	897
Mr. G. L. Aston . .	65	243	66	288	45	209	176	740
Mr. W. Ford . . .	66	230	71	313	41	185	178	728
Mr. W. Butt . . .	42	174	64	276	46	240	152	690
Mr. W. Porter . .	52	204	51	191	44	208	147	603

Mr. C. H. Everett scored 451 on June 23 in the handicap match.

The Eighteenth Grand Annual Crystal Palace Archery Meeting was held on June 28 and 29, 1876.

LADIES	60 Yards		50 Yards		TOTALS	
	Hits	Score	Hits	Score	Hits	Score
Mrs. W. Butt . . .						
Mrs. Kinahan . . .						
Mrs. Marshall . . .						
Mrs. Pond . .						
Miss Berens . . .						
Miss Croker . . .						
Mrs. D. Ainsworth . .						
Mrs. Piers F. Legh . .						
Miss Follett . . .						

GENTLEMEN	100 Yards		80 Yards		60 Yards		TOTALS	
	Hits	Score	Hits	Score	Hits	Score	Hits	Score
Mr. C. H. Everett . .	77	333	69	283	45	209	191	825
Major C. H. Fisher .	65	291	66	294	40	176	171	761
Mr. J. Rogers . .	67	229	66	264	43	213	176	706
Mr. W. Rimington .	69	259	72	274	34	140	175	673
Mr. Eyre W. Hussey .	46	178	56	240	41	207	153	625

Thirty-nine ladies and thirty-five gentlemen shot.

The Thirty-third Grand National Archery Society's Meeting was held on July 5 and 6, 1876, at Sandown Park, near Esher, Surrey.

LADIES	60 Yards		50 Yards		TOTALS	
	Hits	Score	Hits	Score	Hits	Score
Mrs. W. Butt . . .						
Mrs. Marshall . . .						
Mrs. Kinahan . . .						
Miss M. A. Hollins . .						
Mrs. Kane						
Miss Croker . . .						
Mrs. D. Ainsworth . .						
Miss H. Hutchinson . .						
Mrs. Horniblow . . .						

Mrs. Butt won the silver bracer with all the points.

GENTLEMEN	100 Yards		80 Yards		60 Yards		TOTALS	
	Hits	Score	Hits	Score	Hits	Score	Hits	Score
Mr. H. H. Palairet . .	59	233	77	313	45	227	181	773
Major C. H. Fisher .	78	358	60	208	42	204	180	770
Mr. C. H. Everett . .	70	248	56	232	39	203	165	683
Mr. Rogers . . .	51	201	54	240	43	225	148	666
Mr. W. Rimington . .	61	235	59	231	39	163	159	629
Mr. G. E. S. Fryer .	53	195	63	225	38	184	154	604

Mr. H. H. Palairet became the Champion with 8 points after a very close contest during the shooting of the last 3 arrows at 60 yards with Major Fisher, who won the 2 points for hits and score at 100 yards.

In the handicap match on the next day Mrs. Horniblow made 340, and Mr. Everett 427.

Sixty-three ladies and fifty-three gentlemen shot at this meeting.

The Fourteenth Grand Western Archery Meeting was held at Salisbury on August 2 and 3, 1876, when fifty-three ladies and forty gentlemen shot.

LADIES	60 Yards		50 Yards		TOTALS	
	Hits	Score	Hits	Score	Hits	Score
Mrs. Piers F. Legh . .	86	368	46	266	132	634
Miss E. Pinckney . . .	81	345	45	213	126	558
Mrs. Horniblow . . .	78	316	45	223	123	539
Mrs. Kane	65	289	47	233	112	522
Mrs. E. Lister . . .	63	271	40	216	103	487

GENTLEMEN	100 Yards		80 Yards		60 Yards		TOTALS	
	Hits	Score	Hits	Score	Hits	Score	Hits	Score
Mr. H. H. Palairet . .	64	234	64	302	45	229	173	765
Mr. C. H. Everett . .	69	271	59	229	44	204	172	704
Mr. H. Walrond . .	55	201	62	250	46	236	163	687
Mr. J. Penrose . .	56	210	63	259	44	198	163	667
Mr. H. B. Hare . .	44	160	65	285	36	172	145	617
Mr. P. F. Legh . .	49	169	57	231	39	193	145	593

Miss E. Pinckney and Mr. Palairet became Championess and Champion of the West.

The Twenty-third Grand Leamington and Midland Archery Meeting was held on June 27 and 28, 1877. Forty ladies and twenty-seven gentlemen shot.

LADIES	60 Yards		50 Yards		TOTALS	
	Hits	Score	Hits	Score	Hits	Score
Mrs. W. Butt . . .						
Miss M. A. Hollins . .						
Mrs. Kinahan . . .						
Mrs. Piers F. Legh . .						
Miss Legh						
Mrs. D. Ainsworth . .						
Mrs. Acklom . . .						
Mrs. E. Lister . . .						
Miss H. Hutchinson . .						

GENTLEMEN	100 Yards		80 Yards		60 Yards		TOTALS	
	Hits	Score	Hits	Score	Hits	Score	Hits	Score
Mr. H. H. Palairet . . .	66	262	77	363	41	213	184	838
Major C. H. Fisher .	77	299	72	286	44	242	193	827
Mr. H. Elliott. . .	58	220	59	247	37	185	154	652

Mrs. W. Butt scored 365 on June 29 in the handicap match.

The Nineteenth Grand Annual Crystal Palace Archery Meeting was held on July 12 and 13, 1877. Forty-six ladies and forty gentlemen shot.

LADIES	60 Yards		50 Yards		TOTALS	
	Hits	Score	Hits	Score	Hits	Score
Mrs. W. Butt . . .						
Mrs. Kinahan . . .						
Miss Legh						
Mrs. Marshall . . .						
Mrs. Piers F. Legh . .						
Mrs. P. Pinckney . . .						
Mrs. Kane						
Mrs. Hulse						

GENTLEMEN	100 Yards		80 Yards		60 Yards		TOTALS	
	Hits	Score	Hits	Score	Hits	Score	Hits	Score
Major C. H. Fisher .								
Mr. P. Pinckney . .								
Mr. H. H. Palairet . .								
Mr. W. Rimington . .								
Mr. E. N. Snow . .								
Mr. H. Sagar . .								
Mr. H. Walrond . .								
Mr. J. Rogers . .								
Major Lewin, R.E. .								

The Thirty-fourth Grand National Archery Society's Meeting was held at Doncaster, on the Racecourse, on August 8 and 9, 1877.

LADIES	60 Yards		50 Yards		TOTALS	
	Hits	Score	Hits	Score	Hits	Score
Mrs. W. Butt . . .	80	414	46	262	126	676
Miss M. A. Hollins . .	84	376	42	220	126	596
Mrs. D. Ainsworth . .	73	327	45	253	118	580
Mrs. Horniblow . . .	72	316	46	244	118	560
Mrs. E. Lister . . .	70	320	42	216	112	516
Mrs. Marshall . . .	75	319	46	188	121	507
Mrs. Piers F. Legh . .	73	311	44	196	117	507

Mrs. Butt won the silver bracer with $5\frac{1}{2}$ points. Miss Hollins won the point for hits at 60 yards, and made an equal number of gross hits with Mrs. Butt; and Mrs. Horniblow made the same number of hits at 50 yards as Mrs. Butt.

GENTLEMEN	100 Yards		80 Yards		60 Yards		TOTALS	
	Hits	Score	Hits	Score	Hits	Score	Hits	Score
Mr. W. Rimington . .	55	227	70	290	38	186	163	703
Mr. H. H. Palairet . ' .	46	170	61	259	40	220	147	649
Mr. Betham . . .	54	242	54	206	41	179	149	627
Mr. G. E. S. Fryer . .	58	222	53	229	39	159	150	610

Mr. W. Rimington became Champion with 7 points. Mr. Betham won the 2 points for score at 100 yards and hits at 60 yards; Mr. Fryer the point for hits at 100 yards; and Mr. Palairet the point for score at 60 yards.

In the handicap match on the next day—August 10—Mrs. Butt scored 44 hits, 280 sc. and 24 hits, 154 sc. = 68 hits, 434 sc., and Miss Hollins 362. Mr. Palairet scored 400.

The weather on the two first days at this meeting was most unsuitable.

Forty-four ladies and fifty-four gentlemen attended this meeting.

The Fifteenth Grand Western Archery Meeting was held at Bitton, near Teignmouth, on August 29 and 30, 1877, when forty-nine ladies and thirty gentlemen shot.

LADIES	60 Yards		50 Yards		TOTALS	
	Hits	Score	Hits	Score	Hits	Score
Mrs. C. E. Nesham . .	74	360	44	240	118	600
Miss E. Pinckney . . .	75	327	46	240	121	567
Miss C. Radford . . .	82	392	41	173	123	565
Mrs. V. Forbes . . .	71	329	40	202	111	531
Mrs. Gataker . . .	71	301	44	214	115	515
Miss Follett . . .	68	302	41	201	109	503
Miss E. Matthews . .	64	294	40	206	104	500

GENTLEMEN	100 Yards		80 Yards		60 Yards		TOTALS	
	Hits	Score	Hits	Score	Hits	Score	Hits	Score
Major C. H. Fisher .	91	357	66	292	41	201	198	850
Mr. P. Pinckney .	73	251	67	307	42	228	182	786
Mr. H. H. Palairet .	67	263	70	288	44	198	181	749
Mr. O. L. Clare .	75	285	48	186	43	205	166	676
Mr. H. Walrond .	57	219	65	255	43	195	165	669

Miss E. Pinckney and Mr. P. Pinckney—sister and brother —became Championess and Champion of the West.

The Twenty-fourth Grand Leamington and Midland Archery Meeting was held on June 26 and 27, 1878.

Thirty-one ladies and twenty-nine gentlemen shot.

LADIES	60 Yards		50 Yards		TOTALS	
	Hits	Score	Hits	Score	Hits	Score
Mrs. Horniblow . . .	89	399	46	260	135	659
Miss M. A. Hollins . .	80	412	44	206	124	618
Miss Legh . . .	81	375	43	219	124	594
Mrs. Piers F. Legh . .	81	331	45	249	126	580
Mrs. W. Betham . . .	71	311	41	213	112	524

GENTLEMEN	100 Yards		80 Yards		60 Yards		TOTALS	
	Hits	Score	Hits	Score	Hits	Score	Hits	Score
Major C. H. Fisher .	83	359	73	307	41	183	197	849
Mr. C. H. Everett . .	82	298	68	310	44	202	194	810
Mr. Betham . . .	70	278	61	277	29	161	160	716
Mr. *G.* L. Aston .	55	199	65	231	44	214	164	644
Mr. W. Yates Foot .	37	163	61	223	43	223	141	609

On June 28, in the handicap match, Miss Hollins scored 387, and Mr. C. H. Everett 460.

The Twentieth Grand Annual Crystal Palace Archery Meeting was held on July 10 and 11, 1878.

LADIES	60 Yards		50 Yards		TOTALS	
	Hits	Score	Hits	Score	Hits	Score
Mrs. Marshall . . .						
Mrs. Horniblow . . .						
Mrs. D. Ainsworth . .						
Mrs. Piers F. Legh . .						
Miss M. Protheroe . .						
Miss Ellis						
Mrs. Berens . . .						
Miss Benwell . . .						

GENTLEMEN	100 Yards		80 Yards		60 Yards		TOTALS	
	Hits	Score	Hits	Score	Hits	Score	Hits	Score
Mr. H. H. Palairet .								
Mr. W. Rimington . .								
Major C. H. Fisher .								
Mr. Walrond . . .								
Mr. G. W. Chapman .								
Mr. Betham . . .								
Mr. *O.* K. Prescot . .								
Mr. C. H. Everett . .								

Thirty-seven ladies and thirty-four gentlemen shot.

The Thirty-fifth Grand National Archery Society's Meeting was held on July 24 and 25, 1878, at Tunbridge Wells, on the Cricket-ground.

LADIES	60 Yards		50 Yards		TOTALS	
	Hits	Score	Hits	Score	Hits	Score
Mrs. Marshall . . .	87	425	45	267	132	692
Mrs. Horniblow . . .	86	406	46	226	132	632
Mrs. Piers F. Legh . .	85	367	44	246	129	613
Miss Legh	79	369	42	186	121	555
Miss M. A. Hollins . .	78	344	42	190	120	534
Mrs. D. Ainsworth . .	79	319	42	196	121	515
Mrs. E. Lister . . .	71	297	39	199	110	496

Mrs. Marshall won the silver bracer with 6 points ; Mrs. Horniblow having won the point for hits at 50 yards, and tied with Mrs. Marshall for gross hits.

GENTLEMEN	100 Yards		80 Yards		60 Yards		TOTALS	
	Hits	Score	Hits	Score	Hits	Score	Hits	Score
Mr. H. H. Palairet . .								
Mr. O. Leigh Clare .								
Mr. W. Rimington . .								
Mr. C. H. Everett . .								
Major C. H. Fisher .								
Mr. Betham . . .								
Mr. Eyre W. Hussey .								
Mr. Walrond . . .								
Mr. A. Henty . . .								
Mr. G. E. S. Fryer .								
Mr. G. W. Chapman .								

Mr. Palairet became Champion, having won 7 points. Mr. Clare won the point for hits at 80 yards, and Mr. Rimington won the points for hits and score at 60 yards.

In the handicap match on the next day—July 26—Mrs. Piers F. Legh scored 360, and Mr. Rimington 401.

Sixty-two ladies and fifty-six gentlemen shot at thi meeting.

The Sixteenth Grand Western Archery Society's Meeting was held at Weymouth, on August 7 and 8, 1878, on the ground of the Weymouth Archery Society.

LADIES	60 Yards		50 Yards		TOTALS	
	Hits	Score	Hits	Score	Hits	Score
Mrs. Horniblow . . .	74	348	44	244	118	592
Mrs. C. E. Nesham . .	68	336	41	215	109	551
Mrs. Piers F. Legh . .	79	315	43	227	122	542

GENTLEMEN	100 Yards		80 Yards		60 Yards		TOTALS	
	Hits	Score	Hits	Score	Hits	Score	Hits	Score
Mr. Walrond . . .	56	228	73	327	46	260	175	815
Mr. H. H. Palairet. .	70	278	76	328	42	180	188	786
Mr. A. Meyrick . .	45	165	63	261	44	216	152	642
Mr. Piers F. Legh . .	55	219	58	242	39	175	152	636
Mr. E. N. Snow . .	54	200	57	223	38	210	149	633
Mr. C. H. Everett . .	68	254	53	193	39	175	160	622

On August 9, in the handicap match, Mrs. Piers F. Legh made 315 and Mrs. Horniblow 314.

The Twenty-fifth Grand Leamington and Midland Archery Meeting was held in the Jephson Gardens on June 25 and 26, 1879.

Thirty ladies and twenty-five gentlemen shot.

LADIES	60 Yards		50 Yards		TOTALS	
	Hits	Score	Hits	Score	Hits	Score
Mrs. Piers F. Legh . .	89	455	48	288	137	743
Miss M. A. Hollins . .	84	408	43	207	127	615
Mrs. E. Lister . . .	74	356	44	208	118	564
Mrs. Hulse	77	327	40	208	117	535
Miss E. D. Pryce . . .	60	282	42	222	102	504
Mrs. Butt [1]	45	245	23	119	68	364

[1] Mrs. Butt shot only on the first day of the meeting one-half the National Round.

GENTLEMEN	100 Yards		80 Yards		60 Yards		TOTALS	
	Hits	Score	Hits	Score	Hits	Score	Hits	Score
Mr. C. E. Nesham . . .	68	268	63	269	34	156	165	693
Mr. Piers F. Legh . . .	66	258	62	240	42	190	170	688
Mr. H. Sagar . . .	61	251	55	241	36	152	152	644
Mr. E. N. Snow . .	56	218	53	207	42	206	151	631
Mr. Betham . . .	60	210	48	222	39	197	147	629

Miss Hollins, on June 27, in the handicap match, scored 353.

The Twenty-first Grand Annual Crystal Palace Archery Meeting was held on July 10 and 11, 1879.

LADIES	60 Yards		50 Yards		TOTALS	
	Hits	Score	Hits	Score	Hits	Score
Mrs. Marshall . . .						
Mrs. Piers F. Legh . .						
Mrs. C. H. Everett . .						
Mrs. Butt						
Miss H. Hutchinson . .						
Mrs. C. E. Nesham . .						
Mrs. Hulse						
Miss E. D. Pryce . . .						
Miss C. Radford . . .						
Miss F. Shuter . . .						

GENTLEMEN	100 Yards		80 Yards		60 Yards		TOTALS	
	Hits	Score	Hits	Score	Hits	Score	Hits	Score
Mr. W. Rimington . .								
Mr. C. E. Nesham . .								
Mr. E. N. Snow . .								
Mr. H. Sagar . . .								
Mr. Walrond . . .								
Mr. A. T. D. Berrington .								
Mr. C. H. Everett . .								
Mr. H. Elliott . .								
Mr. Eyre W. Hussey .								

Forty-eight ladies and thirty gentlemen shot.

The Thirty-sixth Grand National Archery Society's Meeting was held on August 6 and 7, 1879, at Cheltenham, on the College Cricket-ground.

LADIES	60 Yards		50 Yards		TOTALS	
	Hits	Score	Hits	Score	Hits	Score
Mrs. Marshall . . .						
Mrs. Piers F. Legh . .						
Mrs. Butt . . .						
Mrs. E. Lister . . .						
Miss M. A. Hollins . .						
Mrs. Hulse						
Mrs. C. E. Nesham . .						
Mrs. Hornby . . .						
Miss E. Matthews. . .						
Miss I. Carter . . .						
Miss H. Hutchinson . .						
Lady Harberton . . .						

On this occasion Mrs. Marshall won the silver bracer with the highest score, as she and Mrs. Butt each had 3 points— the former for gross score and for score at 60 yards, and the latter for gross hits and for hits at 60 yards. Mrs. Legh won the points for hits and score at 50 yards.

GENTLEMEN	100 Yards		80 Yards		60 Yards		TOTALS	
	Hits	Score	Hits	Score	Hits	Score	Hits	Score
Mr. W. Rimington . .	58	244	64	304	43	251	165	799
Mr. R. Walters . .	70	256	70	254	47	219	187	729
Mr. P. S. Nevile . .	65	249	61	261	43	183	169	693
Mr. Walrond . . .	53	201	73	265	44	212	170	678
Mr. A. T. D. Berrington.	59	223	56	236	43	203	158	662
Mr. Betham . . .	66	256	47	187	41	201	154	644
Mr. C. H. Everett . .	54	230	58	212	35	159	147	601

Mr. Walters became Champion with $4\frac{1}{2}$ points—gross hits, hits at 100 yards and at 60 yards, and a tie with Mr. Betham for score at 100 yards. Mr. Rimington won 3 points, for gross score and for score at 80 yards; and Mr. Walrond won the point for hits at 80 yards.

Eighty-three ladies and sixty-one gentlemen shot.

Mrs. Butt scored 381, and Mrs. Piers F. Legh 370; Mr. Walters 458, Mr. Berrington 430, and Mr. Rimington 414, in the handicap match on August 8.

The Sixteenth Grand Western Archery Meeting was held at Teignmouth, in Mr. Parson's grounds, on August 13 and 14, 1879.

LADIES	60 Yards		50 Yards		TOTALS	
	Hits	Score	Hits	Score	Hits	Score
Mrs. Butt	89	445	47	299	136	744
Mrs. Piers F. Legh . .	89	469	45	231	134	700
Miss Isabel Carter . .	84	402	44	234	128	636
Miss K. Lowe . . .	77	343	42	220	119	563

GENTLEMEN	100 Yards		80 Yards		60 Yards		TOTALS	
	Hits	Score	Hits	Score	Hits	Score	Hits	Score
Mr. W. Rimington . .	79	327	76	372	45	221	200	920
Mr. Walrond . . .	48	166	72	308	45	235	165	709
Mr. Piers F. Legh . .	53	225	59	251	39	207	151	683
Mr. C. H. Everett . .	71	273	63	249	36	152	170	674
Mr. E. N. Snow .	52	202	59	221	40	210	151	633
Mr. W. Yates Foot .	57	205	61	275	33	151	151	631
Mr. H. Kendall .	58	216	59	247	40	166	157	629

Forty-six ladies and twenty-seven gentlemen shot.

The Twenty-sixth Grand Leamington and Midland Archery Meeting was held in the Jephson Gardens on June 23 and 24, 1880.

Thirty-seven ladies and thirty-three gentlemen shot.

LADIES	60 Yards		50 Yards		TOTALS	
	Hits	Score	Hits	Score	Hits	Score
Mrs. Butt	80	378	46	282	126	660
Mrs. E. Lister . . .	84	404	45	249	129	653
Mrs. Piers F. Legh . .	86	388	47	243	133	631
Miss Legh	78	360	42	246	130	606
Miss M. A. Hollins . .	73	355	39	175	112	530
Miss M. Allen . . .	72	338	40	174	112	512

GENTLEMEN	100 Yards		80 Yards		60 Yards		TOTALS	
	Hits	Score	Hits	Score	Hits	Score	Hits	Score
Mr. W. Rimington . .								
Mr. R. Walters . .								
Mr. J. H. Bridges . .								
Mr. Piers F. Legh . .	64	25						
Mr. G. L. Aston . .	51	19						
Mr. C. E. Nesham . .	74	29						
Mr. G. O. Pardoe . .	46	18						
Mr. Eyre W. Hussey .	62	23						

In the handicap match on June 25 Mrs. Piers F. Legh,. Mrs. E. Lister, and Mrs. Butt scored 367, 364, and 337 respectively, and Mr. C. E. Nesham and Mr. J. H. Bridges 421 and 409.

The Twenty-second Grand Annual Crystal Palace Archery Meeting was held on July 1 and 2, 1880.

GENTLEMEN	100 Yards		80 Yards	60 Yards		TOTALS	
	Hits	Score	Hits	Score	Hits	Score	Hits	Score
Mr. W. Rimington . .								
Mr. C. E. Nesham . .								
Mr. C. H. Everett . .								
Mr. R. Walters . .								
Mr. H. Kendall . .								
Mr. G. O. Pardoe . .								
Mr. Eyre W. Hussey .								
Mr. G. G. Phillips . .								
Mr. P. S. Nevile . .								

LADIES	60 Yards		50 Yards		TOTALS	
	Hits	Score	Hits	Score	Hits	Score
Mrs. Piers F. Legh . .						643
Mrs. Marshall . . .						639
Mrs. Horniblow . . .						639
Mrs. Butt						622
Mrs. Kinahan . . .						606
Miss F. Shuter . . .						597
Miss M. Norton . . .						574
Miss Ellis						567
Miss C. Radford . . .						519
Miss I. Carter . . .						519
Mrs. C. E. Nesham . .	71					502

Fifty-four ladies and twenty-six gentlemen shot.

The Thirty-seventh Grand National Archery Society's Meeting was held on July 28 and 29, 1880, at Shrewsbury.

LADIES	60 Yards		50 Yards		TOTALS	
	Hits	Score	Hits	Score	Hits	Score
Mrs. Piers F. Legh . .						
Mrs. Horniblow . . .						
Mrs. Butt						
Mrs. Marshall . . .						
Mrs. C. H. Everett . .						
Mrs. D. Ainsworth . .						
Miss Legh						
Mrs. Eyre W. Hussey . .						

Mrs. Horniblow, with the second score, won the silver bracer with 4 points—namely, 2 for most hits and 2 for score and hits at 60 yards. Mrs. Legh had 3 points, 2 for highest gross score and 1 for score at 60 yards. Mrs. Butt had 1 point for hits at 50 yards. A very close contest between the three first ladies.

Mr. Palairet became Champion with 9 points.

Mr. Rimington won the point for score at 60 yards.

GENTLEMEN	100 Yards		80 Yards		60 Yards		TOTALS	
	Hits	Score	Hits	Score	Hits	Score	Hits	Score
Mr. H. H. Palairet .	68	272	81	401	46	224	195	897
Mr. C. H. Everett . .	62	248	71	287	43	227	176	762
Mr. W. Rimington. .	57	201	54	192	43	239	154	632
Captain M. Allen . .	43	179	58	226	45	227	146	632
Mr. C. E. Nesham . .	48	164	50	204	40	208	138	576
Mr. G. G. Phillips . .	54	194	52	204	41	177	147	575

Sixty-nine ladies and fifty-seven gentlemen shot at this meeting. The weather and the ground were anything but good.

In the handicap match on the next day—July 30—Mrs. Butt's score was—

60 Yards		50 Yards		TOTALS	
Hits	Score	Hits	Score	Hits	Score
47	289	24	132	– 71	421

Mr. Everett's score was 471.

This meeting was made memorable by the retirement of the Rev. O. Luard from the office of Hon. Secretary of the Grand National Archery Society, after having acted as Secretary at thirty-six meetings—in fact, at every meeting hitherto, except the first in 1844. He was presented with a complimentary scroll, setting out the universal appreciation of his services, and with a purse containing 200 guineas. Mr. Palairet was elected to succeed Mr. Luard as Hon. Secretary.

The Seventeenth Grand Western Archery Meeting was held at Sherborne on August 11 and 12, 1880.

LADIES	60 Yards		50 Yards		TOTALS	
	Hits	Score	Hits	Score	Hits	Score
Miss Ripley	79	389	43	245	122	634
Mrs. D. Ainsworth . .	77	337	43	223	120	560
Miss I. Carter . . .	75	325	42	232	117	557
Miss E. M. Farrington. .	80	362	35	179	115	541

GENTLEMEN	100 Yards		80 Yards		60 Yards		TOTALS	
	Hits	Score	Hits	Score	Hits	Score	Hits	Score
Mr. H. H. Palairet .	77	319	79	403	47	221	203	943
Mr. Walrond . . .	69	307	61	265	42	196	172	768
Mr. C. H. Everett . .	82	322	60	240	41	199	183	761
Mr. O. K. Prescot . .	61	243	63	249	34	152	158	644
Mr. H. P. Okeden . .	41	185	56	242	39	191	136	618

Miss I. Carter and Mr. Palairet became Championess and Champion of the West.

Fifty-four ladies and thirty-two gentlemen shot.

The First Grand Northern Archery Meeting was held at York on September 1 and 2, 1880.

LADIES	60 Yards		50 Yards		TOTALS	
	Hits	Score	Hits	Score	Hits	Score
Mrs. Piers F. Legh . .			45			
Mrs. C. E. Nesham . .			44			
Mrs. H. Clarke . . .			48			
Mrs. Eyre W. Hussey . .			44			
Mrs. W. Yates Foot . .			41			
Mrs. D. Ainsworth . .			48			
Mrs. W. C. Booth . . .			40			
Mrs. Kinahan . . .			35			
Miss M. A. Hollins . .			39			

GENTLEMEN	100 Yards		80 Yards		60 Yards		TOTALS	
	Hits	Score	Hits	Score	Hits	Score	Hits	Score
Mr. W. Rimington . .								
Mr. C. E. Nesham . .								
Mr. J. H. Bridges . .								
Mr. P. S. Nevile . .								
Mr. G. L. Aston . .								
Mr. G. G. Hulme . .								
Mr. G. G. Phillips . .								
Mr. Eyre W. Hussey .								
Mr. G. O. Pardoe . .								

Mrs. H. Clarke and Mr. P. S. Nevile became Championess and Champion of the North.

Fifty-seven ladies and thirty-seven gentlemen shot.

The Twenty-seventh Grand Leamington and Midland Archery Meeting was held on June 22 and 23, 1881.

LADIES	60 Yards		50 Yards		TOTALS	
	Hits	Score	Hits	Score	Hits	Score
Mrs. Piers F. Legh . .	87	471	48	252	135	723
Miss Legh	90	436	46	260	136	696
Mrs. Butt	87	441	45	225	132	666
Miss M. A. Hollins . .	81	367	46	240	127	607
Mrs. Hulse	71	313	40	216	111	529
Mrs. W. Yates Foot . .	68	324	36	184	104	508
Miss H. Hutchinson . .	57	297	38	206	95	503 .

GENTLEMEN	100 Yards		80 Yards		60 Yards		TOTALS	
	Hits	Score	Hits	Score	Hits	Score	Hits	Score
Mr. C. H. Everett . .								
Mr. P. F. Legh . .								
Mr. C. E. Nesham . .								
Mr. E. N. Snow . .								
Mr. G. O. Pardoe . .								
Mr. O. K. Prescot . .								
Mr. H. Sagar . . .								
Mr. W. Ford . . .								

Thirty-four ladies and thirty-four gentlemen shot.

Mr. Everett scored 444 in the handicap match on the next day.

The Twenty-third Grand Annual Crystal Palace Archery Meeting was held on July 7 and 8, 1881.

Thirty-nine ladies and twenty-four gentlemen shot.

LADIES	60 Yards		50 Yards		TOTALS	
	Hits	Score	Hits	Score	Hits	Score
Miss Legh	8					
Mrs. Piers F. Legh . .	8					
Mrs. Butt	8					
Mrs. Eyre W. Hussey . .	7					
Mrs. Marshall . . .						
Miss F. Shuter . . .						
Miss H. Hutchinson .						
Mrs. Horniblow . .	7					
Mrs. Kane	73					
Mrs. P. Pinckney . . .	70					
Mrs. Hulse	75					
Miss Friend	72					
Mrs. W. Yates Foot . .						
Miss E. *O.* Parr . . .						
Mrs. C. E. Nesham . .						

GENTLEMEN	100 Yards		80 Yards		60 Yards		TOTALS	
	Hits	Score	Hits	Score	Hits	Score	Hits	Score
Mr. C. E. Nesham . .								
Mr. J. H. Bridges . .								
Mr. W. Rimington . .								
Mr. P. F. Legh .								
Mr. E. N. Snow .								
Mr. C. H. Everett . .								
Mr. G. *O.* Pardoe . .								
Mr. Eyre W. Hussey .								
Mr. *O.* K. Prescot . .								

The Nineteenth Grand Western Archery Meeting was held at Bath on August 3 and 4, 1881, when seventy-four ladies and forty-five gentlemen shot.

Miss Legh's score of 840 is an achievement never yet approached at a public meeting of two days' duration, and every one of her 144 arrows were in the target. Her scores were—

60 Yards		50 Yards		TOTALS	
Hits	Score	Hits	Score	Hits	Score
48	252	24	156	72	408 the first day,
48	282	24	150	72	432 the second day.

LADIES	60 Yards		50 Yards		TOTALS	
	Hits	Score	Hits	Score	Hits	Score
Miss Legh	96	534	48	306	144	840
Miss I. Carter . . .	84	444	45	245	129	689
Mrs. Butt	84	402	48	264	132	666
Mrs. Eyre W. Hussey . .	76	356	46	256	122	612
Mrs. E. Lister . . .	75	351	47	257	122	608
Mrs. Kane	73	329	43	233	116	562
Miss H. Hutchinson . .	72	314	42	204	114	518

GENTLEMEN	100 Yards		80 Yards		60 Yards		TOTALS	
	Hits	Score	Hits	Score	Hits	Score	Hits	Score
Mr. H. H. Palairet. .								
Mr. C. H. Everett . .								
Major C. H. Fisher .								
Mr. W. Rimington . .								
Captain M. Allen . .								
Mr. E. N. Snow . .								
Mr. H. Kendall . .								
Mr. C. E. Nesham . .								
Mr. G. O. Pardoe . .								
Mr. Perry-Keene . .								
Mr. A. Meyrick . .								

Miss I. Carter and Mr. Palairet became Championess and Champion of the West.

Mr. C. H. Everett scored 477 in the handicap match on the next day, August 5.

The Thirty-eighth Grand National Archery Society's Meeting was held on July 20 and 21, 1881, at Four Oaks Park, Sutton Coldfield, near Birmingham.

Miss Legh won the silver bracer with all the points ; and her score of 763 has only once been beaten by Mrs. Horniblow, in 1873, who made 764, only 1 more.

LADIES	60 Yards		50 Yards		TOTALS	
	Hits	Score	Hits	Score	Hits	Score
Miss Legh	92					
Mrs. Marshall . . .						
Mrs. Butt						
Mrs. Eyre W. Hussey . .						
Mrs. Horniblow . . .						
Mrs. Piers F. Legh . .	70					
Mrs. E. Lister . . .	74					
Mrs. W. Y. Foot . . .	65					
Miss M. A. Hollins . .	72					
Miss Steel	66					

GENTLEMEN	100 Yards		80 Yards		60 Yards		TOTALS	
	Hits	Score	Hits	Score	Hits	Score	Hits	Score
Mr. H. H. Palairet . .								
Mr. J. H. Bridges . .								
Mr. C. H. Everett . .								
Mr. C. E. Nesham . .								
Mr. Piers F. Legh . .								
Mr. W. Rimington . .								
Captain M. Allen . .								
Mr. G. L. Aston . .								
Mr. E. N. Snow . .								
Mr. C. F. Garratt . .								

Mr. Palairet won the Championship with 6 points. Mr. Nesham won the points for hits and score at 100 yards; and Captain Allen the points for hits and score at 60 yards.

Fifty-seven ladies and fifty-six gentlemen shot at this meeting.

In the handicap match on July 22 Mr. Palairet scored 434.

The Second Grand Northern Archery Meeting was held in Croxteth Park, near Liverpool, on August 24, 25, and 26, 1881.

R

LADIES	60 Yards		50 Yards		TOTALS	
	Hits	Score	Hits	Score	Hits	Score
Mrs. Piers F. Legh . .	81	419	42	230	123	649
Mrs. Butt	79	351	43	209	122	560
Mrs. D. Ainsworth . .	68	316	42	204	110	520
Mrs. Eyre W. Hussey . .	71	325	37	183	108	508
Miss Steel	65	303	39	201	104	504

—	100 Yards		80 Yards		60 Yards		TOTALS	
	Hits	Score	Hits	Score	Hits	Score	Hits	Score
Mr. H. H. Palairet . .	59	221	71	329	43	211	173	761

Mrs. D. Ainsworth and Mr. G. Greenwell became Championess and Champion of the North.

The next score was Mr. G. O. Pardoe's of 536. The weather at this meeting was most unfavourable, with storms of wind and almost constant rain.

In 1882 there was no Leamington Archery Meeting, as the Grand National Archery Meeting was held there.

The Twenty-fourth Grand Annual Crystal Palace Archery Meeting was held on June 29 and 30, 1882.

GENTLEMEN	100 Yards		80 Yards		60 Yards		TOTALS	
	Hits	Score	Hits	Score	Hits	Score	Hits	Score
Mr. H. H. Palairet . .								
Mr. W. Rimington . .								
Mr. C. E. Nesham . .								
Mr. R. Walters . .								
Mr. G. O. Pardoe . .								
Mr. C. H. Everett . .								
Mr. Eyre W. Hussey .								
Mr. H. Kendall . .								
Major C. H. Fisher .								
Mr. J. Hayllar . .								

LADIES	60 Yards		50 Yards		TOTALS	
	Hits	Score	Hits	Score	Hits	Score
Miss Legh	8					
Miss I. Carter . . .	8					
Mrs. Piers F. Legh . .						
Miss F. Shuter . . .						
Mrs. Butt						
Mrs. Kinahan . . .						
Mrs. Marshall . . .						
Mrs. Graily Hewitt . .						
Mrs. C. E. Nesham . .						
Miss H. Hutchinson . .						
Miss F. Bardswell . .						
Mrs. C. H. Everett . .						
Mrs. A. Waithman . .						
Mrs. W. Y. Foot . . .						
Miss C. Radford . . .						
Miss Croker						
Mrs. Alex. Smith . . .						
Miss E. O. Parr . . .						
Mrs. Keyworth . . .						

Colonel Lewin acted as Hon. Secretary.

Forty-three ladies and twenty-seven gentlemen shot.

A Public Archery Meeting was held on the Cricket-ground of the Alexandra Park Company on July 6 and 7, 1882.

LADIES	60 Yards		50 Yards		TOTALS	
	Hits	Score	Hits	Score	Hits	Score
Mrs. Butt	80	378	47	265	127	643
Miss Legh	69	329	45	273	114	602
Miss Steel	60	288	44	238	104	526

Nothing could well be worse than the weather during this meeting. The highest gentlemen's scores were Mr. H. Kendall, 151 hits, 625 score, and Mr. C. E. Nesham, 153 hits, 623 score.

Twenty-nine ladies and twenty gentlemen shot.

Better scores were made on the next day in the handicap

match—Miss Legh, 357 ; Mrs. Butt, 350 ; Mrs. P. F. Legh
315 ; and Mrs. Keyworth, 303.

Mr. T. Aldred had the management of this meeting.

The Thirty-ninth Grand National Archery Society's Meeting
was held on July 26 and 27, 1882, in the Shrubland Hall
Grounds (Mrs. Wise's), near Leamington.

LADIES	60 Yards		50 Yards		TOTALS	
	Hits	Score	Hits	Score	Hits	Score
Mrs. Piers F. Legh						
Mrs. Marshall						
Mrs. Horniblow						
Mrs. Butt						
Miss F. Bardswell						
Mrs. W. Y. Foot						
Miss Legh						
Miss F. Shuter						
Miss Steel						
Miss I. Carter						
Miss M. A. Hollins						
Mrs. Kinahan						
Miss Clayton						
Mrs. E. Lister						
Mrs. Hulse						
Mrs. G. Hewitt						

GENTLEMEN	100 Yards		80 Yards		60 Yards		TOTALS	
	Hits	Score	Hits	Score	Hits	Score	Hits	Score
Mr. H. H. Palairet								885
Mr. R. Walters								884
Mr. W. Rimington								794
Mr. W. Ford								770
Mr. O. K. Prescot								764
Mr. C. E. Nesham								725
Mr. C. H. Everett								717
Mr. C. J. Longman								716
Mr. J. H. Bridges								705
Mr. G. O. Pardoe								697
Mr. H. Sagar								629
Captain M. Allen								624
Mr. Piers F. Legh								620
Mr. H. Kendall								611

Mrs. Piers F. Legh won the silver bracer with all the points, except that Mrs. Marshall also made all the hits at 50 yards.

Mr. Palairet won the Championship with 6 points, after a very close contest with Mr. Walters, who won 2 points for score at 80 and at 60 yards, and was only 1 behind in gross score. Mr. Nesham won the point for hits at 100 yards, and Mr. Prescot that for hits at 60 yards.

Sixty-three ladies and fifty-five gentlemen shot at this meeting.

On July 28, in the handicap match, Mr. Pardoe scored 411 and Mr. Walters 410.

The Twentieth Grand Western Archery Meeting was held at Exeter, on the Grammar School Cricket-ground, on August 2 and 3, 1882, when sixty-four ladies and thirty-nine gentlemen shot.

LADIES	60 Yards		50 Yards		TOTALS	
	Hits	Score	Hits	Score	Hits	Score
Miss I. Carter . . .	74	332	42	226	116	558
Mrs. Butt . . .	67	275	46	260	113	535
Mrs. Kinahan . . .	77	353	38	166	115	519
Mrs. Eyre W. Hussey . .	77	343	31	161	108	504
Miss F. Bardswell . .	65	305	41	187	106	492

GENTLEMEN	100 Yards		80 Yards		60 Yards		TOTALS	
	Hits	Score	Hits	Score	Hits	Score	Hits	Score
Mr. H. H. Palairet. .	70	272	73	367	42	184	185	823
Mr. W. Rimington . .	75	291	65	283	41	237	181	811
Mr. O. K. Prescot . .	58	216	64	278	44	208	166	702
Mr. R. Walters . .	60	198	69	301	37	189	166	688
Mr. Perry-Keene . .	63	233	66	300	35	137	164	670
Mr. A. Meyrick . .	59	191	61	239	38	186	158	616
Mr. E. W. Hussey . .	51	179	58	232	43	201	152	612

In the handicap match on the next day Mr. O. K. Prescot scored 480, and Mr. R. Walters 431.

The Third Grand Northern Archery Meeting was held at Harrogate, on the Cricket-ground, on August 23 and 24, 1882.

LADIES	60 Yards		50 Yards		TOTALS	
	Hits	Score	Hits	Score	Hits	Score
Mrs. D. Ainsworth . .	81	365	46	286	127	651
Miss Legh	79	349	41	201	120	550
Mrs. Piers F. Legh . .	73	313	44	228	117	541
Mrs. Kinahan . . .	65	303	40	208	105	511
Mrs. Swire	66	322	37	187	103	509
Mrs. Butt	65	257	46	234	111	491

GENTLEMEN	100 Yards		80 Yards		60 Yards		TOTALS	
	Hits	Score	Hits	Score	Hits	Score	Hits	Score
Mr. C. Perry-Keene .	49	211	57	273	37	183	143	667
Mr. C. H. Everett . .	49	189	62	278	39	165	150	632
Mr. C. E. Nesham . .	44	178	60	278	37	167	141	623
Mr. G. O. Pardoe . .	54	212	59	225	38	158	151	595

Mrs. D. Ainsworth and Mr. Houghton became Championess and Champion of the North.

The Twenty-eighth Grand Leamington and Midland Archery Meeting was held on June 27 and 28, 1883.

Twenty-nine ladies and twenty-two gentlemen shot.

LADIES	60 Yards		50 Yards		TOTALS	
	Hits	Score	Hits	Score	Hits	Score
Mrs. Piers F. Legh . .						
Miss Steel						
Miss F. Bardswell . .						
Mrs. D. Ainsworth . .						
Mrs. E. Lister . . .						
Miss I. Carter . . .						
Miss M. A. Hollins . .						
Mrs. Eyre W. Hussey . .						
Mrs. C. E. Nesham . .						
Mrs. W. Yates Foot . .						
Miss Legh						
Mrs. Keyworth . . .						

GENTLEMEN	100 Yards		80 Yards		60 Yards		TOTALS	
	Hits	Score	Hits	Score	Hits	Score	Hits	Score
Major C. H. Fisher .	75	30						
Mr. C. E. Nesham . .								
Mr. H. Kendall . .								
Mr. T. R. Dunne . .								
Mr. T. T. S. Metcalfe .								
Mr. G. L. Aston . .								
Mr. Eyre W. Hussey .								
Mr. W. Ford . . .								
Hon. A. Hanbury . .								

In the handicap match on June 29 Mrs. Piers F. Legh and Miss Legh scored 374 and 363 respectively, and Mr. C. E. Nesham 398.

The Twenty-fifth Grand Annual Crystal Palace Archery Meeting was held on July 12 and 13, 1883.

LADIES	60 Yards		50 Yards		TOTALS	
	Hits	Score	Hits	Score	Hits	Score
Mrs. Marshall . . .	85					
Miss F. Bardswell . .	83					
Miss Pears	79					
Mrs. D. Ainsworth . .	75					
Miss I. Carter . . .	77					
Miss Steel . . .	71					
Miss H. Hutchinson . .	75					
Mrs. Eyre W. Hussey . .	73					

GENTLEMEN	100 Yards		80 Yards		60 Yards		TOTALS	
	Hits	Score	Hits	Score	Hits	Score	Hits	Score
Major C. H. Fisher .	72	234	81	359	45	235	198	828
Mr. C. E. Nesham . .	64	256	52	232	37	185	153	673
Mr. C. H. Everett . .	54	226	59	257	37	187	150	670
Mr. A. Meyrick . .	45	195	63	297	36	170	144	662
Mr. T. R. Dunne . .	57	225	63	275	38	136	158	636
Mr. W. Rimington . .	42	180	57	243	43	195	142	618

Forty-seven ladies and twenty-nine gentlemen shot.

The Twenty-first Grand Western Archery Meeting was held at Salisbury on July 25 and 26, 1883, when fifty-five ladies and forty-one gentlemen shot.

LADIES	60 Yards		50 Yards		TOTALS	
	Hits	Score	Hits	Score	Hits	Score
Miss Legh	85					
Mrs. Piers F. Legh . .	84					
Miss I. Carter . . .	86					
Miss F. Bardswell . .	79					
Mrs. P. Pinckney . . .	78					
Miss H. Hutchinson . .	80					
Mrs. Eyre W. Hussey . .	83					
Miss C. Radford . . .	79					
Mrs. W. Yates Foot . .	73					

GENTLEMEN	100 Yards		80 Yards		60 Yards		TOTALS	
	Hits	Score	Hits	Score	Hits	Score	Hits	Score
Major C. H. Fisher .	102	406	73	327	43	229	218	962
Mr. H. Kendall . .	76	324	73	309	46	242	195	875
Mr. H. H. Palairet .	66	262	76	322	44	212	186	796
Mr. Eyre W. Hussey .	72	288	69	297	38	192	179	777
Mr. Piers F. Legh .	66	242	59	235	37	199	162	676
Mr. N. Rattray . .	60	218	54	242	39	205	153	665
Mr. Perry Keene .	62	226	59	211	44	212	165	649

Miss I. Carter and Mr. H. H. Palairet became Championess and Champion of the West.

The Fortieth Grand National Archery Society's Meeting was held on August 1 and 2, 1883, at Cheltenham, on the College Cricket-ground.

Sixty-seven ladies and sixty-four gentlemen shot at this meeting.

Mrs. Legh won the silver bracer with 6 points. Miss I. Carter won the point for hits at 50 yards, and Mrs. Ainsworth the point for score at the same distance.

LADIES	60 Yards		50 Yards		TOTALS	
	Hits	Score	Hits	Score	Hits	Score
Mrs. Piers F. Legh						
Miss I. Carter						
Miss Steel						
Mrs. D. Ainsworth						
Mrs. Eyre W. Hussey						
Miss M. A. Hollins						
Miss F. Bardswell						
Miss C. Radford						
Mrs. Horniblow						
Miss Legh						
Miss Pardoe						
Miss H. Hutchinson						
Mrs. E. Lister						
Mrs. Marshall						
Mrs. C. H. Everett						
Mrs. C. E. Nesham						
Mrs. W. Y. Foot						
Miss Hayllar						
Miss Panter						
Miss *Oakley*						
Miss B. *Oakley*						
Mrs. Edgar						

GENTLEMEN	100 Yards		80 Yards		60 Yards		TOTALS	
	Hits	Score	Hits	Score	Hits	Score	Hits	Score
Mr. C. J. Longman								
Mr. Eyre W. Hussey								
Major C. H. Fisher								
Mr. H. H. Palairet								
Captain M. Allen								
Mr. Piers F. Legh								
Mr. C. E. Nesham								
Mr. W. Rimington								
Mr. R. Walters								
Mr. H. Kendall								
Mr. Perry-Keene								
Mr. T. R. Dunne								
Mr. *O*. K. Prescot								
Mr. G. L. Aston								
Mr. Gregson								
Mr. Walrond								
Mr. C. H. Everett								
Mr. A. Meyrick								
Captain C. H. Garnett								

Mr. Longman became Champion with 7 points. Mr. Hussey won the point for hits at 100 yards, Major Fisher the point for score at 100 yards, and Mr. Palairet the point for score at 80 yards. Mr. Longman also won the Spedding Memorial Challenge Cup, now first presented by the Royal Toxophilite Society, to be held by the maker of the highest gross score.

In the handicap match on August 3, Miss Legh scored 416, Major Fisher 508, Mr. Nesham 442, and Mr. Dunne 417.

The Fourth Grand Northern Archery Meeting was held at Derby on August 8, 9, and 10, 1883, when the weather was so unfavourable that the highest lady's score was that of Mrs. Piers F. Legh—490, with 108 hits.

The only notable scores made by gentlemen were—

GENTLEMEN	100 Yards		80 Yards		60 Yards		TOTALS	
	Hits	Score	Hits	Score	Hits	Score	Hits	Score
Mr. F. A. Govett . .	54	220	49	211	39	191	142	622
Captain M. Allen . .	58	238	47	189	41	189	146	616

Mrs. T. Hibbert and Mr. Gregson became Championess and Champion of the North.

The Twenty-ninth Grand Leamington and Midland Archery Meeting was held on June 12 and 13, 1884.

LADIES	60 Yards		50 Yards		TOTALS	
	Hits	Score	Hits	Score	Hits	Score
Mrs. Marshall . . .			48			
Miss M. A. Hollins . .			43			
Mrs. Eyre W. Hussey . .			44			
Miss F. Bardswell . .			44			
Mrs. Horniblow . . .			44			
Mrs. Kinahan . . .			44			
Mrs. W. Yates Foot . .			45			
Miss Steel			44			

GENTLEMEN	100 Yards		80 Yards		60 Yards		TOTALS	
	Hits	Score	Hits	Score	Hits	Score	Hits	Score
Mr. C. E. Nesham . .	1	32						
Mr. C. H. Everett . .								
Mr. J. H. Bridges . .								
Mr. H. J. B. Kendall .								
Mr. Eyre W. Hussey .								
Mr. Gregson . . .								
Mr. C. J. Longman .								
Mr. T. R. Dunne . .								
Mr. G. L. Aston . .								
Mr. F. A. Govett . .								

In the handicap match on June 14 Mr. C. J. Longman scored 401.

Twenty-nine ladies and twenty-seven gentlemen shot at this meeting.

The Twenty-sixth Grand Annual Crystal Palace Archery Meeting was held on July 12 and 13, 1884.

LADIES	60 Yards		50 Yards		TOTALS	
	Hits	Score	Hits	Score	Hits	Score
Mrs. Marshall . . .	83	475	47	269	130	744
Mrs. Piers F. Legh .	79	361	45	259	124	620
Mrs. Eyre W. Hussey .	77	329	41	215	118	544
Miss H. Hutchinson .	71	329	42	194	113	523
Miss Ellis	66	298	44	212	110	510

GENTLEMEN	100 Yards		80 Yards		60 Yards		TOTALS	
	Hits	Score	Hits	Score	Hits	Score	Hits	Score
Major C. H. Fisher .	90						210	
Mr. C. E. Nesham . .	92				4		199	
Mr. C. J. Longman .	69				4		189	
Mr. H. Kendall . .	65				4		173	
Mr. Eyre W. Hussey .	66						178	
Mr. C. H. Everett . .	54						152	
Mr. J. H. Bridges . .	61						164	
Mr. Gregson . . .	78						152	
Mr. T. T. S. Metcalfe .	54						153	

Thirty-eight ladies and twenty-two gentlemen shot at this meeting.

The Twenty-second Grand Western Archery Meeting was held at Taunton on July 23 and 24, 1884.

LADIES	60 Yards		50 Yards		TOTALS	
	Hits	Score	Hits	Score	Hits	Score
Mrs. Eyre W. Hussey . .	72	374	44	246	116	620
Miss I. Carter . . .	67	279	37	197	104	476
Miss F. Bardswell . .	72	282	38	182	110	464
Miss M. Winwood . .	70	298	37	159	107	457

GENTLEMEN	100 Yards		80 Yards		60 Yards		TOTALS	
	Hits	Score	Hits	Score	Hits	Score	Hits	Score
Major C. H. Fisher .								
Mr. C. E. Nesham . .								
Mr. C. J. Longman .								
Mr. F. A. Govett . .								
Mr. Eyre W. Hussey .								
Mr. H. Kendall . .								
Mr. T. T. S. Metcalfe .								
Mr. Gregson . . .								

Mr. and Mrs. Eyre W. Hussey became Champion and Championess of the West.

Fifty ladies and thirty-eight gentlemen shot at this meeting.

In the handicap match on July 25, the only good score was made by Mr. C. E. Nesham, 362.

The Forty-first Grand National Archery Society's Meeting was held on August 6 and 7, 1884, on the Cricket-ground of St. Mark's School (Rev. Stephen Hawtray) at Windsor.

LADIES	60 Yards		50 Yards		TOTALS	
	Hits	Score	Hits	Score	Hits	Score
Mrs. Piers F. Legh . .	88					
Miss Oakley	84					
Miss Legh	80					
Mrs. Marshall . . .						
Miss B. Oakley . . .						
Miss Hayllar . . .						
Mrs. C. E. Nesham . .						
Miss H. Hutchinson . .						
Miss Pears						
Mrs. Horniblow . . .	79					
Miss M. Winwood . .	69					
Miss C. Radford . . .	76					
Miss I. Carter . . .	72					

Mrs. Piers F. Legh won the Challenge bracer with $6\frac{1}{3}$ points. Miss Oakley won 1 point for score at 60 yards; and she and Miss B. Oakley divided the point for hits at 50 yards with Mrs. P. F. Legh.

GENTLEMEN	100 Yards		80 Yards		60 Yards		TOTALS	
	Hits	Score	Hits	Score	Hits	Score	Hits	Score
Major C. H. Fisher .								
Mr. C. E. Nesham . .								
Mr. H. Kendall . .								
Mr. Gregson . . .								
Captain M. Allen . .								
Mr. O. L. Clare [1] .								
Mr. N. Rattray . .								
Mr. J. H. Bridges . .								
Mr. Eyre W. Hussey .								
Mr. F. A. Govett . .								
Mr. G. G. Hulme . .								
Mr. C. J. Longman .								
Mr. T. T. S. Metcalfe .								

Mr. C. E. Nesham won the Champion's medal with 5 points. Major Fisher won the 2 points for gross score and the Spedding Challenge Cup, and 2 more points for score at 80 and at 60 yards. Mr. H. Kendall won the point for hits at 60 yards.

[1] Entered as Mr. Hindley.

In the handicap match on August 8 Mrs. P. F. Legh scored 357, and Miss Legh 354 ; Mr. C. E. Nesham 482, Mr. H. Kendall 411, and Mr. Gregson 406.

Fifty-seven ladies and fifty gentlemen shot at this meeting. The weather was intensely hot.

The Fifth Grand Northern Archery Meeting was held on the West Cliff Cricket-ground at Preston, in Lancashire, on August 27 and 28, 1884.

LADIES	60 Yards		50 Yards		TOTALS	
	Hits	Score	Hit	Score	Hits	Score
Mrs. Piers F. Legh . .	84	432	42	234	126	666
Miss Legh	90	426	45	233	135	659
Mrs. Eyre W. Hussey . .	84	380	47	275	131	655
Mrs. Waithman . . .	70	332	41	223	111	555
Mrs. Swire	66	294	42	230	108	524
Mrs. H. Clarke . . .	64	298	43	217	107	515

GENTLEMEN	100 Yards		80 Yards		60 Yards		TOTALS	
	Hits	Score	Hits	Score	Hits	Score	Hits	Score
Mr. C. E. Nesham . .	81	311	76	382	47	271	204	964
Mr. Gregson . ˙. .	74	320	78	336	42	192	194	848
Mr. Eyre W. Hussey .	74	316	66	280	44	228	184	824
Mr. *O.* L. Clare . .	57	247	63	245	38	176	158	668

Mrs. Waithman and Mr. Gregson became Championess and Champion of the North.

Forty-four ladies and thirty-five gentlemen shot at this meeting.

The Thirtieth Grand Leamington and Midland Archery Meeting was held in the Jephson Gardens on June 10 and 11, 1885, when twenty-nine ladies and thirty-eight gentle-men shot.

LADIES	60 Yards		50 Yards		TOTALS	
	Hits	Score	Hits	Score	Hits	Score
Mrs. Piers F. Legh . .		554				
Miss Steel						
Miss Legh						
Mrs. Eyre W. Hussey . .						
Miss F. Bardswell . .						
Miss B. Oakley . . .						
Mrs. Keyworth . . .						
Mrs. Wade						

GENTLEMEN	100 Yards		80 Yards		60 Yards		TOTALS	
	Hits	Score	Hits	Score	Hits	Score	Hits	Score
Major C. H. Fisher .								
Mr. C. E. Nesham . .								
Mr. Perry-Keene . .								
Mr. R. Walters . .								
Mr. T. T. S. Metcalfe .								
Mr. Gregson . . .								
Mr. Eyre W. Hussey .								
Mr. G. L. Aston . .								
Mr. H. Howman . .								
Mr. Piers F. Legh . .								
Mr. Brodie Hoare . .								
Mr. H. H. Longman .								
Mr. H. Kendall . .								
Mr. G. G. Hulme . .								

Miss Legh scored 352 and Mr. Hussey 390 in the handicap match on June 12.

The Twenty-seventh Grand Annual Crystal Palace Archery Meeting was held on the Cricket-ground on July 9 and 10, 1885, when forty-eight. ladies and twenty-nine gentlemen shot.

Mr. Nesham acted as Hon. Secretary to the meeting.

LADIES	60 Yards		50 Yards		TOTALS	
	Hits	Score	Hits	Score	Hits	Score
Miss Legh						
Mrs. Piers F. Legh . .						
Mrs. Eyre W. Hussey . .						
Miss F. Bardswell . .						
Miss Carlisle . . .						
Miss Pears						
Miss Hayllar . . .						
Mrs. Stilwell. . . .						
Miss Milne						
Mrs. W. Yates Foot . .						
Mrs. Marshall . . .						
Mrs. C. E. Nesham . .						

GENTLEMEN	100 Yards		80 Yards		60 Yards		TOTALS	
	Hits	Score	Hits	Score	Hits	Score	Hits	Score
Mr. C. E. Nesham . .				313				860
Major C. H. Fisher .				351				800
Mr. R. Walters . .				293				738
Mr. C. H. Everett . .				279				732
Mr. Brodie Hoare . .				252				715
Mr. H. Kendall . .				240				700
Mr. Perry-Keene . .				236				697
Mr. T. T. S. Metcalfe .				282				693
Mr. Eyre W. Hussey .				271				678
Mr. Gregson . . .				248				626

The Twenty-third Grand Western Archery Meeting was held at Weymouth on July 22 and 23, 1885, when forty-nine ladies and twenty-eight gentlemen shot.

LADIES	60 Yards		50 Yards		TOTALS	
	Hits	Score	Hits	Score	Hits	Score
Mrs. Eyre W. Hussey . .	80	360	46	250	126	610
Miss F. Bardswell . .	80	354	43	197	123	551
Mrs. P. Pinckney . . .	71	329	43	221	114	550
Mrs. W. Yates Foot . .	83	345	39	201	122	546
Mrs. C. E. Nesham . .	73	317	45	227	118	544
Miss M. Winwood . .	66	282	43	221	109	503

GENTLEMEN	100 Yards		80 Yards		60 Yards		TOTALS	
	Hits	Score	Hits	Score	Hits	Score	Hits	Score
Mr. C. E. Nesham . .	84	324	66	268	46	250	196	842
Mr. R. Walters . .	56	220	66	264	43	209	165	693
Mr. T. T. S. Metcalfe .	56	202	53	193	44	208	153	603
Mr. Eyre W. Hussey .	39	129	66	252	40	196	145	577

Mr. and Mrs. Eyre W. Hussey became Champion and Championess of the West.

Mrs. Hussey and Mr. Nesham scored 367 and 530 respectively in the handicap match on July 24.

The Forty-second Grand National Archery Meeting was held in the College-grounds at Great Malvern on July 29 and 30, 1885, when sixty-four ladies and fifty-one gentlemen shot.

LADIES	60 Yards		50 Yards		TOTALS	
	Hits	Score	Hits	Score	Hits	Score
Mrs. Piers F. Legh . .	88	460	47	289	135	749
Miss Legh	91	417	44	258	135	675
Mrs. Eyre W. Hussey . .	84	386	46	248	130	634
Mrs. Marshall	84	360	42	228	126	588
Miss Steel	77	345	41	197	118	542
Miss B. M. Legh . . .	75	363	42	172	117	535
Miss F. Bardswell . .	72	310	43	217	115	527

GENTLEMEN	100 Yards		80 Yards		60 Yards		TOTALS	
	Hits	Score	Hits	Score	Hits	Score	Hits	Score
Mr. C. E. Nesham . .				316				
Major C. H. Fisher .				310				
Mr. T. T. S. Metcalfe .				310				
Mr. Perry-Keene . .				261				
Mr. R. Walters . .				251				
Mr. H. Kendall . .				270				
Mr. Eyre W. Hussey .				248				
Captain M. Allen . .				252				

S

Mrs. P. F. Legh became the Championess with 6 points, Miss Legh having 1 point for a tie on the gross hits, and 1 point for most hits at 50 yards.

Mr. Nesham won the Champion's medal for most points— 7½—and the Spedding memorial cup with the highest score. Major Fisher won 1 point for hits at 100 yards, and Mr. Perry-Keene won 1½ points, having tied Mr. Nesham with 45 hits at 60 yards, and he won the point for highest score at 60 yards.

Mrs. Eyre W. Hussey and Mrs. P. F. Legh scored 374 and 371 respectively in the handicap match on July 31, and Mr. C. E. Nesham and Mr. Perry-Keene scored 462 and 402 on the same day.

The Sixth Annual Grand Northern Archery Meeting was held at York, on the Gentlemen's Cricket-ground, September 2 and 3, 1885, when forty-eight ladies and thirty-one gentlemen shot.

LADIES	60 Yards		50 Yards		TOTALS	
	Hits	Score	Hits	Score	Hits	Score
Mrs. W. Yates Foot	72	360	44	256	116	616
Mrs. D. Ainsworth	84	392	45	219	129	611
Mrs. Eyre W. Hussey	82	360	44	206	126	566
Miss F. Bardswell	74	294	46	244	120	538
Miss K. Sharpe	70	296	42	233	113	529
Miss M. A. Hollins	61	295	45	225	106	520
Mrs. H. Clarke	70	272	44	234	114	506

GENTLEMEN	100 Yards		80 Yards		60 Yards		TOTALS	
	Hits	Score	Hits	Score	Hits	Score	Hits	Score
Mr. C. E. Nesham	83	343	71	291	46	250	200	884
Mr. Eyre W. Hussey	58	198	73	305	42	248	173	751
Mr. T. T. S. Metcalfe	54	218	64	304	41	225	159	747
Mr. Gregson	42	162	68	276	44	208	154	646
Mr. C. E. Thorpe	56	190	54	276	32	156	142	622

Mrs. D. Ainsworth became the Championess of the North.

Mr. Gregson became the Champion of the North.

In the handicap match on September 4, Mr. Nesham scored 495, Mr. Metcalfe 411, and Mr. Hussey 401.

The Thirty-first Grand Leamington and Midland Archery Meeting was held in the Jephson Gardens on June 9 and 10, 1886, when twenty-three ladies and twenty-eight gentlemen shot.

LADIES	60 Yards		50 Yards		TOTALS	
	Hits	Score	Hits	Score	Hits	Score
Miss Legh	8	409				
Mrs. Kinahan . . .	78	386				
Mrs. Eyre W. Hussey . .	8	354				
Miss F. Bardswell . .		385				
Mrs. Gilmour . . .		369				
Mrs. W. Yates Foot . .		372				
Mrs. D. Ainsworth . .		292				
Mrs. Berens		326				
Mrs. Hibbert . . .		323				
Mrs. Keyworth . . .		318				

GENTLEMEN	100 Yards		80 Yards		60 Yards		TOTALS	
	Hits	Score	Hits	Score	Hits	Score	Hits	Score
Major C. H. Fisher .								
Mr. Perry-Keene . .								
Mr. C. E. Nesham .								
Mr. T. T. S. Metcalfe .								
Mr. Brodie Hoare . .								
Colonel H. A. Burton .								
Mr. R. Walters . .								
Captain Garnett . .								
Mr. C. J. Longman .								
Mr. Gregson . . .								
Mr. G. G. Hulme . .								
Mr. F. N. Garnett . .								

Mr. Perry-Keene scored 474 in the handicap match on June 11.

The Seventh Grand Northern Archery Meeting was held at Lincoln on June 23 and 24, 1886, when twenty-six ladies and nineteen gentlemen shot.

LADIES	60 Yards		50 Yards		TOTALS	
	Hits	Score	Hits	Score	Hits	Score
Mrs. D. Ainsworth . .	82	350	46	248	128	598
Mrs. Eyre W. Hussey . .	75	343	42	242	117	585
Miss F. Bardswell . .	75	375	43	207	118	582
Mrs. Kinahan . . .	78	370	43	207	121	577
Mrs. Waithman . . .	67	301	44	238	111	539

GENTLEMEN	100 Yards		80 Yards		60 Yards		TOTALS	
	Hits	Score	Hits	Score	Hits	Score	Hits	Score
Mr. Perry-Keene . .	88	348	81	377	46	244	215	969
Mr. C. E. Nesham . .	74	286	46	178	44	222	164	686

Mrs. D. Ainsworth and Mr. Gregson (145 hits, 591 score) became Championess and Champion of the North.

Mr. Perry-Keene scored 530 in the handicap match on June 25.

The Twenty-eighth Grand Annual Crystal Palace Archery Meeting was held on the Cricket-ground on July 15 and 16, 1886.

LADIES	60 Yards		50 Yards		TOTALS	
	Hits	Score	Hits	Score	Hits	Score
Mrs. Marshall . . .						
Mrs. D. Ainsworth . .						
Mrs. Kinahan . . .						
Mrs. Haigh						
Miss A. Barton . . .						
Mrs. Keyworth . . .						
Miss Hayllar . . .						
Miss Norton						
Miss F. Bardswell . .						
Miss C. Smith . . .						
Mrs. Kane						
Miss Carlisle . . .						

GENTLEMEN	100 Yards		80 Yards		60 Yards		TOTALS	
	Hits	Score	Hits	Score	Hits	Score	Hits	Score
Mr. Perry-Keene . .	7	3	73					
Mr. Eyre W. Hussey .	5	2	69					
Mr. C. E. Nesham . .	1	2	71					
Mr. T. T. S. Metcalfe .			69					
Mr. J. H. Bridges . .			61					
Colonel H. A. Burton .			65					
Captain M. Allen . .								
Mr. C. H. Everett . .								
Mr. H. Kendall . .								
Mr. Gedge . . .								
Mr. Burrowes . .								
Mr. Erskine . . .								
Mr. Walrond . . .	59	2						
Colonel Lewin . .	58	2						

Fifty-two ladies and thirty-five gentlemen shot.

The Forty-third Grand National and the Twenty-fourth Grand Western Archery Meetings were united and held together at Bath on July 29 and 30, 1886.

LADIES	60 Yards		50 Yards		TOTALS	
	Hits	Score	Hits	Score	Hits	Score
Miss Legh						
Mrs. Eyre W. Hussey . .						
Mrs. Marshall . . .						
Mrs. D. Ainsworth . .						
Miss Steel						
Miss B. Oakley . . .						
Mrs. Gilling						
Mrs. Kinahan . . .						
Miss F. Bardswell . .						
Miss C. Radford . . .						
Miss M. Winwood . .						
Mrs. Horniblow . . .						
Mrs. Berens						
Miss B. M. Legh . . .						
Miss Pedder						
Mrs. Maltby						
Miss Palmer						
Mrs. Gilmour . . .						502

GENTLEMEN	100 Yards		80 Yards		60 Yards		TOTALS	
	Hits	Score	Hits	Score	Hits	Score	Hits	Score
Mr. C. E. Nesham . .	81		76	354				
Major C. H. Fisher .	70		72	344				
Mr. E. Sharpe . .	75		71	303				
Mr. J. H. Bridges . .			68	322				
Colonel H. A. Burton .			60	266				
Mr. Perry-Keene . .			70	290				
Mr. T. T. S. Metcalfe .			66	216				
Mr. F. A. Govett . .			56	232				
Mr. Eyre W. Hussey .			67	259				
Mr. *G. G.* Hulme . .			53	237				
Mr. Gedge . . .			63	263				
Mr. Gregson . . .			73	329				
Mr. Gataker . . .			60	246				
Mr. Piers F. Legh . .			55	253				
Mr. Erskine . . .			57	233				
Mr. R. Walters . .			53	231				
Captain M. Allen . .			60	222				

Ninety-five ladies and sixty-five gentlemen shot.

Miss Legh became the Championess with 7 points, Mrs. Marshall having won the point for hits at 50 yards.

Mrs. Eyre W. Hussey became the Championess of the West.

Mr. C. E. Nesham became the Champion with 9½ points, Major C. H. Fisher having tied with him in the point for hits at 60 yards.

Mr. Perry-Keene became the Champion of the West.

In the handicap match on July 31, Miss Legh scored 391, Miss B. Oakley 363, Mrs. D. Ainsworth 344, Mrs. Marshall 343, and Mrs. Horniblow 337; and on the same day Mr. E. Sharpe scored 429.

ROYAL TOXOPHILITE SOCIETY'S HANDICAP
MEETINGS

A series of meetings extending over two days, the double York Round being shot, commenced in 1881, and the Grand Centenary Archery Meeting of the Royal Toxophilite Society was held in the Society's ground in the Regent's Park, on October 12 and 13, 1881.

GENTLEMEN	100 Yards		80 Yards		60 Yards		TOTALS	
	Hits	Score	Hits	Score	Hits	Score	Hits	Score
Mr. H. H. Palairet .			81					
Mr. W. Rimington . .			75					
Mr. J. H. Bridges . .			75					
Mr. O. K. Prescot [1] .			72					
Mr. Piers F. Legh [1]			69					
Mr. *G. O.* Pardoe [1] . .			77					
Mr. C. H. Everett . .			65					
Major C. H. Fisher .			63					
Mr. H. Kendall . .			64					
Mr. C. J. Longman .			59					
Mr. E. N. Snow . .			52					
Mr. C. E. Nesham . .			55					
Mr. A. Meyrick [1] . .			65					
Colonel Lewin . .			58					
Mr. *O.* L. Clare . .			64					
Mr. A. Newall . .			58					
Mr. Eyre W. Hussey [1] .			57					
Captain M. Allen [1] . .			69					
Mr. Perry-Keene [1] . .			47					

Sixty-five gentlemen shot.

A Grand Annual Handicap Meeting of the Royal Toxophilite Society was held on October 11 and 12, 1882.

[1] Visitors.

| | 100 Yards | | 80 Yards | | 60 Yards | | Totals | |
GENTLEMEN	Hits	Score	Hits	Score	Hits	Score	Hits	Score
Major C. H. Fisher . .							204	890
Mr. C. E. Nesham . .							188	816
Mr. O. L. Clare . .							170	776
Mr. R. Walters . .							188	772
Mr. Piers F. Legh [1] .							174	768
Mr. C. H. Everett . .							181	743
Mr. G. W. Chapman .							150	656
Mr. H. Kendall . .	5						143	639
Mr. G. O. Pardoe [1] . .	4						140	632
Mr. W. Yates Foot .	5						142	626
Mr. C. J. Longman .	5						154	600

Thirty-three gentlemen shot.

The Grand Annual Handicap Meeting of the Royal Toxophilite Society was held on October 11 and 12, 1883.

| | 100 Yards | | 80 Yards | | 60 Yards | | Totals | |
GENTLEMEN	Hits	Score	Hits	Score	Hits	Score	Hits	Score
Mr. C. E. Nesham . .		426	75	337		247		1010
Mr. C. J. Longman .		274	69	305		229		808
Major C. H. Fisher .		313	67	291		185		789
Mr. H. A. Howman [1] .		273	57	259		231		763
Mr. N. Rattray . .		221	71	315		225		761
Mr. F. A. Govett . .		258	66	292		208		758
Mr. O. L. Clare . .		229	69	281		213		723
Mr. Eyre W. Hussey [1] .		291	60	238		189		718
Colonel Lewin . .		203	64	270		211		684
Mr. G. W. Chapman .		224	63	271		164		659
Mr. G. G. Hulme [1] . .		219	57	227		186		632
Captain M. Allen [1] . .		228	57	215		178		621
Mr. C. H. Everett . .		231	54	220		164		615

Twenty-eight gentlemen shot.

The Grand Jubilee and Annual Handicap Meeting of the Royal Toxophilite Society was held on October 9 and 10, 1884.

[1] Visitors.

GENTLEMEN	100 Yards		80 Yards		60 Yards		TOTALS	
	Hits	Score	Hits	Score	Hits	Score	Hits	Score
Mr. C. E. Nesham . .	9	3						
Mr. R. Walters . .	0	2						
Mr. O. L. Clare . .	3	3						
Mr. J. H. Bridges . .	6	2						
Mr. Eyre W. Hussey [1] .								
Mr. C. J. Longman .								
Captain M. Allen [1] . .								
Mr. Gregson [1] . . .								
Mr. T. T. S. Metcalfe .								
Mr. Piers F. Legh [1] .								
Mr. A. Newall . .								
Mr. C. H. Everett . .								
Mr. Walrond . . .								
Mr. G. G. Hulme [1] . .								
Mr. H. Kendall . .								

Forty-nine gentlemen shot.

Nothing could have been more unfavourable than the weather on this occasion. It was wet, stormy, and bitterly cold.

The Grand Annual Autumn Handicap Meeting of the Royal Toxophilite Society was held on October 8 and 9, 1885.

GENTLEMEN	100 Yards		80 Yards		60 Yards		TOTALS	
	Hits	Score	Hits	Score	Hits	Score	Hits	Score
Mr. Perry-Keene [1] . .	69	245	84	384	43	255	196	884
Mr. C. E. Nesham . .	79	273	81	355	45	243	205	871
Mr. R. Walters . .	72	256	78	370	39	203	189	829
Mr. E. Brodie Hoare .	66	274	58	246	43	201	167	721
Mr. H. H. Longman .	61	205	60	268	42	230	163	703
Mr. C. H. Everett . .	63	249	61	259	39	175	163	683
Mr. H. Kendall . .	44	174	52	224	43	233	139	631

Twenty-one gentlemen shot at this meeting.

The Grand Annual Autumn Handicap Meeting of the Royal Toxophilite Society was held on October 14 and 15, 1886.

[1] Visitors.

GENTLEMEN	100 Yards		80 Yards		60 Yards		TOTALS	
	Hits	Score	Hits	Score	Hits	Score	Hits	Score
Mr. C. E. Nesham .								916
Mr. J. H. Bridges .	6							789
Mr. N. Rattray								734
Mr. Walrond .								724
Mr. H. H. Longman								685
Captain M. Allen [1] .								671
Mr. E. Fisher [1]								666
Mr. C. H. Everett .								636
Mr. E. C. Gedge [1] .								610
Mr. A. Henty.								600
Mr. T. T. S. Metcalfe								599

Twenty-one gentlemen shot at this meeting.

SCOTCH PUBLIC MEETINGS

The Eleventh Annual Scottish Archery Meeting was held on the Cricket-ground (Lavilands), near Stirling, on August 4 and 5, 1865.

LADIES	60 Yards		50 Yards		TOTALS	
	Hits	Score	Hits	Score	Hits	Score
Miss Betham . . .	88	424	46	290	134	714
Mrs. Horniblow . . .	82	432	43	253	125	685

GENTLEMEN	100 Yards		80 Yards		60 Yards		TOTALS	
	Hits	Score	Hits	Score	Hits	Score	Hits	Score
Mr. P. Muir . . .	85	315	61	239	44	266	190	820
Mr. J. Murdoch . .	54	194	58	238	39	193	151	625
Mr. P. Murdoch . .	59	243	49	163	40	208	148	614
Mr. J. Allan . . .	52	162	42	206	40	226	134	594

Thirteen ladies and thirty-six gentlemen shot.

[1] Visitors.   [2] Did not complete the shooting at 60 yards.

The Twelfth Annual Scottish National Archery Meeting was held on the County Cricket-ground in Raeburn Place, Stockbridge, Edinburgh, on August 17 and 18, 1866.

	60 Yards		50 Yards		TOTALS	
—	Hits	Score	Hits	Score	Hits	Score
Mrs. Horniblow . . .	82	368	45	241	127	609

GENTLEMEN	100 Yards		80 Yards		Yards		TOTALS	
	Hits	Score	Hit	Score	Hits	Score	Hits	Score
Mr. P. Muir . . .	67	279	63	261	42	212	172	752
Captain Betham . .	47	195	56	232	42	196	145	623

Nine ladies and thirty-eight gentlemen shot.

It was only on these two occasions that the Double Rounds were shot at these meetings.

IRISH PUBLIC MEETINGS

The Second Irish Grand National Archery Meeting was held at Bray, not far from Dublin, on August 12 and 13.

Twenty-three ladies and twenty-eight gentlemen shot.

LADIES	60 Yards		. 50 Yards		TOTALS	
	Hits	Score	Hits	Score	Hits	Score
Mrs. Horniblow . . .	86	428	47	263	133	691
Miss Betham . . .	78	362	47	245	125	607
Miss Warde	69	301	42	218	111	519

GENTLEMEN	100 Yards		80 Yards		60 Yards		TOTALS	
	Hits	Score	Hits	Score	Hits	Score	Hits	Score
Mr. *G.* Edwards .	68	266	77	357	48	298	193	921
Mr. R. W. Atkinson .	69	303	66	298	42	228	177	829
Mr. T. L. Coulson .	60	230	52	248	39	195	151	673
Mr. H. Walters .	63	223	57	235	36	180	156	638
Mr. Macnamara .	46	160	62	254	42	224	150	638
Mr. E. Popham .	54	198	63	287	34	134	151	619
Captain Betham .	48	178	61	263	42	170	151	611

Mr. G. Edwards scored 404 in the handicap match on August 14.

The Third Irish Grand National Archery Meeting was held in the Rotunda Gardens, Dublin, on July 27 and 28, 1864.

LADIES	60 Yards		50 Yards		TOTALS	
	Hits	Score	Hits	Score	Hits	Score
Miss Betham . . .	85	437	42	218	127	655
Miss H. Tarleton . . .	72	320	32	134	104	454

GENTLEMEN	100 Yards		80 Yards		60 Yards		TOTALS	
	Hits	Score	Hits	Score	Hits	Score	Hits	Score
Mr. *G.* Edwards . .	70	276	73	303	48	248	191	827
Captain Betham .	64	234	66	276	43	215	173	725
Mr. Betham . .	58	210	60	246	44	226	162	682
Mr. R. W. Atkinson .	51	179	68	282	42	202	161	663
Mr. Maconchy .	63	215	55	207	40	214	158	636
Mr. H. Elliott .	48	150	59	269	44	200	151	619

Twenty-two ladies and twenty-one gentlemen shot.

The Fourth Irish Grand National Archery Meeting was held in the New Winter Gardens, Dublin, on May 31 and June 1, 1865.

LADIES	60 Yards		50 Yards		TOTALS	
	Hits	Score	Hits	Score	Hits	Score
Miss Betham . . .	85	375	46	264	131	639
Mrs. Ormsby . . .	65	257	41	175	106	432

GENTLEMEN	100 Yards		80 Yards		60 Yards		TOTALS	
	Hits	Score	Hits	Score	Hits	Score	Hits	Score
Mr. G. Edwards . .	50	192	77	387	45	231	172	810
Mr. Betham . . .	74	306	62	248	42	204	178	758
Captain Betham . .	59	227	61	277	39	157	159	661
Captain Whitla . .	59	223	57	237	28	130	144	590

Thirteen ladies and seventeen gentlemen shot.

The Second Grand Leinster Archery Meeting was held in the grounds of the Exhibition Palace, Dublin, on September 19 and 20, 1865.

LADIES	60 Yards		50 Yards		TOTALS	
	Hits	Score	Hits	Score	Hits	Score
Miss Macpherson . . .	75	343	42	220	117	563
Miss Hendley . . .	67	305	41	187	108	492
Miss Betham . . .	66	290	36	200	102	490

GENTLEMEN	100 Yards		80 Yards		60 Yards		TOTALS	
	Hits	Score	Hits	Score	Hits	Score	Hits	Score
Captain Whitla . .	41	149	64	310	40	230	145	689
Mr. Betham . . .	49	197	56	234	39	171	144	602

Twenty-six ladies and sixteen gentlemen shot.

The Fifth Irish Grand National Archery Meeting was held in the New Winter Gardens in Dublin on August 1, 2, and 3, 1866. Eighteen ladies and seventéen gentlemen shot.

LADIES	60 Yards		50 Yards		TOTALS	
	Hits	Score	Hits	Score	Hits	Score
Mrs. Horniblow . . .	86	386	46	268	132	654
Miss Betham . . .	80	378	40	244	120	622
Miss A. Betham . . .	61	291	44	238	105	529

GENTLEMEN	100 Yards		80 Yards		60 Yards		TOTALS	
	Hits	Score	Hits	Score	Hits	Score	Hits	Score
Mr. Betham . . .	63	241	68	272	45	287	176	800
Mr. *G.* Edwards . .	36	134	70	348	45	231	151	713
Mr. R. W. Atkinson .	54	210	57	259	41	213	152	682
Captain Whitla . .	58	226	60	260	40	192	158	678
Captain Betham . .	36	130	60	240	46	238	142	608

The First Ulster Grand Archery Meeting was held at Ulsterville, Belfast, on August 8, 9, and 10, 1866.

LADIES	60 Yards		50 Yards		TOTALS	
	Hits	Score	Hits	Score	Hits	Score
Miss Betham . . .	88	418	46	274	134	692
Mrs. Horniblow . . .	79	349	40	202	119	551
Miss Ada Betham . .	70	320	41	209	111	529

GENTLEMEN	100 Yards		80 Yards		60 Yards		TOTALS	
	Hits	Score	Hits	Score	Hits	Score	Hits	Score
Mr. Betham . . .	72	274	65	257	40	196	177	727
Captain Betham . .	50	172	53	255	41	173	144	600

Eighteen ladies and nine gentlemen shot.

The Third Grand Leinster Archery Meeting was held in the grounds of the Exhibition Palace at Dublin on September 4 and 5, 1866.

LADIES	60 Yards		50 Yards		TOTALS	
	Hits	Score	Hits	Score	Hits	Score
Miss Betham . . .	87	467		287	134	754
Miss L. Quin . . .	74	336	39	191	113	527

GENTLEMEN ·	100 Yards		80 Yards		60 Yards		TOTALS	
	Hits	Score	Hits	Score	Hits	Score	Hits	Score
Mr. Betham . . .	59	209	71	287	41	205	171	701
Captain Betham . .	59	201	71	305	41	195	171	701
Mr. R. W. Atkinson .	54	214	67	305	41	181	162	700
Mr. W. Butt . . .	52	192	50	236	38	172	140	600

Twenty-three ladies and twenty-three gentlemen shot.

The Second Ulster Grand Archery Meeting was held in the grounds of the Armagh Archers, at Armagh, on August 7 and 8, 1867.

LADIES	60 Yards		50 Yards		TOTALS	
	Hits	Score	Hits	Score	Hits	Score
Miss Betham . . .	84	400	48	294	132	694
Miss H. Hutchinson . .	81	367	44	226	125	593
Miss A. Betham . . .	73	329	43	237	116	566
Miss Davison . . .	72	296	42	220	114	516

GENTLEMEN	100 Yards		80 Yards		60 Yards		TOTALS	
	Hits	Score	Hits	Score	Hits	Score	Hits	Score
Mr. Betham . . .	63	281	73	291	43	233	179	805
Mr. R. W. Atkinson .	55	191	56	234	43	231	154	656
Mr. Russell . . .	58	216	58	244	36	162	152	622

Twenty ladies and seventeen gentlemen shot.

The Grand Munster Archery Meeting was held at Limerick, on September 21 and 22, 1867.

LADIES	60 Yards		50 Yards		TOTALS	
	Hits	Score	Hits	Score	Hits	Score
Miss Betham . . .	84	424	48	234	132	658
Miss A. Betham . . .	82	380	46	246	128	626
Miss Warde	64	312	41	225	105	537
Mrs. *Ormsby* . . .	68	294	44	214	112	508

GENTLEMEN	100 Yards		80 Yards		60 Yards		TOTALS	
	Hits	Score	Hits	Score	Hits	Score	Hits	Score
Mr. Betham . . .	63	267	58	246	41	227	162	740
Mr. A. E. Knox . .	60	212	58	270	38	186	156	668
Mr. R. W. Atkinson .	58	204	52	220	37	169	147	593

Twenty-eight ladies and eighteen gentlemen shot.

The Fourth Grand Annual Meeting of the Leinster Archers was held in the grounds of the Exhibition Palace, Dublin, on August 26 and 27, 1867.

LADIES	60 Yards		50 Yards		TOTALS	
	Hits	Score	Hits	Score	Hits	Score
Miss Betham . . .	84	416	46	278	130	694
Miss A. Betham . .	84	390	47	231	131	621
Miss H. Hutchinson . .	75	329	42	224	117	553
Miss Mayne	73	313	46	226	119	539

GENTLEMEN	100 Yards		80 Yards		60 Yards		TOTALS	
	Hits	Score	Hits	Score	Hits	Score	Hits	Score
Mr. Betham . . .	70	282	80	358	45	231	195	871
Mr. A. Knox . . .	63	277	66	252	38	196	167	725
Mr. Russell . . .	53	205	59	299	40	186	152	690
Mr. R. W. Atkinson .	59	217	44	176	45	225	148	618

Twenty-three ladies and seventeen gentlemen shot.

The Sixth Irish Grand National Archery Meeting was held in the grounds of the Exhibition Palace in Dublin, on September 14 and 15, 1867.

LADIES	60 Yards		50 Yards		TOTALS	
	Hits	Score	Hits	Score	Hits	Score
Miss Betham . . .	88	440	47	303	135	743
Miss Ormsby . . .	83	425	44	232	127	657
Miss L. Quin . . .	76	384	47	259	123	643
Miss A. Betham . . .	76	328	46	258	122	586

GENTLEMEN	100 Yards		80 Yards		60 Yards		TOTALS	
	Hits	Score	Hits	Score	Hits	Score	Hits	Score
Mr. Betham . . .	61	269	70	268	44	230	175	767
Mr. Russell . . .	65	247	59	251	38	192	162	690
Mr. N. A. Knox . .	63	253	58	244	34	154	155	651

Fourteen ladies and fourteen gentlemen shot.

The Second Grand Munster Archery Meeting was held in the grounds of Cortigan (Sir Denham Norreys, Bart.), near Mallow, on September 2 and 3, 1868.

LADIES	60 Yards		50 Yards		TOTALS	
	Hits	Score	Hits	Score	Hits	Score
Miss Betham . . .	87	473	48	292	135	765
Miss L. Quin . . .	72	326	43	217	115	543
Miss Ormsby . . .	72	334	40	198	112	532
Mrs. Vansittart . . .	74	326	35	181	109	507

—	100 Yards		80 Yards		60 Yards		TOTALS	
	Hits	Score	Hits	Score	Hits	Score	Hits	Score
Mr. Betham . . .	52	182	65	269	41	219	158	670

Nineteen ladies and twelve gentlemen shot.

The Third Grand Munster Archery Meeting was held in Sir D. Norreys's grounds at Cortigan, near Mallow, on September 8 and 9, 1869.

LADIES	60 Yards		50 Yards		TOTALS	
	Hits	Score	Hits	Score	Hits	Score
Miss Peel	85	373	45	199	130	572
Mrs. V. Forbes . . .	70	308	46	236	116	544
Miss L. Quin . . .	83	359	42	176	125	535
Miss *Ormsby* . . .	73	313	44	220	117	533

—	100 Yards		80 Yards		60 Yards		TOTALS	
	Hits	Score	Hits	Score	Hits	Score	Hits	Score
Mr. Betham . . .	66	232	67	305	41	189	174	726

Twenty-four ladies and fourteen gentlemen shot.

A Grand Leinster Meeting was held in the grounds of the Exhibition Palace, Dublin, on October 6 and 7, 1869.

LADIES	60 Yards		50 Yards		TOTALS	
	Hits	Score	Hits	Score	Hits	Score
Miss H. Hutchinson . .	84	412	46	254	130	666
Mrs. V. Forbes . . .	88	408	46	252	134	660
Miss Mayne	73	323	41	239	114	562
Mrs. C. W. Betham . .	73	333	40	212	113	545
Miss Peel	80	374	38	164	118	538

GENTLEMEN	100 Yards		80 Yards		60 Yards		TOTALS	
	Hits	Score	Hits	Score	Hits	Score	Hits	Score
Mr. Betham . . .	65	285	57	223	42	208	164	716
Mr. McNamara . .	47	183	45	199	43	183	135	565

AMERICAN NATIONAL ARCHERY MEETINGS

The First American National Archery Meeting was held at Chicago on August 12, 13, and 14, 1879. On this occasion the ladies shot forty-eight arrows at each of the distances of 30, 40, and 50 yards. The gentlemen shot forty-eight arrows at 60 yards, and ninety-six arrows at 80 yards, on the first day, and seventy-two arrows at 100 yards on each of the other days; thus making up the quantities of a York Round, though in unusual order. The best results were as follows:—

GENTLEMEN	60 Yards		80 Yards		100 Yards		TOTALS	
	Hits	Score	Hits	Score	Hits	Score	Hits	Score
Mr. W. H. Thompson .	39	155	43	155	68	236	150	546
Mr. T. McMechan . .	35	175	47	177	34	126	116	478
Mr. E. P. Hall . .	37	157	50	178	28	104	115	439
Mr. C. Leach . . .	34	152	38	138	39	149	111	439

The Second Annual American National Archery Meeting was held at Buffalo, near New York, on July 11 and 12 (13 and 14 ?), 1880, when the Round shot by the ladies was forty-eight arrows at each of the distances of 50, 40, and 30 yards; but the gentlemen shot a single York Round on each day. The result of each day's shooting only is given, as the details of the different distances cannot be discovered.

GENTLEMEN	1st Day		2nd Day		Double York Round	
	Hits	Score	Hits	Score	Hits	Score
Mr. L. L. Peddinghaus .	74	346	78	360	152	706
Mr. W. H. Thompson .	82	370	78	332	160	702
Mr. W. Burnham . .	81	331	78	342	159	673
Mr. F. H. Walworth .	68	274	76	316	144	590

The Fourth Annual American National Archery Meeting was held at Chicago on July 11, 12, and 14, 1882, the National and York double Rounds being shot.[1]

LADIES	60 Yards		50 Yards		TOTALS	
	Hits	Score	Hits	Score	Hits	Score
Mrs. A. H. Gibbes . .	63	251	38	198	101	449
Mrs. F. Morrison . . .	—	—	—	—	94	374

GENTLEMEN	100 Yards		80 Yards		60 Yards		TOTALS	
	Hits	Score	Hits	Score	Hits	Score	Hits	Score
Mr. D. A. Nash . .	58	210	65	257	44	246	167	713
Mr. H. S. Taylor . .	55	151	67	275	46	252	168	678
Mr. R. Williams . .	49	179	55	235	44	236	148	650
Mr. W. A. Clark . .	45	197	62	244	41	195	148	636
Mr. W. H. Thompson .	46	178	54	234	44	198	144	610
Mr. F. E. Perry . .	42	148	56	226	39	179	137	553

The Fifth Annual American National Archery Meeting was held at Cincinnati on July 10, 11, and 12, 1883.

GENTLEMEN	100 Yards		80 Yards		60 Yards		TOTALS	
	Hits	Score	Hits	Score	Hits	Score	Hits	Score
Mr. P. Williams . .	76	300	79	371	44	236	199	907
Mr. H. S. Taylor . .	53	191	51	223	45	235	149	649
Mr. W. A. Clark . .	56	192	63	257	39	171	158	620
Mr. D. A. Nash . .	35	135	57	243	45	209	137	587

[1] No report of the meeting in 1881 can be traced.

LADIES	60 Yards		50 Yards		TOTALS	
	Hits	Score	Hits	Score	Hits	Score
Mrs. C. Howell . . .	85	413	47	277	132	690
Mrs. S. A. Whitfield . .	88	436	39	185	127	621
Mrs. T. F. George . .	71	299	45	237	116	536
Mrs. H. M. Pollock . .	76	328	42	198	118	526
Mrs. Arthur	72	296	43	213	115	509

The Sixth Annual American National Archery Meeting was held at Pullman in 1884 on July 8, 9, and 10.

—	60 Yards		50 Yards		TOTALS	
	Hits	Score	Hits	Score	Hits	Score
Mrs. H. Hall . . .	46	204	42	212	88	416

GENTLEMEN	100 Yards		80 Yards		60 Yards		TOTALS	
	Hits	Score	Hits	Score	Hits	Score	Hits	Score
Mr. W. H. Thompson .	63	237	68	314	43	209	174	760
Mr. R. Williams, jun. .	67	251	65	267	43	227	175	745
Mr. C. C. Beach . .	46	176	65	297	44	250	155	723
Mr. H. S. Taylor . .	44	160	50	198	39	181	133	539

The Seventh Annual American National Archery Meeting was held at Eaton, Ohio, on July 7, 8, and 9, 1885.

LADIES	60 Yards		50 Yards		TOTALS	
	Hits	Score	Hits	Score	Hits	Score
Mrs. M. C. Howell . .	75	353	46	252	121	605
Miss J. Pollock . . .	78	300	44	216	122	516
Mrs. J. Arthur . . .	65	271	42	210	107	481

GENTLEMEN	100 Yards		80 Yards		60 Yards		TOTALS	
	Hits	Score	Hits	Score	Hits	Score	Hits	Score
Colonel R. Williams .								
Mr. C. C. Beach . .								
Mr. J. W. B. Siders .								
Mr. W. H. Thompson .								
Mr. W. A. Clark . .								

CHAPTER XIV.

CLUB SHOOTING AND PRIVATE PRACTICE

In the following scores an attempt is made to give authentic specimens of the best shooting of as many as possible of the best archers of the past and present time. Mr. Ford himself mentioned how sadly disheartened and crestfallen he felt on his return from his first Grand National Meeting at Derby, where he had scored 341 with 101 hits in the double York Round, which was far below the score he had anticipated, and warned his readers that shooting at a public meeting was very different from private practice or small match shooting. There are but very few archers who have not met with the same disappoint ment, as will be easily seen when the public and private records here given are compared. Young archers should be strongly recommended to make their public *débuts* as early as pos-sible—as well to work off the novelty and excitement of the scene as to compare the methods and results of other archers—before they have established great local reputations, which may run the greater risk of being fatally exploded from the very over-anxiety which is employed to keep or increase those reputations in public.

The erroneous practice of shooting trial arrows before the commencement of the regular round has been mostly given up of late years, being altogether discountenanced by the rules of the private practice club, and disallowed at all the public meetings.

In fact, it was a most dangerous practice at the public meetings, where, in former years, before the match shooting commenced, or when it was finished those who had to cross the ground ran no little risk of being shot by some of the industrious archers, who, not satisfied with the round allotted to the day, were threshing out themselves and their bows, not with shooting at the targets, but mostly at a piece of white paper placed about so far from themselves as an arrow would fall when supposed to have passed through the gold at the particular distance at which these zealots were ever engaged in the apparently hopeless search of the 'range' or a 'point of aim.'

The earliest grand score on the testified York Round in the books of the Royal Toxophilite Society belonged to *Mr. H. C. Mules,* and was shot on August 24, 1856.

Hits	Score	Hits	Score	Hits	Score		Hits	Score
50	240	42	232	23	131	=	115	603

He also has scores of 116 hts. 500 sc. and 106 hts. 508 sc. in the books made in 1858. This was surpassed by *Mr. H. A. Ford* on November 3, 1858, in the Toxophilite grounds ·

Hits	Score	Hits	Score	Hits	Score		Hits	Score
47	227	46	258	24	138	=	117	623

and the score of *Mr. G. E. S. Fryer,* made in the same grounds on August 2, 1872, of

Hits	Score	Hits	Score	Hits	Score		Hits	Score
59	289	44	218	24	132	=	127	639

went further, and still remains unsurpassed.

This last-mentioned score took, and still holds, the *Wilkin son practice medal,* which was given to the Royal Toxophilite Society in 1866, and was first taken by *Mr. T. Boulton* with

Hits	Score	Hits	Score	Hits	Score		Hits	Score
43	175	40	186	24	148	=	107	509

who afterwards improved his holding of it by making

Hits	Score	Hits	Score	Hits	Score		Hits	Score
48	206	46	208	23	133	=	117	547

On July 6, 1867, *Mr. W. Spottiswoode* scored

Hits	Score	Hits	Score	Hits	Score		Hits	Score
50	244	41	201	23	129	=	114	574

and took and held it until it was transferred to Mr. Fryer in 1872.

The full details of *Mr. H. A. Ford's* best private-practice score of 809 with 137 hits have been already given.

He also records a score in which the only arrow missed was the 59th, shot at 100 yards, the particular of the score being

Hits	Score	Hits	Score	Hits	Score		Hits	Score
71	335	48	272	24	158	=	143	765

When shooting with the Royal Toxophilite Society on June 23, 1854, the round being 96 arrows at 100 yards, 72 arrows at 80 yards, and 48 arrows at 60 yards, he made the following score :

Hits	Score	Hits	Score	Hits	Score		Hits	Score
79	373	71	325	47	313	=	197	1011

His best double York Round, made privately, seems to be as follows :

Hits	Score	Hits	Score	Hits	Score		Hits	Score
61	295	48	306	24	186	=	133	787
63	299	46	278	24	168	=	133	745
		Total				.	266	1532

His best scoring at 100 yards is represented by 371 with 69 hits—

G.	R.	B.	BK.	W.
12	17	19	14	7

from his second best York Round score of

Hits	Score	Hits	Score	Hits	Score		Hits	Score
69	371	48	274	24	154	=	141	799

his best score at 80 yards being 306 with all the 48 hits,

G.	R.	B.	BK.	W.
10	19	15	2	2

and his best at 60 yards 186,

G.	R.	B.
10	13	1

Mr. H. A. Ford himself reports one of his own most extraordinary feats as follows : ' Not but what I have been the originator of a respectable fluke or two myself in my time. For instance, on the second day of the first Grand National Meeting at Shrewsbury in 1854, an old archer, Mr. Hughes, offered a silver bracer as a prize for most golds at any one end, 100 yards to take precedence of 80, and 80 yards of 60.   In a very few minutes two gentlemen, Messrs. Garnett and Hilton, if I remember rightly, got two ; but this was not enough, the third arrow being destined to go there as well.   Accordingly, but a few rounds after, my friend Chance came to my aid, and so the whole three went into the desired spot.   Now the combination here was curious.   But once during my archery experience has a special prize been offered for a feat of this particular nature, and upon that occasion, and that occasion only in a match, have three golds been got at one end, by one shooter, at 100 yards' (' Archer's Register,' 1864).

Mr. Bramhall gives a good idea of Mr. Ford's indomitable perseverance. ' If,' he says, ' I reported a good score, he persevered until he had beaten it—e.g. in 1853, March 7, I completed 409 following hits at 60 yards.   He soon sent me a report of a little over 600 ' (' Archer's Register,' 1881).

Mr. John Bramhall's best single York Round was made November 25, 1851 ·

Hits	Score	Hits	Score	Hits	Score	Hits	Score
61	317	41	223	23	135	125	675

In 1849 the average of the 54 York Rounds he shot was 453 score from 103 hits ; in 1850 it was 502 from 110 hits in 70 rounds ; in 1851 it was 561 from 117 hits in 64 rounds ; in 1852 it was 575 from 117 hits in 52 rounds ; and in 1853 it was 567 from 114 hits in 38 rounds.   In shooting at 100 yards he has made 4 golds in consecutive hits, and often 3 at one end. At 80 yards his best in 48 arrows was 47 hits 273 score ; and he has made 55 consecutive hits at 80, and 5 following golds. At 60 yards his best record is 24 hits 172 score—409 consecutive hits and 5 following golds. His best double York Round was :

Hits	Score	Hits	Score	Hits	Score		Hits	Score
107	535	91	497	48	290	=	256	1322

shot on June 26 and July 1, 1852.

Mr. E. A. Holmes (champion 1865 and 1870) made his best score on the single York Round in private practice at Harrow, soon after the Grand National Meeting at Brighton in 1867, which is as follows :

Hits	Score	Hits	Score	Hits	Score		Hits	Score
66	284	46	206	22	132	−	134	622

Mr. C. E. Nesham (Royal Toxophilite Society), champion 1884-5-6, has 13 York Rounds scores on the Royal Toxophilite Society's books of over 500, of which the highest is :

Hits	Score	Hits	Score	Hits	Score		Hits	Score
55	281	41	187	22	126	=	118	594

made on May 5, 1887.

In private practice at Bournemouth he scored, on May 14, 1883,

Hits	Score	Hits	Score	Hits	Score		Hits	Score
63	281	43	243	22	108		128	632

and

Hits	Score	Hits	Score	Hits	Score		Hits	Score
53	269	41	203	22	122	−	116	594

made in the Regent's Park, March 6, 1884.

On twenty-three other occasions, in private and in club matches, he has scored 500 and upwards. Of these, in the Royal Toxophilite Society's books, are :

Hits	Score	Hits	Score	Hits	Score		Hits	Score
46	228	47	253	20	110	=	113	591

shot on October 16, 1884, and

Hits	Score	Hits	Score	Hits	Score		Hits	Score
50	224	44	220	24	148	=	118	592

shot on October 29, 1885.

Major *C. H. Fisher's* (Champion 1871-2-3-4, and made highest score at Windsor in 1884 when Mr. Nesham became champion) best York Round score in the books of the Royal Toxophilite Society, made on July 2, 1885, is as follows ·

Hits	Score	Hits	Score	Hits	Score		Hits	Score
53	239	42	192	24	136	=	119	557

and his next best, made on October 20, 1871, is

Hits	Score	Hits	Score	Hits	Score		Hits	Score
47	227	42	194	23	113	=	112	534

His best private practice score on the York Round is the fol- lowing ·

Hits	Score	Hits	Score	Hits	Score		Hits	Score
49	227	45	243	24	158	=	862	118

made on May 25, 1872 ; and he reports that this Round was shot too quickly, and might have been improved if he had taken more pains.

He has made the following good double rounds in practice, namely ·

	Hits	Score
May 27 and 28, 1873	235	1079
July 23 and 24, 1874	235	1123

and in 1876 ·

	Hits	Score	Hits	Score	Hits	Score		Hits	Score
June 12,	50	196	43	213	23	103		116	512
„ 13,	46	194	45	233	23	113	=	114	540
Totals . .							.	230	1052

and in 1877 a single York Round ·

	Hits	Score	Hits	Score	Hits	Score		Hits	Score
Sept. 7,	55	241	44	202	23	125		122	568

Mr. T. T. S. Metcalfe's (Royal Toxophilite Society) best single York Round is :

Hits	Score	Hits	Score	Hits	Score		Hits	Score
54	258	37	173	19	93	−	100	524

made on May 22, 1886, in private practice.

Mr. C. H. Everett's best single York Rounds appear to be ·

	Hits	Score	Hits	Score	Hits	Score		Hits	Score
Aug. 9, 1880	45	179	41	229	22	114	=	108	522
April 2, 1883	48	180	42	222	24	134	−	114	536
„ 16, „	54	214	37	177	24	158	=	115	549

made in private practice.

At a meeting of the Royal Toxophilite Society on October 4, 1874, he scored :

Hits	Score	Hits	Score	Hits	Score		Hits	Score
45	187	40	190	23	123	=	108	500

and again in the Regent's Park on September 30, 1880

Hits	Score	Hits	Score	Hits	Score	Hits	Score
52	192	41	209	23	109	116	510

and on October 14, 1880 :

Hits	Score	Hits	Score	Hits	Score		Hits	Score
50	224	38	166	22	116	=	110	506

Mr. W. J. Richardson (Royal Toxophilite Society) has a good score on the York Round in the books of the Royal Toxophilite Society, made on June 7, 1860 ·

Hits	Score	Hits	Score	Hits	Score		Hits	Score
44	190	39	193	21	133	=	104	516

as also has *Mr. W. Rimington* (Royal Toxophilite Society) champion 1868–69 and 1877 ·

Hits	Score	Hits	Score	Hits	Score		Hits	Score
48	206	42	178	24	120	=	114	504

made on July 2, 1869.

Col. H. F. C. Lewin's (Royal Toxophilite Society) best

scores have been made in private practice at Eltham, in the late Mr. Mill's grounds, and are :

Hits	Score	Hits	Score	Hits	Score		Hits	Score
41	199	38	194	21	115	=	100	508

made on November 3, 1870, and

Hits	Score	Hits	Score	Hits	Score	Hits	Score
50	226	36	146	24	136	110	508

made in 1869.

Mr. G. E. S. Fryer (Champion in 1875, Royal Toxophilite Society), besides his excellent score of 639 with 127 hits, has another very good York Round score in the books of the Royal Toxophilite Society, made on June 3, 1873 :

Hits	Score	Hits	Score	Hits	Score		Hits	Score
55	235	47	249	24	138	=	126	622

He made another fine York Round on August 15, 1873, in private practice :

Hits	Score	Hits	Score	Hits	Score		Hits	Score
54	238	46	218	24	150	=	124	606

and in the books of the Royal Toxophilite Society in 1874, on May 27 :

Hits	Score	Hits	Score	Hits	Score		Hits	Score
50	200	42	242	23	129	=	115	571

on June 17 :

Hits	Score	Hits	Score	Hits	Score		Hits	Score
58	242	44	200	23	155	=	125	597

and on July 1 ·

Hits	Score	Hits	Score	Hits	Score		Hits	Score
48	184	45	243	24	132	=	117	559

Mr. H. H. Palairet's (Champion in 1876, Royal Toxophilite Society) best scores on the York Round appear to be the following ·

Hits	Score	Hits	Score	Hits	Score		Hits	Score
53	241	45	239	24	108	=	122	588

made at a West Berks Meeting at Great Marlow (Colonel Wethered's) on June 20, 1882, and this score is the York Round ' record ' of the West Berks Archers.

In private practice on July 15, 1875, he scored ·

Hits	Score	Hits	Score	Hits	Score		Hits	Score
54	252	43	205	23	121	=	120	578

showing a very good score at 100 yards; and on July 30 he scored 46 hits 264 score in the 48 arrows at 80 yards.

His best shooting at 60 yards appears to have been made on July 24, 1874, when, shooting 96 arrows, he scored 579 with 95 hits.

Mr. C. J. Longman's (Champion in 1883, Royal Toxophilite Society) best York Round score in the books of the Royal Toxophilite Society is dated November 1, 1883, and is as follows :

Hits	Score	Hits	Score	Hits	Score		Hits	Score
49	199	41	189	23	149	−	113	537

and his best private practice scores made in the same grounds are ·

Hits	Score	Hits	Score	Hits	Score		Hits	Score
55	249	41	213	23	129		119	591
46	204	46	220	24	148	=	116	572
		Totals	.	.	.	.	235	1163

made on June 17 and 18, 1884, respectively.

Mr. H. H. Longman's (Royal Toxophilite Society) best York Round score made in private practice in the Royal Toxophilite Society's grounds on March 30, 1887, is as follows ·

Hits	Score	Hits	Score	Hits	Score		Hits	Score
51	223	41	191	21	91	=	113	505

Mr. Piers F. Legh
some good single York

	Hits	Score		Hits	Score
July 14, 1879	45	181	=	109	529
„ 19, 1880	41	177	=	109	509
Sept 20, „	51	223	=	113	527

Mr. R. Walters (Champion in 1879, Royal Toxophilite Society) has made some good scores in private practice, of which the best appear to be as follows ·

	Hits	Score	Hits	Score	Hits	Score		Hits	Score
Oct. 25, 1884	48	184	43	211	23	133	−	114	528
Aug. 15, 1885	45	187	44	214	24	126	=	113	527

Mr. J. H. Bridges' (Royal Toxophilite Society) best single York Rounds in private practice are:

	Hits	Score	Hits	Score	Hits	Score		Hits	Score
Oct. 7, 1881	39	181	42	222	24	120	=	105	523
June 8, 1884							=	118	546

At 100 yards, in 72 arrows, he has made

	Hits	Score
April 2, 1884　.　.	55	261

At 80 yards, in 48 arrows, he has made:

	Hits	Score
January 27, 1887 .	45	263
April 12, 1887　　.	48	216

At 60 yards, in 24 arrows:

	Hits	Score
April 23, 1884　.	24	166

and in 100 arrows at 60 yards:

	Hits	Score
September 18, 1879	100	586
April 23, 1884　.　.　.　.	99	627

It will be observed that nearly all Mr. Bridges' practice occurs early or late in the season, as cricket absorbs much of his attention in the summer.

Mr. L. R. Erskine (Royal Toxophilite Society) has made some good single York Rounds in private·practice, viz.:

	Hits	Score	Hits	Score	Hits	Score		Hits	Score
Nov. 8, 1886	49	195	41	215	22	122	=	112	532
Mar. 1, 1887	50	210	46	222	23	117	=	119	549
„　5, „	53	231	46	198	24	126	=	123	555
„ 11, „	52	220	45	227	23	133		120	580

The full particulars of *Mr. O. K. Prescot's* (Royal Toxophilite Society) best private practice double York Round score of 1197 cannot be given, as they have been lost or destroyed. It was shot in two-days of September 1867. The first total score was 621, and the score at 100 yards was 256—200 having been made in the first 4 dozen. The second round was 567, and, in this round, the score at 80 yards was 249. The most annoying thing about the round was that the last arrow at 60 yards missed the target, when a black even would have brought the total up to 1200.

Mr. H. J. B. Kendall's (Royal Toxophilite Society) best score in the York Round was made in private practice on August 14, 1884:

Hits	Score	Hits	Score	Hits	Score	Hits	Score
46	222	46	228	22	118	— 114	568

On this occasion the 2 arrows not counted at 80 yards went through weak places in the target.

He also made 52 hits 224 score at 100 yards on Aug 28, 1884.

On July 5, 1877, he made 3 golds in one end at 100 yards in the course of the Summer Handicap match of the Royal Toxophilite Society, repeating the feat performed by Mr. H. A. Ford at Shrewsbury in 1854.

Mr. O. Leigh Clare (Royal Toxophilite Society) has made some good private practice, viz. ·

	Hits	Score	Hits	Score	Hits	Score	Hits	Score
July 23, 1879,	52	266	43	193	23	109	— 118	568

in the single York Round; and in 72 arrows at 100 yards ·

	Hits	Score
October 12, 1878 . . .	56	250

also in 48 arrows at 80 yards ·

	Hits	Score
July 13, 1878 . . .	42	212

Mr. C. J. Perry-Keene made the following fine score

in private practice on July 24, 1886, in the single York
Round :—

Hits	Score	Hits	Score	Hits	Score		Hits	Score
57	225	45	229	24	150	=	126	604

and two other good scores made by him are ·

	Hits	Score	Hits	Score	Hits	Score		Hits	Score
May 6, 1886,	43	217	40	188	23	119	=	106	524
„ 7, „	51	215	45	199	24	152	=	120	566
April 18, 1887,	48	202	44	230	24	124	=	116	556

In private practice *Mr. F. A. Govett* (Royal Toxophilite
Society) made ·

	Hits	Score	Hits	Score	Hits	Score		Hits	Score
October 12, 1883,	50	204	38	184	21	113	=	109	501

and on May 29, at one of the meetings of the same society, he
made :

Hits	Score	Hits	Score	Hits	Score		Hits	Score
52	198	41	209	24	114	=	117	521

Again, in private practice, he made on April 11, 1884 ·

· Hits	Score	Hits	Score	Hits	Score		Hits	Score
38	174	43	215	23	123	=	104	512

On September 23, 1886, *Mr. F. L. Govett* (Royal Toxophilite Society) scored in private practice :

Hits	Score	Hits	Score	Hits	Score		Hits	Score
47	227	40	176	24	130	=	111	533

Mr. F. Townsend's (Woodman of Arden) best York Round
score appears to be as follows ·

Hits	Score	Hits	Score	Hits	Score		Hits	Score
49	237	33	177	22	102	=	104	516

made on December 27, 1862.

He seldom practised the York Round, and never allowed
his archery practice to interfere with his other numerous
avocations.

Mr. W. Spottiswoode, P.R.S. (Royal Toxophilite Society), has another good score on the Society's books :

Hits	Score	Hits	Score	Hits	Score		Hits	Score
50	194	38	194	22	124	−	110	512

made on May 30, 1867.

Captain A. P. Moore, who made the highest score in 1849, at Derby, when Mr. H. A. Ford was first champion, reports that his best score in a single York Round was in private practice ·

Hits	Score	Hits	Score	Hits	Score		Hits	Score
65	309	44	230	24	152	=	133	691

and that he has made 316 score with 56 hits and 304 score with 64 hits in the 72 arrows at 100 yards.

His best performance at 80 yards was 254 score with 44 hits in the 48 shots, and at 60 yards his best score was 164 with the 24 hits. His best double York Round was 1288 with 252 hits, mentioned by Mr. H. A. Ford. In the month of March 1852 he shot 14 rounds, and their average was· 557 score with 115 hits.

Two very good records of *Mr. Charles Garnett's* (Royal Toxophilite Society) shooting at 100 yards are ·

Hits	Score		Hits	Score
58	288	and	61	269

72 arrows being shot on each occasion.

He says : ' I shot a distance of 304 yards on a calm day with an 85-lb. bow and four-and-ninepenny 28-inch arrow. I could not get a flight-arrow to stand the bow, or I should probably have shot further, as the four-and-ninepenny arrow was one of the old pattern and heavily feathered.'

Captain C. H. Garnett's (John o' Gaunt Bowmen) best score in the York Round amounted to 522, but he has been unable to find a record of the details. The following is another good score made by him on November 17, 1873 :

Hits	Score	Hits	Score	Hits	Score		Hits	Score
48	202	34	182	23	127	=	105	511

In October of the same year, in 72 arrows at 100 yards he made 48 hits 220 score, and made 3 golds in one end.

He reports that his father, Mr. H. Garnett, shooting with the John o' Gaunt Bowmen on one occasion, scored 500 in the York Round.

Another John o' Gaunt Bowman, *Mr. B. P. Gregson*, has scored as much as 497 in the York Round.

A good St. George's Round (of 36 arrows at each distance) made by *Mr. Marr* is :

100 Yards		80 Yards		60 Yards		TOTALS		
Hits	Score	Hits	Score	Hits	Score		Hits	Score
24	114	32	118	35	181	−	101	413

another by *Mr. Heath* :

100 Yards		80 Yards		60 Yards		TOTALS		
Hits	Score	Hits	Score	Hits	Score		Hits	Score
25	89	31	139	35	203	=	91	431

A good St. George's Round made by *Mr. E. Maitland* (Champion in 1848, Royal Toxophilite Society) is :

100 Yards		80 Yards		60 Yards		TOTALS		
Hits	Score	Hits	Score	Hits	Score		Hits	Score
25	97	34	190	36	196	=	95	483

and he says: ' I tried hard to catch up Mr. H. A. Ford on my return to England from Australia in 1858 but had scarcely got within 25 per cent. of his scores when I broke down from overwork—bows too strong, and practice too unremitting.   He said if I did not beat him, there was no one else in the field to do it.   I don't think I ever should, because I had not his indomitable steadiness and threw away many a shot on a chance : for I was a rapid shooter.   I never dwelt on the aim as he did.'

Mr. T. L. Coulson (Royal Toxophilite Society) recorded his first score of 500 on the single York Round on May 1, 1861, on November 18, 1862 :

Hits	Score	Hits	Score	Hits	Score	Hits	Score
	228	−	207	−	130	105	565

and on October 21, 1865 :

Hits	Score	Hits	Score	Hits	Score		Hits	Score
56	224	44	198	24	136	=	124	558

On January 13, 1869, he made 3 golds in one end at 100 yards.

Mr. J. A. Froude (Royal Toxophilite Society) says : ' I did once make [a score of] over 500 [in the single York Round] in a private match ; but only once, and the record of it has long vanished.   Richardson and Spedding were both shooting on that occasion, and I, for a miracle, in that single instance beat Richardson.'   This probably happened about 1860.

It is generally believed that the private practice of *Mr. G. Edwards* (Champion in 1860-1-2-4-6) was far beyond his public shooting.   He has been heard to say that, though Mr. Ford had been able to land only 71 of the 72 arrows shot at 100 yards in the target (missing his 59th arrow), he (Mr G. E.) had put all his 72 arrows into the target at the same distance.   There is no reason to disbelieve his positive state ment that on one occasion, shooting 24 arrows at 60 yards, he put every one of them in the red circle.

' Some of the scores made by *Mr. Edward Mason* in private practice were very large, and it is to be regretted that no actual details can be given.   It is well known, however, that on several occasions he made a score of over 1000 on the double York Round, and were the figures available they could not fail to be of wide interest' ('Archers' Register,' 1882-3).

Mr. Peter Muir (Champion 1845-7 and 1863) was a most successful shot at all distances, short as well as long, but probably seldom, if ever, practised the York Round.   Mr H. A. Ford gives as his best score the following, made at the distance of from 20 to 30 yards, 2 shots, 2 hits—a hawk and a crow (fact).

Mr. E. Meyrick says : ' It is true that I have seen *Escott* hurl his eight-shilling arrows from a bow of 80 lbs. and ten-shilling arrows from a 100-lb. bow, but then he could not do much hitting.   I should think something authentic must exist of my old friend *Marsh's* long shot of 360 yards up and down. He would hit half his arrows at 100 yards very often,' as may be seen from the extracts given from his actual scores.

A point of interest in *Mr. W. Butt's* (Royal Toxophilite Society) shooting is, that he shot with both hands, though only on one occasion did he shoot two rounds on the same day, one with each hand. This was at a West Berks meeting at Coombe Wood, Surrey (Sir W. Baynes), as follows :

Hits	Score	Hits	Score	Hits	Score		Hits	Score	
34	134	28	122	21	105	–	83	361	Right-handed
16	68	23	77	21	95	=	60	240	Left-handed

His best right-handed shooting was as follows ·

80 Yards		60 Yards	
Hits	Score	Hits	Score
43	215	24	158

shot on October 3 1863 ; and on October 9 1863, in 110 arrows at 60 yards :

Hits	Score	G.	R.	B.	Bk.	W.
110	640	19	32	39	15	5

On February 8, 1864, in a York Round ·

Hits	Score	Hits	Score	Hits	Score		Hits	Score
48	216	42	172	23	113	=	113	501

and on March 12, 1864, at 80 yards 41 hits 207 score in the 48 arrows.

Shooting left-handed, his best scores in the books of the Royal Toxophilite Society are 47 hits 201 score, in 72 arrows at 100 yards, on the first half of the shooting on the Crunden Day on April 18, 1867 ; and on May 30 in the same year in the York Round :

Hits	Score	Hits	Score	Hits	Score		Hits	Score
44	206	36	154	24	138	=	104	498

and on October 5 1876, at 60 yards, 24 hits with 160 score— ' record ' for 60 yards shooting in the York Round at the meetings of the Royal Toxophilite Society.

Mr. Macnamara made good scores at the public meetings, but it is believed that his shooting in private practice was of infinitely higher quality. He took to shooting left-handed afterwards, but without much success in public.

Mr. G. L. Aston also has been at different periods a successful shot, both right-handed and left-handed, at the public meetings.

About thirty years ago *Mr. Aubrey Patton* shot so well that Mr. H. A. Ford took the trouble to explain in the pages of the *Field* that he had not yet been beaten by him; but Mr. Patton's regimental duties took him out of reach of more archery practice.

Mr. E. Sharpe (John o' Gaunt Bowmen) made

Hits	Score	Hits	Score	Hits	Score		Hits	Score
48	240	36	164	22	112	=	106	516

in private practice October 2, 1886.

No attempt has yet been made to collect the records of the many excellent scores that have been made by numerous ladies in club matches, or in private practice; but it is believed that, owing to the ladies' shooting at the public meetings being more like their club and private practice, in that it occupies an afternoon only, and is not spun out all over the day, as is the case with the gentlemen, the ladies' public shooting more fairly represents the best they can do; yet many ladies have scored over 400 in the half of the National Round who have not yet approached the 800 which both Mrs. and Miss Legh have shown to be attainable at a public meeting in the National Round. A few samples of their accuracy of aim can however be here given as specimens of what might be contributed to another edition of this book.

Mrs. Butt, shooting in private practice in the Jephson Gardens, at Leamington, on June 10, 1870, made

60 Yards		50 Yards		Totals	
Hits	Score	Hits	Score	Hits	Score
48	280	24	168	72	448

and, in the course of this score at 50 yards, made 6 consecutive golds in one double end.

Miss Ripley (now Mrs. Bradford), shooting at a Prize Meeting of the Torbay Archers, on August 5, 1871, is reported to have scored

60 Yards		50 Yards		Totals	
Hits	Score	Hits	Score	Hits	Score
46	292	24	170	— 70	462

Mrs. Piers F. Legh, shooting at home on September 9, 1881, scored

60 Yards		50 Yards		Totals	
Hits	Score	Hits	Score	Hits	Score
48	316	24	162	⇒ 72	478

Doubtless many other archers have already made noteworthy scores in the course of their private practice. These scores and the many others hereafter to be made, as much as possible better than any herein given, the editor (with Mr. H. A. Ford's adieu of ' Farewell and shoot well ') will gladly record in the fourth edition.

PRINTED BY
SPOTTISWOODE AND CO., NEW-STREET SQUARE
LONDON

A Classified Catalogue
OF WORKS IN
GENERAL LITERATUR
PUBLISHED BY
LONGMANS, GREEN, & CO.
39 PATERNOSTER ROW, LONDON, E.C.
91 AND 93 FIFTH AVENUE, NEW YORK, AND 32 HORNBY ROAD, BOM

CONTENTS.

INDEX OF AUTHORS AND EDITORS.

History, Politics, Polity, Political Memoirs, &c.

Abbott.—*A History of Greece.* By Evelyn Abbott, M.A., LL.D.

Part I.—From the Earliest Times to the Ionian Revolt. Crown 8vo., 10s. 6d.

Part II.—500-445 B.C. Crown 8vo., 10s. 6d.

Part III.—From the Peace of 445 B.C. to the Fall of the Thirty at Athens in 403 B.C. Crown 8vo., 10s. 6d.

Abbott.—*Tommy Cornstalk:* being Some Account of the Less Notable Features of the South African War from the Point of View of the Australian Ranks. By J. H. M. Abbott. Crown 8vo., 5s. net.

Acland and Ransome.—*A Handbook in Outline of the Political History of England to* 1896. Chronologically Arranged. By the Right Hon. A. H. Dyke Acland, and Cyril Ransome, M.A. Crown 8vo., 6s.

Allgood. — *China War,* 1860: *Letters and Journals.* By Major-General G. Allgood, C.B., formerly Lieut. G. Allgood, 1st Division China Field Force. With Maps, Plans, and Illustrations. Demy 4to. 12s. 6d. net.

Annual Register (The). A Review of Public Events at Home and Abroad, for the year 1902. 8vo., 18s.

Volumes of the *Annual Register* for the years 1863-1901 can still be had. 18s. each.

Arnold.—*Introductory Lectures on Modern History.* By Thomas Arnold, D.D., formerly Head Master of Rugby School. 8vo., 7s. 6d.

Ashbourne.—*Pitt: Some Chapters on His Life and Times.* By the Right Hon. Edward Gibson, Lord Ashbourne, Lord Chancellor of Ireland. With 11 Portraits. 8vo., gilt top, 21s.

Ashley (W. J.)

English Economic History and Theory. Crown 8vo., Part I., 5s. Part II., 10s. 6d.

Surveys, Historic and Economic. Crown 8vo., 9s. net.

Bagwell.—*Ireland under the Tudors.* By Richard Bagwell, LL.D. (3 vols.) Vols. I. and II. From the first invasion of the Northmen to the year 1578. 8vo., 32s. Vol. III. 1578-1603. 8vo., 18s.

Baillie.—*The Oriental Club,* Hanover Square. By Alexande Baillie. With 6 Photogravure Por and 8 Full-page Illustrations. Crown 25s. net.

Besant.—*The History of Lon* By Sir Walter Besant. With 74 trations. Crown 8vo., 1s. 9d. Or b as a School Prize Book, gilt edges, 2s.

Bright.—*A History of Engl* By the Rev. J. Franck Bright, D.D.

Period I. *Mediæval Monarchy:* 449-1485. Crown 8vo., 4s. 6d.

Period II. *Personal Monarchy.* 1688. Crown 8vo., 5s.

Period III. *Constitutional Monar* 1689-1837. Crown 8vo., 7s. 6d.

Period IV. *The Growth of Democ* 1837-1880. Crown 8vo., 6s.

Bruce.—*The Forward Policy its Results;* or, Thirty-five Years' amongst the Tribes on our North-We Frontier of India. By Richard Bruce, C.I.E. With 28 Illustrations a Map. 8vo., 15s. net.

Buckle.—*History of Civilisa in England.* By Henry Thomas Buc

Cabinet Edition. 3 vols. Crown 8vo.,

'*Silver Library*' *Edition.* 3 vols. C 8vo., 10s. 6d.

Burke. — *A History of Sp from the Earliest Times to Death of Ferdinand the Cath* By Ulick Ralph Burke, M.A. E by Martin A. S. Hume. With 6 2 vols. Crown 8vo., 16s. net.

Caroline, Queen.—*Caroline Illustrious, Queen-Consort of Ge II. and Sometime Queen Regen* Study of Her Life and Time. By W Wilkins, M.A., F.S.A., Author of ' Love of an Uncrowned Queen'. 2 8vo., 36s.

Casserly. — *The Land of Boxers;* or, China under the Allies. Captain Gordon Casserly. With Illustrations and a Plan. 8vo., 10s. 6d.

Chesney.—*Indian Polity:* a Vie the System of Administration in India. General Sir George Chesney, K. With Map showing all the Administr Divisions of British India. 8vo., 21s.

History, Politics, Polity, Political Memoirs, &c.—*contin.*

Churchill (Winston Spencer, M.P.).

The River War: an Historical Account of the Reconquest of the Soudan. Edited by Colonel F. Rhodes, D.S.O. With Photogravure Portrait of Viscount Kitchener of Khartoum, and 22 Maps and Plans. 8vo., 10s. 6d. net.

The Story of the Malakand Field Force, 1897. With 6 Maps and Plans. Crown 8vo., 3s. 6d.

London to Ladysmith viâ Pretoria. Crown 8vo., 6s.

Ian Hamilton's March. With Portrait of Major-General Sir Ian Hamilton, and 10 Maps and Plans. Crown 8vo., 6s.

Corbett (Julian S.).

Drake and the Tudor Navy, with a History of the Rise of England as a Maritime Power. With Portraits, Illustrations and Maps. 2 vols. Crown 8vo., 16s.

The Successors of Drake. With 4 Portraits (2 Photogravures) and 12 Maps and Plans. 8vo., 21s.

Creighton (M., D.D., Late Lord Bishop of London).

A History of the Papacy from the Great Schism to the Sack of Rome, 1378-1527. 6 vols. Cr. 8vo., 5s. net each.

Queen Elizabeth. With Portrait. Crown 8vo., 5s. net.

Historical Essays and Reviews. Edited by Louise Creighton. Crown 8vo., 5s. net.

Dale.—*The Principles of English Constitutional History.* By Lucy Dale, late Scholar of Somerville College, Oxford. Crown 8vo., 6s.

De Tocqueville.—*Democracy in America.* By Alexis de Tocqueville. Translated by Henry Reeve, C.B., D.C.L. 2 vols. Crown 8vo., 16s.

Falkiner.—*Studies in Irish History and Biography*, Mainly of the Eighteenth Century. By C. Litton Falkiner. 8vo., 12s. 6d. net.

Fitzmaurice. — *Charles Will Ferdinand, Duke of Brunswick* Historical Study. By Lord Ed Fitzmaurice. With Map and 2 Port 8vo., 6s. net.

Fuller.—*Egypt and the Hin Land.* By Frederic W. Fuller. Frontispiece and Map of Egypt and Sudan. Crown 8vo., 6s. net.

History, Politics, Polity, Political Memoirs, &c.—*continu*

Gardiner (SAMUEL RAWSON, D.C.L., LL.D.)—*continued.*

A HISTORY OF THE COMMONWEALTH AND THE PROTECTORATE. 1649-1656. 4 vols. Crown 8vo., 5s. net each.

THE STUDENT'S HISTORY OF ENG-LAND. With 378 Illustrations. Crown 8vo., gilt top, 12s.

Also in Three Volumes, price 4s. each.

WHAT GUNPOWDER PLOT WAS. With 8 Illustrations. Crown 8vo., 5s.

CROMWELL'S PLACE IN HISTORY. Founded on Six Lectures delivered in the University of Oxford. Cr. 8vo., 3s. 6d.

OLIVER CROMWELL. With Frontis-piece. Crown 8vo., 5s. net.

German Empire (The) of To-day : Outlines of its Formation and Development. By 'VERITAS'. Crown 8vo., 6s. net.

Graham.—*ROMAN AFRICA :* an Out-line of the History of the Roman Occupa-tion of North Africa, based chiefly upon Inscriptions and Monumental Remains in that Country. By ALEXANDER GRAHAM, F.S.A., F.R.I.B.A. With 30 reproductions of Original Drawings by the Author, and 2 Maps. 8vo., 16s. net.

Greville.—*A JOURNAL OF THE REIGNS OF KING GEORGE IV., KING WILLIAM IV., AND QUEEN VICTORIA.* By CHARLES C. F. GREVILLE, formerly Clerk of the Council. 8 vols. Crown 8vo., 3s. 6d. each.

Gross.—*THE SOURCES AND LITERA-TURE OF ENGLISH HISTORY, FROM THE EARLIEST TIMES TO ABOUT 1485.* By CHARLES GROSS, Ph.D. 8vo., 18s. net.

Hamilton.—*HISTORICAL RECORD OF THE 14TH (KING'S) HUSSARS,* from A.D. 1715 to A.D. 1900. By Colonel HENRY BLACK-BURNE HAMILTON, M.A., Christ Church, Oxford ; late Commanding the Regiment. With 15 Coloured Plates, 35 Portraits, etc., in Photogravure, and 10 Maps and Plans. Crown 4to., gilt edges, 42s. net.

Hill.—*LIBERTY DOCUMENTS.* With Contemporary Exposition and Critical Com-ments drawn from various Writers. Selected and Prepared by MABEL HILL. Edited with an Introduction byALBERT BUSHNELL HART, Ph.D. Large Crown 8vo., 7s. 6d. net.

HARVARD HISTORICAL STUDIE

THE SUPPRESSION OF THE AFRI SLAVE TRADE TO THE UNITED STATE AMERICA, 1638-1870. By W. E. B. BOIS, Ph.D. 8vo., 7s. 6d.

THE CONTEST OVER THE RATIFICA OF THE FEDERAL CONSTITUTION IN MA CHUSETTS. By S. B. HARDING,A.M. 8vc

A CRITICAL STUDY OF NULLIFICA IN SOUTH CAROLINA. By D. F. HOUS A.M. 8vo., 6s.

NOMINATIONS FOR ELECTIVE OF IN THE UNITED STATES. By FREDE W. DALLINGER, A.M. 8vo., 7s. 6d.

A BIBLIOGRAPHY OF BRITISH M CIPAL HISTORY, INCLUDING GILDS PARLIAMENTARY REPRESENTATION. CHARLES GROSS, Ph.D. 8vo., 12s.

THE LIBERTY AND FREE SOIL PAR IN THE NORTH WEST. By THEODOR SMITH, Ph.D. 8vo, 7s. 6d.

THE PROVINCIAL GOVERNOR IN ENGLISH COLONIES OF NORTH AME By EVARTS BOUTELL GREENE. 8vo., 7s

THE COUNTY PALATINE OF DURH a Study in Constitutional History. By G LARD THOMAS LAPSLEY, Ph.D. 8vo., 10s

THE ANGLICAN EPISCOPATE AND AMERICAN COLONIES. By ARTHUR CROSS, Ph.D., Instructor in History ir University of Michigan. 8vo., 10s. 6d,

History, Politics, Polity, Political Memoirs, &c.—*continu*

Hunter (Sir WILLIAM WILSON).

A HISTORY OF BRITISH INDIA.
Vol. I.—Introductory to the Overthrow of the English in the Spice Archipelago, 1623. With 4 Maps. 8vo., 18s. Vol. II.—To the Union of the Old and New Companies under the Earl of Godolphin's Award, 1708. 8vo., 16s.

THE INDIA OF THE QUEEN, and other Essays. Edited by Lady HUNTER. With an Introduction by FRANCIS HENRY SKRINE, Indian Civil Service (Retired). 8vo., 9s. net.

Ingram.—*A CRITICAL EXAMINATION OF IRISH HISTORY.* From the Elizabethan Conquest to the Legislative Union of 1800. By T. DUNBAR INGRAM, LL.D. 2 vols. 8vo., 24s.

Joyce.—*A SHORT HISTORY OF IRELAND*, from the Earliest Times to 1603. By P. W. JOYCE, LL.D. Crown 8vo., 10s. 6d.

Kaye and Malleson.—*HISTORY OF THE INDIAN MUTINY*, 1857-1858. By Sir JOHN W. KAYE and Colonel G. B. MALLESON. With Analytical Index and Maps and Plans. 6 vols. Crown 8vo., 3s. 6d. each.

Lang (ANDREW).

THE MYSTERY OF MARY STUART. With 6 Photogravure Plates (4 Portraits) and 15 other Illustrations. 8vo., 18s. net.

JAMES THE SIXTH AND THE GOWRIE MYSTERY. With Gowrie's Coat of Arms in colour, 2 Photogravure Portraits and other Illustrations. 8vo., 12s. 6d. net.

PRINCE CHARLES EDWARD STUART, THE YOUNG CHEVALIER. With Photogravure Frontispiece. Cr. 8vo., 7s. 6d. net.

Laurie.—*HISTORICAL SURVEY OF PRE-CHRISTIAN EDUCATION.* By S. S. LAURIE, A.M., LL.D. Crown 8vo., 7s. 6d.

Lecky (The Rt. Hon. WILLIAM E. H.)

HISTORY OF ENGLAND IN THE EIGHTEENTH CENTURY.

Library Edition. 8 vols. 8vo. Vols. I. and II., 1700-1760, 36s.; Vols. III. and IV., 1760-1784, 36s.; Vols. V. and VI., 1784-1793, 36s.; Vols. VII. and VIII., 1793-1800, 36s.

Cabinet Edition. ENGLAND. 7 vols. Crown 8vo., 5s. net each. IRELAND. 5 vols. Crown 8vo., 5s. net each.

Lecky (The Rt. Hon. WILLIAM E. —*continued.*

LEADERS OF PUBLIC OPINION IRELAND: FLOOD—GRATTAN—O' NELL. 2 vols. 8vo., 25s. net.

HISTORY OF EUROPEAN MOR FROM AUGUSTUS TO CHARLEMAGN. vols. Crown 8vo., 10s. net.

A SURVEY OF ENGLISH ETH Being the First Chapter of the 'Hi of European Morals'. Edited, Introduction and Notes, by W. A. H Crown 8vo., 3s. 6d.

HISTORY OF THE RISE AND IN. ENCE OF THE SPIRIT OF RATIONALIS EUROPE. 2 vols. Crown 8vo., 10s.

DEMOCRACY AND LIBERTY.
Library Edition. 2 vols. 8vo., 36s. Cabinet Edition. 2 vols. Cr. 8vo., 10s

Lieven.—*LETTERS OF DOROTH PRINCESS LIEVEN, DURING HER RESID IN LONDON*, 1812-1834. Edited by LIC G. ROBINSON. With 2 Photogravure traits. 8vo., 14s. net.

Lowell.—*GOVERNMENTS AND I TIES IN CONTINENTAL EUROPE.* B LAWRENCE LOWELL. 2 vols. 8vo.,

Lumsden's Horse, Records o Edited by H. H. S. PEARSE. With a I and numerous Portraits and Illustratio the Text. 4to., 21s. net.

Lynch.—*THE WAR OF THE CIV SATIONS: BEING A RECORD OF ' A FOR. DEVIL'S' EXPERIENCES WITH THE AL IN CHINA.* By GEORGE LYNCH, Sp Correspondent of the 'Sphere,' etc. Portrait and 21 Illustrations. Crown 6s. net.

Macaulay (Lord).

THE LIFE AND WORKS OF L MACAULAY.
'Edinburgh' Edition. 10 vols. 8vo.,6s.e
Vols. I.-IV. HISTORY OF ENGLANL
Vols. V.-VII. ESSAYS, BIOGRAPL INDIAN PENAL CODE, CONTRIBUT TO KNIGHT'S 'QUARTERLY MAGAZ.
Vol. VIII. SPEECHES, LAYS OF ANC ROME, MISCELLANEOUS POEMS.
Vols. IX. and X. THE LIFE LETTERS OF LORD MACAULAY. Sir G. O. TREVELYAN, Bart.

Macaulay (Lord)—*continued.*

THE WORKS.

'Albany' Edition. With 12 Portraits. 12 vols. Large Crown 8vo., 3s. 6d. each.

Vols. I.-VI. HISTORY OF ENGLAND, FROM THE ACCESSION OF JAMES THE SECOND.

Vols. VII.-X. ESSAYS AND BIOGRAPHIES.

Vols. XI.-XII. SPEECHES, LAYS OF ANCIENT ROME, ETC., AND INDEX.

Cabinet Edition. 16 vols. Post 8vo., £4 16s.

Library Edition. 5 vols. 8vo., £4.

HISTORY OF ENGLAND FROM THE ACCESSION OF JAMES THE SECOND.

Popular Edition. 2 vols. Cr. 8vo., 5s.
Student's Edition. 2 vols. Cr. 8vo., 12s.
People's Edition. 4 vols. Cr. 8vo., 16s.
'Albany' Edition. With 6 Portraits. 6 vols. Large Crown 8vo., 3s. 6d. each.
Cabinet Edition. 8 vols. Post 8vo., 48s.
'Edinburgh' Edition. 4 vols. 8vo., 6s. each.

CRITICAL AND HISTORICAL ESSAYS, WITH LAYS OF ANCIENT ROME, etc., in 1 volume.

Popular Edition. Crown 8vo., 2s. 6d.
'Silver Library' Edition. With Portrait and 4 Illustrations to the 'Lays'. Cr. 8vo., 3s. 6d.

CRITICAL AND HISTORICAL ESSAYS.

Student's Edition. 1 vol. Cr. 8vo., 6s.
'Trevelyan' Edition. 2 vols. Cr. 8vo., 9s.
Cabinet Edition. 4 vols. Post 8vo., 24s.
'Edinburgh' Edition. 3 vols. 8vo., 6s. each.
Library Edition. 3 vols. 8vo., 36s.

ESSAYS, which may be had separately, sewed, 6d. each ; cloth, 1s. each.

Addison and Walpole.	Frederick the Great.
Croker's Boswell's Johnson.	Ranke and Gladstone.
Hallam's Constitutional History.	Lord Bacon.
	Lord Clive.
Warren Hastings.	Lord Byron, and The
The Earl of Chatham (Two Essays).	Comic Dramatists of the Restoration.

MISCELLANEOUS WRITINGS, SPEECHES AND POEMS.
Popular Edition. Crown 8vo., 2s. 6d.
Cabinet Edition. 4 vols. Post 8vo., 24s.

SELECTIONS FROM THE WRITINGS OF LORD MACAULAY. Edited, with Occasional Notes, by the Right Hon. Sir G. O. TREVELYAN, Bart. Crown 8vo., 6s.

Mackinnon (JAMES, Ph.D.).

THE HISTORY OF EDWARD THIRD. 8vo., 18s.

THE GROWTH AND DECLINE OF T FRENCH MONARCHY. 8vo., 21s. net.

Mallet.—MALLET DU PAN AND T FRENCH REVOLUTION. By BERNA MALLET. With Photogravure Portra 8vo., 12s. 6d. net.

May.—THE CONSTITUTIONAL HI TORY OF ENGLAND since the Accessi of George III. 1760-1870. By Sir THOM ERSKINE MAY, K.C.B. (Lord Farnboroug 3 vols. Cr. 8vo., 18s.

Montague. — THE ELEMENTS ENGLISH CONSTITUTIONAL HISTORY. F. C. MONTAGUE, M.A. Crown 8vo., 3s.

Moran.—THE THEORY AND PRA TICE OF THE ENGLISH GOVERNMENT. THOMAS FRANCIS MORAN, Ph.D., Profess of History and Economics in Purdue U versity, U.S. Crown 8vo., 5s. net.

Nash.—THE GREAT FAMINE A ITS CAUSES. By VAUGHAN NASH. Wi 8 Illustrations from Photographs by t Author, and a Map of India showing t Famine Area. Crown 8vo., 6s.

Owens College Essays.—Edit by T. F. TOUT, M.A., Professor of Histo in the Owens College, Victoria Universit and JAMES TAIT, M.A., Assistant Lectur in History. With 4 Maps. 8vo., 12s. 6d. n

Pears.—THE DESTRUCTION OF T GREEK EMPIRE AND THE STORY OF T CAPTURE OF CONSTANTINOPLE BY T TURKS. By EDWIN PEARS, LL.B. Wi 3 Maps and 4 Illustrations. 8vo., 18s. n

History, Politics, Polity, Political Memoirs, &c.—*continu*

Powell and Trevelyan. — *The Peasants' Rising and the Lollards:* a Collection of Unpublished Documents. Edited by Edgar Powell and G. M. Trevelyan. 8vo., 6s. net.

Randolph.—*The Law and Policy of Annexation*, with Special Reference to the Philippines; together with Observations on the Status of Cuba. By Carman F. Randolph. 8vo., 9s. net.

Rankin (Reginald).

The Marquis d'Argenson; and Richard the Second. 8vo., 10s. 6d. net.

A Subaltern's Letters to His Wife. (The Boer War.) Crown 8vo., 3s. 6d.

Ransome.—*The Rise of Constitutional Government in England.* By Cyril Ransome, M.A. Crown 8vo., 6s.

Seebohm (Frederic, LL.D., F.S.A.).

The English Village Community. With 13 Maps and Plates. 8vo., 16s.

Tribal Custom in Anglo-Saxon Law: being an Essay supplemental to (1) 'The English Village Community,' (2) 'The Tribal System in Wales'. 8vo., 16s.

Seton-Karr.—*The Call to Arms,* 1900-1901; or a Review of the Imperial Yeomanry Movement, and some subjects connected therewith. By Sir Henry Seton-Karr, M.P. With a Frontispiece by R. Caton-Woodville. Crown 8vo., 5s. net.

Shaw.—*A History of the English Church during the Civil Wars and under the Commonwealth*, 1640-1660. By William A. Shaw, Litt.D. 2 vols. 8vo., 36s.

Sheppard. — *The Old Royal Palace of Whitehall.* By Edgar Sheppard, D.D., Sub-Dean of H.M. Chapels Royal, Sub-Almoner to the King. With 6 Photogravure Plates and 33 other Illustrations. Medium 8vo., 21s. net.

Smith.—*Carthage and the Carthaginians.* By R. Bosworth Smith, M.A. With Maps, Plans, etc. Cr. 8vo., 3s. 6d.

Stephens. — *A History of the French Revolution.* By H. Morse Stephens. 8vo. Vols. I. and II. 18s. each.

Sternberg. — *My Experiences the Boer War.* By Adalbert C Sternberg. With Preface by Lieut. G. F. R. Henderson. Crown 8vo., 5s.

Stubbs.—*History of the Uni sity of Dublin.* By J. W. Stubbs. 12s. 6d.

Stubbs. — *Historical Introi tions to the 'Rolls Series'.* William Stubbs, D.D., formerly Bi of Oxford, Regius Professor of Mo History in the University. Collected Edited by Arthur Hassall, M.A. 12s. 6d. net.

Biography, Personal Memoirs, &c.

Bacon.—*THE LETTERS AND LIFE OF FRANCIS BACON, INCLUDING ALL HIS OCCASIONAL WORKS.* Edited by JAMES SPEDDING. 7 vols. 8vo., £4 4s.

Bagehot.—*BIOGRAPHICAL STUDIES.* By WALTER BAGEHOT. Crown 8vo., 3s. 6d.

Blount. — *THE MEMOIRS OF SIR EDWARD BLOUNT, K.C.B., ETC.* Edited by STUART J. REID, Author of 'The Life and Times of Sydney Smith,' etc. With 3 Photogravure Plates. 8vo., 10s. 6d. net.

Bowen.—*EDWARD BOWEN: A MEMOIR.* By the Rev. the Hon. W. E. BOWEN. With Appendices, 3 Photogravure Portraits and 2 other Illustrations. 8vo., 12s. 6d. net.

Carlyle.—*THOMAS CARLYLE: A History of his Life.* By JAMES ANTHONY FROUDE.

1795-1835. 2 vols. Crown 8vo., 7s.
1834-1881. 2 vols. Crown 8vo., 7s.

Crozier.—*MY INNER LIFE:* being a Chapter in Personal Evolution and Autobiography. By JOHN BEATTIE CROZIER, LL.D. 8vo., 14s.

Dante.—*THE LIFE AND WORKS OF DANTE ALLIGHIERI:* being an Introduction to the Study of the 'Divina Commedia'. By the Rev. J. F. HOGAN, D.D. With Portrait. 8vo., 12s. 6d.

Danton.—*LIFE OF DANTON.* By A. H. BEESLY. With Portraits. Cr. 8vo., 6s.

De Bode.— *THE BARONESS DE BODE,* 1775-1803. By WILLIAM S. CHILDE-PEMBERTON. With 4 Photogravure Portraits and other Illustrations. 8vo., gilt top, 12s. 6d. net.

Erasmus.

LIFE AND LETTERS OF ERASMUS. By JAMES ANTHONY FROUDE. Crown 8vo., 3s. 6d.

THE EPISTLES OF ERASMUS, from his Earliest Letters to his Fifty-first Year, arranged in Order of Time. English Translations, with a Commentary. By FRANCIS MORGAN NICHOLS. 8vo., 18s. net.

Faraday.—*FARADAY AS A DISCOVERER.* By JOHN TYNDALL. Crown 8vo., 3s. 6d.

Fénelon : his Friends and his Enemies, 1651-1715. By E. K. SANDERS. With Portrait. 8vo., 10s. 6d.

Fox. — *THE EARLY HISTORY CHARLES JAMES FOX.* By the Right Sir G. O. TREVELYAN, Bart. Crown 3s. 6d.

Granville.—*SOME RECORDS OF LATER LIFE OF HARRIET, COUN GRANVILLE.* By her Granddaughter, Hon. Mrs. OLDFIELD. With 17 Port 8vo., gilt top, 16s. net.

Grey. — *MEMOIR OF SIR GEO GREY, BART, G.C.B.,* 1799-1882. MANDELL CREIGHTON, D.D., late Bishop of London. With 3 Port Crown 8vo., 6s. net.

Hamilton.—*LIFE OF SIR WILL HAMILTON.* By R. P. GRAVES. 8vo. 3 15s. each. ADDENDUM. 8vo., 6d. sew

Harrow School Register (T 1801-1900. Second Edition, 1901. E by M. G. DAUGLISH, Barrister-at- 8vo. 10s. net.

Havelock.—*MEMOIRS OF SIR HE HAVELOCK, K.C.B.* By JOHN C MARSHMAN. Crown 8vo., 3s. 6d.

Haweis.—*MY MUSICAL LIFE.* By Rev. H. R. HAWEIS. With Portrait of Ric Wagner and 3 Illustrations. Cr. 8vo., 6s.

Higgins.—*THE BERNARDS OF AB TON AND NETHER WINCHENDON:* A Fa History. By Mrs. NAPIER HIGGINS Vols. 8vo., 21s. net.

Hunter.—*THE LIFE OF SIR WILL WILSON HUNTER, K.C.S.I., M.A., L* Author of 'A History of British India, By FRANCIS HENRY SKRINE, F.S.S. 6 Portraits (2 Photogravures) and 4 c Illustrations. 8vo., 16s. net.

Luther. — *LIFE OF LUTHER.* JULIUS KÖSTLIN. With 62 Illustrat and 4 Facsimilies of MSS. Cr. 8vo., 3s.

Biography, Personal Memoirs, &c.—*continued.*

Macaulay.—*THE LIFE AND LETTERS OF LORD MACAULAY.* By the Right Hon. Sir G. O. TREVELYAN, Bart.

Popular Edition. 1 vol. Cr. 8vo., 2s. 6d.
Student's Edition 1 vol. Cr. 8vo., 6s.
Cabinet Edition. 2 vols. Post 8vo., 12s.
'*Edinburgh' Edition.* 2 vols. 8vo.,6s. each.
Library Edition. 2 vols. 8vo., 36s.

Marbot. — *THE MEMOIRS OF THE BARON DE MARBOT.* 2 vols. Cr. 8vo., 7s.

Max Müller (F.)

THE LIFE AND LETTERS OF THE RIGHT HON. FRIEDRICH MAX MÜLLER. Edited by his Wife. With Photogravure Portraits and other Illustrations. 2 vols., 8vo., 32s. net.

MY AUTOBIOGRAPHY : a Fragment. With 6 Portraits. 8vo., 12s. 6d.

AULD LANG SYNE. Second Series. 8vo., 10s. 6d.

CHIPS FROM A GERMAN WORKSHOP. Vol. II. Biographical Essays. Cr. 8vo., 5s.

Meade.—*GENERAL SIR RICHARD MEADE AND THE FEUDATORY STATES OF CENTRAL AND SOUTHERN INDIA.* By THOMAS HENRY THORNTON. With Portrait, Map and Illustrations. 8vo., 10s. 6d. net.

Morris. — *THE LIFE OF WILLIAM MORRIS.* By J. W. MACKAIL. With 2 Portraits and 8 other Illustrations by E. H. NEW, etc. 2 vols. Large Crown 8vo., 10s. net.

On the Banks of the Seine. By A. M. F., Author of '*Foreign Courts and Foreign Homes'.* Crown 8vo., 6s.

Paget.—*MEMOIRS AND LETTERS OF SIR JAMES PAGET.* Edited by STEPHEN PAGET, one of his sons. With Portrait. 8vo., 6s. net.

Place.—*THE LIFE OF FRANCIS PLACE,* 1771-1854. By GRAHAM WALLAS, M.A. With 2 Portraits. 8vo., 12s.

Powys.—*PASSAGES FROM THE DIARIES OF MRS. PHILIP LYBBE POWYS, OF HARDWICK HOUSE, OXON.* 1756-1808. Edited by EMILY J. CLIMENSON. 8vo., gilt top, 16s.

Râmakrishna : *HIS LIFE AND SAYINGS.* By the Right Hon. F. MAX MÜLLER. Crown 8vo., 5s.

Rich.—*MARY RICH, COUNTESS OF WARWICK* (1625-1678): Her Family and Friends. By C. FELL SMITH. With 7 Photogravure Portraits and 9 other Illustrations. 8vo., gilt top, 18s. net.

Rochester, and other Lite Rakes of the Court of Charles II. some Account of their Surroundings the Author of 'The Life of Sir K Digby,' The Life of a Prig,' etc. W Portraits. 8vo., 16s.

Romanes.—*THE LIFE AND LET OF GEORGE JOHN ROMANES, M.A., I F.R.S.* Written and Edited by his With Portrait and 2 Illustrations. Cr 5s. net.

Russell. —*SWALLOWFIELD ANI OWNERS.* By CONSTANCE LADY RU: of Swallowfield Park. With 15 Photog Portraits and 36 other Illustrations. gilt edges, 42s. net.

Seebohm.—*THE OXFORD REFOR —JOHN COLET, ERASMUS, AND T: MORE :* a History of their Fellow- By FREDERIC SEEBOHM. 8vo., 14s.

Shakespeare. — *OUTLINES OF LIFE OF SHAKESPEARE.* By J. O. I WELL-PHILLIPPS. With Illustratior Facsimiles. 2 vols. Royal 8vo., 21s

Tales of my Father.—By A. } Crown 8vo., 6s.

Tallentyre.—*THE WOMEN OF SALONS,* and other French Portraits S. G. TALLENTYRE. With 11 Photog Portraits. 8vo., 10s. 6d. net.

Victoria, Queen, 1819-1901. RICHARD R. HOLMES, M.V.O., With Photogravure Portrait. Crow gilt top, 5s. net.

Walpole.—*SOME UNPUBLI. LETTERS OF HORACE WALPOLE.* by Sir SPENCER WALPOLE, K.C.B. 2 Portraits. Crown 8vo., 4s. 6d. net.

Wellington.—*LIFE OF THE OF WELLINGTON.* By the Rev. GLEIG, M.A. Crown 8vo., 3s. 6d.

Wilkins (W. H.).

CAROLINE THE ILLUSTRIOUS, Q CONSORT OF GEORGE II. AND SON QUEEN-REGENT : a Study of He and Time. 2 vols. 8vo., 36s.

THE LOVE OF AN UNCRO QUEEN : Sophie Dorothea, Cons George I., and her Correspondenc Philip Christopher, Count Königs With Portraits and Illustrations. 12s. 6d. net.

Travel and Adventure, the Colonies, &c.

Arnold.—*Seas and Lands.* By Sir EDWIN ARNOLD. With 71 Illustrations. Crown 8vo., 3s. 6d.

Baker (Sir S. W.).

Eight Years in Ceylon. With 6 Illustrations. Crown 8vo., 3s. 6d.

The Rifle and the Hound in Ceylon. With 6 Illusts. Cr. 8vo., 3s. 6d.

Ball (JOHN).

The Alpine Guide. Reconstructed and Revised on behalf of the Alpine Club, by W. A. B. COOLIDGE.

Vol. I., *The Western Alps*: the Alpine Region, South of the Rhone Valley, from the Col de Tenda to the Simplon Pass. With 9 New and Revised Maps. Crown 8vo., 12s. net.

Hints and Notes, Practical and Scientific, for Travellers in the Alps: being a Revision of the General Introduction to the 'Alpine Guide'. Crown 8vo., 3s. net.

Bent.—*The Ruined Cities of Mashonaland*: being a Record of Excavation and Exploration in 1891. By J. THEODORE BENT. With 117 Illustrations. Crown 8vo., 3s. 6d.

Brassey (The Late Lady).

A Voyage in the 'Sunbeam'; Our Home on the Ocean for Eleven Months.

Cabinet Edition. With Map and 66 Illustrations. Cr. 8vo., gilt edges, 7s. 6d.
'Silver Library' Edition. With 66 Illustrations. Crown 8vo., 3s. 6d.
Popular Edition. With 60 Illustrations. 4to., 6d. sewed, 1s. cloth.
School Edition. With 37 Illustrations. Fcp., 2s. cloth, or 3s. white parchment.

Sunshine and Storm in the East.

Popular Edition. With 103 Illustrations. 4to., 6d. sewed, 1s. cloth.

In the Trades, the Tropics, and the 'Roaring Forties'.

Cabinet Edition. With Map and 220 Illustrations. Cr. 8vo., gilt edges, 7s. 6d.

Cockerell.—*Travels in Southern Europe and the Levant*, 1810-1817. By C. R. COCKERELL, Architect, R.A. Edited by his Son, SAMUEL PEPYS COCKERELL. With Portrait. 8vo.

Fountain (PAUL).

The Great Deserts and Forests of North America. With a Preface by W. H. HUDSON, Author of 'The Naturalist in La Plata,' etc. 8vo., 9s. 6d. net.

The Great Mountains and Forests of South America. With Portrait and 7 Illustrations. 8vo., 10s. 6d. net.

Travel and Adventure, the Colonies, &c.—*continued.*

Knight (E. F.)—*continued.*

WHERE THREE EMPIRES MEET: a Narrative of Recent Travel in Kashmir, Western Tibet, Baltistan, Ladak, Gilgit, and the adjoining Countries. With a Map and 54 Illustrations. Cr. 8vo., 3s. 6d.

THE 'FALCON' ON THE BALTIC: a Voyage from London to Copenhagen in a Three-Tonner. With 10 Full-page Illustrations. Crown 8vo., 3s. 6d.

Lees.—*PEAKS AND PINES:* another Norway Book. By J. A. LEES. With 63 Illustrations and Photographs. Cr. 8vo., 6s.

Lees and Clutterbuck.—B.C. 1887: *A RAMBLE IN BRITISH COLUMBIA.* By J. A. LEES and W. J. CLUTTERBUCK. With Map and 75 Illustrations. Crown 8vo., 3s. 6d.

Lynch. — *ARMENIA :* Travels and Studies. By H. F. B. LYNCH. With 197 Illustrations (some in tints) reproduced from Photographs and Sketches by the Author, 16 Maps and Plans, a Bibliography, and a Map of Armenia and adjacent countries. 2 vols. Medium 8vo., gilt top, 42s. net.

Nansen.—*THE FIRST CROSSING OF GREENLAND.* By FRIDTJOF NANSEN. With 143 Illustrations and a Map. Crown 8vo., 3s. 6d.

Rice.—*OCCASIONAL ESSAYS ON TIVE SOUTH INDIAN LIFE.* By STA P. RICE, Indian Civil Service. 8vo., 1c

Smith.—*CLIMBING IN THE BRI ISLES.* By W. P. HASKETT SMITH. Illustrations and Numerous Plans.

Part I. *ENGLAND.* 16mo., 3s. net.

Part II. *WALES AND IRELAND.* 1 3s. net.

Spender.—*TWO WINTERS IN ₄ WAY:* being an Account of Two Hol spent on Snow-shoes and in Sleigh Dr₂ and including an Expedition to the L By A. EDMUND SPENDER. With 40 Ill tions from Photographs. 8vo., 10s. 6c

Stephen. — *THE PLAY-GROUNL EUROPE* (The Alps). By Sir L STEPHEN, K.C.B. With 4 Illustra Crown 8vo., 3s. 6d.

Three in Norway. By Tw Them. With a Map and 59 Illustra Crown 8vo., 2s. boards, 2s. 6d. cloth.

Tyndall.—(JOHN).

THE GLACIERS OF THE ALPS. ₄ 61 Illustrations. Crown 8vo., 6s. 6a

HOURS OF EXERCISE IN THE ₄ With 7 Illustrations. Cr. 8vo., 6s. 6a

Sport and Pastime.
THE BADMINTON LIBRARY.

Edited by HIS GRACE THE (EIGHTH) DUKE OF BEAUFORT, K.G., and A. E. T. WATSON.

ARCHERY. By C. J. LONGMAN and Col. H. WALROND. With Contributions by Miss LEGH, Viscount DILLON, etc. With 2 Maps, 23 Plates and 172 Illustrations in the Text. Crown 8vo., cloth, 6s. net; half-bound, with gilt top, 9s. net.

ATHLETICS. By MONTAGUE SHEARMAN. With Chapters on Athletics at School by W. BEACHER THOMAS; Athletic Sports in America by C. H. SHERRILL; a Contribution on Paper-chasing by W. RYE, and an Introduction by Sir RICHARD WEBSTER (Lord ALVERSTONE). With 12 Plates and 37 Illustrations in the Text. Cr. 8vo., cloth, 6s. net; half-bound, with gilt top, 9s. net.

BIG GAME SHOOTING. CLIVE PHILLIPPS-WOLLEY.

Vol. I. AFRICA AND AMEF With Contributions by Sir SAMUE BAKER, W. C. OSWELL, F. C. SE etc. With 20 Plates and 57 Illustra in the Text. Crown 8vo., cloth, 6s half-bound, with gilt top, 9s. net.

Vol. II. EUROPE, ASIA, AND ARCTIC REGIONS. With Con tions by Lieut.-Colonel R. H PERCY, Major ALGERNON C. H PERCY, etc. With 17 Plates and 56 trations in the Text. Crown 8vo., 6s. net; half-bound, with gilt top, 9

Sport and Pastime—*continued.*

THE BADMINTON LIBRARY—*continued.*

Edited by HIS GRACE THE (EIGHTH) DUKE OF BEAUFORT, K.G., and A. E. T. WATSON.

ILLIARDS. By Major W. BROAD-FOOT, R.E. With Contributions by A. H. BOYD, SYDENHAM DIXON, W. J. FORD, etc. With 11 Plates, 19 Illustrations in the Text, and numerous Diagrams. Crown 8vo., cloth, 6s. net; half-bound, with gilt top, 9s. net.

OURSING AND FALCONRY. By HARDING COX, CHARLES RICHARDSON, and the Hon. GERALD LASCELLES. With 20 Plates and 55 Illustrations in the Text. Crown 8vo., cloth, 6s. net; half-bound, with gilt top, 9s. net.

RICKET. By A. G. STEEL and the Hon. R. H. LYTTELTON. With Contributions by ANDREW LANG, W. G. GRACE, F. GALE, etc. With 13 Plates and 52 Illustrations in the Text. Crown 8vo., cloth, 6s. net; half-bound, with gilt top, 9s. net.

YCLING. By the EARL OF ALBEMARLE and G. LACY HILLIER. With 19 Plates and 44 Illustrations in the Text. Crown 8vo., cloth, 6s. net; half-bound, with gilt top, 9s. net.

DANCING. By Mrs. LILLY GROVE. With Contributions by Miss MIDDLETON, The Hon. Mrs. ARMYTAGE, etc. With Musical Examples, and 38 Full-page Plates and 93 Illustrations in the Text. Crown 8vo., cloth, 6s. net; half-bound, with gilt top, 9s. net.

DRIVING. By His Grace the (Eighth) DUKE of BEAUFORT, K.G. With Contributions by A. E. T. WATSON the EARL OF ONSLOW, etc. With 12 Plates and 54 Illustrations in the Text. Crown 8vo., cloth, 6s. net; half-bound, with gilt top, 9s. net.

FENCING, BOXING, AND WRESTLING. By WALTER H. POLLOCK, F. C. GROVE, C. PREVOST, E. B. MITCHELL, and WALTER ARMSTRONG. With 18 Plates and 24 Illustrations in the Text. Crown 8vo., cloth, 6s. net; half-bound, with gilt top, 9s. net.

GOLF. By HORACE G. HUTCHINSON. With Contributions by the Rt. Hon. A. J. BALFOUR, M.P., Sir WALTER SIMPSON, Bart., ANDREW LANG, etc. With 34 Plates and 56 Illustrations in the Text. Crown 8vo., cloth, 6s. net; half-bound, with gilt top, 9s. net.

HUNTING. By His Grace the (Eighth) DUKE OF BEAUFORT, K.G., and MOWBRAY MORRIS. With Contributions by the EARL OF SUFFOLK AND BERKSHIRE, Rev. E. W. L. DAVIES, G. H. LONGMAN, etc. With 5 Plates and 54 Illustrations in the Text. Crown 8vo., cloth, 6s. net; half-bound, with gilt top, 9s. net.

Sport and Pastime—*continued*.

THE BADMINTON LIBRARY—*continued*.

Edited by HIS GRACE THE (EIGHTH) DUKE OF BEAUFORT, K.G.,
and A. E. T. WATSON.

MOUNTAINEERING. By C. T. DENT. With Contributions by the Right Hon. J. BRYCE, M.P., Sir MARTIN CONWAY, D. W. FRESHFIELD, C. E. MATTHEWS, etc. With 13 Plates and 91 Illustrations in the Text. Crown 8vo., cloth, 6s. net; half-bound, with gilt top, 9s. net.

POETRY OF SPORT (THE).— Selected by HEDLEY PEEK. With a Chapter on Classical Allusions to Sport by ANDREW LANG, and a Special Preface to the BADMINTON LIBRARY by A. E. T. WATSON. With 32 Plates and 74 Illustrations in the Text. Crown 8vo., cloth, 6s. net; half-bound, with gilt top, 9s. net.

RACING AND STEEPLE-CHASING. By the EARL OF SUFFOLK AND BERKSHIRE, W. G. CRAVEN, the Hon. F. LAWLEY, ARTHUR COVENTRY, and A. E. T. WATSON. With Frontispiece and 56 Illustrations in the Text. Crown 8vo., cloth, 6s. net; half-bound, with gilt top, 9s. net.

RIDING AND POLO. By Captain ROBERT WEIR, J. MORAY BROWN, T. F. DALE, THE LATE DUKE OF BEAUFORT, THE EARL OF SUFFOLK AND BERKSHIRE, etc. With 18 Plates and 41 Illusts. in the Text. Crown 8vo., cloth, 6s. net; half-bound, with gilt top, 9s. net.

ROWING. By R. P. P. ROWE and C. M. PITMAN. With Chapters on Steering by C. P. SEROCOLD and F. C. BEGG; Metropolitan Rowing by S. LE BLANC SMITH; and on PUNTING by P. W. SQUIRE. With 75 Illustrations. Crown 8vo., cloth, 6s. net; half-bound, with gilt top, 9s. net.

SHOOTING.

Vol. I. FIELD AND COVERT. By LORD WALSINGHAM and Sir RALPH PAYNE-GALLWEY, Bart. With Contributions by the Hon. GERALD LASCELLES and A. J. STUART-WORTLEY. With 11 Plates and 95 Illustrations in the Text. Crown 8vo., cloth, 6s. net; half-bound, with gilt top, 9s. net.

Vol. II. MOOR AND MARSH. By LORD WALSINGHAM and Sir RALPH PAYNE-GALLWEY, Bart. With Contributions by LORD LOVAT and Lord CHARLES LENNOX KERR. With 8 Plates and 57 Illustrations in the Text. Crown 8vo., cloth, 6s. net; half-bound, with gilt top, 9s. net.

SEA FISHING. By JOHN BICK DYKE, Sir H. W. GORE-BOOTH, A C. HARMSWORTH, and W. SENIOR. W Full-page Plates and 175 Illusts. in the Crown 8vo., cloth, 6s. net; half-boun gilt top, 9s. net.

SKATING, CURLING, TO GANING. By J. M. HEATHCOTE, TEBBUTT, T. MAXWELL WITHAM, JOHN KERR, ORMOND HAKE, HEN BUCK, etc. With 12 Plates and 272 trations in the Text. Crown 8vo., clo net; half-bound, with gilt top, 9s. net

SWIMMING. By ARCHIBALD CLAIR and WILLIAM HENRY, Hon. Secs Life-Saving Society. With 13 Plates a Illustrations in the Text. Crown 8vo., 6s. net; half-bound, with gilt top, 9s.

TENNIS,   LAWN   TEN RACKETS AND FIVES. By J. M C. G. HEATHCOTE, E. O. PLEYDELL VERIE, and A. C. AINGER. With Contrib by the Hon. A. LYTTELTON, W. C. SHALL, Miss L. DOD, etc. With 14 Plat 65 Illustrations in the Text. Crown cloth, 6s. net; half-bound, with gil 9s. net.

YACHTING.

Vol. I. CRUISING, CONSTRUC OF YACHTS, YACHT RA RULES, FITTING-OUT, etc. I EDWARD SULLIVAN, Bart., THE EA PEMBROKE, LORD BRASSEY, K.C. E. SETH-SMITH, C.B., G. L. WATS T. PRITCHETT, E. F. KNIGHT, etc. 21 Plates and 93 Illustrations i Text. Crown 8vo., cloth, 6s. net; bound, with gilt top, 9s. net.

Vol. II. YACHT CLUBS, YA ING IN AMERICA AND COLONIES, YACHT RACING, By R. T. PRITCHETT, THE MARQU DUFFERIN AND AVA, K.P., THE EA ONSLOW, JAMES MCFERRAN, etc. 35 Plates and 160 Illustrations i Text. Crown 8vo., cloth, 9s. net; bound, with gilt top, 9s. net.

Sport and Pastime—*continued.*
FUR, FEATHER, AND FIN SERIES.
Edited by A. E. T. WATSON.
Crown 8vo., price 5s. each Volume, cloth.

₊ *The Volumes are also issued half-bound in Leather, with gilt top.* *Price 7s. 6d. net e*

THE PARTRIDGE. Natural History, by the Rev. H. A. MACPHERSON; Shooting, by A. J. STUART-WORTLEY; Cookery, by GEORGE SAINTSBURY. With 11 Illustrations and various Diagrams. Crown 8vo., 5s.

THE GROUSE. Natural History, by the Rev. H. A. MACPHERSON; Shooting, by A. J. STUART-WORTLEY; Cookery, by GEORGE SAINTSBURY. With 13 Illustrations and various Diagrams. Crown 8vo., 5s.

THE PHEASANT. Natural History, by the Rev. H. A. MACPHERSON; Shooting, by A. J. STUART-WORTLEY; Cookery, by ALEXANDER INNES SHAND. With 10 Illustrations and various Diagrams. Crown 8vo., 5s.

THE HARE. Natural History, by the Rev. H. A. MACPHERSON; Shooting, by the Hon. GERALD LASCELLES; Coursing, by CHARLES RICHARDSON; Hunting, by J. S. GIBBONS and G. H. LONGMAN; Cookery, by Col. KENNEY HERBERT. With 9 Illustrations. Crown 8vo., 5s.

RED DEER.—Natural History, the Rev. H. A. MACPHERSON; Deer S ing, by CAMERON OF LOCHIEL; Hunting, by Viscount EBRING Cookery, by ALEXANDER INNES SH With 10 Illustrations. Crown 8vo., 5s

THE SALMON. By the Hon. A GATHORNE-HARDY. With Chapters o Law of Salmon Fishing by CLAUD DOU PENNANT; Cookery, by ALEXANDER I SHAND. With 8 Illustrations. Cr. 8vc

THE TROUT. By the MARQU OF GRANBY. With Chapters on the B ing of Trout by Col. H. CUSTANCE; Cookery, by ALEXANDER INNES SH With 12 Illustrations. Crown 8vo., 5s

THE RABBIT. By JAMES EDM HARTING. Cookery, by ALEXANDER I SHAND. With 10 Illustrations. Cr. 8vc

PIKE AND PERCH. By WIL SENIOR ('Redspinner,' Editor of 'Field'). With Chapters by JOHN BIC DYKE and W. H. POPE; Cookery ALEXANDER INNES SHAND. With 1 lustrations. Crown 8vo., 5s.

Alverstone and Alcock.—*SURREY CRICKET:* its History and Associations. Edited by the Right Hon. LORD ALVERSTONE, L.C.J., President, and C.W. ALCOCK, Secretary, of the Surrey County Cricket Club. With 48 Illustrations. 8vo., 16s. net.

Bickerdyke.—*DAYS OF MY LIFE ON WATER, FRESH AND SALT;* and other Papers. By JOHN BICKERDYKE. With Photo-etching Frontispiece and 8 Full-page Illustrations. Crown 8vo., 3s. 6d.

Blackburne. — *MR. BLACKBURNE'S GAMES AT CHESS.* Selected, Annotated and Arranged by Himself. Edited, with a Biographical Sketch and a brief History of Blindfold Chess, by P. ANDERSON GRAHAM. With Portrait of Mr. Blackburne. 8vo., 7s. 6d. net.

Dead Shot (The): or, Sportsman's Complete Guide. Being a Treatise on the Use of the Gun, with Rudimentary and Finishing Lessons in the Art of Shooting Game of all kinds. Also Game-driving, Wildfowl and Pigeon-shooting, Dog-breaking, etc. By MARKSMAN. With numerous Illustrations. Crown 8vo., 10s. 6d.

Sport and Pastime—*continued.*

Gathorne - Hardy. — *AUTUMNS IN ARGYLESHIRE WITH ROD AND GUN.* By the Hon. A. E. GATHORNE-HARDY. With 8 Illustrations by ARCHIBALD THORBURN. 8vo., 6s. net.

Graham.—*COUNTRY PASTIMES FOR BOYS.* By P. ANDERSON GRAHAM. With 252 Illustrations from Drawings and Photographs. Cr. 8vo., gilt edges, 3s. net.

Hutchinson.—*THE BOOK OF GOLF AND GOLFERS.* By HORACE G. HUTCHINSON. With Contributions by Miss AMY PASCOE, H. H. HILTON, J. H. TAYLOR, H. J. WHIGHAM, and Messrs. SUTTON & SONS. With 71 Portraits from Photographs. Large crown 8vo., gilt top, 7s. 6d. net.

Lang.—*ANGLING SKETCHES.* By ANDREW LANG. With 20 Illustrations. Crown 8vo., 3s. 6d.

Lillie.—*CROQUET UP TO DATE.* Containing the Ideas and Teachings of the Leading Players and Champions. By ARTHUR LILLIE. With Contributions by Lieut.-Col. the Hon. H. NEEDHAM, C. D. LOCOCK, etc. With 19 Illustrations (15 Portraits), and numerous Diagrams. 8vo., 10s. 6d. net.

Locock.—*SIDE AND SCREW :* being Notes on the Theory and Practice of the Game of Billiards. By C. D. LOCOCK. With Diagrams. Crown 8vo., 5s. net.

Longman.—*CHESS OPENINGS.* By FREDERICK W. LONGMAN. Fcp. 8vo., 2s. 6d.

Mackenzie.—*NOTES FOR HUNTING MEN.* By Captain CORTLANDT GORDON MACKENZIE. Crown 8vo., 2s. 6d. net.

Madden.—*THE DIARY OF MASTER WILLIAM SILENCE :* a Study of Shakespeare and of Elizabethan Sport. By the Right Hon. D. H. MADDEN, Vice-Chancellor of the University of Dublin. 8vo., gilt top, 16s.

Maskelyne.—*SHARPS AND FLATS :* a Complete Revelation of the Secrets of Cheating at Games of Chance and Skill. By JOHN NEVIL MASKELYNE, of the Egyptian Hall. With 62 Illustrations. Crown 8vo., 6s.

Millais (JOHN GUILLE).

THE WILD-FOWLER IN SCOTLAND. With a Frontispiece in Photogravure by Sir J. E. MILLAIS, Bart., P.R.A., 8 Photogravure Plates, 2 Coloured Plates and 50 Illustrations from the Author's Drawings and from Photographs. Royal 4to., gilt top, 30s. net.

Millais (JOHN GUILLE)—*contin*

THE NATURAL HISTORY OF BRITISH SURFACE - FEEDING L With 6 Photogravures and 66 Pla in Colours) from Drawings by the A ARCHIBALD THORBURN, and from graphs. Royal 4to.,cloth,gilt top,£6

Modern Bridge.—By 'Slam'. a Reprint of the Laws of Bridge, as a by the Portland and Turf Clubs. gilt edges, 3s. 6d. net.

Park.—*THE GAME OF GOLF.* WILLIAM PARK, Jun., Champion (1887-89. With 17 Plates and 26 Il tions in the Text. Crown 8vo., 7s. 6.

Payne-Gallwey (Sir RALPH, E

THE CROSS-BOW : Mediæval Modern ; Military and Sporting Construction, History and Manage with a Treatise on the Balista and pult of the Ancients. With 220 Il tions. Royal 4to., £3 3s. net.

LETTERS TO YOUNG SHOOTERS (Series). On the Choice and use of With 41 Illustrations. Crown 8vo.,

LETTERS TO YOUNG SHOOTERS (Se Series). On the Production, Preserv and Killing of Game. With Dire in Shooting Wood-Pigeons and Bre in Retrievers. With Portrait an Illustrations. Crown 8vo., 12s. 6d.

LETTERS TO YOUNG SHOO (Third Series.) Comprising a Natural History of the Wildfowl are Rare or Common to the E Islands, with complete directio Shooting Wildfowl on the Coast Inland. With 200 Illustrations. (8vo., 18s.

Pole.—*THE THEORY OF THE MO SCIENTIFIC GAME OF WHIST.* By W POLE, F.R.S. Fcp. 8vo., gilt edges, 2

Proctor.—*HOW TO PLAY WE WITH THE LAWS AND ETIQUETT WHIST.* By RICHARD A. PROCTOR. (8vo., gilt edges, 3s. net.

Ronalds.—*THE FLY-FISHER'S E MOLOGY.* By ALFRED RONALDS. W coloured Plates. 8vo., 14s.

Selous.—*SPORT AND TRAVEL, J AND WEST.* By FREDERICK COURT SELOUS. With 18 Plates and 35 Ill tions in the Text. Medium 8vo., 12s. 6

Warner.—*CRICKET IN AUSTRAL* being Record of the Tour of the E Team, 1902-3. By PELHAM F. WA With numerous Illustrations from F graphs. Crown 8vo.

Mental, Moral, and Political Philosophy.

LOGIC, RHETORIC, PSYCHOLOGY, &C.

Abbott.—*THE ELEMENTS OF LOGIC.*
By T. K. ABBOTT, B.D. 12mo., 3s.

Aristotle.

THE ETHICS: Greek Text, Illustrated
with Essay and Notes. By Sir ALEXAN-
DER GRANT, Bart. 2 vols. 8vo., 32s.

*AN INTRODUCTION TO ARISTOTLE'S
ETHICS.* Books I.-IV. (Book X. c. vi.-ix.
in an Appendix). With a continuous
Analysis and Notes. By the Rev. E.
MOORE, D.D. Crown 8vo., 10s. 6d.

Bacon (FRANCIS).

COMPLETE WORKS. Edited by R. L.
ELLIS, JAMES SPEDDING and D. D.
HEATH. 7 vols. 8vo., £3 13s. 6d

LETTERS AND LIFE, including all his
occasional Works. Edited by JAMES
SPEDDING. 7 vols. 8vo., £4 4s.

THE ESSAYS: with Annotations. By
RICHARD WHATELY, D.D. 8vo., 10s. 6d.

THE ESSAYS: with Notes. By F.
STORR and C. H. GIBSON. Cr. 8vo., 3s. 6d.

THE ESSAYS: with Introduction,
Notes, and Index. By E. A. ABBOTT, D.D.
2 Vols. Fcp. 8vo., 6s. The Text and Index
only, without Introduction and Notes, in
One Volume. Fcp. 8vo., 2s. 6d.

Bain (ALEXANDER).

MENTAL AND MORAL SCIENCE : a
Compendium of Psychology and Ethics.
Crown 8vo., 10s. 6d.
Or separately,
Part I. PSYCHOLOGY AND HISTORY OF
PHILOSOPHY. Crown 8vo., 6s. 6d.
Part II. THEORY OF ETHICS AND ETHICAL
SYSTEMS. Crown 8vo., 4s. 6d.

LOGIC. Part I. *DEDUCTION.* Cr. 8vo.,
4s. Part II. *INDUCTION.* Cr. 8vo., 6s. 6d.

THE SENSES AND THE INTELLECT.
8vo., 15s.

THE EMOTIONS AND THE WILL.
8vo., 15s.

PRACTICAL ESSAYS. Cr. 8vo., 2s.

*DISSERTATIONS ON LEADING PHILO-
SOPHICAL TOPICS.* 8vo.

Baldwin.—*A COLLEGE MANUAL
RHETORIC.* By CHARLES SEARS BALDW
A.M., Ph.D. Crown 8vo., 4s. 6d.

Brooks.—*THE ELEMENTS OF MIN*
being an Examination into the Nature
the First Division of the Elementary S
stances of Life. By H. JAMYN BROO
8vo., 10s. 6d. net.

Brough.—*THE STUDY OF MENT*
SCIENCE : Five Lectures on the Uses a
Characteristics of Logic and Psycholo
By J. BROUGH, LL.D. Crown 8vo, 2s. 1

Crozier (JOHN BEATTIE).

CIVILISATION AND PROGRESS : bei
the Outlines of a New System of Politi
Religious and Social Philosophy. 8vo.,

*HISTORY OF INTELLECTUAL DEV
OPMENT:* on the Lines of Modern Evoluti

Vol. I. 8vo., 14s.

Vol. II. (*In preparation.*)

Vol. III. 8vo., 10s. 6d.

Davidson.—*THE LOGIC OF DEFI
TION,* Explained and Applied. By WILL
L. DAVIDSON, M.A. Crown 8vo., 6s.

Green (THOMAS HILL).—THE WO
OF. Edited by R. L. NETTLESHIP.

Vols. I. and II. Philosophical Works. 8
16s. each.

Vol. III. Miscellanies. With Index to
three Volumes, and Memoir. 8vo., 2)

*LECTURES ON THE PRINCIPLES
POLITICAL OBLIGATION.* With Pre
by BERNARD BOSANQUET. 8vo., 5s.

Gurnhill.—*THE MORALS OF SUICI*
By the Rev. J. GURNHILL. B.A. Vol
Crown 8vo., 5s. net. Vol. II., Crown 8
5s. net.

Mental, Moral and Political Philosophy—*continued*

LOGIC, RHETORIC, PSYCHOLOGY, &C.

Hodgson (SHADWORTH H.).

TIME AND SPACE: A Metaphysical
Essay. 8vo., 16s.

THE THEORY OF PRACTICE: an
Ethical Inquiry. 2 vols. 8vo., 24s.

THE PHILOSOPHY OF REFLECTION.
2 vols. 8vo., 21s.

THE METAPHYSIC OF EXPERIENCE.
Book I. General Analysis of Experience;
Book II. Positive Science; Book III.
Ana ysis of Conscious Action; Book IV.
The Real Universe. 4 vols. 8vo., 36s. net.

Hume.—THE PHILOSOPHICAL WORKS
OF DAVID HUME. Edited by T. H. GREEN
and T. H. GROSE. 4 vols. 8vo., 28s. Or
separately, ESSAYS. 2 vols. 14s. TREATISE
OF HUMAN NATURE. 2 vols. 14s.

James (WILLIAM, M.D., LL.D.).

THE WILL TO BELIEVE, and Other
Essays in Popular Philosophy. Crown
8vo., 7s. 6d.

THE VARIETIES OF RELIGIOUS EX-
PERIENCE: a Study in Human Nature.
Being the Gifford Lectures on Natural
Religion delivered at Edinburgh in 1901-
1902. 8vo., 12s. net.

TALKS TO TEACHERS ON PSYCHO-
LOGY, AND TO STUDENTS ON SOME OF
LIFE'S IDEALS. Crown 8vo., 4s. 6d.

Justinian.—THE INSTITUTES OF
JUSTINIAN: Latin Text, chiefly that of
Huschke, with English Introduction, Trans-
lation, Notes, and Summary. By THOMAS
C. SANDARS, M.A. 8vo., 18s.

Kant (IMMANUEL).

CRITIQUE OF PRACTICAL REASON,
AND OTHER WORKS ON THE THEORY OF
ETHICS. Translated by T. K. ABBOTT,
B.D. With Memoir. 8vo., 12s. 6d.

FUNDAMENTAL PRINCIPLES OF THE
METAPHYSIC OF ETHICS. Translated by
T. K. ABBOTT, B.D. Crown 8vo, 3s.

INTRODUCTION TO LOGIC, AND HIS
ESSAY ON THE MISTAKEN SUBTILTY OF
THE FOUR FIGURES. Translated by T.
K. ABBOTT. 8vo., 6s

Kelly.—GOVERNMENT OR HUMAN
EVOLUTION. By EDMOND KELLY, M.A.,
F.G.S. Vol. I. Justice. Crown 8vo., 7s. 6d.
net. Vol. II. Collectivism and Individualism.
Crown 8vo., 10s. 6d. net.

Killick.—HANDBOOK TO MILL'S
SYSTEM OF LOGIC. By Rev. A. H.
KILLICK, M.A. Crown 8vo., 3s. 6d.

Ladd (GEORGE TRUMBULL).

PHILOSOPHY OF CONDUCT: a Trea
of the Facts, Principles and Idea
Ethics. 8vo., 21s.

ELEMENTS OF PHYSIOLOGICAL *
CHOLOGY. 8vo., 21s.

OUTLINES OF DESCRIPTIVE PSY
LOGY: a Text-Book of Mental Scienc
Colleges and Normal Schools. 8vo.,

OUTLINES OF PHYSIOLOGICAL *
CHOLOGY. 8vo., 12s.

PRIMER OF PSYCHOLOGY. Cr. 8
5s. 6d.

Lecky(WILLIAM EDWARD HARTPO

THE MAP OF LIFE: Conduct
Character. Crown 8vo., 5s. net.

HISTORY OF EUROPEAN MO
FROM AUGUSTUS TO CHARLEMAGN
vols. Crown 8vo., 10s. net.

A SURVEY OF ENGLISH ETH
being the First Chapter of W. I
Lecky's 'History of European Mo
Edited, with Introduction and Not
W. A. HIRST. Crown 8vo., 3s. 6d.

HISTORY OF THE RISE AND IN
ENCE OF THE SPIRIT OF RATION.
IN EUROPE. 2 vols. Cr. 8vo., 10s.

DEMOCRACY AND LIBERTY.
Library Edition. 2 vols. 8vo., 36s
Cabinet Edition. 2 vols. Cr. 8vo., 10

Lutoslawski.—THE ORIGIN
GROWTH OF PLATO'S LOGIC. W
Account of Plato's Style and of the Ch
logy of his Writings. By WINC
LUTOSLAWSKI. 8vo., 21s.

Max Müller (F.).

THE SCIENCE OF THOUGHT. 8vo.

THE SIX SYSTEMS OF INDIAN *
OSOPHY. 8vo., 18s.

THREE LECTURES ON THE VED.
PHILOSOPHY. Crown 8vo., 5s.

Mill (JOHN STUART).

A SYSTEM OF LOGIC. Cr. 8vo., 3

ON LIBERTY. Crown 8vo., 1s.

CONSIDERATIONS ON REPRESE
TIVE GOVERNMENT. Crown 8vo.,

UTILITARIANISM. 8vo., 2s. 6d

EXAMINATION OF SIR WIL
HAMILTON'S PHILOSOPHY. 8vo.,

NATURE, THE UTILITY OF RELI
AND THEISM. Three Essays. 8vo

Mental, Moral, and Political Philosophy—*continued.*

LOGIC, RHETORIC, PSYCHOLOGY, &C.

Monck. — *An Introduction to Logic.* By William Henry S. Monck, M.A. Crown 8vo., 5s.

Myers.—*Human Personality and its Survival of Bodily Death.* By Frederic W. H. Myers. 2 vols. 8vo., 42s. net.

Pierce.—*Studies in Auditory and Visual Space Perception*: Essays on Experimental Psychology. By A. H. Pierce. Crown 8vo., 6s. 6d. net.

Richmond.—*The Mind of a Child.* By Ennis Richmond. Cr. 8vo., 3s. 6d. net.

Romanes.—*Mind and Motion and Monism.* By George John Romanes, Cr. 8vo., 4s. 6d.

Sully (James).

An Essay on Laughter: its Forms, its Cause, its Development and its Value. 8vo., 12s. 6d. net.

The Human Mind: a Text-book of Psychology. 2 vols. 8vo., 21s.

Outlines of Psychology. Crown 8vo., 9s.

The Teacher's Handbook of Psychology. Crown 8vo., 6s. 6d.

Studies of Childhood. 8vo., 10s. 6d.

Children's Ways: being Selections from the Author's 'Studies of Childhood'. With 25 Illustrations. Crown 8vo., 4s. 6d.

Sutherland. — *The Origin and Growth of the Moral Instinct.* By Alexander Sutherland, M.A. 2 vols. 8vo., 28s.

Swinburne. — *Picture Logic*: an Attempt to Popularise the Science of Reasoning. By Alfred James Swinburne, M.A. With 23 Woodcuts. Cr. 8vo., 2s. 6d.

Thomas. — *Intuitive Suggestion.* By J. W. Thomas, Author of 'Spiritual Law in the Natural World,' etc. Crown 8vo., 3s. 6d. net.

Webb.—*The Veil of Isis*: a Series of Essays on Idealism. By Thomas E. Webb, LL.D., Q.C. 8vo., 10s. 6d.

Weber.—*History of Philosophy* By Alfred Weber, Professor in the University of Strasburg. Translated by Frank Thilly, Ph.D. 8vo., 16s.

Whately (Archbishop).

Bacon's Essays. With Annotations, 8vo., 10s. 6d.

Elements of Logic. Cr. 8vo., 4s. 6d.

Elements of Rhetoric. Cr. 8vo., 4s. 6d.

Zeller (Dr. Edward).

The Stoics, Epicureans, and Sceptics. Translated by the Rev. O. J. Reichel, M.A. Crown 8vo., 15s.

Outlines of the History of Greek Philosophy. Translated by Sarah F. Alleyne and Evelyn Abbott, M.A., LL.D. Crown 8vo., 10s. 6d.

Plato and the Older Academy. Translated by Sarah F. Alleyne and Alfred Goodwin, B.A. Crown 8vo., 18s.

Socrates and the Socratic Schools. Translated by the Rev. O. J. Reichel, M.A. Crown 8vo., 10s. 6d.

Aristotle and the Earlier Peripatetics. Translated by B. F. C. Costelloe, M.A., and J. H. Muirhead, M.A. 2 vols. Crown 8vo., 24s.

STONYHURST PHILOSOPHICAL SERIES.

A Manual of Political Economy. By C. S. Devas, M.A. Crown 8vo., 7s. 6d.

First Principles of Knowledge. By John Rickaby, S.J. Crown 8vo., 5s.

General Metaphysics. By John Rickaby, S.J. Crown 8vo., 5s.

Logic. By Richard F. Clarke, S.J. Crown 8vo., 5s.

Moral Philosophy (Ethics and Natural Law). By Joseph Rickaby, S.J. Crown 8vo., 5s.

Natural Theology. By Bernard Boedder, S.J. Crown 8vo., 6s. 6d.

Psychology. By Michael Maher, S.J., D.Litt., M.A. (Lond.). Cr. 8vo., 6s. 6d.

History and Science of Language, &c.

Davidson.—*LEADING AND IMPORT-ANT ENGLISH WORDS:* Explained and Exemplified. By WILLIAM L. DAVIDSON, M.A. Fcp. 8vo., 3s. 6d.

Farrar.—*LANGUAGE AND LANGUAGES.* By F. W. FARRAR, D.D., late Dean of Canterbury. Crown 8vo., 6s.

Graham. — *ENGLISH SYNONYMS,* Classified and Explained: with Practical Exercises. By G. F. GRAHAM. Fcp. 8vo., 6s.

Max Müller (F.).

THE SCIENCE OF LANGUAGE. 2 vols. Crown 8vo., 10s.

Max Müller (F.)—*continued.*

BIOGRAPHIES OF WORDS, AND TH. HOME OF THE ARYAS. Crown 8vo., 5:

CHIPS FROM A GERMAN WORKSHOF Vol. III. *ESSAYS ON LANGUAGE AN LITERATURE.* Crown 8vo., 5s.

LAST ESSAYS. First Series. Essay on Language, Folk-lore and other Sul jects. Crown 8vo., 5s.

Roget.—*THESAURUS OF ENGLIS, WORDS AND PHRASES.* Classified an Arranged so as to Facilitate the Expressio of Ideas and assist in Literary Compositio By PETER MARK ROGET, M.D., F.R.S With full Index. Crown 8vo., 9s. net.

Political Economy and Economics.

Ashley (W. J.).

ENGLISH ECONOMIC HISTORY AND THEORY. Crown 8vo., Part I., 5s. Part II., 10s. 6d.

SURVEYS, HISTORIC AND ECONOMIC. Crown 8vo., 9s. net.

THE ADJUSTMENT OF WAGES: a Study on the Coal and Iron Industries of Great Britain and the United States. With 4 Maps. 8vo.

Bagehot.—*ECONOMIC STUDIES.* By WALTER BAGEHOT. Crown 8vo., 3s. 6d.

Barnett.—*PRACTICABLE SOCIALISM:* Essays on Social Reform. By SAMUEL A. and HENRIETTA BARNETT. Crown 8vo., 6s.

Devas.—*A MANUAL OF POLITICAL ECONOMY.* By C. S. DEVAS, M.A. Cr. 8vo., 7s. 6d. (*Stonyhurst Philosophical Series.*)

Dewey.—*FINANCIAL HISTORY OF THE UNITED STATES.* By DAVIS RICH DEWEY. Crown 8vo., 7s. 6d. net.

Lawrence.—*LOCAL VARIATIONS IN WAGES.* By F. W. LAWRENCE, M.A. With Index and 18 Maps and Diagrams. 4to., 8s.6d.

Leslie.—*ESSAYS ON POLITICAL ECO-NOMY.* By T. E. CLIFFE LESLIE, Hon. LL.D., Dubl. 8vo., 10s. 6d.

Macleod (HENRY DUNNING).

BIMETALLISM. 8vo., 5s. net.

THE ELEMENTS OF BANKING. Cr. 8vo., 3s. 6d.

Macleod (HENRY DUNNING)—*conta*

THE THEORY AND PRACTICE O BANKING. Vol. I. 8vo., 12s. Vol. II. 14

THE THEORY OF CREDIT. 8vc In 1 Vol., 30s. net; or separately, Vo I., 10s. net. Vol. II., Part I., 10s. ne Vol II., Part II. 10s. net.

INDIAN CURRENCY. 8vo., 2s. 6d. ne

Mill.—*POLITICAL ECONOMY.* B JOHN STUART MILL. *Popular Edition.* C 8vo.,3s.6d. *Library Edition.* 2 vols. 8vo.,30

Mulhall.—*INDUSTRIES AND WEALT. OF NATIONS.* By MICHAEL G. MULHAL F.S.S. With 32 Diagrams. Cr. 8vo., 8s. 6

Symes. — *POLITICAL ECONOMY:* Short Text-book of Political Econom With Problems for Solution, Hints fc Supplementary Reading, and a Suppl mentary Chapter on Socialism. By J. 1 SYMES, M.A. Crown 8vo., 2s. 6d.

Toynbee.—*LECTURES ON THE IF DUSTRIAL REVOLUTION OF THE 18TH CEI TURY IN ENGLAND.* By ARNOLD TOYNBEI 8vo., 10s. 6d.

Webb (SIDNEY and BEATRICE).

THE HISTORY OF TRADE UNIONISM With Map and Bibliography. 8vo., 7s. 6 net.

INDUSTRIAL DEMOCRACY: a Stud in Trade Unionism. 2 vols. 8vo., 12s. ne

PROBLEMS OF MODERN INDUSTRI 8vo., 5s. net.

Evolution, Anthropology, &c.

Avebury.—*The Origin of Civilisation*, and the Primitive Condition of Man. By the Right Hon. LORD AVEBURY. With 6 Plates and 20 Illustrations. 8vo., 18s.

Clodd (EDWARD).

The Story of Creation: a Plain Account of Evolution. With 77 Illustrations. Crown 8vo., 3s. 6d.

A Primer of Evolution: being a Popular Abridged Edition of 'The Story of Creation'. With Illustrations. Fcp. 8vo., 1s. 6d.

Lang and Atkinson. — *Social Origins*. By ANDREW LANG, M.A., LL.D.; and *Primal Law*. By J. J. ATKINSON. 8vo., 10s. 6d. net.

Packard.—*Lamarck, the Founder of Evolution*: his Life and Work, with Translations of his Writings on Organic Evolution. By ALPHEUS S. PACKARD, M.D., LL.D. With 10 Portrait and other Illustrations. Large Crown 8vo., 9s. net.

Romanes (GEORGE JOHN).

Essays. Ed. by C. LLOYD MORG(Crown 8vo., 5s. net.

An Examination of Weism ism. Crown 8vo., 6s.

Darwin, and after Darwin Exposition of the Darwinian Theory, Discussion on Post-Darwinian Quest

Part I. THE DARWINIAN THEORY. Portrait of Darwin and 125 Illustrat Crown 8vo., 10s. 6d.

Part II. POST-DARWINIAN QUESTI Heredity and Utility. With Portr the Author and 5 Illustrations. Cr. 10s. 6d.

Part III. Post-Darwinian Questi Isolation and Physiological Selec Crown 8vo., 5s.

The Science of Religion, &c.

Balfour. — *The Foundations of Belief*; being Notes Introductory to the Study of Theology. By the Right Hon. ARTHUR JAMES BALFOUR. Cr. 8vo., 6s. net.

Baring-Gould.—*The Origin and Development of Religious Belief.* By the Rev. S. BARING-GOULD. 2 vols. Crown 8vo., 3s. 6d. each.

Campbell.—*Religion in Greek Literature.* By the Rev. LEWIS CAMPBELL, M.A., LL.D. 8vo., 15s.

Davidson.—*Theism*, as Grounded in Human Nature, Historically and Critically Handled. Being the Burnett Lectures for 1892 and 1893, delivered at Aberdeen. By W. L. DAVIDSON, M.A., LL.D. 8vo., 15s.

James.—*The Varieties of Religious Experience*: a Study in Human Nature. Being the Gifford Lectures on Natural Religion delivered at Edinburgh in 1901-1902. By WILLIAM JAMES, LL.D., etc. 8vo., 12s. net.

Lang (ANDREW).

Magic and Religion. 8vo., 10s. 6d.

Custom and Myth: Studies of Early Usage and Belief. With 15 Illustrations. Crown 8vo., 3s. 6d.

Myth, Ritual, and Religion. 2 vols. Crown 8vo., 7s.

Lang (ANDREW)—*continued.*

Modern Mythology: a Repl Professor Max Müller. 8vo., 9s.

The Making of Religion. Cr. 5s. net.

Leighton.—*Typical Modern ceptions of God*; or, The Absolu German Romantic Idealism and of En Evolutionary Agnosticism. By Jo ALEXANDER LEIGHTON, Professor of P sophy in Hobart College, U.S. Crown 3s. 6d. net.

Max Müller (The Right Hon.

The Silesian Horseherd (' *Pferdebürla*'): Questions of the answered by F. MAX MÜLLER. T lated by OSCAR A. FECHTER; May North Jakima, U.S.A. With a Pr by J. ESTLIN CARPENTER.

Chips from a German Works Vol. IV. Essays on Mythology and lore. Crown 8vo., 5s.

The Six Systems of In Philosophy. 8vo., 18s.

Contributions to the Scienc Mythology. 2 vols. 8vo., 32s.

The Origin and Growth of R gion, as illustrated by the Religio India. The Hibbert Lectures, deli at the Chapter House, Westmi Abbey, in 1878. Crown 8vo., 5s.

The Science of Religion, &c.—*continued.*

Max Müller (The Right Hon. F.)—*continued.*

INTRODUCTION TO THE SCIENCE OF RELIGION: Four Lectures delivered at the Royal Institution. Crown 8vo., 5s.

NATURAL RELIGION. The Gifford Lectures, delivered before the University of Glasgow in 1888. Crown 8vo., 5s.

PHYSICAL RELIGION. The Gifford Lectures, delivered before the University of Glasgow in 1890. Crown 8vo., 5s.

ANTHROPOLOGICAL RELIGION. The Gifford Lectures, delivered before the University of Glasgow in 1891. Cr. 8vo., 5s.

THEOSOPHY, OR PSYCHOLOGICAL RELIGION. The Gifford Lectures, delivered before the University of Glasgow in 1892. Crown 8vo., 5s.

Max Müller (The Right Hon. F.) *continued.*

THREE LECTURES ON THE VEDÂ PHILOSOPHY, delivered at the R Institution in March, 1894. Cr. 8vo.

LAST ESSAYS. Second Serie Essays on the Science of Relig Crown 8vo., 5s.

Oakesmith. — *THE RELIGION PLUTARCH:* a Pagan Creed of Apos Times. An Essay. By JOHN OAKESM D.Litt., M.A. Crown 8vo., 5s. net.

Wood-Martin (W. G.).
TRACES OF THE ELDER FAITHS IRELAND: a Folk-lore Sketch. A H book of Irish Pre-Ch istian Tradit With 192 Illustrations. 2 vols. 30s. net.

PAGAN IRELAND: an Archæolog Sketch. A Handbook of Irish Christian Antiquities. With 512 trations. 8vo., 15s.

Classical Literature, Translations, &c.

Abbott.—*HELLENICA.* A Collection of Essays on Greek Poetry, Philosophy, History, and Religion. Edited by EVELYN ABBOTT, M.A., LL.D. Crown 8vo., 7s. 6d.

Æschylus.—*EUMENIDES OF ÆSCHYLUS.* With Metrical English Translation. By J. F. DAVIES. 8vo., 7s.

Aristophanes. — *THE ACHARNIANS OF ARISTOPHANES,* translated into English Verse. By R. Y. TYRRELL. Crown 8vo., 1s.

Becker (W. A.), Translated by the Rev. F. METCALFE, B.D.

GALLUS: or, Roman Scenes in the Time of Augustus. With Notes and Excursuses. With 26 Illustrations. Crown 8vo., 3s. 6d.

CHARICLES: or, Illustrations of the Private Life of the Ancient Greeks. With Notes and Excursuses. With 26 Illustrations. Crown 8vo., 3s. 6d.

Campbell.—*RELIGION IN GREEK LITERATURE.* By the Rev. LEWIS CAMPBELL, M.A., LL.D., Emeritus Professor of Greek, University of St. Andrews. 8vo., 15s.

Cicero.—*CICERO'S CORRESPONDENCE.* By R. Y. TYRRELL. Vols. I., II., III., 8vo., each 12s. Vol. IV., 15s. Vol. V., 14s. Vol. VI., 12s. Vol. VII. Index, 7s. 6d.

Harvard Studies in Classi Philology. Edited by a Committee o Classical Instructors of Harvard Univer Vols. XI., 1900; XII., 1901; XIII., 1 8vo., 6s. 6d. net each.

Hime.—*LUCIAN, THE SYRIAN TIRIST.* By Lieut.-Col. HENRY W. L. H (late) Royal Artillery. 8vo., 5s. net.

Homer.—*THE ODYSSEY OF HOM* Done into English Verse. By WILI MORRIS. Crown 8vo., 5s. net.

Horace.—*THE WORKS OF HOR. RENDERED INTO ENGLISH PROSE.* Life, Introduction and Notes. By WILI COUTTS, M.A. Crown 8vo., 5s. net.

Lang.—*HOMER AND THE EPIC.* ANDREW LANG. Crown 8vo., 9s. net.

Lucian. — *TRANSLATIONS F LUCIAN.* By AUGUSTA M. CAMPB DAVIDSON, M.A. Edin. Crown 8vo., 5s.

Ogilvie.—*HORAE LATINAE:* Stu in Synonyms and Syntax. By the ROBERT OGILVIE, M.A., LL.D., H.M. C Inspector of Schools for Scotland. E by ALEXANDER SOUTER, M.A. Wi Memoir by JOSEPH OGILVIE, M.A., L 8vo., 12s. 6d. net.

Classical Literature, Translations, &c.—*continued.*

Rich.—*A DICTIONARY OF ROMAN AND GREEK ANTIQUITIES.* By A. RICH, B.A. With 2000 Woodcuts. Crown 8vo., 6s. net.

Sophocles.—Translated into English Verse. By ROBERT WHITELAW, M.A., Assistant Master in Rugby School. Cr. 8vo., 8s. 6d.

Theophrastus.—*THE CHARACTERS OF THEOPHRASTUS:* a Translation, with Introduction. By CHARLES E. BENNETT and WILLIAM A. HAMMOND, Professors in Cornell University. Fcp. 8vo., 2s. 6d. net.

Tyrrell. — *DUBLIN TRANSLATIONS INTO GREEK AND LATIN VERSE.* Edited by R. Y. TYRRELL. 8vo., 6s.

Virgil.

THE POEMS OF VIRGIL. Translated into English Prose by JOHN CONINGTON. Crown 8vo., 6s.

Virgil—*continued.*

THE ÆNEID OF VIRGIL. Transla[t] into English Verse by JOHN CONINGT[ON]. Crown 8vo., 6s.

THE ÆNEIDS OF VIRGIL. Done i[n] English Verse. By WILLIAM MOR[RIS]. Crown 8vo., 5s. net.

THE ECLOGUES AND GEORGICS [OF] VIRGIL. Translated into English Pr[ose] by J. W. MACKAIL, Fellow of Ba[lliol] College, Oxford. 16mo., 5s.

Wilkins.—*THE GROWTH OF* [THE] HOMERIC POEMS. By G. WILKINS. 8vo.

Poetry and the Drama.

Arnold.—*THE LIGHT OF THE WORLD:* or, The Great Consummation. By Sir EDWIN ARNOLD. With 14 Illustrations after HOLMAN HUNT. Crown 8vo., 5s. net.

Bell (MRS. HUGH).

CHAMBER COMEDIES: a Collection of Plays and Monologues for the Drawing Room. Crown 8vo., 5s. net.

FAIRY TALE PLAYS, AND HOW TO ACT THEM. With 91 Diagrams and 52 Illustrations. Crown 8vo., 3s. net.

RUMPELSTILTZKIN: a Fairy Play in Five Scenes (Characters, 7 Male; 1 Female). From 'Fairy Tale Plays and How to Act Them'. With Illustrations, Diagrams and Music. Cr. 8vo., sewed, 6d.

Bird. — *RONALD'S FAREWELL,* and other Verses. By GEORGE BIRD, M.A., Vicar of Bradwell, Derbyshire. Fcp. 8vo., 4s. 6d. net.

Cochrane.—*COLLECTED VERSES.* ALFRED COCHRANE, Author of 'The [Kes]trel's Nest, and other Verses,' 'Lev[e] Plectro,' etc. With a Frontispiece by H[ugh] FORD. Fcp. 8vo.

Dabney.—*THE MUSICAL BASIS* [OF] VERSE: a Scientific Study of the P[rin]ciples of Poetic Composition. By J. [P.] DABNEY. Crown 8vo., 6s. 6d. net.

Graves. — *CLYTÆMNESTRA.* [A] TRAGEDY. By ARNOLD F. GRAVES. W[ith] a Preface by ROBERT Y. TYRRELL, Lit[t.] Crown 8vo., 5s. net.

Hither and Thither: Songs a[nd] Verses. By the Author of 'Times [and] Days,' etc. Fcp. 8vo., 5s.

Ingelow (JEAN).

POETICAL WORKS. Complete [in] One Volume. Crown 8vo., gilt top, 6s.

LYRICAL AND OTHER POEMS. Sel[ec]ted from the Writings of JEAN INGEL[OW]. Fcp. 8vo., 2s. 6d. cloth plain, 3s. cloth [gilt]

Poetry and the

Keary.—*The Brothers :* a Fairy Masque. By C. F. Keary. Cr. 8vo., 4s. net.

Lang (Andrew).

Grass of Parnassus. Fcp. 8vo., 2s. 6d. net.

The Blue Poetry Book. Edited by Andrew Lang. With 100 Illustrations. Crown 8vo., gilt edges, 6s.

Lecky.—*Poems.* By the Right Hon. W. E. H. Lecky. Fcp. 8vo., 5s.

Lytton (The Earl of), (Owen Meredith).

The Wanderer. Cr. 8vo., 10s. 6d.

Lucile. Crown 8vo., 10s. 6d.

Selected Poems. Cr. 8vo., 10s. 6d.

Macaulay.—*Lays of Ancient Rome, with 'Ivry' and 'The Armada'.* By Lord Macaulay.

Illustrated by G. Scharf. Fcp. 4to., 10s. 6d.

———————— Bijou Edition. 18mo., 2s. 6d. gilt top.

———————— Popular Edition. Fcp. 4to., 6d. sewed, 1s. cloth.

Illustrated by J. R. Weguelin. Crown 8vo., 3s. net.

Annotated Edition. Fcp. 8vo., 1s. sewed, 1s. 6d. cloth.

MacDonald.—*A Book of Strife, in the form of the Diary of an Old Soul :* Poems. By George MacDonald, LL.D. 18mo., 6s.

Morris (William).

POETICAL WORKS—Library Edition. Complete in 11 volumes. Crown 8vo., price 5s. net each.

The Earthly Paradise. 4 vols. Crown 8vo., 5s. net each.

The Life and Death of Jason. Crown 8vo., 5s. net.

The Defence of Guenevere, and other Poems. Crown 8vo., 5s. net.

The Story of Sigurd the Volsung, and The Fall of the Niblungs. Cr. 8vo., 5s. net.

The Tale of Beowulf, some King of the Folk of the Wederg Translated by William Morris : J. Wyatt. Crown 8vo., 5s. net.

Certain of the Poetical Works may : had in the following Editions :—

The Earthly Paradise.

Popular Edition. 5 vols. 12mo., or 5s. each, sold separately.

The same in Ten Parts, 25s.; or : each, sold separately.

Cheap Edition, in 1 vol. Crown 6s. net.

Poems by the Way. Square o 8vo., 6s.

. For Mr. William Morris's ot Works, see pp. 27, 28, 37 and 4

Morte Arthur: an Alliterative I of the Fourteenth Century. Edited the Thornton MS., with Introd Notes and Glossary. By Mary Ma Banks. Fcp. 8vo., 3s. 6d.

Nesbit.—*Lays and Legends.* Nesbit (Mrs. Hubert Bland). Series. Crown 8vo., 3s. 6d. Second With Portrait. Crown 8vo., 5s.

Ramal.—*Songs of Childhood* Walter Ramal. With a Fronti from a Drawing by Richard Doyle. 8vo., 3s. 6d. net.

Riley. — *Old Fashioned R* Poems. By James Whitcomb 12mo., gilt top, 5s.

Romanes.—*A Selection from Poems of George John Romanes,* LL.D., F.R.S. With an Introduct T. Herbert Warren, President o dalen College, Oxford. Crown 8vo.,

Poetry and the Drama—*continued.*

Savage-Armstrong.—*BALLADS OF DOWN.* By G. F. SAVAGE-ARMSTRONG, M.A., D.Litt. Crown 8vo., 7s. 6d.

Shakespeare.

BOWDLER'S FAMILY SHAKESPEARE. With 36 Woodcuts. 1 vol. 8vo., 14s. Or in 6 vols. Fcp. 8vo., 21s.

THE SHAKESPEARE BIRTHDAY BOOK. By MARY F. DUNBAR. 32mo., 1s. 6d.

Stevenson.—*A CHILD'S GARDEN OF VERSES.* By ROBERT LOUIS STEVENSON. Fcp. 8vo., gilt top, 5s.

Trevelyan.—*CECILIA GONZAGA* Drama. By R. C. TREVELYAN. 8vo., 2s. 6d. net.

Wagner.—*THE NIBELUNGEN R*. Done into English Verse by REGIN RANKIN, B.A., of the Inner Temple, Ba ter-at-Law.

Vol. I. Rhine Gold, The Valkyrie. 8vo., gilt top, 4s. 6d.

Vol. II. Siegfried, The Twilight of Gods. Fcp. 8vo., gilt top, 4s. 6d.

Fiction, Humour, &c.

Anstey (F.).

VOCES POPULI. (Reprinted from 'Punch'.)

First Series. With 20 Illustrations by J. BERNARD PARTRIDGE. Cr. 8vo., gilt top, 3s. net.

Second Series. With 25 Illustrations by J. BERNARD PARTRIDGE. Cr. 8vo., gilt top, 3s. net.

THE MAN FROM BLANKLEY'S, and other Sketches. (Reprinted from 'Punch'.) With 25 Illustrations by J. BERNARD PARTRIDGE. Cr. 8vo., gilt top, 3s. net.

Bailey (H. C.).

MY LADY OF ORANGE: a Romance of the Netherlands in the Days of Alva. With 8 Illustrations. Crown 8vo., 6s.

KARL OF ERBACH : a Tale of the Thirty Years' War. Crown 8vo., 6s.

Beaconsfield (The Earl of).

NOVELS AND TALES. Complete in 11 vols. Crown 8vo., 1s. 6d. each, or in sets, 11 vols., gilt top, 15s. net.

Vivian Grey.	Contarini Fleming ;
The Young Duke; Count Alarcos: a Tragedy.	The Rise of Iskan- der.
Alroy ; Ixion in Heaven ; The In- fernal Marriage ; Popanilla.	Sybil. Henrietta Temple. Venetia. Coningsby. Lothair.
Tancred.	Endymion.

NOVELS AND TALES. THE HUGH-ENDEN EDITION. With 2 Portraits and 11 Vignettes. 11 vols. Crown 8vo., 42s.

Bottome.—*LIFE, THE INTERPRE7* By PHYLLIS BOTTOME. Crown 8vo., 6

Churchill.—*SAVROLA :* a Tale of Revolution in Laurania. By WINS SPENCER CHURCHILL, M.P. Cr. 8vo.,

Crawford.—*THE AUTOBIOGRAPH*1 *A TRAMP.* By J. H. CRAWFORD. Wi Photogravure Frontispiece 'The Vagra by FRED. WALKER, and 8 other Illu tions. Crown 8vo., 5s. net.

Creed.—*THE VICAR OF ST. LUK* By SIBYL CREED. Crown 8vo., 6s.

Davenport.—*BY THE RAMPARTS JEZREEL :* a Romance of Jehu, Kin Israel. By ARNOLD DAVENPORT. Frontispiece by LANCELOT SPEED. Cr 8vo., 6s.

Dougall.—*BEGGARS ALL.* By DOUGALL. Crown 8vo., 3s. 6d.

Fiction, Humour, &c.—*continued.*

Dyson.—*THE GOLD-STEALERS:* a Story of Waddy. By EDWARD DYSON, Author of 'Rhymes from the Mines,' etc. Crown 8vo., 6s.

Farrar (F. W., late DEAN OF CANTERBURY).

DARKNESS AND DAWN: or, Scenes in the Days of Nero. An Historic Tale. Cr. 8vo., gilt top, 6s. net.

GATHERING CLOUDS : a Tale of the Days of St. Chrysostom. Cr. 8vo., gilt top, 6s. net.

Fowler (EDITH H.).

THE YOUNG PRETENDERS. A Story of Child Life. With 12 Illustrations by Sir PHILIP BURNE-JONES, Bart. Crown 8vo., 6s.

THE PROFESSOR'S CHILDREN. With 24 Illustrations by ETHEL KATE BURGESS. Crown 8vo., 6s.

Francis (M. E.).

FIANDER'S WIDOW. Cr. 8vo., 6s.

YEOMAN FLEETWOOD. With Frontispiece. Crown 8vo., 3s. net.

PASTORALS OF DORSET. With 8 Illustrations. Crown 8vo., 6s.

THE MANOR FARM. With Frontispiece by CLAUD C. DU PRÉ COOPER. Crown 8vo., 6s.

Froude.—*THE TWO CHIEFS OF DUNBOY:* an Irish Romance of the Last Century. By JAMES A. FROUDE. Cr. 8vo., 3s. 6d.

Haggard (H. RIDER).

ALLAN QUATERMAIN. With 31 Illustrations. Crown 8vo., 3s. 6d.

ALLAN'S WIFE. With 34 Illustrations. Crown 8vo., 3s. 6d.

Haggard (H. RIDER)—*continued*

BEATRICE. With Frontispiece Vignette. Crown 8vo., 3s. 6d.

BLACK HEART AND WHITE HE AND OTHER STORIES. With 33 Illu tions. Crown 8vo., 3s. 6d.

CLEOPATRA. With 29 Illustratic Crown 8vo., 3s. 6d.

COLONEL QUARITCH, V.C. W Frontispiece and Vignette. Cr. 8vo., 3.

DAWN. With 16 Illustrations. 8vo., 3s. 6d.

DR. THERNE. Crown 8vo., 3s.

ERIC BRIGHTEYES. With 51 II trations. Crown 8vo., 3s. 6d.

HEART OF THE WORLD. With Illustrations. Crown 8vo., 3s. 6d.

JOAN HASTE. With 20 Illustratic Crown 8vo., 3s. 6d.

LYSBETH. With 26 Illustratic Crown 8vo., 6s.

MAIWA'S REVENGE. Cr. 8vo., 1s

MONTEZUMA'S DAUGHTER. Wit Illustrations. Crown 8vo., 3s. 6d.

MR. MEESON'S WILL. With Illustrations. Crown 8vo.. 3s. 6d.

NADA THE LILY. With 23 Illu tions. Crown 8vo., 3s. 6d.

PEARL-MAIDEN : a Tale of Fall of Jerusalem. With 16 Illustrat Crown 8vo., 6s.

SHE. With 32 Illustrations. Cr 8vo., 3s. 6d.

SWALLOW : a Tale of the Great T With 8 Illustrations. Crown 8vo., 3

THE PEOPLE OF THE MIST. V 16 Illustrations. Crown 8vo., 3s. 6d

THE WITCH'S HEAD. With Illustrations. Crown 8vo., 3s. 6d

Fiction, Humour, &c.—*continued.*

Haggard and Lang.—*THE WORLD'S DESIRE.* By H. RIDER HAGGARD and ANDREW LANG. With 27 Illustrations. Crown 8vo., 3s. 6d.

Harte.—*IN THE CARQUINEZ WOODS.* By BRET HARTE. Crown 8vo., 3s. 6d.

Hope.—*THE HEART OF PRINCESS OSRA.* By ANTHONY HOPE. With 9 Illustrations. Crown 8vo., 3s. 6d.

Howard.—*THE FAILURE OF SUCCESS.* By Lady MABEL HOWARD. Crown 8vo., 6s.

Hutchinson.—*A FRIEND OF NELSON.* By HORACE G. HUTCHINSON. Cr. 8vo., 6s.

Jerome.—*SKETCHES IN LAVENDER: BLUE AND GREEN.* By JEROME K. JEROME, Author of 'Three Men in a Boat,' etc. Crown 8vo., 3s. 6d.

Joyce.—*OLD CELTIC ROMANCES.* Twelve of the most beautiful of the Ancient Irish Romantic Tales. Translated from the Gaelic. By P. W. JOYCE, LL.D. Crown 8vo., 3s. 6d.

Lang (ANDREW).

A MONK OF FIFE; a Story of the Days of Joan of Arc. With 13 Illustrations by SELWYN IMAGE. Crown 8vo., 3s. 6d.

THE DISENTANGLERS. With 7 Full-page Illustrations by H. J. FORD. Crown 8vo., 6s.

Lyall (EDNA).

THE HINDERERS. Crown 8vo., 2s. 6d.

THE AUTOBIOGRAPHY OF A SLANDER. Fcp. 8vo., 1s. sewed.
Presentation Edition. With 20 Illustrations by LANCELOT SPEED. Crown 8vo., 2s. 6d. net.

DOREEN. The Story of a Singer. Crown 8vo., 6s.

WAYFARING MEN. Crown 8vo., 6s.

HOPE THE HERMIT: a Romance of Borrowdale. Crown 8vo., 6s.

Marchmont.—*IN THE NAME O WOMAN:* a Romance. By ARTHUR MARCHMONT. With 8 Illustrations. C 8vo., 6s.

Mason and Lang. —*PARSON KE* By A. E. W. MASON and ANDREW L Crown 8vo., 3s. 6d.

Max Müller. — *DEUTSCHE L₁* (GERMAN LOVE): Fragments from Papers of an Alien. Collected by F. MÜLLER. Translated from the Germa G. A. M. Crown 8vo., gilt top, 5s.

Melville (G. J. WHYTE).

The Gladiators.	Holmby Hous
The Interpreter.	Kate Coventry
Good for Nothing.	Digby Grand.
The Queen's Maries.	General Boun

Crown 8vo., 1s. 6d. each.

Merriman.—*FLOTSAM:* A Stor the Indian Mutiny. By HENRY S MERRIMAN. With Frontispiece and nette by H. G. MASSEY. Cr. 8vo., 3s.

Morris (WILLIAM).

THE SUNDERING FLOOD. Cr. 8 7s. 6d.

THE WATER OF THE WONDR ISLES. Crown 8vo., 7s. 6d.

THE WELL AT THE WORLD'S 2 vols. 8vo., 28s.

THE WOOD BEYOND THE WO Crown 8vo., 6s. net.

THE STORY OF THE GLITTER PLAIN, which has been also called Land of the Living Men, or The Ac the Undying. Square post 8vo., 5s.

THE ROOTS OF THE MOUNTA wherein is told somewhat of the Liv the Men of Burgdale, their Friends, Neighbours, their Foemen, and Fellows-in-Arms. Written in Prose Verse. Square crown 8vo., 8s.

Fiction, Humour, &c.—*continued.*

Morris (WILLIAM)—*continued.*

A TALE OF THE HOUSE OF THE WOLFINGS, and all the Kindreds of the Mark. Written in Prose and Verse. Square crown 8vo., 6s.

A DREAM OF JOHN BALL, AND A KING'S LESSON. 16mo., 2s. net.

NEWS FROM NOWHERE; or, An Epoch of Rest. Being some Chapters from an Utopian Romance. Post 8vo., 1s. 6d.

THE STORY OF GRETTIR THE STRONG. Translated from the Icelandic by EIRÍKR MAGNÚSSON and WILLIAM MORRIS. Cr. 8vo., 5s. net.

THREE NORTHERN LOVE STORIES, AND OTHER TALES. Translated from the Icelandic by EIRÍKR MAGNÚSSON and WILLIAM MORRIS. Crown 8vo., 6s. net.

.* For Mr. William Morris's other Works, see pp. 24, 37 and 40.

Newman (Cardinal).

LOSS AND GAIN: The Story of a Convert. Crown 8vo., 3s. 6d.

CALLISTA: A Tale of the Third Century. Crown 8vo., 3s. 6d.

Phillipps-Wolley.—*SNAP:* a Legend of the Lone Mountain. By C. PHILLIPPS-WOLLEY. With 13 Illustrations. Crown 8vo., 3s. 6d.

Portman.—*STATION STUDIES:* being the Jottings of an African Official. By LIONEL PORTMAN. Crown 8vo., 5s. net.

Sewell (ELIZABETH M.).

A Glimpse of the World.	Amy Herbert.
Laneton Parsonage.	Cleve Hall.
Margaret Percival.	Gertrude.
Katharine Ashton.	Home Life.
The Earl's Daughter.	After Life.
The Experience of Life.	Ursula. Ivors.

Cr. 8vo., cloth plain, 1s. 6d. each. Cloth extra, gilt edges, 2s. 6d. each.

Sheehan. — *LUKE DELMEGE.* the Rev. P. A. SHEEHAN, P.P., Aut] 'My New Curate'. Crown 8vo., 6s

Somerville (E. Œ.) and F (MARTIN).

SOME EXPERIENCES OF AN R.M. With 31 Illustrations by F SOMERVILLE. Crown 8vo., 6s.

ALL ON THE IRISH SHORE: Sketches. With Illustrations by E SOMERVILLE. Crown 8vo., 6s.

THE REAL CHARLOTTE. C 8vo., 3s. 6d.

THE SILVER FOX. Cr. 8vo., 3.

Stebbing.—*RACHEL WULFSTAN* other Stories. By W. STEBBING, aut] 'Probable Tales'. Crown 8vo., 4s. 6

Stevenson (ROBERT LOUIS).

THE STRANGE CASE OF DR. JE AND MR. HYDE. Fcp. 8vo., 1s. 1s. 6d. cloth.

THE STRANGE CASE OF JEKYLL AND MR. HYDE; WITH FABLES. Crown 8vo., bound in bu with gilt top, 5s. net.

'*Silver Library*' Edition. Crow 3s. 6d.

MORE NEW ARABIAN NIGHTS— DYNAMITER. By ROBERT LOUIS S1 SON and FANNY VAN DE GRIFT S1 SON. Crown 8vo., 3s. 6d.

THE WRONG BOX. By RC LOUIS STEVENSON and LLOYD OSBC Crown 8vo., 3s. 6d.

Fiction, Humour, &c.—*continued.*

Suttner.—*Lay Down Your Arms* (*Die Waffen Nieder*): The Autobiography of Martha von Tilling. By BERTHA VON SUTTNER. Translated by T. HOLMES. Cr. 8vo., 1s. 6d.

Trollope (ANTHONY).

The Warden. Cr. 8vo., 1s. 6d.

Barchester Towers. Cr.8vo.,1s.6d.

Walford (L. B.).

Stay-at-Homes. Crown 8vo., 6s.

Charlotte. Crown 8vo., 6s.

One of Ourselves. Cr. 8vo., 6s.

The Intruders. Crown 8vo., 2s. 6d.

Leddy Marget. Crown 8vo., 2s. 6d.

Iva Kildare: a Matrimonial Problem. Crown 8vo., 2s. 6d.

Mr. Smith: a Part of his Life. Crown 8vo., 2s. 6d.

The Baby's Grandmother. Cr. 8vo., 2s. 6d.

Cousins. Crown 8vo., 2s. 6d.

Troublesome Daughters. Cr. 8vo., 2s. 6d.

Pauline. Crown 8vo., 2s. 6d.

Dick Netherby. Cr. 8vo., 2s. 6d.

The History of a Week. Cr. 8vo. 2s. 6d.

A Stiff-necked Generation. Cr. 8vo. 2s. 6d.

Nan, and other Stories. Cr. 8vo., 2s. 6d.

Walford (L. B.)—*continued.*

The Mischief of Monica. 8vo., 2s. 6d.

The One Good Guest. Cr. 8 2s. 6d.

'*Ploughed,*' and other Stori Crown 8vo., 2s. 6d.

The Matchmaker. Cr. 8vo., 2s.

Ward.—*One Poor Scruple.* Mrs. WILFRID WARD. Crown 8vo., 6s.

Weyman (STANLEY).

The House of the Wolf. W Frontispiece and Vignette. Crown 8 3s. 6d.

A Gentleman of France. W Frontispiece and Vignette. Cr. 8vo.,

The Red Cockade. With Fron piece and Vignette. Crown 8vo., 6s.

Shrewsbury. With 24 Illus tions by CLAUDE A. SHEPPERSON. 8vo., 6s.

Sophia. With Frontispiece. Cro 8vo., 6s.

Yeats (S. LEVETT).

The Chevalier D'Auriac. Cro 8vo., 3s. 6d.

The Traitor's Way. Cr. 8vo.,

Yoxall.—*The Rommany Stone.* J. H. YOXALL, M.P. Crown 8vo., 6s.

Popular Science (Natural History, &c.).

Butler.—*OUR HOUSEHOLD INSECTS.* An Account of the Insect-Pests found in Dwelling-Houses. By EDWARD A. BUTLER, B.A., B.Sc. (Lond.). With 113 Illustrations. Crown 8vo., 3s. 6d.

Furneaux (W.).

THE OUTDOOR WORLD; or The Young Collector's Handbook. With 18 Plates (16 of which are coloured), and 549 Illustrations in the Text. Crown 8vo., gilt edges, 6s. net.

BUTTERFLIES AND MOTHS (British). With 12 coloured Plates and 241 Illustrations in the Text. Crown 8vo., gilt edges, 6s. net.

LIFE IN PONDS AND STREAMS. With 8 coloured Plates and 331 Illustrations in the Text. Crown 8vo., gilt edges, 6s. net.

Hartwig (GEORGE).

THE SEA AND ITS LIVING WONDERS. With 12 Plates and 303 Woodcuts. 8vo., gilt top, 7s. net.

THE TROPICAL WORLD. With 8 Plates and 172 Woodcuts. 8vo., gilt top, 7s. net.

THE POLAR WORLD. With 3 Maps, 8 Plates and 85 Woodcuts. 8vo., gilt top, 7s. net.

THE SUBTERRANEAN WORLD. With 3 Maps and 80 Woodcuts. 8vo., gilt top, 7s. net.

Helmholtz.—*POPULAR LECTURES ON SCIENTIFIC SUBJECTS.* By HERMANN VON HELMHOLTZ. With 68 Woodcuts. 2 vols. Cr. 8vo., 3s. 6d. each.

Hudson (W. H.).

HAMPSHIRE DAYS. With numous Illustrations from Drawings BRYAN HOOK, etc. 8vo., 10s. 6d. n

BIRDS AND MAN. Large cro 8vo., 6s. net.

NATURE IN DOWNLAND. With Plates and 14 Illustrations in the Tex A. D. MCCORMICK. 8vo., 10s. 6d. ne

BRITISH BIRDS. With a Cha on Structure and Classification by FF E. BEDDARD, F.R.S. With 16 Plate of which are Coloured), and over 100 I trations in the Text. Crown 8vo., edges, 6s. net.

Millais.—*THE NATURAL HISTOR THE BRITISH SURFACE FEEDING-DU* By JOHN GUILLE MILLAIS, F.Z.S., With 6 Photogravures and 66 Plates (Colours) from Drawings by the Au ARCHIBALD THORBURN, and from Ph graphs. Royal 4to., £6 6s.

Proctor (RICHARD A.).

LIGHT SCIENCE FOR LEISURE HO Familiar Essays on Scientific Subj Crown 8vo., 3s. 6d.

ROUGH WAYS MADE SMOOTH. Fa liar Essays on Scientific Subjects. Cr 8vo., 3s. 6d.

PLEASANT WAYS IN SCIENCE. Cr 8vo, 3s. 6d.

NATURE STUDIES. By R. A. PR TOR, GRANT ALLEN, A. WILSON, FOSTER and E. CLODD. Cr. 8vo., 3s.

LEISURE READINGS. By R. A. PF TOR, E. CLODD, A. WILSON, T. FOS and A. C. RANYARD. Cr. 8vo., 3s. 6d

. For Mr. Proctor's other books see p and 35, and Messrs. Longmans & Co.'s C logue of Scientific Works.

Popular Science (Natural History, &c.)—*continued.*

Stanley.—*A FAMILIAR HISTORY OF BIRDS.* By E. STANLEY, D.D., formerly Bishop of Norwich. With 160 Illustrations. Cr. 8vo., 3s. 6d.

Wood (Rev. J. G.).

HOMES WITHOUT HANDS: A Description of the Habitations of Animals, classed according to their Principle of Construction. With 140 Illustrations. 8vo., gilt top, 7s. net.

INSECTS AT HOME : A Popular Account of British Insects, their Structure, Habits and Transformations. With 700 Illustrations. 8vo., gilt top, 7s. net.

Wood (Rev. J. G.)—*continued.*

INSECTS ABROAD : A Popular A count of Foreign Insects, their Structu Habits and Transformations. With 6 Illustrations. 8vo., 7s. net.

OUT OF DOORS; a Selection Original Articles on Practical Natu History. With 11 Illustrations. Cr. 8v 3s. 6d.

PETLAND REVISITED. With Illustrations. Cr. 8vo., 3s. 6d.

STRANGE DWELLINGS: a Descripti of the Habitations of Animals, abridg from 'Homes without Hands'. With Illustrations. Cr. 8vo., 3s. 6d.

Works of Reference.

Gwilt.—*AN ENCYCLOPÆDIA OF ARCHITECTURE.* By JOSEPH GWILT, F.S.A. With 1700 Engravings. Revised (1888), with Alterations and Considerable Additions by WYATT PAPWORTH. 8vo., 21s. net.

Longmans' *GAZETTEER OF THE WORLD.* Edited by GEORGE G. CHISHOLM, M.A., B.Sc. Imperial 8vo., 18s. net cloth ; 21s. half-morocco.

Maunder (SAMUEL).

BIOGRAPHICAL TREASURY. With Supplement brought down to 1889. By Rev. JAMES WOOD. Fcp. 8vo., 6s.

THE TREASURY OF BIBLE KNOWLEDGE. By the Rev. J. AYRE, M.A. With 5 Maps, 15 Plates, and 300 Woodcuts. Fcp. 8vo., 6s.

TREASURY OF KNOWLEDGE AND LIBRARY OF REFERENCE. Fcp. 8vo., 6s.

Maunder (SAMUEL)—*continued.*

THE TREASURY OF BOTANY. Edit by J. LINDLEY, F.R.S., and T. MOOF F.L.S. With 274 Woodcuts and 20 St Plates. 2 vols. Fcp. 8vo., 12s.

Willich.--*POPULAR TABLES* for givir information for ascertaining the value Lifehold, Leasehold, and Church Propert the Public Funds, etc. By CHARLES WILLICH. Edited by H. BENCE JONE Crown 8vo., 10s. 6d.

Children's Books.

borg.—*CLEAN PETER AND THE
LDREN OF GRUBBYLEA.* By OTTILIA
LBORG. Translated from the Swedish
Mrs. GRAHAM WALLAS. With 23
ured Plates. Oblong 4to., boards,
d. net.

's Adventures. — By G. R.
h 8 Illustrations by JOHN HASSALL.
vn 8vo., 3s. 6d.

n.—*THE BOOK OF SAINTS AND
NDLY BEASTS.* By ABBIE FARWELL
WN. Wi h 8 Illustrations by FANNY Y.
Y. Crown 8vo., 4s. 6d. net.

land.—*TWO LITTLE RUNAWAYS.*
pted from the French of LOUIS DES-
ERS. By JAMES BUCKLAND. With 110
strations by CECIL ALDIN. Cr. 8vo., 6s.

e (Rev. A. D.).

WY THE FAIR; or, The First
hronicle of Æscendune. Cr. 8vo., silver
p, 2s. net.

FGAR THE DANE; or, The Second
hronicle of Æscendune. Cr. 8vo., silver
p, 2s. net.

E RIVAL HEIRS: being the Third
d Last Chronicle of Æscendune. Cr.
o., silver top, 2s. net.

E HOUSE OF WALDERNE. A Tale
the Cloister and the Forest in the Days
the Barons' Wars. Crown 8vo., silver
p, 2s. net.

IAN FITZ-COUNT. A Story of
allingford Castle and Dorchester
bbey. Cr. 8vo., silver top, 2s. net.

ty (G. A.).—EDITED BY

LE LOGS: A Story-Book for Boys.
y VARIOUS AUTHORS. With 61 Illus-
ations. Crown 8vo., gilt edges, 3s. net.

LE TIDE YARNS: a Story-Book
r Boys. By VARIOUS AUTHORS. With
5 Illustrations. Cr. 8vo., gilt edges, 3s.
et.

Lang (ANDREW).—EDITED BY.

THE BLUE FAIRY BOOK. With 138
Illustrations. Crown 8vo., gilt edges, 6s.

ThE RED FAIRY BOOK. With 100
Illustrations. Crown 8vo., gilt edges, 6s.

THE GREEN FAIRY BOOK. With 99
Illustrations. Crown 8vo., gilt edges, 6s.

THE GREY FAIRY BOOK. With 65
Illustrations. Crown 8vo., gilt edges, 6s.

THE YELLOW FAIRY BOOK. With
104 Illustrations. Cr. 8vo., gilt edges, 6s.

THE PINK FAIRY BOOK. With 67
Illustrations. Crown 8vo., gilt edges, 6s.

THE VIOLET FAIRY BOOK. With 8
Coloured Plates and 54 other Illustrations.
Crown 8vo., gilt edges, 6s.

THE BLUE POETRY BOOK. With 100
Illustrations. Crown 8vo., gilt edges, 6s.

THE TRUE STORY BOOK. With 66
Illustrations. Crown 8vo., gilt edges, 6s.

THE RED TRUE STORY BOOK. With
100 Illustrations. Cr. 8vo., gilt edges, 6s.

THE ANIMAL STORY BOOK. With
67 Illustrations. Cr. 8vo., gilt edges, 6s.

THE RED BOOK OF ANIMAL STORIES.
With 65 Illustrations. Crown 8vo., gilt
edges, 6s.

*THE ARABIAN NIGHTS ENTERTAIN-
MENTS.* With 66 Illustrations. Cr. 8vo.,
gilt edges, 6s.

THE BOOK OF ROMANCE. With 8
Coloured Plates and 44 other Illustrations.
Crown 8vo., gilt edges, 6s.

l-yall.—*THE BURGES LETTERS:* a
Record of Child Life in the Sixties. By
EDNA LYALL. With Coloured Frontispiece
and 8 other Full-page Illustrations by
WALTER S. STACEY. Crown 8vo., 2s. 6d.

Children's Books—*continued.*

Murray. — *FLOWER LEGENDS FOR CHILDREN.* By HILDA MURRAY (the Hon. Mrs. MURRAY of Elibank). Pictured by J. S. ELAND. With numerous Coloured and other Illustrations. Oblong 4to., 6s.

Penrose. — *CHUBBY: A NUISANCE.* By Mrs. PENROSE. With 8 Illustrations by G. G. MANTON. Crown 8vo., 3s. 6d.

Praeger (ROSAMOND).

THE ADVENTURES OF THE THREE BOLD BABES: HECTOR, HONORIA AND ALISANDER. A Story in Pictures. With 24 Coloured Plates and 24 Outline Pictures. Oblong 4to., 3s. 6d.

THE FURTHER DOINGS OF THE THREE BOLD BABES. With 24 Coloured Pictures and 24 Outline Pictures. Oblong 4to., 3s. 6d.

Roberts. — *THE ADVENTURES OF CAPTAIN JOHN SMITH :* Captain of Two Hundred and Fifty Horse, and sometime President of Virginia. By E. P. ROBERTS. With 17 Illustrations and 3 Maps. Crown 8vo., 5s. net.

Stevenson.—*A CHILD'S GARDEN OF VERSES.* By ROBERT LOUIS STEVENSON. Fcp. 8vo., gilt top, 5s.

Tappan.—*OLD BALLADS IN PROSE.* By EVA MARCH TAPPAN. With 4 Illustrations by FANNY Y. CORY. Crown 8vo., gilt top, 4s. 6d. net.

Upton (FLORENCE K. AND BERTHA).

THE ADVENTURES OF TWO DUTCH DOLLS AND A 'GOLLIWOGG'. With 31 Coloured Plates and numerous Illustrations in the Text. Oblong 4to., 6s.

THE GOLLIWOGG'S BICYCLE CLUB. With 31 Coloured Plates and numerous Illustrations in the Text. Oblong 4to., 6s.

THE GOLLIWOGG AT THE SEASIDE. With 31 Coloured Plates and numerous Illustrations in the Text. Oblong 4to., 6s.

THE GOLLIWOGG IN WAR. With 31 Coloured Plates. Oblong 4to., 6s.

THE GOLLIWOGG'S POLAR ADVENTURES. With 31 Coloured Plates. Oblong 4to., 6s.

THE GOLLIWOGG'S AUTO-GO-CART. With 31 Coloured Plates and numerous Illustrations in the Text. Oblong 4to., 6s.

THE GOLLIWOGG'S AIR-SHIP. With 30 Coloured Pictures and numerous Illustrations in the Text. Oblong 4to., 6s.

THE VEGE-MEN'S REVENGE. With 31 Coloured Plates and numerous Illustrations in the Text. Oblong 4to., 6s.

Wemyss.—*' THINGS WE THOUGHT OF ':* Told from a Child's Point of View. By MARY C. E. WEMYSS, Author of 'All About All of Us '. With 8 Illustrations in Colour by S. R. PRAEGER. Crown 8vo., 3s. 6d.

The Silver Library.

CROWN 8VO. 3s. 6d. EACH VOLUME.

Arnold's (Sir Edwin) Seas and Lands. With 71 Illustrations. 3s. 6d.

Bagehot's (W.) Biographical Studies. 3s. 6d.

Bagehot's (W.) Economic Studies. 3s. 6d.

Bagehot's (W.) Literary Studies. With Portrait. 3 vols., 3s. 6d. each.

Baker's (Sir S. W.) Eight Years in Ceylon. With 6 Illustrations. 3s. 6d.

Baker's (Sir S. W.) Rifle and Hound in Ceylon. With 6 Illustrations. 3s. 6d.

Baring-Gould's (Rev. S.) Curious Myths of the Middle Ages. 3s. 6d.

Baring-Gould's (Rev. S.) Origin and Development of Religious Belief. 2 vols. 3s. 6d. each.

Becker's (W. A.) Gallus : or, Roman Scenes in the Time of Augustus. With 26 Illus. 3s. 6d.

Becker's (W. A.) Charicles : or, Illustrations of the Private Life of the Ancient Greeks. With 26 Illustrations. 3s. 6d.

Bent's (J. T.) The Ruined Cities of Mashonaland. With 117 Illustrations. 3s. 6d.

Brassey's (Lady) A Voyage in the 'Sunbeam'. With 66 Illustrations. 3s. 6d.

Buckle's (H. T.) History of Civilisation in England. 3 vols. 10s. 6d.

Churchill's (Winston S.) The Story of the Malakand Field Force, 1897. With 6 Maps and Plans. 3s. 6d.

Clodd's (E.) Story of Creation: a Plain Account of Evolution. With 77 Illustrations. 3s. 6d.

Conybeare (Rev. W. J.) and Howson's (Very Rev. J. S.) Life and Epistles of St. Paul. With 46 Illustrations. 3s. 6d.

Dougall's (L.) Beggars All : a Novel. 3s. 6d.

Doyle's (Sir A. Conan) Micah Clarke. A Tale of Monmouth's Rebellion. With 10 Illusts. 3s. 6d.

The Silver Library—*continued.*

Doyle's (Sir A. Conan) The Captain of the Polestar, and other Tales. 3s. 6d.

Doyle's (Sir A. Conan) The Refugees: A Tale of the Huguenots. With 25 Illustrations. 3s 6d.

Doyle's (Sir A. Conan) The Stark Munro Letters. 3s. 6d.

Froude's (J. A.) The History of England, from the Fall of Wolsey to the Defeat of the Spanish Armada. 12 vols. 3s. 6d. each.

Froude's (J. A.) The English in Ireland. 3 vols. 10s. 6d.

Froude's (J. A.) The Divorce of Catherine of Aragon. 3s. 6d.

Froude's (J. A.) The Spanish Story of the Armada, and other Essays. 3s. 6d.

Froude's (J. A.) English Seamen in the Sixteenth Century. 3s. 6d.

Froude's (J. A.) Short Studies on Great Subjects. 4 vols. 3s. 6d. each.

Froude's (J. A.) Oceana, or England and Her Colonies. With 9 Illustrations. 3s. 6d.

Froude's (J. A.) The Council of Trent. 3s. 6d.

Froude's (J. A.) The Life and Letters of Erasmus. 3s. 6d.

Froude's (J. A.) Thomas Carlyle: a History of his Life.
1795-1835. 2 vols. 7s. 1834-1881. 2 vols. 7s.

Froude's (J. A.) Cæsar: a Sketch. 3s. 6d.

Froude's (J. A.) The Two Chiefs of Dunboy: an Irish Romance of the Last Century. 3s. 6d.

Froude's (J. A.) Writings, Selections from. 3s. 6d.

Gleig's (Rev. G. R.) Life of the Duke of Wellington. With Portrait. 3s. 6d.

Greville's (C. C. F.) Journal of the Reigns of King George IV., King William IV., and Queen Victoria. 8 vols., 3s. 6d. each.

Haggard's (H. R.) She: A History of Adventure. With 32 Illustrations. 3s. 6d.

Haggard's (H. R.) Allan Quatermain. With 20 Illustrations. 3s. 6d.

Haggard's (H. R.) Colonel Quaritch, V.C.: a Tale of Country Life. With Frontispiece and Vignette. 3s. 6d.

Haggard's (H. R.) Cleopatra. With 29 Illustrations. 3s. 6d.

Haggard's (H. R.) Eric Brighteyes. With 51 Illustrations. 3s. 6d.

Haggard's (H. R.) Beatrice. With Frontis and Vignette. 3s. 6d.

Haggard's (H. R.) Black Heart and White H With 33 Illustrations. 3s. 6d.

Haggard's (H. R.) Allan's Wife. With 34 trations. 3s. 6d.

Haggard (H. R.) Heart of the World. 15 Illustrations. 3s. 6d.

Haggard's (H. R.) Montezuma's Daughter. 25 Illustrations. 3s. 6d.

Haggard's (H. R.) Swallow: a Tale of the (Trek. With 8 Illustrations. 3s. 6d.

Haggard's (H. R.) The Witch's Head. 16 Illustrations. 3s. 6d.

Haggard's (H. R.) Mr. Meeson's Will. 16 Illustrations. 3s. 6d.

Haggard's (H. R.) Nada the Lily. Wit Illustrations. 3s. 6d.

Haggard's (H. R.) Dawn. With 16 Illusts. 3

Haggard's (H. R.) The People of the Mist. 16 Illustrations. 3s. 6d.

Haggard's (H. R.) Joan Haste. With 20 trations. 3s. 6d.

Haggard (H. R.) and Lang's (A.) The Wc Desire. With 27 Illustrations. 3s. 6d.

Harte's (Bret) In the Carquinez Woods other Stories. 3s. 6d.

Helmholtz's (Hermann von) Popular Lec on Scientific Subjects. With 68 Illustra 2 vols. 3s. 6d. each.

Hope's (Anthony) The Heart of Princess (With 9 Illustrations. 3s. 6d.

Howitt's (W.) Visits to Remarkable Pl With 80 Illustrations. 3s. 6d.

Jefferies' (R.) The Story of My Heart: Autobiography. With Portrait. 3s. 6d

Jefferies' (R.) Field and Hedgerow. Portrait. 3s. 6d.

Jefferies' (R.) Red Deer. With 17 Illusts. 3

Jefferies' (R.) Wood Magic: a Fable. Frontispiece and Vignette by E. V. B. 3

Jefferies (R.) The Toilers of the Field. Portrait from the Bust in Salisbury Cathe 3s. 6d.

Kaye (Sir J.) and Malleson's (Colonel) His of the Indian Mutiny of 1857-8. 6 3s. 6d. each.

Knight's (E. F.) The Cruise of the 'Ale the Narrative of a Search for Treasur the Desert Island of Trinidad. Wit Maps and 23 Illustrations. 3s. 6d.

The Silver Library—*continued.*

Knight's (E. F.) Where Three Empires Meet: a Narrative of Recent Travel in Kashmir, Western Tibet, Baltistan, Gilgit. With a Map and 54 Illustrations. 3s. 6d.

Knight's (E. F.) The 'Falcon' on the Baltic: a Coasting Voyage from Hammersmith to Copenhagen in a Three-Ton Yacht. With Map and 11 Illustrations. 3s. 6d.

Köstlin's (J.) Life of Luther. With 62 Illustrations and 4 Facsimiles of MSS. 3s. 6d.

Lang's (A.) Angling Sketches. With 20 Illustrations. 3s. 6d.

Lang's (A.) Custom and Myth: Studies of Early Usage and Belief. 3s. 6d.

Lang's (A.) Cock Lane and Common-Sense. 3s. 6d.

Lang's (A.) The Book of Dreams and Ghosts. 3s. 6d.

Lang's (A.) A Monk of Fife: a Story of the Days of Joan of Arc. With 13 Illustrations. 3s. 6d.

Lang's (A.) Myth, Ritual, and Religion. 2 vols. 7s.

Lees (J. A.) and Clutterbuck's (W. J.) B.C. 1887, A Ramble in British Columbia. With Maps and 75 Illustrations. 3s. 6d

Levett-Yeats' (S.) The Chevalier D'Auriac. 3s. 6d.

Macaulay's (Lord) Complete Works. 'Albany' Edition. With 12 Portraits. 12 vols. 3s. 6d. each.

Macaulay's (Lord) Essays and Lays of Ancient Rome, etc. With Portrait and 4 Illustrations to the 'Lays'. 3s. 6d.

Macleod's (H. D.) Elements of Banking. 3s. 6d.

Marshman's (J. C.) Memoirs of Sir Henry Havelock. 3s. 6d.

Mason (A. E. W.) and Lang's (A.) Parson Kelly. 3s. 6d.

Merivale's (Dean) History of the Romans under the Empire. 8 vols. 3s. 6d. each.

Merriman's (H. S. Flotsam: A Tale of the Indian Mutiny. 3s. 6d.

Mill's (J. S.) Political Economy. 3s. 6d.

Mill's (J. S.) System of Logic. 3s. 6d.

Milner's (Geo.) Country Pleasures: the Chronicle of a Year chiefly in a Garden. 3s. 6d.

Nansen's (F.) The First Crossing of Greenland. With 142 Illustrations and a Map. 3s. 6d.

Phillipps-Wolley's (C.) Snap: a Legend of the Lone Mountain With 13 Illustrations. 3s. 6d.

Proctor's (R. A.) The Orbs Around Us. 3s.

Proctor's (R. A.) The Expanse of Heaven. 3s.

Proctor's (R. A.) Light Science for Leisu Hours. 3s. 6d.

Proctor's (R. A.) The Moon. 3s. 6d.

Proctor's (R. A.) Other Worlds than Ours. 3s.

Proctor's (R. A.) Our Place among Infiniti a Series of Essays contrasting our Lit Abode in Space and Time with the Infinit around us. 3s. 6d.

Proctor's (R. A.) Other Suns than Ours. 3s.

Proctor's (R. A.) Rough Ways made Smoo 3s. 6d.

Proctor's (R.A.) Pleasant Ways in Science. 3s.

Proctor's (R. A.) Myths and Marvels of tronomy. 3s. 6d.

Proctor's (R. A.) Nature Studies. 3s. 6d.

Proctor's (R. A.) Leisure Readings. By R. PROCTOR, EDWARD CLODD, ANDR WILSON, THOMAS FOSTER, and A. RANYARD. With Illustrations. 3s. 6d.

Rossetti's (Maria F.) A Shadow of Dante. 3s.

Smith's (R. Bosworth) Carthage and the Cart ginians. With Maps, Plans, etc. 3s. 6d

Stanley's (Bishop) Familiar History of Bir With 160 Illustrations. 3s. 6d.

Stephen's (Sir Leslie) The Playground of Euro (The Alps). With 4 Illustrations. 3s. 6d.

Stevenson's (R. L.) The Strange Case of Jekyll and Mr. Hyde; with other Fables. 3s.

Stevenson (R. L.) and Osbourne's (Ll.) T Wrong Box. 3s. 6d.

Cookery, Domestic Management, &c.

Acton. — *MODERN COOKERY.* By ELIZA ACTON. With 150 Woodcuts. Fcp. 8vo., 4s. 6d.

Angwin.—*SIMPLE HINTS ON CHOICE OF FOOD,* with Tested and Economical Recipes. For Schools, Homes, and Classes for Technical Instruction. By M. C. ANGWIN, Diplomate (First Class) of the National Union for the Technical Training of Women, etc. Crown 8vo., 1s.

Ashby.—*HEALTH IN THE NURSERY.* By HENRY ASHBY, M.D., F.R.C.P., Physician to the Manchester Children's Hospital. With 25 Illustrations. Crown 8vo., 3s. net.

Bull (THOMAS, M.D.).

HINTS TO MOTHERS ON THE MANAGEMENT OF THEIR HEALTH DURING THE PERIOD OF PREGNANCY. Fcp. 8vo., sewed, 1s. 6d. ; cloth, gilt edges, 2s. net.

THE MATERNAL MANAGEMENT OF CHILDREN IN HEALTH AND DISEASE. Fcp. 8vo., sewed, 1s. 6d. ; cloth, gilt edges, 2s. net.

De Salis (Mrs.).

À LA MODE COOKERY : Up-to-date Recipes. With 24 Plates (16 in Colour). Crown 8vo., 5s. net.

CAKES AND CONFECTIONS À LA MODE. Fcp. 8vo., 1s. 6d.

DOGS : A Manual for Amateurs. Fcp. 8vo., 1s. 6d.

DRESSED GAME AND POULTRY À LA MODE. Fcp. 8vo., 1s. 6d.

DRESSED VEGETABLES À LA MODE. Fcp. 8vo., 1s 6d.

DRINKS À LA MODE. Fcp. 8vo., 1s.6d.

De Salis (Mrs.)—*continued.*

ENTRÉES À LA MODE. Fcp. 1s. 6d.

FLORAL DECORATIONS. Fcp. 1s. 6d.

GARDENING À LA MODE. Fcp. Part I., Vegetables, 1s. 6d. Par Fruits, 1s. 6d.

NATIONAL VIANDS À LA MODE. 8vo., 1s. 6d.

NEW-LAID EGGS. Fcp. 8vo., 1

OYSTERS À LA MODE. Fcp. 1s. 6d.

PUDDINGS AND PASTRY À LA M Fcp. 8vo., 1s. 6d.

SAVOURIES À LA MODE. Fcp. 1s.6d.

SOUPS AND DRESSED FISH MODE. Fcp. 8vo., 1s. 6d.

SWEETS AND SUPPER DISHES MODE. Fcp. 8vo., 1s. 6d.

TEMPTING DISHES FOR SMAL. COMES. Fcp. 8vo., 1s. 6d.

WRINKLES AND NOTIONS EVERY HOUSEHOLD. Crown 8vo.,

Lear.—*MAIGRE COOKERY.* By SIDNEY LEAR. 16mo., 2s.

Poole.—*COOKERY FOR THE DIAB* By W. H. and Mrs. POOLE. With P by Dr. PAVY. Fcp. 8vo., 2s. 6d.

Rotheram. — *HOUSEHOLD COO* RECIPES. By M. A. ROTHERAM, First Diplomée, National Training Sch Cookery, London ; Instructress to th fordshire County Council. Crown 8v

---

The Fine Arts and Music.

Burne-Jones.—*THE BEGINNING OF THE WORLD :* Twenty-five Pictures by Sir EDWARD BURNE-JONES, Bart. Medium 4to., Boards, 7s. 6d. net.

Burns and Colenso.—*LIVING ANATOMY.* By CECIL L. BURNS, R.B.A., and ROBERT J. COLENSO, M.A., M.D. 40 Plates, 11¼ by 8¾ ins., each Plate containing Two Figures—(a) A Natural Male or Female Figure ; (b) The same Figure Anatomatised. In a Portfolio, 7s. 6d. net.

Hamlin.—*A TEXT-BOOK OF HISTORY OF ARCHITECTURE.* By A. HAMLIN, A.M. With 229 Illustr Crown 8vo., 7s. 6d.

Haweis (Rev. H. R.).

MUSIC AND MORALS. With Po of the Author. Crown 8vo., 6s. ne

MY MUSICAL LIFE. With Po of Richard Wagner and 3 Illustr Crown 8vo., 6s. net.

The Fine Arts and Music—*continued.*

Huish, Head, and Longman.—
SAMPLERS AND TAPESTRY EMBROIDERIES.
By MARCUS B. HUISH, LL.B.; also 'The
Stitchery of the Same,' by Mrs. HEAD;
and 'Foreign Samplers,' by Mrs. C. J.
LONGMAN. With 30 Reproductions in
Colour, and 40 Illustrations in Mono-
chrome. 4to., £2 2s. net.

Hullah.—THE HISTORY OF MODERN
MUSIC. By JOHN HULLAH. 8vo., 8s. 6d.

Jameson (Mrs. ANNA).

SACRED AND LEGENDARY ART, containing Legends of the Angels and Arch-
angels, the Evangelists, the Apostles, the
Doctors of the Church, St. Mary Mag-
dalene, the Patron Saints, the Martyrs,
the Early Bishops, the Hermits, and the
Warrior-Saints of Christendom, as represented in the Fine Arts. With 19 Etchings
and 187 Woodcuts. 2 vols. 8vo., 20s. net.

LEGENDS OF THE MONASTIC ORDERS,
as represented in the Fine Arts, comprising the Benedictines and Augustines,
and Orders derived from their Rules, the
Mendicant Orders, the Jesuits, and the
Order of the Visitation of St. Mary. With
11 Etchings and 88 Woodcuts. 1 vol.
8vo., 10s. net.

LEGENDS OF THE MADONNA, OR
BLESSED VIRGIN MARY. Devotional with
and without the Infant Jesus, Historical
from the Annunciation to the Assumption,
as represented in Sacred and Legendary
Christian Art. With 27 Etchings and
165 Woodcuts. 1 vol. 8vo., 10s. net.

THE HISTORY OF OUR LORD, as exemplified in Works of Art, with that of
His Types, St. John the Baptist, and
other persons of the Old and New Testa-
ment. Commenced by the late Mrs.
JAMESON; continued and completed by
LADY EASTLAKE. With 31 Etchings
and 281 Woodcuts. 2 vols. 8vo., 20s. net.

Kristeller. — ANDREA MANTEGNA.
By PAUL KRISTELLER. English Edition by
S. ARTHUR STRONG, M.A., Librarian to the
House of Lords, and at Chatsworth. With
26 Photogravure Plates and 162 Illustrations
in the Text. 4to., gilt top, £3 10s. net.

Macfarren. — LECTURES ON HAR-
MONY. By Sir GEORGE A. MACFARREN.
8vo., 12s.

Morris (WILLIAM).

ARCHITECTURE, INDUSTRY AND
WEALTH. Collected Papers. Crown
8vo., 6s. net.

HOPES AND FEARS FOR ART. Five
Lectures delivered in Birmingham, London, etc., in 1878-1881. Cr 8vo., 4s. 6d.

AN ADDRESS DELIVERED AT THE
DISTRIBUTION OF PRIZES TO STUDENTS
OF THE BIRMINGHAM MUNICIPAL SCHOOL
OF ART ON 21ST FEBRUARY, 1894. 8vo.,
2s. 6d. net. (*Printed in 'Golden' Type.*)

SOME HINTS ON PATTERN-DESIGN-
ING: a Lecture delivered at the Working
Men's College, London, on 10th Decem-
ber, 1881. 8vo., 2s. 6d. net. (*Printed in
'Golden' Type.*)

ARTS AND ITS PRODUCERS (1888)
AND THE ARTS AND CRAFTS OF TO-DAY
(1889). 8vo., 2s. 6d. net. (*Printed in
'Golden' Type.*)

ARCHITECTURE AND HISTORY, AND
WESTMINSTER ABBEY. Two Papers
read before the Society for the Protection
of Ancient Buildings. 8vo., 2s. 6d. net.
(*Printed in 'Golden' Type.*)

ARTS AND CRAFTS ESSAYS. By
Members of the Arts and Crafts Exhibition
Society. With a Preface by WILLIAM
MORRIS. Crown 8vo., 2s. 6d. net.
⁎ For Mr. William Morris's other
Works, see pp. 24, 27, 28 and 40.

Robertson.—OLD ENGLISH SONGS
AND DANCES. Decorated in Colour by W.
GRAHAM ROBERTSON. Royal 4to., 42s. net.

Vanderpoel. — COLOUR PROBLEMS:
a Practical Manual for the Lay Student of
Colour. By EMILY NOYES VANDERPOEL.
With 117 Plates in Colour. Square 8vo.,
21s. net.

Van Dyke.—A TEXT-BOOK ON THE
HISTORY OF PAINTING. By JOHN C. VAN
DYKE. With 110 Illustrations. Cr. 8vo., 6s.

Wellington.—A DESCRIPTIVE AND
HISTORICAL CATALOGUE OF THE COLLEC-
TIONS OF PICTURES AND SCULPTURE AT
APSLEY HOUSE, LONDON. By EVELYN,
Duchess of Wellington. Illustrated by 52
Photo-Engravings, specially executed by
BRAUN, CLÉMENT, & Co., of Paris. 2 vols.,
royal 4to., £6 6s. net.

Willard. — HISTORY OF MODERN
ITALIAN ART. By ASHTON ROLLINS
WILLARD. Part I. Sculpture. Part II.
Painting. Part III. Architecture. With
Photogravure Frontispiece and numerous
full-page Illustrations. 8vo., 21s. net.

Miscellaneous and Critical Works.

Auto da Fé and other Essays: some being Essays in Fiction. By the Author of 'Essays in Paradox' and 'Exploded Ideas'. Crown 8vo., 5s.

Bagehot.—*LITERARY STUDIES.* By WALTER BAGEHOT. With Portrait. 3 vols. Crown 8vo., 3s. 6d. each.

Baker. — *EDUCATION AND LIFE:* Papers and Addresses. By JAMES H. BAKER, M.A., LL.D. Crown 8vo., 4s. 6d.

Baring-Gould.—*CURIOUS MYTHS OF THE MIDDLE AGES.* By Rev. S. BARING-GOULD. Crown 8vo., 3s. 6d.

Baynes. — *SHAKESPEARE STUDIES,* and other Essays. By the late THOMAS SPENCER BAYNES, LL.B., LL.D. With a Biographical Preface by Professor LEWIS CAMPBELL. Crown 8vo., 7s. 6d.

Bonnell. — *CHARLOTTE BRONTÈ, GEORGE ELIOT, JANE AUSTEN:* Studies in their Works. By HENRY H. BONNELL. Crown 8vo., 7s. 6d. net.

Booth.—*THE DISCOVERY AND DECIPHERMENT OF THE TRILINGUAL CUNEIFORM INSCRIPTIONS.* By ARTHUR JOHN BOOTH, M.A. With a Plan of Persepolis. 8vo. 14s. net.

Charities Register, The Annual, *AND DIGEST:* being a Classified Register of Charities in or available in the Metropolis. 8vo., 5s. net.

Christie.—*SELECTED ESSAYS.* By RICHARD COPLEY CHRISTIE, M.A., Oxon. Hon. LL.D., Vict. With 2 Portraits and 3 other Illustrations. 8vo., 12s. net.

Dickinson.—*KING ARTHUR IN CORNWALL.* By W. HOWSHIP DICKINSON, M.D. With 5 Illustrations. Crown 8vo., 4s. 6d.

Essays in Paradox. By the Author of 'Exploded Ideas ' and 'Times and Days '. Crown 8vo., 5s.

Evans.—*THE ANCIENT STONE IMPLEMENTS, WEAPONS AND ORNAMENTS OF GREAT BRITAIN.* By Sir JOHN EVANS, K.C.B. With 537 Illustrations. 8vo., 10s. 6d. net.

Exploded Ideas, *AND OTHER ESSAYS.* By the Author of 'Times and Days '. Cr. 8vo., 5s.

Frost. — *A MEDLEY BOOK.* GEORGE FROST. Crown 8vo., 3s.

Geikie.—*THE VICAR AND HIS FR* Reported by CUNNINGHAM GEIKI LL.D. Crown 8vo., 5s. net.

Gilkes. — *THE NEW REVOL* By A. H. GILKES, Master of College. Fcp. 8vo., 1s. net.

Hoenig. — *INQUIRIES CONC* *THE TACTICS OF THE FUTURE.* B HOENIG. With 1 Sketch in the Te Maps. Translated by Captain H. M. 8vo., 15s. net.

Hutchinson.—*DREAMS AND MEANINGS.* By HORACE G. HUTC 8vo., gilt top, 9s. 6d. net.

Jefferies (RICHARD).

FIELD AND HEDGEROW: Wi trait. Crown 8vo., 3s. 6d.

THE STORY OF MY HEART Autobiography. Crown 8vo., 3s.

RED DEER. With 17 Illustr Crown 8vo., 3s. 6d.

THE TOILERS OF THE FIELD. 8vo., 3s. 6d.

WOOD MAGIC: a Fable. 8vo., 3s. 6d.

Miscellaneous and Critical Works—*continued.*

ohnson (J. & J. H.).

The Patentee's Manual : a Treatise on the Law and Practice of Letters Patent. 8vo., 10s. 6d.

An Epitome of the Law and Practice connected with Patents for Inventions, with a reprint of the Patents Acts of 1883, 1885, 1886 and 1888. Crown 8vo., 2s. 6d.

oyce.—*The Origin and History of Irish Names of Places.* By P. W. Joyce, LL.D. 2 vols. Crown 8vo., 5s. each.

ang (Andrew).

Letters to Dead Authors. Fcp. 8vo., 2s. 6d. net.

Books and Bookmen. With 2 Coloured Plates and 17 Illustrations. Fcp. 8vo., 2s. 6d. net.

Old Friends. Fcp. 8vo., 2s. 6d. net.

Letters on Literature. Fcp. 8vo., 2s. 6d. net.

Essays in Little. With Portrait of the Author. Crown 8vo., 2s. 6d.

Cock Lane and Common-Sense. Crown 8vo., 3s. 6d.

The Book of Dreams and Ghosts. Crown 8vo., 3s. 6d.

Maryon.—*How the Garden Grew.* By Maud Maryon. With 4 Illustrations. Crown 8vo., 5s. net.

Matthews.—*Notes on Speech-Making.* By Brander Matthews. Fcp. 8vo., 1s. 6d. net.

Max Müller (The Right Hon. F.).

Collected Works. 18 vols. Crown 8vo., 5s. each.

Vol. I. *Natural Religion:* the Gifford Lectures, 1888.

Vol. II. *Physical Religion:* the Gifford Lectures, 1890.

Vol. III. *Anthropological Religion:* the Gifford Lectures, 1891.

Vol. IV. *Theosophy;* or, Psychological Religion: the Gifford Lectures, 1892.

Chips from a German Workshop.

Vol. V. Recent Essays and Addresses.

Vol. VI. Biographical Essays.

Vol. VII. Essays on Language and Literature.

Vol. VIII. Essays on Mythology and Folk-lore.

Vol. IX. *The Origin and Growth of Religion*, as Illustrated by the Religions of India: the Hibbert Lectures, 1878.

Vol. X. *Biographies of Words, and the Home of the Aryas.*

Vol. XV. *Râmakrishna:* his Life and Sayings.

Vol. XVI. *Three Lectures on the Vedânta Philosophy*, 1894.

Vol. XVII. *Last Essays.* First Series. Essays on Language, Folk-lore, etc.

Vol. XVIII. *Last Essays.* Second Series. Essays on the Science of Religion.

Miscellaneous and Critical Works—*continued.*

Milner.—*COUNTRY PLEASURES :* the Chronicle of a Year chiefly in a Garden. By GEORGE MILNER. Crown 8vo., 3s. 6d.

Morris.—*SIGNS OF CHANGE.* Seven Lectures delivered on various Occasions. By WILLIAM MORRIS. Post 8vo., 4s. 6d.

Parker and Unwin.—*THE ART OF BUILDING A HOME :* a Collection of Lectures and Illustrations. By BARRY PARKER and RAYMOND UNWIN. With 68 Full-page Plates. 8vo., 10s. 6d. net.

Pollock.—*JANE AUSTEN :* her Contemporaries and Herself. By WALTER HERRIES POLLOCK. Cr. 8vo., 3s. 6d. net.

Poore (GEORGE VIVIAN, M.D.).

ESSAYS ON RURAL HYGIENE. With 13 Illustrations. Crown 8vo., 6s. 6d.

THE DWELLING HOUSE. With 36 Illustrations. Crown 8vo., 3s. 6d.

THE EARTH IN RELATION TO THE PRESERVATION AND DESTRUCTION OF CONTAGIA : being the Milroy Lectures delivered at the Royal College of Physicians in 1899, together with other Papers on Sanitation. With 13 Illustrations. Crown 8vo., 5s.

COLONIAL AND CAMP SANITATION. With 11 Illustrations. Cr. 8vo., 2s. net.

Rossetti.—*A SHADOW OF DANTE :* being an Essay towards studying Himself, his World and his Pilgrimage. By MARIA FRANCESCA ROSSETTI. Crown 8vo., 3s. 6d.

Seria Ludo. By a DILETTANTE. Post 4to., 5s. net.

** *Sketches and Verses, mainly reprinted from the St. James's Gazette.*

Shadwell. — *DRINK : TEMPERANCE AND LEGISLATION.* By ARTHUR SHADWELL, M.A., M.D. Crown 8vo., 5s. net.

Soulsby (LUCY H. M.).

STRAY THOUGHTS ON READING. Fcp. 8vo., 2s. 6d. net.

STRAY THOUGHTS FOR GIRLS. 16mo., 1s. 6d net.

Soulsby (LUCY H. M.)—*contin*

STRAY THOUGHTS FOR MOTHER TEACHERS. Fcp. 8vo., 2s. 6d. ne

STRAY THOUGHTS FOR INV. 16mo., 2s. net.

STRAY THOUGHTS ON CHARA Fcp. 8vo., 2s. 6d. net.

Southey.—*THE CORRESPONDEN ROBERT SOUTHEY WITH CAROLINE B(* Edited by EDWARD DOWDEN. 8vo.,

Stevens.—*ON THE STOWAGE OF AND THEIR CARGOES.* With Informat garding Freights, Charter-Parties, et(ROBERT WHITE STEVENS. 8vo., 21s

Thuillier.—*THE PRINCIPLES OF DEFENCE, AND THEIR APPLICATION ? CONDITIONS OF TO-DAY.* By Capt: F. THUILLIER, R.E. With Maps and 8vo., 12s. 6d. net.

Turner and Sutherland.—*TH: VELOPMENT OF AUSTRALIAN LITERA* By HENRY GYLES TURNER and ALEX SUTHERLAND. With Portraits and Il tions. Crown 8vo., 5s.

Warwick.—*PROGRESS IN WO EDUCATION IN THE BRITISH EMPIRE :* the Report of Conferences and a Co held in connection with the Educa Section, Victorian Era Exhibition. 1 by the COUNTESS OF WARWICK. Cr. 8

Weathers.—*A PRACTICAL GUI GARDEN PLANTS.* By JOHN WEAT F.R.H.S. With 159 Diagrams. 8vo net.

Whittall.—*FREDERICK THE G. ON KINGCRAFT,* from the Original N script ; with Reminiscences and T Stories. By Sir J. WILLIAM WHIT President of the British Chamber of merce of Turkey. 8vo., 7s. 6d. net.

Printed in Great Britain
by Amazon

26062335R00196